D1397973

Sustaining and Sharing Economic Growth in Tanzania

Sustaining and Sharing Economic Growth in Tanzania

Edited by

Robert J. Utz

THE WORLD BANK
Washington, D.C.

©2008 The International Bank for Reconstruction and Development / The World Bank
1818 H Street, NW
Washington, DC 20433
Telephone: 202-473-1000
Internet: www.worldbank.org
E-mail: feedback@worldbank.org

All rights reserved

1 2 3 4 10 09 08 07

This volume is a product of the staff of the International Bank for Reconstruction and Development / The World Bank. The findings, interpretations, and conclusions expressed in this volume do not necessarily reflect the views of the Executive Directors of The World Bank or the governments they represent.

The World Bank does not guarantee the accuracy of the data included in this work. The boundaries, colors, denominations, and other information shown on any map in this work do not imply any judgement on the part of The World Bank concerning the legal status of any territory or the endorsement or acceptance of such boundaries.

Rights and Permissions

The material in this publication is copyrighted. Copying and/or transmitting portions or all of this work without permission may be a violation of applicable law. The International Bank for Reconstruction and Development / The World Bank encourages dissemination of its work and will normally grant permission to reproduce portions of the work promptly.

For permission to photocopy or reprint any part of this work, please send a request with complete information to the Copyright Clearance Center Inc., 222 Rosewood Drive, Danvers, MA 01923, USA; telephone: 978-750-8400; fax: 978-750-4470; Internet: www.copyright.com.

All other queries on rights and licenses, including subsidiary rights, should be addressed to the Office of the Publisher, The World Bank, 1818 H Street, NW, Washington, DC 20433, USA; fax: 202-522-2422; e-mail: pubrights@worldbank.org.

ISBN: 978-0-8213-7195-4
eISBN: 978-0-8213-7196-1
DOI: 10.1596/978-0-8213-7195-4

Library of Congress Cataloging-in-Publication Data

Utz, Robert J.
   Sustaining and sharing economic growth in Tanzania / Robert J. Utz.
     p. cm.
   ISBN 978–0–8213–7195–4 (alk. paper)—ISBN 978–0–8213–7196–1 (electronic)
   1. Tanzania—Economic policy. 2. Poverty—Tanzania. I. Title.

HC885.U89 2007
338.96789—dc22

                        2007022160

Contents

The Benefits of Malnutrition Interventions: Empirical Evidence and Lessons to Tanzania by Adolf F. Mkenda
Causes of Malnutrition and Tanzania's Nutrition Programs: Past and Present by Tanzania Food and Nutrition Centre

Part II: Statistical Tables

Part III: Summary of Main Findings and Recommendations

BOXES

FIGURES

Foreword

Promoting growth, reducing poverty and inequity, and improving opportunities for people are central to the World Bank Group's objectives in Tanzania. The World Bank Group is strongly committed to supporting these objectives and the detailed programs and policies needed to achieve them as portrayed in the government of Tanzania's National Strategy for Growth and Reduction of Poverty—also called MKUKUTA.

Economic transformation in countries such as Tanzania is not at all easy. Working closely with other development partners, the World Bank Group supports government and private efforts in this regard—with financial support and policy advice. Tanzania's progress thus far is very promising. It is one of the few countries in Sub-Saharan Africa to have recorded sound macroeconomic management and rapid economic growth, which averaged 6 percent per year since 2000. The big challenge now is to sustain this impressive growth performance and ensure it is shared more broadly, so as to increase economic opportunities throughout Tanzania.

This book is designed to contribute to the government's thinking on how best to translate broad MKUKUTA policy objectives into practical tactics and programs well suited to Tanzania's economic priorities and to the removal of key institutional and infrastructure bottlenecks. The volume aims to respond to three fundamental questions: (a) what factors explain Tanzania's recent acceleration in economic growth, (b) how well has the accelerated growth translated into reduced poverty, and (c) what needs to be done to sustain growth that is also pro-poor.

It gives me great personal satisfaction to note the important achievements to date in Tanzania and to know that the World Bank Group has contributed to these in some small measure. Clearly much more remains to be done before Tanzania is on an established path to sustained and shared economic growth, but I am confident the authorities, in partnership with the private sector, will continue to progress.

Tanzania can meet its poverty reduction goals assuming enlightened leadership maintains the strong commitment to its growth and poverty reduction agenda and ensures a clear, strong, and effective partnership with the private sector.

Judy O'Connor
Country Director for Tanzania and Uganda
World Bank

Acknowledgments

This book is based on a Country Economic Report that was undertaken jointly by the Tanzanian Ministry of Planning, Economy, and Empowerment (MPEE) and the World Bank (WB), with support from the African Development Bank and various local and international researchers. The report was prepared under the overall supervision of Enos Bukuku (Permanent Secretary, Ministry of Infrastructure Development, previously Permanent Secretary, MPEE), Charles Mutalemwa (Permanent Secretary, MPEE), Judy O'Connor (WB Country Director for Uganda and Tanzania), and Kathie Krumm (WB Sector Manager, Poverty Reduction and Economic Management Unit for East Africa and the Horn), who provided substantive inputs, comments, and support at all stages of the preparation process. The World Bank team was led by Robert J. Utz (WB Senior Economist, Poverty Reduction and Economic Management for East Africa and the Horn), who also edited this publication. The government team was initially led by Arthur Mwakapugi (Permanent Secretary, Ministry of Energy and Mining, previously Director for Macroeconomics, MPEE), followed by Laston Msongole (Director of Macroeconomics, MPEE).

This book is a compilation of chapters written by authors from the African Development Bank (Peter Mwanakatwe), COWI Consultants (Kerstin Pfliegner), independent consultancies (Marianne Simonsen and Annabella Skof), and the World Bank (Jean-Eric Aubert, Vandana Chandra, Louise Fox, Henry Gordon, Johannes Hoogeveen, Pooja Kacker, Ying Li, Allister Moon, Philip Mpango, Ravi Ruparel, Anuja Utz, Robert J. Utz, and Michael Wong).

Significant inputs and background studies were prepared by Harold Alderman (WB), Luc Christiaensen (WB), Gabriel Demombynes (WB), Thomas Hansen (COWI Consultants), Vivian Hofmann (consultant), Flora Kessy (Economic and Social Research Foundation [ESRF]), Blandina Kilama (Research on Poverty Alleviation [REPOA]), Ronald Kopicki (WB), Kassim Kulindwa (University of Dar es Salaam), Jorgen Levin (Öerebro University, Sweden), Wietze Lindenboom (REPOA), Robert Mahamba (University of Dar es Salaam), Adolf Mkenda (University of Dar es Salaam), Mariacristina Rossi (University of Rome Tor Vergata), Alexander Sarris (Food and Agriculture Organization of the United Nations), Klaas Schwarz (United Nations Educational, Scientific, and Cultural Organization Institute for Water Education [UNESCO-IHE]), Meine Pieter van Dijk (UNESCO-IHE), and Goodwill Wanga (consultant). The background studies can be found on the CD-ROM accompanying this book and are listed in the table of contents and bibliograhy. Also on the CD-ROM are the Appendixes of

Statistical Tables prepared by Emmanuel Mungunasi (WB) and a Summary of Main Findings and Recommendations by Robert J. Utz.

We gratefully acknowledge generous support by the governments of Austria, Denmark, the Netherlands, and Sweden for the preparation of this study. InfoDev financed a study on growth, competitiveness, and information and communications technology carried out by OTF Group consultants. The book benefited also from participation in the "growth path" project led by Roberto Zagha (WB), in cooperation with Harvard University, which helped to sharpen the growth diagnostic.

Insightful and challenging comments were provided at various stages of the preparation process by peer reviewers Benno Ndulu (WB); Josephat Kweka (WB, previously ESRF); Erik Thorbecke, Steven Younger, and David Sahn (Cornell University); and Dani Rodrik (Harvard University). During the consultations held in Dar es Salaam, the following people served as discussants for the draft background studies: Haidari Amani (ESRF), Robert Mabele (University of Dar es Salaam), Amon Mbelle (University of Dar es Salaam), Adolf Mkenda (University of Dar es Salaam), Peter Noni (Bank of Tanzania), and Brian van Arkadie (ESRF). Detailed comments were also provided by members of the World Bank country team, including Mavis Ampah, on the topic of information and communications technology; Mathew Glasser, on decentralization and local government; Indumathie Hewawasam, on natural resource management; Keith Hinchliffe, on education; Denyse Morin, on institutional reforms; Karen Rasmussen, Duncan Reynolds, and Arun Sanghvi, on energy; and Dieter Schelling, on transport.

Preparation of the original report included several rounds of consultations in Tanzania organized by the MPEE. In initial consultations in September 2003 and July 2004, the team defined and agreed on the scope and focus of the study as well as on collaborative arrangements. The main mission took place in November 2004 and included field visits to Kigoma, Lindi, and Mtwara. In March 2005, a series of workshops in Dar es Salaam, Dodoma, Morogoro, and Moshi were organized to obtain feedback and input on the draft background studies before drafting the main report. At that stage, the MPEE organized a review meeting with permanent secretaries and senior officials from a large number of ministries for a briefing on the consultations and a discussion of the emerging main messages and recommendations. The team would like to express its sincere gratitude to all who have provided valuable comments, and input during the consultations.

Production of the final report was aided by Mary-Anne Mwakangale (WB) and Arlette Sourou (WB), who provided dedicated logistical support. Arlette Sourou was also responsible for word processing and physical production of the report. Publications Professionals edited the material. Production of the book was managed in the World Bank Office of the Publisher. Tomoko Harata (WB) designed the cover.

Original Report

World Bank. 2007. "Tanzania: Sustaining and Sharing Economic Growth—Country Economic Memorandum and Poverty Assessment (in Two Volumes)." Report 39021-TZ, Poverty Reduction and Economic Management for East Africa and the Horn, World Bank, Washington, DC.

Abbreviations

T Sh	Tanzanian shillings (exchange rate effective as of January 18, 2007, was US$1.00 = T Sh 1,285.1)
AIDS	acquired immune deficiency syndrome
ASDP	Agricultural Sector Development Programme
ASDS	Agricultural Sector Development Strategy
BCI	Business Competitiveness Index
CBO	community-based organization
CDTT	Centre for the Development and Transfer of Technology
CET	common external tariff
CPIA	Country Policy and Institutional Assessment
DADG	District Agricultural Development Grant
DADP	District Agricultural Development Plan
DANIDA	Danish International Development Agency
DAWASA	Dar es Salaam Water and Sewerage Authority
DHS	Demographic and Health Survey
DRD	Department of Research and Development
EAC	East African Community
EEZ	Exclusive Economic Zone
EWURA	Energy and Water Utilities Regulatory Authority
FDI	foreign direct investment
GCI	Global Competitiveness Index
GDP	gross domestic product
GLS	gray leaf spot
GNI	gross national income
HBS	Household Budget Survey
HIPC	Heavily Indebted Poor Countries (Initiative)
HIV	human immunodeficiency virus
ICOR	incremental capital output ratio
ICRG	International Country Risk Guide
ICT	information and communication technology
ILD	Instituto Libertad y Democracia
ILO	International Labour Organization
IMF	International Monetary Fund

ISO	International Standards Organization
IT	information technology
KAM	Knowledge Assessment Methodology
KEI	Knowledge Economy Index
MAC	Ministry of Agriculture and Cooperatives
MAFS	Ministry of Agriculture and Food Security
MAFSC	Ministry of Agriculture, Food Security, and Cooperatives
MBICU	Mbinga Cooperative Union
MCM	Ministry of Cooperatives and Marketing
MDG	Millennium Development Goal
MLD	Ministry of Livestock Development
MNRT	Ministry of Natural Resources and Tourism
MSMEs	micro- , small, and medium enterprises
MTEF	Medium-Term Expenditure Framework
MVIWATA	Mtandao wa Vikundi vya Wakulima Tanzania
MWLD	Ministry of Water and Livestock Development
NARS	National Agricultural Research System
NEER	nominal effective exchange rate
NGO	nongovernmental organization
NPV	net present value
NSGRP	National Strategy for Growth and Reduction of Poverty
ODA	official development assistance
OECD	Organisation for Economic Co-operation and Development
PASS	Private Agricultural Sector Support
PBRs	Plant Breeder's Rights
PC	personal computer
PEDP	Primary Education Development Program
PORALG	President's Office–Regional Administration and Local Government
PRSP	Poverty Reduction Strategy Paper
R&D	research and development
REER	real effective exchange rate
ROSCAs	rotating savings and credit associations
S&T	science and technology
SACCO	savings and credit cooperative
SACMEQ	Southern and Eastern Africa Consortium for Monitoring Educational Quality
SADC	South African Development Community
SEDP	Secondary Education Development Program
SMEs	small and medium enterprises
SPILL	Strategic Plan for Implementation of Land Legislation
TAFOPA	Tanzania Food Processors Association
TAI	Technology Achievement Index
TANAPA	Tanzania National Parks
TANESCO	Tanzania Electricity Supply Company
TANROADS	Tanzania National Roads Agency

TASISO	Tanzania Small Industrialists Society
TAZARA	Tanzania-Zambia Railway
TBS	Tanzania Bureau of Standards
TCRA	Tanzania Communications Regulatory Authority
TFP	total factor productivity
TICTS	Tanzania International Container Terminal Services
TNBC	Tanzania National Business Council
TPA	Tanzania Port Authority
TRC	Tanzania Railways Corporation
TRCHS	Tanzania Reproductive and Child Health Survey
TTCL	Tanzania Telecommunications Company Limited
TVET	technical and vocational education and training
UNCTAD	United Nations Conference on Trade and Development
UNDP	United Nations Development Programme
UNIDO	United Nations Industrial Development Organization
USAID	U.S. Agency for International Development
VAT	value added tax
VIBINDO	Vikundi vya Biashara Ndogondogo (Small Industries and Petty Traders Association)
WUA	water user association
ZRDC	zonal research and development centers

Overview

Robert J. Utz

Tanzania's National Strategy for Growth and Reduction of Poverty (NSGRP) emphasizes the importance of fostering economic growth for poverty reduction. It sets an ambitious target of 6 to 8 percent annual economic growth to achieve rapid reduction in poverty. This book focuses on three issues that are central to the success of Tanzania's poverty reduction efforts:

- What factors explain Tanzania's recent acceleration in economic growth?

- Has the accelerated economic growth translated into reduced poverty?

- What must be done to sustain economic growth that is pro-poor?

The book presents evidence from the macroeconomic, sectoral, firm, and household levels that sheds light on these questions. This summary provides an overview of the main findings and recommendations.

What Factors Explain Tanzania's Recent Acceleration in Economic Growth?

The average annual growth of Tanzania's gross domestic product (GDP) of 6.0 percent during 2000 to 2005 has been high, not only compared with its own historical growth performance but also compared with international growth rates. Growth rates increased across all sectors, with industry growing by 8.7 percent, services by 5.9 percent, and agriculture by 4.8 percent during the same period. Mining (growth rate of 15.2 percent), construction (10 percent), manufacturing (7.0 percent), and trade hotels and restaurants (6.9 percent) were the fastest-growing subsectors. The contribution of the various sectors to growth, which depends on both the growth rate of the sector and its share in the economy, shows that agriculture contributed 2.3 percentage points, services 2.1 percentage points, and industry 1.6 percentage points of the average annual growth of 6.0 percent during 2000 to 2005. The analysis of the sectoral contributions to the increase in the average GDP growth rate from 2.5 percent during 1990 to 1994 to 6.0 percent during 2000 to 2005 confirms that growth accelerated in all sectors. Growth in the service sector contributed 1.4 percentage points to the increase, industry 1.3 percentage points, and agriculture 0.8 percentage point.

The implementation of a comprehensive set of macroeconomic and structural reforms laid the foundation for the recent growth acceleration. These reforms enhanced the incentives for private sector activities and led to improved efficiency of resource allocation and use in the economy. The domestic and foreign private sectors as well as Tanzania's development partners reacted to the improvements in the economic and incentive regime in a variety of ways that explain the increase in economic growth. A central element of Tanzania's recent growth performance is large inflows of private and public capital that were triggered by the reforms undertaken by the government.

The transition of Tanzania to a market economy began in the mid-1980s with an initial focus on the liberalization of the economy through the removal of constraints on private sector activities and the abolition of controls on prices and exchange and interest rates. The reforms also included a restructuring of the public sector and an ambitious privatization program. In the mid-1990s, the reform agenda was augmented by a strong focus on macroeconomic stability and the quality of public financial management. Initially, this effort involved sharp cuts in government expenditures to minimize the government's domestic and nonconcessional borrowing. These cuts served as the basis for a prudent monetary policy that reduced the rate of inflation to well below 10 percent. Subsequently, reform efforts focused on improving Tanzania's tax system and public financial management to improve allocative and operational efficiency of public expenditures and to minimize resource leakages. An important result of prudent monetary and fiscal policy, combined with financial sector reforms, is the recovery of credit to the private sector, which grew by more than 30 percent annually in recent years. The environment for economic growth is thus vastly improved, and current government efforts are targeting higher levels of investment in human capital and physical infrastructure, improvements in the business environment, and strengthening of government capacity.

The intensification of reforms since 1995 and improvements in the business environment, as well as sector-specific reforms—especially in the mining sector—have triggered an increase in foreign direct investment (FDI) and aid inflows. FDI has increased rapidly since the mid-1990s and reached about US$542 million or 5 percent of GDP by 1999, partly driven by large investments in mining and privatization-related investments. Following the completion of considerable investments in the mining sector and the major privatizations, FDI declined to US$375 million by 2005, or 2.5 percent of GDP, a level that is still high in comparison with that of most other African countries. The sectors that received the bulk of the FDI showed the highest growth rates, including mining, manufacturing, and trade and tourism, which together attracted about 75 percent of FDI during 1999 to 2001.

The reforms implemented by the government also triggered a continuous increase in aid inflows that, together with improved domestic revenue collection, supported the increase in government spending from 16 percent of GDP in 1999/2000 to 26 percent in 2005/06. National accounting statistics suggest that this increase in government spending contributed significantly to the acceleration in economic growth. In the short term, the increased demand for goods and services by the government led to increased use of available capacity. For example, the rehabilitation and expansion of administrative, economic, and social infrastructure are reflected in the fast growth of the construction sector by about 10 percent annually during 2000 to 2005. Fast growth in the service sector is also partly related to increased government expenditures. In addition to these direct effects of increased government spending, traditional multiplier effects translate increases in government spending into increased demand for goods and services in all sectors. In the medium to long term, if government spending contributes effectively to the building of human capital and the expansion of economic infrastructure, then sustained levels of increased government spending have the potential to expand the productive capacity of the economy.

A noteworthy development is the rapid growth of the informal sector—particularly in Dar es Salaam—as the result of various factors. These include the liberalization of the economy, the tolerance of many informal sector activities that were previously illegal, the need for laid-off government workers and migrants to generate new income-earning opportunities, and the increased demand for informal sector products and services as a trickle-down effect from growth in the formal economy.

Another significant economic development during the past decade has been the rapid expansion of mining and gold exports, whose share in total exports increased from 4 percent in 1998 to 56 percent in 2005. However, the contribution of mining to overall growth was only 0.4 percentage point, reflecting the relatively small size of the mining sector, as well as the high import dependence of the sector for machinery and its very limited domestic backward and forward links. Aside from gold, fish, and tourism, the value of exports remains low and volatile. Between 1995 and 2001, the real effective exchange rate appreciated by almost 50 percent and then returned to its 1995 level. The real appreciation has had a significant influence on the competitiveness of Tanzania's tradables sector. Although merchandise exports declined during 1995 to 2001, they started a recovery in parallel to the recent real depreciation. To date, exports other than gold and fish have played a relatively small role as a dynamic source of growth and learning and have seen little diversification. Thus, a key challenge for the Tanzanian economy is to strengthen its export competitiveness. Doing so would ensure that, aside from the dynamic growth effects of a strong export sector, exports will provide an important demand stimulus for the economy, especially because the scope for continued increases of government spending as the primary demand stimulus is clearly limited.

The analysis of factor inputs suggests that the acceleration in economic growth is not so much grounded in a rapid expansion of human and physical capital but is primarily due to an increase in cultivated land in the agriculture sector and increased factor productivity for the other sectors. The increase in total factor productivity reflects both increased capacity use in response to increased aggregate demand and economic efficiency gains in the wake of the removal of economic distortions. Innovation and technological change have so far played only small roles in improving Tanzania's total factor productivity, mainly in the form of FDI but also as some encouraging innovations emerging from the agricultural research system. At the firm level, there is some evidence that the structural reforms have resulted in a more dynamic and competitive private sector. Increased competition in the private sector is evidenced by an increasing number of firms exiting and entering the market. The fact that firms entering the market are typically more competitive than those that exit is an important driver of the increase in total factor productivity registered at the aggregate level.

Although the contribution of human and physical capital accumulation to economic growth has been relatively small, the recent increases in school enrollment can be expected to be reflected in higher economic growth in the future. Public investment has recovered from an average of about 3 percent of GDP during the late 1990s to about 8 percent of GDP in recent years. The analysis of public investment suggests, however, that only about one-third of it was used on public infrastructure such as roads or electricity, while the remainder was devoted to the rehabilitation and expansion of administrative and social infrastructure. Private sector investment had been stagnant at about 11 percent until 2002 but increased to 14 percent by 2005, reflecting increased investor confidence in response to sustained implementation of investor-friendly reforms and increased demand.

Drawing on the review of Tanzania's recent growth performance, this book assesses the prospects for sustained high growth and the key challenges that need to be addressed. Policy-based growth projections suggest that growth of 6 to 8 percent per year is feasible. However, some of the factors behind the recent growth acceleration are unlikely to be sustainable in the medium to long term. The demand-side impulses of foreign aid and government spending depend on ever-increasing amounts of aid and government spending. There is also a clear limit to the extent that agricultural production can be increased solely by increasing the land under cultivation. Signs of environmental and social stress (especially between pastoralists and agriculturalists) of increased land use already exist in some areas of Tanzania. Similarly, the effect of reform-induced efficiency gains on economic growth will diminish when the higher level of efficiency has been reached.

Thus, for Tanzania to achieve sustained high growth, increases in government spending and expansion of land under cultivation need to be gradually replaced by increased productivity, savings, and investment by the private sector as primary drivers of growth. Sustained economic growth will depend on the ability of the economy to diversify and to increase its international competitiveness. Diversification requires efforts both to enhance the capacity to innovate and to find new areas of economic activity where Tanzanian enterprises can successfully compete. Enhancing international competitiveness requires measures that enhance productivity and reduce the cost of doing business at the microeconomic level and macroeconomic policies that ensure a competitive exchange rate as well as interest rates and access to capital that are not distorted by high public demand for funds.

Has the Accelerated Economic Growth Translated into Reduced Poverty?

Sustained economic growth is critical to achieving progress in poverty reduction. The mechanisms through which the poor contribute to and participate in economic growth include the following:

- Increased incomes from the main sources of livelihood of the poor

- New income-generating opportunities for the poor

- Reduced vulnerability to shocks that affect the incomes of the poor
- Increased government revenue for pro-poor expenditures
- Increased private transfers and strengthened social safety nets.

In addition, the book examines the effectiveness of measures that support the poor in efforts to accumulate human and physical capital, which would enhance their prospects of contributing to economic growth.

Modest per capita GDP growth rates during the early and mid-1990s resulted in equally modest poverty reduction. In 2001, government estimates show 35 percent of the population living in poverty. The potential effect of the recent GDP growth acceleration has not yet been captured in available poverty data. Ownership of assets such as improved housing, radios, and bicycles by the poor has also increased. The expansion of access to free primary education has also clearly benefited the poor. The analysis of growth incidence suggests that expenditures of all income groups grew at about the same pace, probably because growth in agriculture, which is the source of income for most of the poor, was similar to growth in other sectors during 1991 to 2000. Since 2000, growth in the industry and service sectors has been higher than in the agriculture sector, which may have caused an increase in inequality.

The Household Budget Survey data show large regional differences in poverty reduction. Although poverty dropped from 28.1 percent to 17.6 percent in Dar es Salaam, in other urban areas poverty declined only from 28.7 percent to 26 percent and in rural areas from 40.8 percent to 38.7 percent. The faster pace of poverty reduction in Dar es Salaam reflects Tanzania's pattern of growth. In particular, Dar es Salaam accounts for about 50 percent of the FDI stock and flows, and as the seat of central government and most donor agencies, it also benefits disproportionately from the increase in aid inflows. Although central government expenditures increased from 18 percent to 25.6 percent of GDP between 2000 and 2005, transfers to local governments increased only from 2.9 percent to 3.3 percent of GDP during that period. Growth in the formal sector in Dar es Salaam also supported an increase in the size and incomes in the informal sector, which contributed significantly to poverty reduction during the period from 1991/92 to 2000/01.

More than 80 percent of Tanzania's poor derive their livelihoods from agriculture. Between 1991 and 2000, the agriculture sector grew by an average of 3.5 percent, which suggests per capita growth of less than 1 percent. The increase in per capita expenditure by farm households is equally modest at 7.3 percent during the period from 1991/92 to 2000/01. Nonetheless, because most of the poor derive their livelihood from agriculture, this modest increase explains more than half of the total decline in poverty observed during that period. Between 2000 and 2005, growth in the agriculture sector accelerated to an average of 4.8 percent annually, which according to poverty simulations, is likely to have generated a further drop in rural poverty. The study argues that given Tanzania's agricultural potential, there is significant scope for reducing poverty by measures that would foster growth in agriculture and thus the incomes of farmers.

Another path out of poverty is the movement from agriculture to other sources of income, possibly combined with migration from rural to urban areas. Data suggest that the shift from agriculture to nonagricultural activities in rural areas has been an important contributor to poverty reduction. Informal sector activities have been an important entry point for the poor to engage in nonagricultural activities. Rural-urban migration has also contributed to poverty reduction. However, its quantitative significance was less than that of the other channels, probably because most of the migrants are from households above the poverty line. But migration is only one path in which fast urban growth can benefit the poor in rural areas. Indirect channels include higher demand for rural products, wage effects, and transfers. However, the fact that rural growth and poverty reduction lag significantly behind urban growth and poverty reduction suggests that these links are still weak.

Nevertheless, urban-rural links can also result in a deepening of urban-rural differences. There is evidence that rural migrants are typically better educated than the average rural population, leading to a widening of the education gap as these migrants move from rural to urban areas. A large share of financial savings collected by banks in rural areas flows toward Dar es Salaam, funding credit to the private sector and government in Dar es Salaam, as well as overseas investments by the banking sector. Although the mobility of human and financial resources toward opportunities where the returns are highest is supportive of high economic growth in Tanzania, measures that counteract an increasing marginalization of the rural poor in Tanzania's growth process are needed. Such measures would include enhanced rural access to quality education and policies that support agriculture.

The book highlights instances in which the lack of integration of rural areas in the economy significantly reduced rural growth. Key among these instances is the access of rural areas to markets as well as to agricultural inputs. For example, surveys carried out in the Kilimanjaro and Ruvuma regions suggest that lack of access to agricultural inputs results in low agricultural productivity and, consequently, limited progress in rural poverty reduction. This limited access to agricultural inputs is the result of two equally important problems: (a) limited access to input credit and (b) lack of a rural input supply infrastructure that would allow farmers to purchase these inputs.

These results suggest that rural development and informal sector activities are the primary direct drivers of poverty reduction in Tanzania, where the informal sector has been an important transmission mechanism that allowed the poor to participate in economic growth opportunities originating in the formal and public sectors. This interpretation is reinforced by the fact that although economic growth was significantly higher in urban areas than in rural areas in the period from 1990/01 to 2000/01, modest rural growth has clearly dominated the faster urban growth with respect to its effect on poverty reduction. Furthermore, even in an environment of relatively high growth differences between rural and urban areas, the contribution of migration and other urban-rural links to poverty reduction has been relatively modest.

Appropriate tax and public expenditure policies play an important role in fostering shared growth. As the book highlights, enhancement of the domestic revenue base through sustained economic growth is central to the sustainable financing of public expenditures and reduction of aid dependence in the medium to long term. In turn, tax policies have a direct influence on the level of investment and economic activities.

Similarly, public expenditures play an important role not only in improving the environment for economic growth, but also in enhancing the access and quality of public services for the poor.

Overall, the Tanzanian tax policy is assessed as being sound and not inimical to growth. However, several measures could enhance the contribution of the tax system to fostering shared growth. First, there remains an urban bias in the tax system: effective tax rates are higher for farmers than for businesses, which are mostly urban. In particular, the crop cess collected by local authorities imposes a relatively heavy tax burden on agriculture. Second, the presumptive tax regime for small businesses is one of the most sophisticated in the region. Nonetheless, it is regressive for small businesses that do not keep records. Third, there are significant weaknesses in the taxation of natural resources, which result in both distortions to the sustainable exploitation of natural resources and suboptimal collection of revenue.

Social sector expenditures have seen significant increases in recent years. However, incidence analysis suggests that only in the education sector have public expenditures been pro-poor. In other sectors, such as water, primarily nonpoor households benefited from improved quality and access to services. The focus on social expenditures also limited the availability of funds for growth-enhancing expenditures.

What Must Be Done to Sustain Economic Growth That Is Pro-Poor?

The review of Tanzania's recent growth performance suggests that enhancing the pace of structural change and diversification and increasing the international competitiveness of the economy remain the key challenges for sustaining growth. The poverty analysis highlights the importance of a productive agriculture sector and of a conducive environment for the activities of micro- , small, and medium enterprises (MSMEs) as key elements of a shared-growth strategy. It also emphasizes that participation of the poor in the growth process requires that policies support the accumulation by the poor of primarily human capital and physical and financial capital. Finally, the book underscores the importance of appropriate policies and institutions to manage the design and implementation of a shared-growth strategy, as well as resources for their implementation. Here the book discusses not only the management of public finances but also the equally important management of natural resources. Improved governance of Tanzania's natural resources, strengthened capacity to ensure that tax and expenditure policies are supportive of a shared-growth agenda, and a better institutional coordination framework for development and implementation of a growth strategy require attention in Tanzania's quest for sustainable shared growth.

To sustain and share economic growth across all income groups of society, Tanzania will need to preserve achievements, consolidate ongoing reforms, and strengthen institutional capacity for both policy advice and program implementation. It will also be important to guard against backsliding in the face of pressures from vested interests or impatience with the pace of poverty reduction.

The sectoral distribution of growth has a significant effect on the pace of poverty reduction and inequality. Tanzania's comparative advantage in agricultural production and its large potential to enhance agricultural productivity provide a good basis for a focus on agriculture and agriculture-related activities as the central element of its efforts to reduce poverty. Agricultural activities are the source of livelihood for 75 percent of the population, more than 40 percent of whom are poor. Efforts to reduce poverty must focus on measures that will help the poor to (a) generate more income from their current agricultural products, (b) shift their production to more profitable agricultural products, and (c) shift to income-generating opportunities outside of agriculture in both rural and urban areas. In addition, a decline in prices attributable to productivity increases benefits poor people who are net buyers of agricultural products.

Increasing agricultural incomes requires policies that target both improvements in market access and increases in agricultural productivity. Enhancing rural infrastructure remains critical to ensure market access for farmers. It is equally important to ensure that institutional arrangements are in place that link farmers to domestic and international markets. An example of reforms in this area would be to ensure that the crop boards function efficiently, with a clear separation of public and private functions, and that they are accountable to farmers. Regulations such as mandatory auctions and single license rules for coffee potentially harm the efficiency of markets and reduce farm incomes.

Scaled-up investment in agricultural research and a reform of Tanzania's extension service have important roles to play in supporting farmers in the move to raising crops that yield higher returns. The study highlights the large productivity losses attributable to human diseases that make health intervention an important element of efforts to increase agricultural productivity. In addition to improving farm-level productivity, the focus needs to be on promoting downstream activities such as agroprocessing and enhancing links to domestic and foreign markets. Efforts toward raising agricultural productivity must also take into account the general question of the impact that risks have on agricultural activity in general and the more specific consideration of the capacity of the poor to grow out of poverty.

Increased income-generating opportunities in nonagricultural activities, especially in rural areas, are also important for poverty reduction and for the medium- to long-term structural transformation of the economy. Providing opportunities for Tanzanians to move out of the agriculture sector can be expected to improve the labor productivity in the sector and to provide higher incomes for those moving out of the sector. MSMEs, often in the informal economy, provide an important entry point for the poor to engage in industrial and service sector activities. Measures that support MSMEs are thus important. Such measures would target easier access to credit and public recognition and support for informal sector activities, instead of the frequently observed harassment of informal sector operators. Formalization should be primarily incentive based in the case of microenterprises.

This book highlights the importance of the manufacturing sector as a potential dynamic driver of diversification and growth. Analysis of firm-level data from the enterprise survey suggests that, in order of priority, the five leading factors that affect firm growth and that deserve special attention by policy makers are (a) access to and cost of financial capital; (b) access to technology to improve productivity; (c) infrastructure, especially energy; (d) skilled labor; and (e) the regulatory environment for business activities.

Because firm growth is intricately tied to growth in exports, an aggressive and proactive policy stance promoting manufactured exports is likely to have the greatest effect on manufacturing growth in Tanzania and is recommended. The rationale for this selective approach is motivated by today's global reality: if a firm cannot compete in the global market (that is, if it cannot export), it is unlikely to survive too long in Tanzania's domestic or Africa's regional markets, which are flooded with cheaper imports from low-cost and high-skills producers such as those from East and South Asia. The policy implications of an export-oriented stance have several overlaps with factors that promote growth in nonexporting firms, but an aggressive focus on incentives that facilitate the expansion of existing firms and promote new entrants in the export sector is likely to yield the most benefits.

Priority areas that require improved policies or scaling up of expenditures include investing in infrastructure; enhancing access to finance, notably for the rural and MSME sectors; and building an effective interface between the public and private sectors, because the economy currently suffers from ineffective regulation, bureaucracy, and corruption. Focus on these issues promises increased economic activities in areas that the private sector can readily support. This advice may seem tantamount to recommending *everything*—that is, redressing *all* barriers to production presently facing *all* manufacturing firms in Tanzania. But it is not. To circumvent the high financial and time costs and the government's limited implementation capacity, the book recommends focus and pragmatism in catering to existing and potential exporters. A sound strategy for delivering physical inputs (such as infrastructure) and financial inputs (which will make bank finance more accessible) includes the identification of spatial locations where export activity is most prevalent and where exporters are most likely to locate. The government is pursuing this strategy through export processing zones and special economic zones. However, in rolling out this strategy, it will be important to sequence these activities by initially addressing problems of existing zones before new ones are created. A review of Tanzania's export processing zones highlights infrastructure weaknesses, especially reliable access to electricity and water, as a main constraint for firms located in those zones (World Bank 2005f). The targeted improvement of infrastructure services to the manufacturing sector thus needs to be a priority in Tanzania's efforts to spur growth and structural transformation. Spatial targeting helps in targeting exports. This approach would render public support in a financially feasible and timely manner for fast-growing exporters and potential new entrants into the export business.

Sustained economic growth will increasingly depend on the capacity of economic actors to innovate, to produce an increased array of goods and services, and to accelerate the pace of technological change. It will require, foremost, a greater focus on investment in human resource development (and vast improvement in secondary, technical, and tertiary education), as well as strengthening of the innovation environment and Tanzania's fledgling information and communication technology (ICT) infrastructure.

Tanzania's natural resource endowment could be an important source of growth and poverty reduction. Strengthening the governance of natural resource use and the backward and forward links to other activities is critical to ensure that Tanzania benefits from the exploitation of its natural resources. In addition, improved governance arrangements are important for the sustainable exploitation of renewable resources such as fish or forests and are necessary to minimize the impact of negative externalities such as that of commercial fishing and mining on their artisanal counterparts.

A shared-growth strategy also requires a focus on the capacity of the poor to contribute to—and participate in—economic growth. This strategy includes opportunities to build human capital through measures that center on equitable access to, and improved quality of, education (primary, secondary, and technical), nutrition, and health services; to reduce the burden of communicable diseases; to improve child nutritional status; and to reduce maternal mortality by helping women achieve their desired family size. Other measures include supporting household savings and investment through development of appropriate finance and ancillary institutions, especially in rural areas. Limited social protection measures can also play a role in mitigating the impact of large shocks that may create poverty traps for the poor.

Regional differences in economic performance reflect not only inherent differences in economic potential, but also factors such as past investments in infrastructure and human resources, local governance, and connectivity. Data suggest some degree of convergence in per capita incomes across regions. However, in most regions, the growth performance remains intimately linked to the fortunes of individual crops. Several policy lessons emerge from the analysis of subnational growth patterns. First is the importance of capturing local knowledge to fully exploit growth opportunities. This lesson suggests that decentralization not only is a means for improved service delivery, but also has an important role to play in the implementation of Tanzania's growth strategy. Local knowledge about growth opportunities is critical for a series of public interventions to foster growth, ranging from infrastructure investments to targeted, crop-specific interventions in the agriculture sector. Second, local governments have a significant effect on the business environment, ranging from their attitude toward the informal sector to local tax policy and administration, licensing, land management, and so forth. Finally, attention to subnational growth is important to identify successful strategies that can be scaled up and replicated in other parts of the country. The study argues that the regional distribution of public investment should be determined by the growth opportunities, whereas distributional objectives should be primarily pursued through targeting of access to education.

As the book highlights, Tanzania has been successful in establishing a sound basis for sustained and shared economic growth through the implementation of a broad reform agenda. Tanzania's strategic frameworks for growth and poverty reduction, including the National Development Vision 2025, the Medium-Term Plan for Growth and Poverty Reduction, and the NSGRP, adequately identify core interventions that are needed to sustain economic growth. These interventions include the strengthening of economic infrastructure, scaling up of human resource development from an initial focus on primary education to secondary and higher education, and the implementation of reforms to strengthen the business environment. In many key areas, specific reform programs are in place, including the Business Environment Strengthening Program in Tanzania, the Agricultural Sector Development Program, the Primary and Secondary Education Development Program, and the Second-Generation Financial

Sector Reform Program. The book broadly endorses this reform program, and it highlights three elements of the reform agenda that deserve increased attention:

- Enhancing international competitiveness and accelerating diversification

- Making growth pro-poor

- Managing policies and resources for shared growth.

Enhancing International Competitiveness and Accelerating Diversification

Enhancing international competitiveness and accelerating diversification with a focus on macroeconomic management, infrastructure, access and cost of credit, the regulatory environment for private sector activities, human resource development, the innovation environment, and the rollout and use of ICT involve the following:

- *Resolve infrastructure bottlenecks.* Recurrent energy shortages are the most visible constraint to economic growth. However, general underinvestment in the development and maintenance of transport infrastructure, especially in the rail sector and for rural roads, also holds back growth, particularly in rural areas. In addition to scaled-up investment, there is an urgent need to get appropriate policy and regulatory frameworks in place, which would support greater participation by the private sector in selected areas of infrastructure development, operation, and maintenance.

- *Devote greater attention to fostering structural transformation.* To sustain its economic growth, Tanzania will increasingly need to broaden the range of goods and services it produces. The role of government in the process of structural transformation is not to identify new growth opportunities, but rather to support the identification and exploitation of opportunities by the private sector. This effort will require scaling up of investment in higher education, with the availability of skilled labor already being a constraint to economic growth. FDI and the import of technology are the primary sources of new technology for Tanzania. However, a strengthening of Tanzania's research and development systems, especially in agriculture, also has an important role to play in the adaptation and dissemination of new technologies. Finally, greater access to ICT is an important tool to accelerate the acquisition of technology and knowledge. In addition, microeconomic evidence supports a direct link between greater use of ICT, especially cell phones, and the productivity of farms and rural enterprises. In addition to economywide support, there is also some scope for more direct support at the sector and firm levels. An example of such support would be the establishment of a matching grant scheme for the introduction of business activities that are new to Tanzania.

- *Develop an urban strategy.* Urban areas play an important role in the economic growth process. Thus, an important challenge is not only to sustain the good performance of Dar es Salaam, but also to enhance the role of regional urban centers as hubs of economic activity. Such an urban strategy would define the role of urban areas in Tanzania's economy, as well as the necessary investments and an appropriate institutional and fiscal framework that would allow the implementation of such an urban strategy.

Making Growth Pro-Poor

Making growth pro-poor highlights reforms that would accelerate growth of the agriculture sector; expand income-generating opportunities in micro-, small, and medium-size enterprises; and strengthen the capacity of the poor to participate in and contribute to economic growth:

- *Ensure that reforms benefit rural areas.* To date, the effect of reforms undertaken has been visible primarily in urban areas, especially Dar es Salaam, while rural areas have seen much less systemic improvement in growth performance and poverty reduction. The book highlights five areas in which reform programs should scale up the focus on rural areas. First, improved access to markets is central to increasing real incomes of the rural population. Such access requires investments in road infrastructure and in storage and market facilitation (standards and business climate). The second area is financial sector reform. Despite the overall progress made, rural areas remain largely cut off from access to financial services, which, in turn, has been identified as a key constraint to both farm and off-farm activities in rural areas. The third area is public expenditure reform. In this area, the increases in the overall resource envelope have accrued primarily to central government agencies and, to a much lesser extent, to local governments. Progress in the development of a sound intergovernmental fiscal framework is a necessary precondition to strengthening the development, operation, and maintenance of local infrastructure and delivery of local services, which, in turn, directly affect rural growth and poverty reduction. Fourth are government policies and expenditures to support agriculture. Here the book suggests that public expenditures on research and extension or irrigation can play an important role in supporting the sector. However, scaling up the public support for agriculture needs to be grounded in a careful analysis of the effectiveness of expenditure programs. Finally, a better integration of rural areas in the growth process will require an effort to draw effectively on local knowledge in the development and implementation of regional and district growth strategies. This effort will require an increased focus of Tanzania's decentralization program on economic growth, in addition to the provision of social services.

- *Encourage micro-, small, and medium-size enterprise activities.* Microenterprises, mostly in the informal economy, not only are an important source of income for many Tanzanians, but also are an important entry point for Tanzanians into entrepreneurial activities. The primary focus should be on facilitating and supporting such activities. Facilitating the transition to the formal sector is important, but the move should be voluntary unless the primary motive for being in the informal sector is clearly tax evasion.

- *Devote greater attention to the effect of social expenditures.* The book highlights that the substantial increase in public expenditures since the late 1990s has directly benefited the poor to only a limited extent. This situation calls for a revision of spending priorities and targeting approaches to ensure that public expenditures do benefit the poor.

Managing Policies and Resources for Shared Growth

Managing policies and resources for shared growth means strengthening institutions to develop and implement a growth strategy and to harness both public finances and natural resources toward the objective of sustained shared growth:

- *Strengthen the capacity for the implementation of Tanzania's reform agenda.* As high-lighted throughout the book, Tanzania has made great strides in establishing a vastly improved economic and incentive regime for economic activities. However, in many areas where appropriate policies and regulations are in place, their effectiveness is hindered by limited implementation capacity. Enhancing implementation capacity will rely on the continued implementation of public sector reforms, but the increased use of the private sector, when appropriate, is an important way to realize reform objectives. Examples range from an increased role of the private sector in the provision of agricultural support services to the contracting-out of capacity at the National Audit Office.

- *Strengthen the management of the growth process.* The book highlights the importance of developing and strengthening institutions that are able to coordinate the formulation and implementation of a shared-growth (pro-poor) strategy in Tanzania. This effort includes the ongoing strengthening of the budget process to examine and prioritize investments in infrastructure. Given the large regional differences in productive potential, strengthening institutions that are able to respond to these differences will be critical.

- *Strengthen analytic underpinnings and participation in the design of growth policies.* The NSGRP suggests a very welcome greater focus on economic growth, supported by a scaling up of expenditures that would support accelerated growth, ranging from increased infrastructure investments to subsidies for agricultural inputs or credits to targeted segments of the economy. In addition, the government is implementing a range of specific programs, such as Tanzania's Mini Tiger Plan 2020, the Property and Business Formalization Programme, and the National Economic Empowerment Policy. For these measures to be effective, they must be grounded in a solid analytic basis that supports the choice and prioritization of specific strategies and expenditure policies. Strong processes for stakeholder inputs, adequate governance arrangements for expenditure programs at the sectoral level, and a strong monitoring and evaluation system are of central importance. Although these issues have received significant attention in the social sectors, they are yet to be fully developed for growth-enhancing expenditure programs.

- *Ensure the effectiveness of government interventions through appropriate governance arrangements.* The book highlights a range of government interventions and supports the government's proactive efforts that complement the focus on creating an enabling environment for private sector activities. Recent government interventions—such as targeted credit guarantee schemes, export processing zones, and targeted agricultural subsidies—are innovative efforts with the potential to foster growth, but they also carry significant risks. These risks include the potential for governance problems that could make such interventions ineffective or even counterproductive. The book suggests a range of measures that would improve the likelihood of success of government interventions.

- *Pay greater attention to the management of natural resources.* Tanzania's natural resource endowment could be an important source of growth and poverty reduction. Governance of natural resource use, as well as the backward and forward links to other activities, must be strengthened if Tanzania is to benefit from the exploitation of its natural resources. Moreover, governance arrangements must be improved for the sustainable exploitation of renewable resources such as fish or forests. Strengthening governance can minimize the impact of negative externalities such as commercial fishing and mining on their artisanal counterparts. Finally, improved governance should aim at an equitable sharing of natural resource rents.

Issues for Further Study

Finally, it is important to highlight a set of issues that are raised in the book but that need further analytic work to inform policy:

- A better understanding of private sector consumption and saving behavior, because private saving has remained relatively low and has thus limited the domestic accumulation of assets

- A better understanding of population dynamics and their effect on economic growth

- A better understanding of the relatively large movements in the real exchange rate and their effect on economic performance and trade

- A better understanding of economic developments at the regional and district levels.

PART I
Poverty Reduction and Growth: Recent Performance and Prospects

1

A Decade of Reforms, Macroeconomic Stability, and Economic Growth

Robert J. Utz

Per capita gross domestic product (GDP) growth was negative in Tanzania during the first half of the 1990s, but it has accelerated subsequently and reached 4 percent in recent years. Looking at long-term trends (figure 1.1), we see that 1985 was a turning point in the secular trend in Tanzania's economic performance, when Tanzania embarked on a market-oriented reform program. Tanzania's economic performance since 1985 provides a strong endorsement for the policies pursued since then by successive governments. The reversal of the negative long-term trend and the gradual acceleration in growth are consistent with the gradual broadening and deepening of reforms that has taken place and the cautious but steady private sector response to those reforms. The temporary slump in economic growth during the early 1990s was caused by a weakening of macroeconomic policies. This slowdown highlights the fragility of growth in poor countries such as Tanzania and the importance of sustaining macroeconomic stability, a cornerstone of Tanzania's growth strategy.

In the mid-1990s, Tanzania resumed its reform course with a clear and sustained commitment to macroeconomic stability through sound fiscal and monetary policies as the foundation for economic growth. Macroeconomic stabilization was accompanied by wide-ranging structural reforms, including privatization of state-owned enterprises, liberalization of the agriculture sector, efforts to improve the business environment, and strengthening of public expenditure management (box 1.1). Those reforms have resulted in sustained high growth.

With an average growth rate of 5.2 percent between 1998 and 2003, Tanzania's performance was close to that of South Asia (5.4 percent) and South East Asia (5.6 percent) (table 1.1). However, though Tanzania was able to catch up to the South and East Asian nations with respect to real economic growth, a relatively wide gap remains when growth is measured on a per capita basis. That gap reflects different rates of population growth. On a per capita basis, Tanzania grew by a respectable 2.7 percent. However, South and East Asia grew by 3.6 percent and 4.6 percent, respectively.

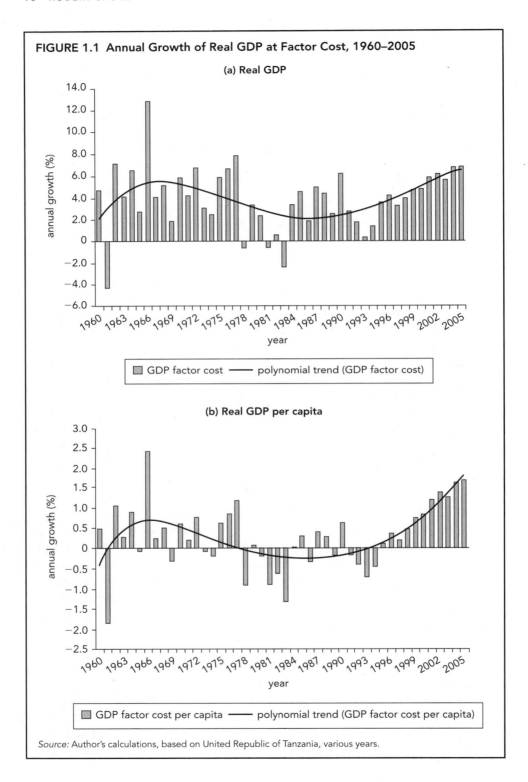

FIGURE 1.1 Annual Growth of Real GDP at Factor Cost, 1960–2005

(a) Real GDP

(b) Real GDP per capita

Source: Author's calculations, based on United Republic of Tanzania, various years.

BOX 1.1 Overview of Structural Reforms in Tanzania

Financial Sector

During the past decade, the financial sector has seen significant change. From being the sole preserve of state-owned financial institutions, it has gone through a process of privatization and has been opened up to new entrants. The two largest state-owned banks have been successfully privatized: a 70 percent stake of National Bank of Commerce and a 49 percent stake of National Microfinance Bank. Those sales have contributed to increased efficiency and competition in the banking sector and to narrowed interest spreads and a fairly rapid increase in credit to the private sector. Financial sector reforms also involved the strengthening of the legal and regulatory framework, including for microfinance, as well as a strengthening of supervision by the Bank of Tanzania. The recent establishment of a credit rating agency is a further step in enhancing the efficiency of financial intermediation in Tanzania. The main challenges for the sector include further reduction in interest spreads and enhanced access to credit by the private sector, especially in rural areas. The government has prepared a comprehensive plan—the Action Plan for Second-Generation Financial Sector Reforms—and has begun implementing it.

Parastatal Sector

Tanzania has been aggressively implementing its privatization agenda. The privatization of manufacturing and commercial parastatal entities was virtually complete by 2000 and a solid success.

The reform and development of public-private partnerships in the infrastructure sector proved much more difficult. At the end of the 1990s, Tanzania launched the privatization of its infrastructure enterprises. By 2003, five key infrastructure enterprises had some form of private participation:

- Tanzania Electricity Supply Corporation (TANESCO)
- Tanzania International Container Terminal Services (TICTS)
- Dar es Salaam Water and Sewerage Authority (DAWASA)
- Tanzania Telecommunications Company Limited (TTCL)
- Air Tanzania, the national airline

However, by early 2007, only the private sector participation in TICTS was still in place and considered to be successful, whereas private sector participation in DAWASA and in Air Tanzania had been dissolved and that of TANESCO was not renewed as a result of performance. As for the two railroads, Tanzania Railways Corporation (TRC) was under negotiation, and negotiations regarding Tanzania-Zambia Railway (TAZARA) had not yet started, as was the case for the harbor authority (Tanzania Port Authority, or TPA).

Trade Policies and Institutions

Reforms of trade policies have taken place mainly in the context of regional agreements, including those of the South African Development Community (SADC) and the East African Community (EAC). Tanzania adopted the common external tariff (CET) of the EAC in January 2005 and lowered its average tariff from 13.8 percent to 12.3 percent; however, it further raised the dispersion of protection. The lowering of the maximum rate of the CET from the current 25 percent to 20 percent, as is expected to happen by 2010 in accordance with the Customs Union Protocol, should help correct some of the dispersion of protection. On the export side, the main issue pertains to export taxes. International experience has shown that export taxes and bans have generally failed to achieve industrial development objectives, have led to informal trade, and have frequently hurt smallholders, who receive lower prices as a result.

(continued)

BOX 1.1 *(continued)*

Factor Markets: Labor and Land

The revision of land and labor legislation is complete, with most of the emphasis on the reform of institutions. The main challenge now is to implement the new legislation. In the case of land reform, the implementation process is expected to be lengthy and costly.

Infrastructure: Power Sector and Transportation

The establishment of the executive agency, Tanzania National Roads Agency (TANROADS), with responsibility for the trunk road network has been a major step forward for the transportation sector. However, a clear separation of the responsibilities of the Ministry of Works, TANROADS, and the districts is needed. The overlap of responsibilities hampers effective road maintenance and development activities. The current formulation of a new Road Act offers a real opportunity to establish a more appropriate policy and institutional framework and to provide the basis for accelerated infrastructure development.

Detailed work on the restructuring of the power sector has been carried out, but the implementation of the restructuring has been delayed, partly as a consequence of developments in the international energy market. A drought-related energy crisis in 2006 focused attention on structural weaknesses in the sector. Reform of the policy and institutional framework for the power sector is essential to ensure the effectiveness of future investments in the sector.

Public Institutions Interfacing with the Private Sector

Red tape, corruption, and overly burdensome regulatory and licensing requirements are among the main constraints to private sector development in Tanzania. The government has started reviewing regulations, focusing on removing obstacles and reorganizing the most important tasks of government. In practical terms, this effort requires (a) harmonization of local government taxation to remove excessive tax burden on private enterprise, (b) streamlining of work permit procedures, (c) review and amendment of licensing legislation to reduce the cost of business establishment and continuation, (d) review and revision of export-import procedures to reduce time costs and corruption-related costs, and (e) design and implementation of a program for enhancing access to commercial courts by small and medium enterprises. Tanzania has reformed the legal framework for regulatory institutions. The effectiveness of those newly established regulatory institutions, especially given the current oversight arrangements, needs to be closely monitored.

Sectoral growth rates have accelerated across the board from 2000 to 2005 (table 1.2). Industry has been the most dynamic sector. The construction sector grew by an average of 10 percent during that period. This strong performance is partly attributable to public investment in infrastructure, but investment in residential and business structures has also increased. Gold mining expanded rapidly as several gold mines started production. However, its overall contribution to economic growth remains small. The manufacturing sector has started to recover, growing at an average of 7 percent per year from 2000 to 2005.

Growth of agriculture averaged 4.8 percent from 2000 to 2005—which is more than 1 percentage point higher than during the period from 1995 to 1999. Within agriculture, fishing was the most dynamic sector. However, crops remain the mainstay

TABLE 1.1 Real GDP Growth Rates, 1988–2003

(percent)

Country/region	Annual real GDP growth			Annual real per capita GDP growth		
	1988–93	1993–98	1998–2003	1988–93	1993–98	1998–2003
Country						
Côte d'Ivoire	0.3	13.0	−0.3	−3.1	9.7	−1.8
Ghana	4.6	4.3	4.4	2.0	1.5	2.4
Kenya	3.1	2.5	1.0	0.1	0.0	−1.2
Tanzania	**3.6**	**3.0**	**5.2**	**0.4**	**0.1**	**2.7**
Uganda	6.0	7.6	5.8	2.1	4.7	3.1
Region						
East Asia and Pacific	8.6	7.7	5.6	6.9	6.4	4.6
Latin America and the Caribbean	2.1	3.6	1.2	0.2	1.9	−0.3
South Asia	5.3	5.7	5.4	3.2	3.7	3.6
Sub-Saharan Africa	1.3	2.9	3.0	−1.4	0.3	0.6

Source: World Bank, World Development Indicators database.

TABLE 1.2 Sources of Growth and Production, 1990–2005

(percent)

Type of economic activity	Average annual growth rate			Average contribution to growth		
	1990–94	1995–99	2000–05	1990–94	1995–99	2000–05
Agriculture	*3.1*	*3.6*	*4.8*	*1.5*	*1.8*	*2.3*
Crops	3.2	3.9	4.8	1.1	1.4	1.7
Livestock	2.5	2.7	4.1	0.2	0.2	0.3
Forestry and hunting	2.8	2.4	4.0	0.1	0.1	0.1
Fishing	3.4	3.7	6.7	0.1	0.1	0.2
Industry	*2.0*	*5.4*	*9.0*	*0.3*	*0.9*	*1.6*
Mining and quarrying	11.8	14.8	15.2	0.1	0.2	0.4
Manufacturing	0.4	4.6	7.3	0.0	0.4	0.6
Electricity and water	4.0	5.7	4.4	0.1	0.1	0.1
Electricity	4.5	6.3	4.5	0.1	0.1	0.1
Water	0.8	1.9	3.5	0.0	0.0	0.0
Construction	2.2	3.5	10.3	0.1	0.2	0.5
Services	*1.9*	*3.8*	*6.1*	*0.7*	*1.3*	*2.1*
Trade, hotels, and restaurants	2.0	4.5	7.1	0.3	0.7	1.2
Transportation and communication	3.6	4.8	6.0	0.2	0.2	0.3
Financial and business	2.9	3.6	4.5	0.3	0.4	0.4
Finance and insurance	2.6	3.5	3.9	0.1	0.1	0.1
Real estate	3.0	3.7	4.8	0.2	0.2	0.3
Business	3.6	4.5	5.6	0.0	0.0	0.0
Public administration and other	1.9	1.6	4.1	0.2	0.1	0.3
Public administration	0.6	−0.2	2.8	0.0	0.0	0.1
Education	4.9	4.2	6.6	0.1	0.0	0.1
Health	3.9	3.6	5.8	0.0	0.0	0.0
Other	4.7	6.0	5.3	0.1	0.1	0.1
Less financial services (index measured)	5.7	3.4	3.2	−0.3	−0.2	−0.2
Total GDP (factor cost)	2.5	4.0	6.0	2.5	4.0	6.0

Source: Author's calculations, based on United Republic of Tanzania, various years.

TABLE 1.3 Structural Change of the Tanzanian Economy, 1990–2005

(percent)

Sector	Average annual growth rate			Share of GDP			
	1990–94	1995–99	2000–05	1990	1995	2000	2005
Agriculture	3.1	3.6	4.8	50	51	48	46
Industry	2.0	5.4	9.0	16	15	17	20
Services	1.9	3.8	6.1	35	35	35	35
Total GDP (factor cost)	2.5	4.0	6.0	100	100	100	100

Source: Author's calculations, based on United Republic of Tanzania, various years.
Note: Total may not equal 100 because of rounding.

of the Tanzanian economy and output grew by 4.8 percent during 2000 to 2005, thereby contributing 1.7 percentage points to Tanzania's overall growth.

The service sector grew by 6.1 percent, representing a significant improvement as compared with the growth of the sector during the previous five-year period. Growth was particularly strong in the areas of trade, transportation, and communication.

Sectoral growth patterns have resulted in modest structural change of the Tanzanian economy (table 1.3). The relatively fast growth of industry has led to an increase by 2 percentage points in its contribution to GDP, and as of 2005 it accounts for 20 percent of GDP. Most of the increased contribution of industry to GDP is attributable to the expansion of the mining and construction sectors. Gains in manufacturing were more modest. Conversely, the share of agriculture has fallen by 2 percentage points from 48 percent in 2000 to 46 percent in 2005.

Rapid expansion of nontraditional exports, especially of gold and fish, plus a recovery of exports of manufactured goods, has led to rapid export growth (figure 1.2). However, even though exports of gold rose from virtually nothing to about 5 percent of GDP, their contribution to economic growth has been only around 0.4 percentage point. There is concern that both the gold and fishing industries are reaching the limits of expansion of natural resource extraction, with only limited prospects of future growth. The environmental impact of these industries is also a concern. Exports of agricultural products declined since the mid-1990s and started to recover only recently. Exports of manufactured goods have recovered in recent years, from about US$30 million in 1999 to US$156 million in 2005, which is only 23 percent higher than the value of export of manufactured goods that had already been achieved in 1996. A key challenge for the Tanzanian economy is thus to strengthen and diversify its export base.

Improved Macroeconomic Fundamentals

Since 1995, Tanzania has successfully pursued a policy of macroeconomic stabilization. This policy has resulted in low inflation and accelerated economic growth. At the core of Tanzania's stabilization efforts is fiscal consolidation. In 1996/97, Tanzania adopted a cash budget system, under which expenditures are strictly limited to available resources from domestic revenue and foreign aid. This system virtually eliminated net domestic borrowing. In parallel to the country's regaining fiscal control,

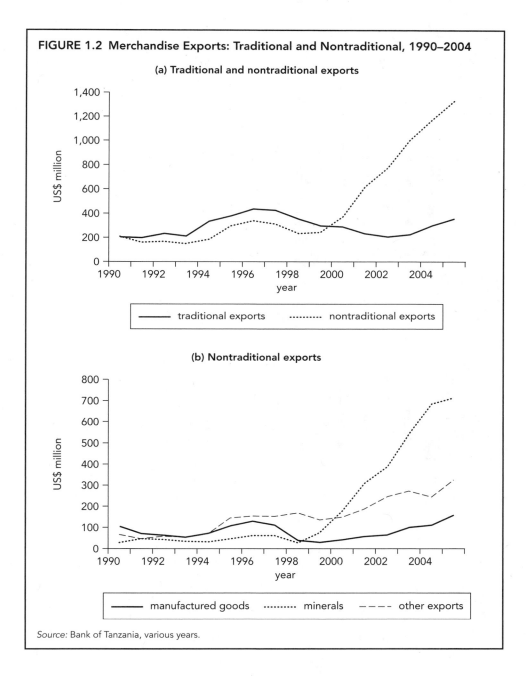

FIGURE 1.2 Merchandise Exports: Traditional and Nontraditional, 1990–2004

(a) Traditional and nontraditional exports

— traditional exports   ·········· nontraditional exports

(b) Nontraditional exports

——— manufactured goods   ·········· minerals   ———— other exports

Source: Bank of Tanzania, various years.

donor assistance in the form of grants and concessional lending increased substantially. Such assistance financed the increase in government expenditures from about 16 percent of GDP in 1997/98 to more than 24 percent in 2004/05 (figure 1.3).[1]

Tanzania's tax system has undergone significant reform, including the replacement of the sales tax with a value added tax in 1998, the elimination of nuisance taxes, the removal of tax exemptions, the adoption of a new income tax act in 2004, and the rationalization of local government taxes. A program to strengthen tax administration

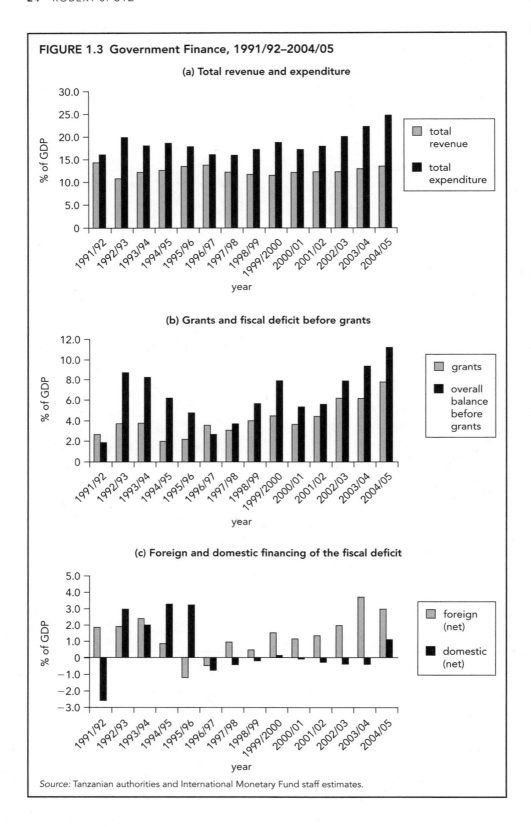

FIGURE 1.3 Government Finance, 1991/92–2004/05

(a) Total revenue and expenditure

(b) Grants and fiscal deficit before grants

(c) Foreign and domestic financing of the fiscal deficit

Source: Tanzanian authorities and International Monetary Fund staff estimates.

accompanied the reform and resulted in a gradual increase in domestic revenue from 11.3 percent of GDP in 1999/2000 to 13.3 percent in 2004/05.

Fiscal consolidation has provided the space for sound monetary policy, aimed at price stability. Annual monetary growth was 30 to 40 percent during the first half of the 1990s, but it dropped to below 10 percent at the start of Tanzania's stabilization program. In parallel, the rate of inflation declined continuously from about 40 percent in 1995 to around 5 percent in recent years. Monetary growth started to accelerate again in recent years, mainly because of the large inflows of foreign aid, which were only partially sterilized. It is interesting to note that higher monetary growth did not result in increased inflation, reflecting both the faster economic growth and the increased monetization and deepening of financial markets in recent years (figure 1.4). Nonetheless,

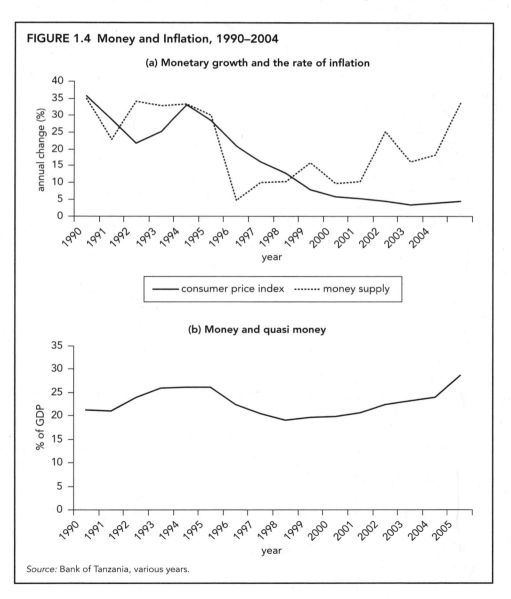

FIGURE 1.4 Money and Inflation, 1990–2004

(a) Monetary growth and the rate of inflation

consumer price index   ········ money supply

(b) Money and quasi money

Source: Bank of Tanzania, various years.

the money-to-GDP ratio is still low in Tanzania compared with that in other African countries. M2, which is a measure of the money supply, stood at 21.6 percent of GDP in Tanzania. In Kenya it was 40.0 percent, Mozambique 29.6 percent, and Uganda 19.0 percent.

Credit to the private sector has started to recover, but it is still low. Credit as a share of GDP declined dramatically from about 35 percent to GDP in 1993 to 8 percent in 2003, but it recovered to 15 percent by 2005, as shown in panel (a) of figure 1.5. Most of this decline is due to the fiscal consolidation, which resulted in a reduction in credit to the public sector from 23 percent of GDP in 1993 to 0.2 percent in 2004. Credit to the private sector contracted from about 15 percent of GDP to only 3 percent in 1996. However, since then it has steadily recovered and stood at 11 percent of GDP in 2005. The tightening led to a significant increase in real interest rates. Panel (b) of figure 1.5 shows that lending rates increased from 5 percent in 1993 to 15 percent by 2000, but they declined subsequently to 10 percent as the money supply was allowed to grow faster.

Large foreign aid inflows have financed an increase in public sector investment during the past five years, but the ratio of private investment to GDP has been fairly constant since 1995. Following successful fiscal stabilization efforts in the mid-1990s, which included significant cuts in public investment, capital formation declined to 16.3 percent of GDP in 1997. As shown in panel (a) of figure 1.6, it has recovered since then, however, reaching 22 percent of GDP in 2005. This recovery is primarily due to an increase in public sector investment from 3.2 percent of GDP in 1997 to 7.5 percent in 2005. While public sector investment increased, private sector investment fluctuated between 12 and 13 percent of GDP and only in 2005 increased to 14.4 percent. The increase in public sector investment affected primarily investment in buildings and other works. As panel (b) of figure 1.6 shows, investment in equipment fluctuated between 7 and 9 percent of GDP since 1996, showing, however, a sustained upward trend in recent years.

Since 1995, Tanzania has also benefited from significant inflows of foreign direct investment (FDI). A survey of direct foreign investment (Bank of Tanzania 2004b) provides more detailed information on FDI. The value of the foreign investment stock was estimated to have risen from US$1.7 billion in 1998 to US$2.6 billion in 2001. Manufacturing is the biggest recipient of FDI and accounts for about 34 percent of the stock of FDI. Mining accounted for 28 percent and tourism for 8.1 percent of the stock of FDI at the end of 1999. Agriculture, despite its importance and potential, accounts for only 6.7 percent of the FDI stock in Tanzania.

Public investment has witnessed a dramatic shift from low-return investment by parastatal enterprises to investment by the central government in public infrastructure. During the first half of the 1990s, parastatal enterprises accounted for most of the public sector investment. The privatization of most parastatals has led to a virtual disappearance of this form of low-return investments. As panel (c) of figure 1.6 illustrates, public sector investment is now almost exclusively investment by the central government. Such investment includes the rehabilitation of government facilities in all areas and the expansion of the infrastructure for social service provision (in particular the construction of classrooms, as well as investments in roads, water, and power).

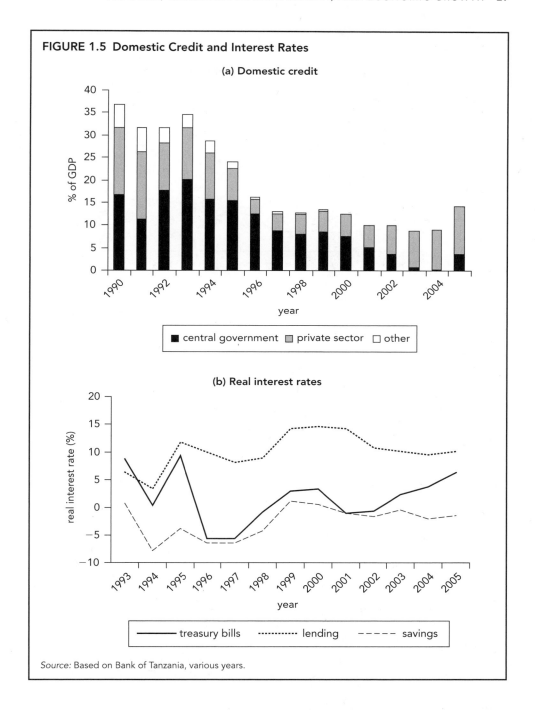

FIGURE 1.5 Domestic Credit and Interest Rates

(a) Domestic credit

y-axis: % of GDP

x-axis: year

Legend: ■ central government ■ private sector □ other

(b) Real interest rates

y-axis: real interest rate (%)

x-axis: year

Legend: —— treasury bills ·········· lending – – – – savings

Source: Based on Bank of Tanzania, various years.

Domestic saving has shown a dramatic increase from −5 percent of GDP in 1993 to almost 15 percent in 2005 (see figure 1.7). The increase in saving is almost entirely the result of increased public sector saving. Between 1990 and 2005, public sector consumption declined from 18 percent of GDP to 7 percent. During that period, private

FIGURE 1.6 Capital Formation, 1995–2005

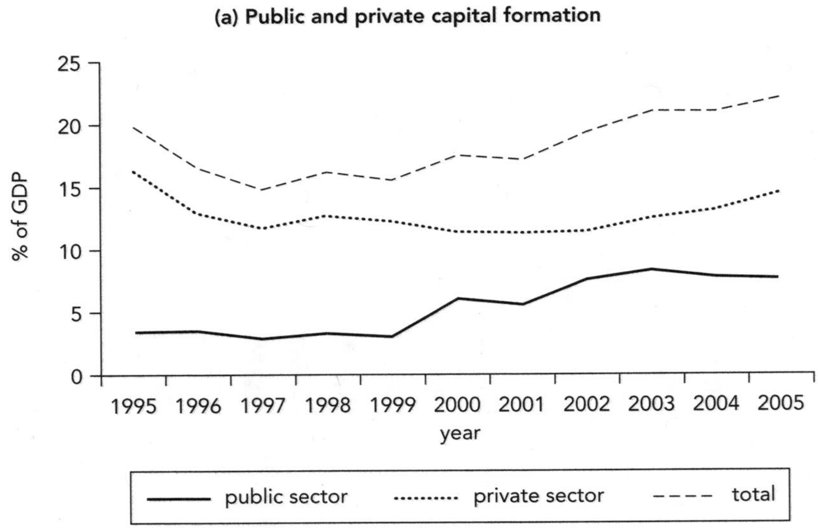

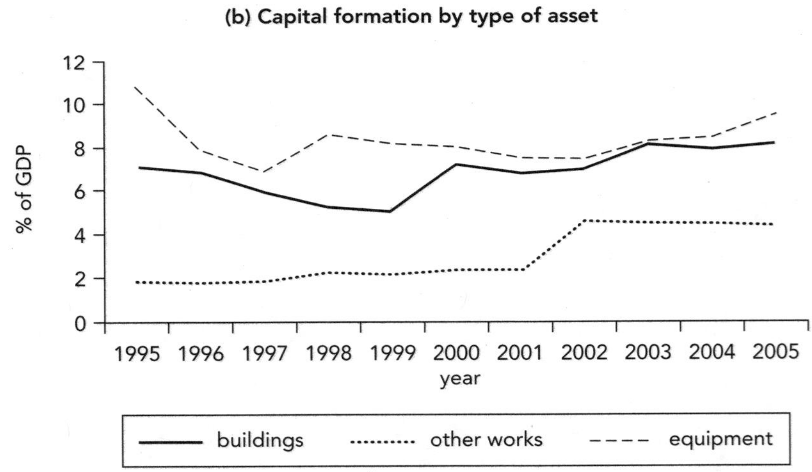

(a) Public and private capital formation

(b) Capital formation by type of asset

(continued)

sector consumption increased initially from 83 percent of GDP in 1990 to 88 percent in 1999, but it dropped subsequently to 80 percent by 2005. The difference between savings and investment, which corresponds to the current account deficit, declined dramatically since the early 1990s.

In an international comparison, Tanzania's savings rate is still low. The average savings rate for Sub-Saharan Africa is 18 percent. However, the economic literature (for example, Rodrik 2000) suggests that increases in the savings rate are typically the result of accelerated economic growth rather than being a driver of economic growth.

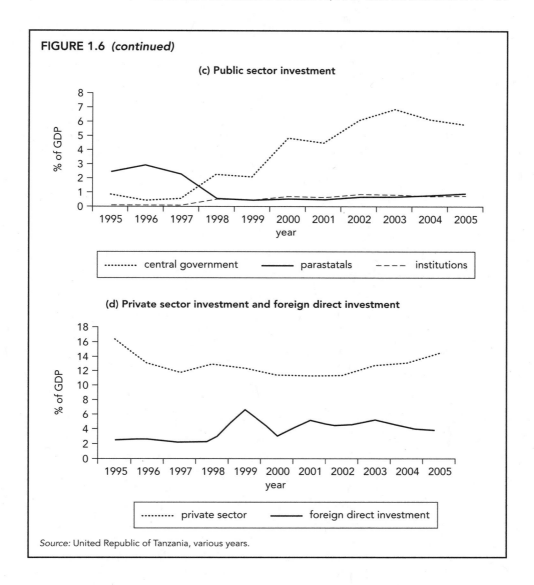

FIGURE 1.6 *(continued)*

(c) Public sector investment

.... central government   ——— parastatals   – – – – institutions

(d) Private sector investment and foreign direct investment

.... private sector   ——— foreign direct investment

Source: United Republic of Tanzania, various years.

Consequently, measures to stimulate saving have a lesser priority than those aimed directly at stimulating growth and investment.

Macroeconomic stabilization has also resulted in a slowdown of the depreciation of the nominal effective exchange rate (NEER) and an appreciation of the real effective exchange rate (REER) between 1996 and 2001. Since 2001, both the NEER and the REER have been depreciating, as panel (a) of figure 1.8 demonstrates, and the 2004 level of the REER is considered to be consistent with equilibrium in the external accounts (IMF 2004). The current account (exclusive and inclusive of current transfers) and the overall balance of payments have improved significantly since 1993, as shown in panel (b) of figure 1.8. The current account deficit (excluding grants) has declined from 35 percent of GDP in 1993 to only 4 percent in 2002. The current

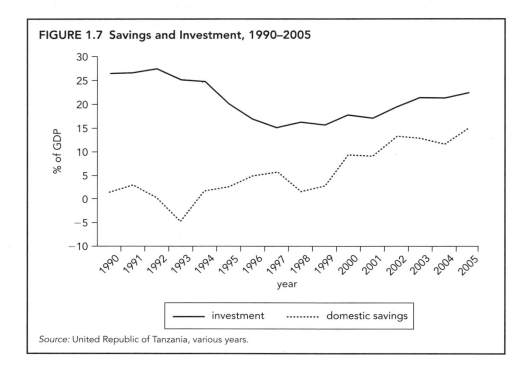

FIGURE 1.7 Savings and Investment, 1990–2005

Source: United Republic of Tanzania, various years.

account balance after grants improved from a deficit of 26 percent in 1993 to 0 percent in 2002. Subsequently, partly on account of the absorption of increasing aid flows, the current account deficit increased again to 12 percent by 2005. The improvement in the external accounts coincides with an extended period of strong appreciation of the REER, suggesting that the positive effect of overall macroeconomic stabilization and structural reforms outweighed the exchange rate appreciation.

Panel (a) of figure 1.9 shows that external debt declined dramatically during the 1990s, from more than 130 percent of GDP in 1990 to 60 percent in 2004. In parallel, debt service also declined from a peak of almost 40 percent of exports to 4 percent in 2004. Following implementation of the Enhanced Highly Indebted Poor Countries Initiative and the Multilateral Debt Relief Initiatives, Tanzania's debt sustainability indicators are well below the debt sustainability thresholds. The net present value of debt-to-export ratio is estimated to be 64 percent in 2006. At the same time, as panel (b) of figure 1.9 shows, gross international reserves increased more than threefold between 1997 and 2005 and stand now at US$2.0 billion or more than five months of import coverage.

Determinants of Economic Growth in Tanzania

This section explores two questions. First, what has been the contribution of the main factors of production—that is, capital per worker and education per worker—to the recent growth performance? Second, what have been the demand-side factors that triggered Tanzania's growth acceleration? Growth accounting is a widely used method

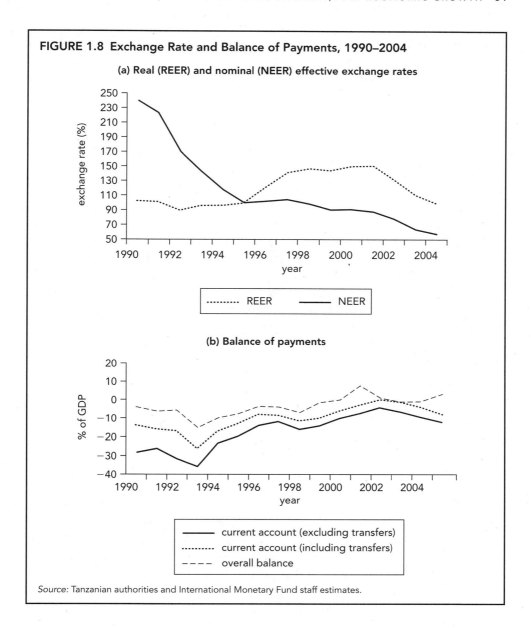

FIGURE 1.8 Exchange Rate and Balance of Payments, 1990–2004

(a) Real (REER) and nominal (NEER) effective exchange rates

(b) Balance of payments

Source: Tanzanian authorities and International Monetary Fund staff estimates.

to estimate the contribution of human and physical capital as well as total factor productivity to economic growth. The analysis requires estimates of the human and the physical capital stock:[2]

- *Human capital.* Human capital is typically estimated on the basis of average years of schooling. Between 1992 and 2001, average years of education among Tanzania's adult population increased from 3.8 years to 4.2 years. According to Cohen and Soto (2001), Tanzania's average number of years of schooling in 2000 was higher than that of Uganda (3.22), but lower than that of Kenya (5.80) and far from that of South Africa (7.22).

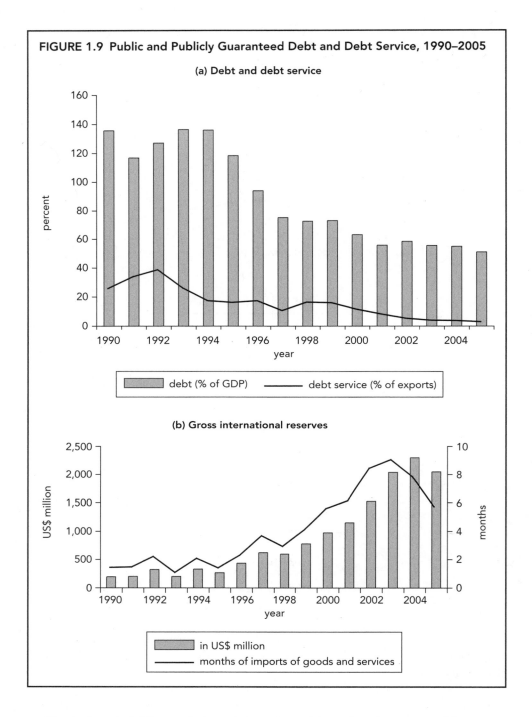

FIGURE 1.9 Public and Publicly Guaranteed Debt and Debt Service, 1990–2005

(a) Debt and debt service

debt (% of GDP) ———— debt service (% of exports)

(b) Gross international reserves

in US$ million
———— months of imports of goods and services

- *Physical capital.* The capital stock is estimated by using the perpetual inventory method. After the capital stock is estimated for an initial period,[3] estimates for subsequent periods are obtained by assuming a certain rate of annual depreciation[4] and by adding new investment. However, in many instances, the value of an investment will not automatically add an equivalent amount to the capital stock.[5] Among the reasons for this discrepancy are poor investment decisions and overpriced investment cost. For Tanzania, it is likely that in the past government investment did not add commensurately to the productive capital stock. Examples abound, such as the Morogoro shoe factory, which never produced at more than 4 percent of its production capacity. Once the government decided to privatize such enterprises, their sales value, if they could be sold at all, was typically low and in many cases negative. In the case of investments in infrastructure, the rate of depreciation quite likely exceeded the commonly assumed rate of 5 percent on account of insufficient investments in maintenance and rehabilitation.

Thus, 1985, when Tanzania abandoned its socialist policies and started to introduce market reforms, might be an appropriate year for the reestimation of the capital stock.[6] Given the paucity of data, we examine two scenarios. Under the first scenario, the actual capital stock in 1985 is assumed to be only 50 percent of the estimated capital stock. Under the second scenario, it is assumed to be 75 percent. With respect to the growth accounting exercise, a lower initial capital stock implies reduced absolute amounts of depreciation and, thus, higher levels of net investment[7] and additions to the capital stock. In turn, the share of growth attributed to capital will be higher, and the share attributed to factor productivity will be lower, with a lower initial capital stock. The contribution of education remains unaffected by changes in the capital stock (see table 1.4).[8]

The growth accounting calculations suggest that the recent acceleration of economic growth is primarily due to more rapid accumulation of physical capital and increased factor productivity, as shown in figure 1.10. From 1995 to 1999, the ratio of investment to GDP declined from 19.9 percent to 15.5 percent, and the contribution of capital accumulation was negative. After 1999, both public and private sector investment increased significantly, reaching 22.2 percent of GDP by 2005. During that period, private and public sector investment increased by 2.1 and 4.4 percentage points, respectively. However, national accounts data may not fully reflect the significant increase in FDI that Tanzania has witnessed since the mid-1990s. Although there was virtually no FDI until the early 1990s, by 2000 FDI was more than US$500 million, or about 5 percent of GDP. An investment report prepared by the Bank of Tanzania (2004b) shows that most of the FDI flows go into mining (30 percent); manufacturing (31 percent); and wholesale and retail trade, including tourism (14 percent), with agriculture receiving only a small share (7 percent) of total FDI.[9] The sectors that were the main beneficiaries of

TABLE 1.4 Decomposition of Tanzania's Growth, 1995–2005: Depreciation of Initial Capital Stock by 0, 25, and 50 Percent

(percent)

Adjustment in capital stock	Output per worker	Contribution		
		Physical capital	Education	Factor productivity
0	2.31	0.34	0.73	1.24
25	2.31	0.58	0.73	1.00
50	2.31	0.88	0.73	0.70

Source: Author's calculations.

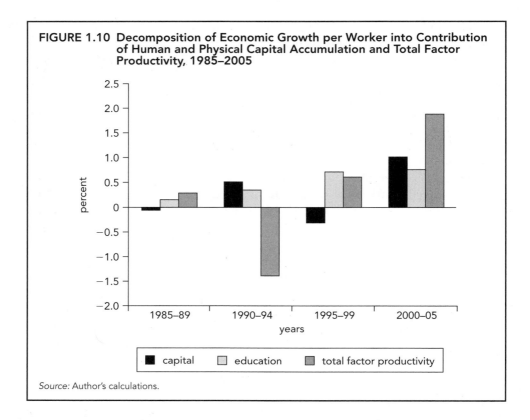

FIGURE 1.10 Decomposition of Economic Growth per Worker into Contribution of Human and Physical Capital Accumulation and Total Factor Productivity, 1985–2005

Source: Author's calculations.

FDI flows are also those that showed the highest growth rates in the past five years. The FDI survey also shows the increasing importance of regional FDI flows from member countries of the South African Development Community and the East African Community (primarily South Africa, but also Kenya). Such flows account for 42.2 percent of total FDI flows in 2001, compared with 52.2 percent from Organisation for Economic Co-operation and Development countries. In 2004, FDI had declined to about 2.4 percent of GDP, because the major investments in the mining sector had been completed and privatization-related FDI had declined.

Recent investments in education have a relatively long gestation period before they will lead to an effective increase in the human capital of Tanzania; hence, the contribution of human capital to growth is still small. However, if recent trends in expanding primary and secondary education are sustained, the contribution of human capital to growth is likely to increase.

The share of growth that cannot be explained by human and physical capital accumulation is labeled *total factor productivity,* but it contains a variety of different factors that contributed to growth. First, it covers the increase in land under cultivation in response to improved incentives for agricultural production, which has been a major contributor to growth in the agriculture sector. It also includes increases in capacity utilization as a result of increases in aggregate demand. Enhanced efficiency of resource allocation and use is another important component of the observed increase in factor productivity in Tanzania. Analysis of the manufacturing sector suggests that increased productivity in the sector is the result of accelerated exit and entry of firms. As older, inefficient firms leave, new, more productive firms enter the sector. All those factors contribute to bringing Tanzania's economy closer to its production frontier. Productivity increases that lead to an expansion of the production frontier, such as the adoption of improved technologies, have been of lesser importance, but a number of cases in which new technologies have been successfully introduced demonstrate the scope for future growth impulses. Such technologies include innovations introduced through FDI but also the results of Tanzania's agricultural research system.

To interpret the findings of the growth accounting exercise for Tanzania, one may find comparisons to other countries useful. Table 1.5 compares the contribution of capital, education, and factor productivity to growth in Tanzania with results obtained for other regions. Several interesting facts are apparent from this table. First, average growth rates varied significantly during the 1990s. The Asian economies performed strongest, led by China, where output per worker grew by 8.8 percent. On the other end of the spectrum, the African countries in the sample saw their output per worker decline by 0.2 percent. The wide variation in growth rates is reflected in similarly large variations in the contributions of capital and factor productivity. For the Asian economies, capital formation clearly played an important role, and it appears that, in general, faster growth of output per worker is associated with higher growth in capital per worker. On the other hand, the contribution of factor productivity seems to be less clear cut. For example, in the case of China, almost 60 percent of the country's growth is explained by enhanced factor productivity, whereas in other East Asian economies, only about 20 percent of growth is explained by increases in factor productivity. The contribution of education to growth shows less variability across regions. The contribution ranges in a rather narrow band between 0.2 percent and 0.5 percent.

The increase in average years of education during the past decade is reflected in a relative large contribution of human capital to growth. However, compared with the

TABLE 1.5 Sources of Growth, by Region, 1990–2000

(percent)

Country or region	Output per worker	Contribution		
		Physical capital	Education	Factor productivity
Tanzania[a]	2.4	0.4 to 0.9	0.7	0.8 to 1.3
Africa	−0.2	−0.1	0.4	−0.5
China	8.8	3.2	0.3	5.1
East Asia (except China)	3.4	2.3	0.5	0.5
Latin America	0.9	0.2	0.3	0.4
Middle East	0.8	0.3	0.5	0.0
South Asia	2.8	1.2	0.4	1.2
World	3.5	1.2	0.3	1.9
Industrial countries	1.5	0.8	0.2	0.5

Source: Data for Tanzania, author's calculations; other data, Bosworth and Collins 2003.
a. Data for Tanzania are for 1995–2005.

performance of other countries, Tanzania's performance during the 1990s appears to be plagued by several weaknesses. First, the contribution of capital formation seems to be low, even when we allow for the fact that the initial capital stock may have been lower than suggested by the commonly used estimates. In addition, the data also suggest scope for greater increases in factor productivity, although estimates for more recent years actually suggest that factor productivity has indeed increased in Tanzania to levels achieved by other regions. However, it is likely that this recent upturn in factor productivity is the result of demand-side factors and efficiency gains from reforms that have moved Tanzania closer to its production frontier; there is little evidence that the increased factor productivity indeed represents technological change that would increase Tanzania's productive capacity on a sustainable basis.

On the demand side, aid-financed public sector investment has provided an important stimulus for economic growth. These growth impulses have translated into growth in consumption and also higher demand for imports (table 1.6).

Increased government spending has been an important engine of economic growth (see box 1.2), contributing 3.8 percentage points to the overall growth of 6.8 percent of GDP at market prices during the period from 2000 to 2005. Figure 1.11 shows dramatically different trajectories for the growth rates of GDP at market prices, including and excluding government spending. Overall GDP at market prices shows the familiar acceleration of economic growth in Tanzania over the past 15 years. However, GDP net of public sector expenditure shows a markedly different growth path. There, growth during the period from 1995 to 2005 was 4.5 percent, compared with 4.8 percent during the first half of the 1990s. Most of the increase in government

TABLE 1.6 Sources of Growth: Expenditure, 1990–2005

(percent)

Economic activity	Average annual growth rate			Average contribution to growth		
	1990–94	1995–99	2000–05	1990–94	1995–99	2000–05
GDP (market prices)	2.5	3.8	7.0			
Consumption	2.1	6.0	5.4	2.1	6.2	5.6
Private consumption	2.6	5.7	4.0	2.1	5.0	3.4
Government consumption	−0.3	7.3	10.9	0.0	1.2	2.2
Gross domestic investment	5.8	−1.3	15.3	1.2	−0.3	3.5
Net exports	−1.4	−2.1	9.1	0.4	0.4	−1.7
Exports of goods and nonfactor services	12.1	5.4	19.4	1.6	1.0	5.0
Imports of goods and nonfactor services	−3.2	−1.4	−15.0	−1.3	−0.6	−6.7
Statistical discrepancy	−37.4	−285.0	4.3	−1.2	−2.6	−0.4
Investment by type of asset						
Construction	2.1	−4.4	18.9	0.2	−0.4	1.8
Machinery and vehicles	9.9	1.0	12.5	1.0	0.1	1.6
Investment by sector						
Private	20.5	−0.3	11.6	2.3	0.0	1.9
Public	−11.5	−5.0	25.9	−1.0	−0.2	1.5

Source: Author's calculations, based on United Republic of Tanzania, various years.

BOX 1.2 Government Spending and Economic Growth

Government spending affects economic activity both through its demand-side effects and its supply-side effects. The magnitude and time pattern of demand-side effects depend on whether there are unused capacities in the economy and whether changes in government spending are temporary or permanent. In the case of excess capacity, increases in government expenditure add to economic activity directly through the added demand in the form of government purchases, as well as through multiplier effects on private sector consumption. Empirical estimates of this demand-side effect for developing countries (Hemming, Kell, and Mahfouz 2002; Schclarek 2003) suggest that these demand effects are typically larger in developing than in industrial countries. If the increase in government expenditure exceeds unused capacity, it is likely to exert inflationary pressures in the short run and—if increases in government expenditure are considered to be permanent—to induce an expansion in the productive capacity of the economy.

Public expenditures also affect aggregate supply. Government spending—especially government investment in economic infrastructure, human capital, or research and development—can increase the productive capacity of the economy. Whereas the demand-side effects typically occur in the short term, supply-side effects have a longer gestation period. In addition, though demand-side effects affect only the level of economic activity, supply-side effects have the potential to lead to a sustained increase in the growth rate.

Separate from the effect of government spending on economic activity is the effect of the way government spending is financed. In general, higher taxation and domestic borrowing have a negative impact on economic activity. The effect of donor financing—separate from that of the associated increase in government spending—is primarily through its effect on the exchange rate.

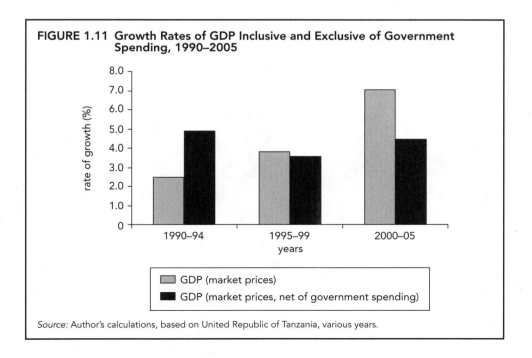

FIGURE 1.11 Growth Rates of GDP Inclusive and Exclusive of Government Spending, 1990–2005

GDP (market prices)

GDP (market prices, net of government spending)

Source: Author's calculations, based on United Republic of Tanzania, various years.

spending is financed from increased aid inflows to Tanzania. In the national accounts data, this situation is reflected in a widening of net exports during the period from 2000 to 2005.

Figure 1.12 presents the contribution of private and public expenditure to economic growth and shows a picture similar to that in figure 1.11. The contribution of private expenditure to growth increased only from 4.5 percentage points during the period between 1990 and 1994 to 5.3 percentage points during the period between 2000 and 2005. However, the direct contribution of government spending to economic growth increased dramatically during that period. Public sector reforms during the first half of the 1990s involved a significant reduction in the size of government and thus slowed down growth of GDP. The period from 1995 to 1999 saw a slight recovery of government spending, and the contribution to GDP growth was 1 percentage point. The period from 2000 to 2005 saw a sharp increase in government spending, and its direct contribution to overall GDP growth was 3.8 percent.[10] The contribution of the sum of net exports and unrecorded trade and the statistical discrepancy has been negative and increasing during the three periods. This finding suggests that the demand-side impulses emanating from increased government spending have only partly translated into higher domestic production but have also contributed to increased imports and a widening current account deficit.

Although exports have been rising rapidly, this effect has been more than offset by the increase in imports (table 1.6). The increase in exports is primarily due to the rapid expansion of gold production, which fostered large imports of capital goods and equipment. The net effect of the increase in gold production, as seen in the contribution of mining to growth, was only 0.4 percentage point.

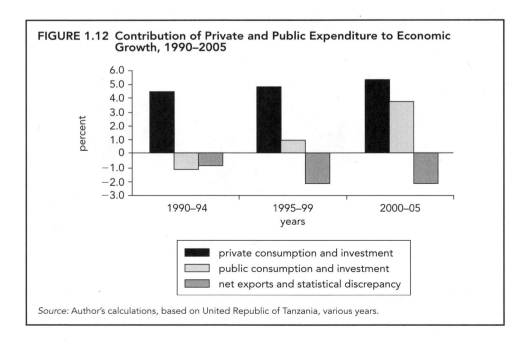

FIGURE 1.12 Contribution of Private and Public Expenditure to Economic Growth, 1990–2005

private consumption and investment
public consumption and investment
net exports and statistical discrepancy

Source: Author's calculations, based on United Republic of Tanzania, various years.

Conclusions

Successful macroeconomic stabilization and the implementation of a broad range of structural reforms have resulted in a steady acceleration in economic growth during the past decade. This achievement is a strong endorsement for continuation of the reform course with macroeconomic stability, clear definition of the roles of the public and private sectors, market-determined prices, and openness of the economy as the foundation for private sector–driven growth. Increasing inflows of foreign aid have supported Tanzania's reform efforts and have contributed significantly to the recent growth acceleration by stimulating domestic demand. However, the review of growth and macroeconomic performance also highlights vulnerabilities that need to be addressed if growth is to be sustained.

Most of the growth acceleration can be explained by demand-side effects of foreign aid, as well as by greater efficiency of the economy. However, the growth effect of efficiency gains is likely to diminish over time, and aid inflows cannot be expected to increase indefinitely. Thus, an important element focus of future reforms needs to be on strengthening the investment climate at the firm and farm levels.

Also, the fact that increasing aid inflows have provided an important demand-side stimulus to the economy highlights the vulnerability of the economy to fluctuations in aid flows and underpins the importance of using aid to strengthen the competitiveness of the economy through investments in infrastructure and the implementation of reforms that would increase competitiveness.

In addition, the growth in exports is primarily due to increased natural resource exploitation—namely, exploitation of gold and fish—while exports of agricultural products and manufactured goods account for a declining share of exports. Diversification of exports is thus critical with respect to the dynamic effect of greater integration into international markets both as a driver of innovation and technological change and as an important source for efficiency gains and scale effects achieved by producing for a larger market.

Finally, reforms and the acceleration in economic growth have so far shown only a limited effect on the lives of the poor. In the next chapter, we review the link between growth and poverty and analyze Tanzania's poverty profile with the objective of identifying reform strategies that would ensure pro-poor growth.

Notes

1. Developments in government finance are monitored and reviewed under the annual Public Expenditure Review process.
2. Estimates of human capital are based on Bosworth and Collins (2003), who provide data up to 2000 by averaging time series for years of schooling assembled by Barro and Lee (2000) and Cohen and Soto (2001) and applying a rate of return of 7 percent to years of schooling. Estimates of the capital stock are also drawn from Bosworth and Collins (2003).
3. Nehru and Dhareshwar (1993) provide estimates of the capital stock for a large number of countries, including Tanzania.

4. We assume an annual rate of depreciation of 5 percent.

5. For a detailed discussion, see Pritchett (2000).

6. Even after 1985 until the mid-1990s, public sector investment and investment by parastatal entities were relatively large. Therefore, it might indeed be appropriate to discount up to 50 percent of public sector investment during that period.

7. *Net investment* is gross investment minus depreciation.

8. This effect is purely a consequence of the underlying growth accounting methodology. It is likely that a lower ratio of capital to qualified labor would imply higher returns to capital and lower returns to qualified labor.

9. Shares represent the average distribution of FDI by sector, 1999–2001 (Bank of Tanzania 2004b).

10. To the extent that increased government spending fell on imports, the effect on growth is reduced.

2
The Challenge of Reducing Poverty

Johannes Hoogeveen, Louise Fox, and Marianne Simonsen

During the 1990s, the poverty headcount in Tanzania remained roughly the same as a percentage of the population, but the severity of poverty seems to have been reduced (box 2.1). According to the data from two household surveys (National Bureau of Statistics 1993, 2002), the national poverty headcount declined from about 38 percent to 35 percent. However, because the 1991/92 survey had a small sample size and the 2000/01 survey had some sampling issues, that difference is within the margin of error for the two surveys and, therefore, we cannot conclude with certainty that poverty declined. The reduction in the severity of poverty at the national level shows a 10 percent decline in the poverty gap (average distance of the poor to the poverty line) and a 20 percent decline in the poverty gap squared (severity), but that difference is not significant for the same reason (see table 2.1).

The modest decline in the national poverty levels conceals large regional differences in levels of poverty and changes during the decade, as can be seen in table 2.2. At the strata level (rural areas, other urban areas, and Dar es Salaam), there was an important decline in poverty in the Dar es Salaam region even as the population grew. Disaggregating the data further into seven regional zones, other urban areas, and rural areas,[1] the picture becomes even more heterogeneous. In addition to that in Dar es Salaam, a significant decline in poverty occurred in the southern highlands, in both urban and rural areas (see table 2.2). In the northern highlands, poverty increased in rural areas but remained constant in urban areas, whereas the opposite occurred in the lake districts. In the case of the southern highlands, the decline in poverty was quite a reversal in fortune. However, because of the small sample size of the 1991/92 survey, estimates of changes in poverty at the zone level are imprecise and should be interpreted with great care. The more precise changes in table 2.2 are in bold (that is they are significant at the 5 percent level).

In sum, the extent of poverty reduction during the 1990s seems to be uneven, with major gains in some areas and an overall worsening in others. Understanding the sources of those differences and analyzing them could yield insights into the effects on households of the economic roller coaster of the 1990s. Unfortunately, the data

---

BOX 2.1 Is Tanzania's Poverty Line Too Low?

The Tanzania poverty line applied in 2001 was T Sh 7,253 per adult equivalent per 28 days (December 2000 prices), which is equivalent to US$0.79 per capita per day, using the international purchasing power parity conversion. That figure is considerably less than the US$1.08, or "dollar-a-day," poverty line often used in international poverty comparisons. If one were to calculate poverty in Tanzania using the dollar-a-day poverty line, then the poverty line expressed in local currency would be T Sh 9,900 and the poverty incidence would be around 57.5 percent, considerably more than the 35.6 percent used in Tanzania.

One can compare Tanzania's poverty line with that used elsewhere in the region. Uganda's poverty line, for instance, is higher and equivalent to US$1.12 per capita per day. Application of that poverty line to Tanzania gives a poverty incidence of 59.8 percent. One can safely conclude that Tanzania's poverty line is low from an international and a regional perspective.

Source: World Bank staff calculations.

TABLE 2.1 Poverty Indexes, 1991/92–2000/01

(percent)

Location	Population share 1991/92	Population share 2000/01	Poverty headcount 1991/92	Poverty headcount 2000/01	Poverty gap 1991/92	Poverty gap 2000/01	Poverty gap squared 1991/92	Poverty gap squared 2000/01
Tanzania	100.0	100.0	38.6	35.3	11.8	10.4	5.3	4.4
Rural	82.1	79.0	40.8	38.6	12.7	11.5	5.8	4.9
Other urban	12.6	13.6	28.7	25.9	8.0	7.7	3.2	3.4
Dar es Salaam	5.3	**7.4**	28.1	**17.6**	7.5	**4.1**	3.0	1.6
Geographic zone								
Coastal	12.8	12.8	40	34.7	11.8	8.7	4.8	3.2
Rural	10.8	10.7	44.1	36.7	13.1	9.2	5.4	3.4
Urban	2	2.1	17.9	24.9	4.8	6.2	1.7	2.4
Northern highlands	10.1	11.0	20.2	36.1	3.0	**10.9**	0.9	**4.7**
Rural	9.3	9.4	20.4	**38.7**	3.0	**11.9**	0.8	**5.2**
Urban	0.8	1.6	18.4	20.8	3.7	5.3	1.3	2.0
Lake	35.1	37.4	37.0	39.0	12.3	12.9	5.7	5.8
Rural	31.3	32.9	39.6	39.8	13.3	13.0	6.2	5.9
Urban	3.8	4.4	15.2	**32.7**	4.4	**11.5**	2.0	**5.5**
Central	9.4	8.3	48.8	42.4	16.1	11.8	7.6	5.0
Rural	9.0	7.3	49.5	44.8	16.5	12.5	7.8	5.4
Urban	0.4	**1.0**	34.5	24.1	9.5	6.2	3.6	2.3
Southern highlands	15.3	14.0	46.6	25.8	15.9	**6.0**	7.8	**2.1**
Rural	11.0	11.2	48.2	**28.0**	16.9	**6.6**	8.8	**2.3**
Urban	4.3	2.8	42.7	**16.9**	13.2	**3.7**	5.4	**1.3**
South	11.9	9.1	43.9	43.2	11.2	13.0	4.2	5.4
Rural	10.3	7.5	44.0	45.7	11.6	13.6	4.3	5.6
Urban	1.2	1.6	42.6	31.2	8.3	9.9	2.9	4.4

Source: Based on Household Budget Survey 1991/92 (National Bureau of Statistics 1993) and Household Budget Survey 2000/01 (National Bureau of Statistics 2002).
Note: **Bold** typeface indicates that the difference across years is significant at the 5 percent level.

TABLE 2.2 Poverty Status in Tanzania, 1991/92–2000/01

(percent)

Location	Population share		Poverty headcount	
	1991/92	2000/01	1991/92	2000/01
Tanzania	100.0	100.0	38.6	35.3
Rural areas	82.1	79.0	40.8	38.6
Other urban areas	12.6	13.6	28.7	25.9
Dar es Salaam	5.3	**7.4**	28.1	**17.6**
Geographic zone				
Coastal	12.8	12.8	40.0	34.7
Northern highlands	10.1	11.0	20.2	**36.1**
Lake	35.1	37.4	37.0	39.0
Central	9.4	8.3	48.8	42.4
Southern highlands	15.3	14.0	46.6	**25.8**
South	11.9	9.1	43.9	43.2

Source: Based on Household Budget Survey 1991/92 (National Bureau of Statistics 1993) and Household Budget Survey 2000/01 (National Bureau of Statistics 2002).
Note: **Bold** typeface indicates that the difference between the two surveys is significant at the 5 percent level.

quality is not adequate for that type of analysis. A new survey will be needed to provide a basis for such analysis. In the rest of this chapter, we usually show data disaggregated by the three strata (rural areas, other urban areas, and Dar es Salaam) only.

Economic Inequality, Poverty, and Growth

In the simplest terms, poverty reduction results from (a) an increase in per capita household income and (b) the share of this increase that goes to the poor. That simple identity can be further disaggregated by region of the country or other relevant household group. The change in income that goes to the poor is measured by the change in share of the poor in total consumption, but it is also helpful to look at the change in common measures of inequality, including the Gini coefficient and the Theil index, the latter of which is decomposable and so is often the measure of choice. In this section, we look at the role those two components of poverty reduction played in the observed results.

The small growth in per capita consumption recorded in the household survey data during the period from 1992 to 2001 is caused by a poor economic growth performance during that period (see figure 2.1). Real GDP grew at an average of 3.6 percent, which resulted in annual per capita growth of only 0.7 percent when combined with a high annual rate of population increase of 2.9 percent. We must note that the household survey data provide only two snapshots in time and fail to represent the full evolution of poverty between 1992 and 2001. What actually happened to average household consumption during that period? We do not know the answer, but one way to estimate it would be to assume that it tracked economic growth during that period. By applying macroeconomic growth data to the microlevel household survey

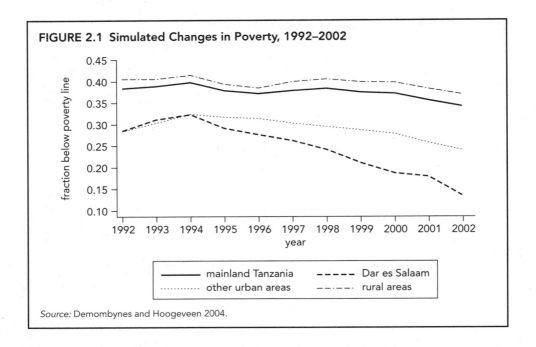

FIGURE 2.1 Simulated Changes in Poverty, 1992–2002

Source: Demombynes and Hoogeveen 2004.

data, we can simulate changes in consumption year by year.[2] As noted earlier, income growth varied substantially during that period. If poverty tracks that growth—especially if poverty in the rural areas tracks growth in the agricultural sector—then poverty most likely rose between 1992 and 1994 and then fell in the final years of the decade. As with other analyses, the pattern shown in figure 2.1 suggests that national poverty incidence is mostly determined by rural poverty incidence.

Table 2.3 suggests a widening poverty gap between urban areas—especially Dar es Salaam—and rural areas. Between 1991/92 and 2000/01, the share of Dar es Salaam's population in the lower (national) quintiles declined, while the share of Dar es Salaam's population in the highest national expenditure quintile jumped from 23.5 percent to 43 percent. At the same time, in rural areas the share of the population in the lowest quintiles increased marginally, while that in the highest quintile decreased. In other urban areas, inequality seems to have increased, because both the share of the population in the lowest and that in the highest national quintile increased, while the share of the population in the middle quintiles decreased. However, the extent to which the cost of living in urban areas and that in rural areas have diverged may be less than these numbers suggest. The same holds true for changes across quintiles, to the extent that the consumption baskets by quintile differ significantly. Table 2.4 shows the increase in the components of the consumer price index. Rent, which has increased by more than 600 percent, is an important component of urban consumption baskets, whereas clothing and footwear, furniture and utensils, or personal care and health, which showed more modest price increases, are likely to claim a larger share in the expenditure baskets of the rural population. Similarly, these items are likely to claim a larger share of the expenditure baskets of the poor population than of those of the better-off population.

TABLE 2.3 Distribution of the Population by Strata by National Quintile, 1991/92–2000/01

(percentage of population)

Quintile	Dar es Salaam		Other urban areas		Rural areas	
	1991/92	2000/01	1991/92	2000/01	1991/92	2000/01
Poorest	12.7	**8.2**	13.1	14.4	21.5	22.1
2nd	16.5	12.2	16.6	15.6	20.8	21.5
3rd	22.8	**17.3**	19.1	14.9	20.0	21.1
4th	24.4	**19.2**	19.9	22.7	19.7	19.6
Richest	23.5	**43.0**	31.3	32.4	18.0	15.7

Source: Based on Household Budget Survey 1991/92 (National Bureau of Statistics 1993) and Household Budget Survey 2000/01 (National Bureau of Statistics 2002).
Note: **Bold** typeface signifies that the difference across years is significant at the 5 percent level.

TABLE 2.4 Increase in Consumer Prices between 1991 and 2001

(percent)

Product	Increase
Food	221
Drinks and tobacco	363
Rent	614
Fuel and light	723
Clothing and footwear	63
Furniture and utensils	204
Household operation	87
Personal care and health	103
Recreation and entertainment	145
Transportation	340

Source: Bank of Tanzania 2004a.

The growth incidence curve is another way of representing that story. Figure 2.2 shows the growth rates of consumption for the entire distribution. The vertical line represents the poverty line. The curve shows that growth was positive for poor and non-poor households alike, which is indicated by the fact that the growth incidence curve is above zero at all points. The flatness of the curve indicates that growth was evenly distributed and not highly concentrated among either high-income or low-income households. The slight rise at the far right of the curve is attributable to the larger gains in Dar es Salaam, in particular among high-income households in the capital.

Reflecting the consumption changes noted above, the national measures of inequality—the Gini coefficient and the Theil index (see table 2.5)—changed modestly. We can calculate those indices by region (with the same caveats as before). Not surprisingly, in places such as northern highlands, where the rural areas suffered relative to the urban areas, inequality increased. For the country in general, which in 2000/01 had a Gini coefficient of 0.34, the level of inequality is low compared to other African countries.[3]

The Theil index can be decomposed into within- and between-group inequality (see Shorrocks 1984).[4] Table 2.6 shows the share of the between-group inequality of total

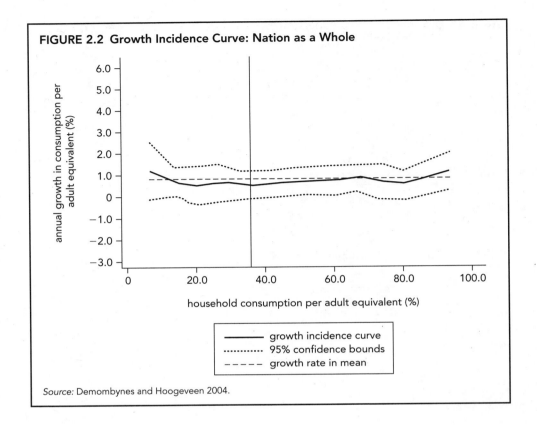

FIGURE 2.2 Growth Incidence Curve: Nation as a Whole

Source: Demombynes and Hoogeveen 2004.

TABLE 2.5 Gini Coefficient and Theil Index, 1991/92–2000/01

	Gini		Theil	
Location	1991/92	2000/01	1991/92	2000/01
Tanzania	0.33	0.34	0.185	0.199
Rural areas	0.33	0.32	0.184	0.177
Other urban areas	0.34	0.35	0.201	0.214
Dar es Salaam	0.30	**0.34**	0.152	**0.208**
Geographic zone				
Coastal	0.34	**0.30**	0.204	0.165
Northern highlands	0.26	**0.32**	0.120	0.170
Lake	0.33	0.34	0.191	0.207
Central	0.30	0.34	0.161	0.185
Southern highlands	0.37	**0.32**	0.244	**0.169**
South	0.29	**0.33**	0.157	0.197

Source: Based on Household Budget Survey 1991/92 (National Bureau of Statistics 1993) and Household Budget Survey 2000/01 (National Bureau of Statistics 2002).
Note: **Bold** typeface signifies that the difference across years is significant at the 5 percent level.

TABLE 2.6 Share of Inequality Created by Between-Group Differences in Tanzania, 1991/92–2000/01

(percentage of total inequality)

Group	Theil index	
	1991/92	2000/01
Dar es Salaam, other urban areas, and rural areas	2.0	6.5
Geographic zones	2.8	5.2
Education levels	4.7	12.0
Household sizes	18.2	15.8

Source: Based on Household Budget Survey 1991/92 (National Bureau of Statistics 1993) and Household Budget Survey 2000/01 (National Bureau of Statistics 2002).

inequality for different groups of the population. Although the within-group estimate contributes the bulk of the inequality for all groupings, the share of inequality between groups has also widened.[5] Inequality between households classified by the education level of the head of household increased the most, with geographic inequality also increasing. Inequality between geographic zones is higher than in Mozambique but much lower than in Uganda. The widening inequality by education level of head of households may reflect increased returns to education at the upper levels relative to the lower levels, or it may be caused by factors correlated with education (for example, living in an urban area).

What has been the effect on poverty of the increase in inequality within and between regions? The change in poverty can be decomposed into a growth component, an inequality component, and a residual component (Datt and Ravallion 1992). Table 2.7 shows such a decomposition for mainland Tanzania, Dar es Salaam, other urban areas, and rural areas. In that table, the growth impact refers to the change in the poverty headcount brought by growth in household consumption per capita as reported in the survey (in Tanzania, a reduction of 8.4 percentage points in the poverty headcount). The inequality impact is the change in the poverty headcount caused by the change in the distribution of per capita consumption as measured by the household survey (an increase of 5.5 percentage points in the poverty headcount). If the change is negative (for example, −8.4 percentage points), it is a positive contribution to poverty reduction (a reduction in the headcount).

Growth has clearly decreased poverty, but at the same time, higher inequality has worked in the opposite direction. Outside of Dar es Salaam, both the consumption growth and the inequality change are small, such that they almost cancel out one another. In Dar es Salaam, inequality increased, but household consumption growth occurred as well, and the poor benefited substantially from this growth. Thus, despite the much larger increase in inequality in Dar es Salaam, poor households gained more than in other areas where the inequality increase was more modest. In other words, although the rising inequality in Tanzania is somewhat of an issue, increasing overall income growth across the country in the poor households is an even greater issue. Income inequality does not seem to have been an impediment to growth in Dar es Salaam.

TABLE 2.7 Decomposition of Change in Poverty in Tanzania, 1991/92–2000/01

(percentage points)

Aspect of change	Tanzania	Dar es Salaam	Other urban areas	Rural areas
Poverty 1991	38.6	28.1	28.7	40.8
Poverty 2001	35.4	17.6	26.0	38.7
Total change in poverty	−3.2	−10.5	−2.7	−2.1
Growth impact	−8.4	−18.4	−6.6	−5.3
Inequality impact	5.5	12.4	4.0	2.7
Residual	−0.2	−4.5	−0.2	0.6
Urban-rural decomposition				
Change in poverty in Dar es Salaam	−0.6			
Change in poverty in other urban areas	−0.3			
Change in poverty in rural areas	−1.7			
Total intraregional effect	−2.6			
Population-shift effect	−0.4			
Interaction effect	−0.2			
Type of employment				
Change in poverty in farming and fishing	−2.0	1.1	−0.2	−2.5
Change in poverty in paid employment	−0.4	−7.9	−0.9	0.2
Change in poverty in self-employment	−0.6	−5.8	−0.9	−0.2
Change in poverty in family employment	0.1	−0.2	0.2	0.0
Change in poverty in noneconomic activity	0.0	0.1	−0.1	0.1
Total intrasectoral effect	−2.9	−12.6	−1.8	−2.5
Population-shift effect	−0.6	0.6	−0.8	−0.7
Interaction effect	0.4	1.5	−0.2	1.2

Source: Based on Household Budget Survey 1991/92 (National Bureau of Statistics 1993) and Household Budget Survey 2000/01 (National Bureau of Statistics 2002).

Alternatively, the change in poverty can be decomposed into regional composition effects. There are intraregional effects, population-shift effects, and interaction effects (see Huppi and Ravallion 1991). Those effects are depicted in the second part of table 2.7. During the period from 1991/92 to 2000/01, poverty declined substantially in Dar es Salaam and other urban areas. That decline attracted people from rural areas, resulting in a 4.0 percent population growth rate in other urban areas, compared with 2.7 percent in rural areas. Despite those population inflows and the substantial urban poverty reduction, only 0.4 percentage point of the total drop in national poverty of 3.2 percentage points (12 percent) can be attributed to a shift in the population from poorer rural areas to wealthier urban sectors. This finding suggests that the majority of migrants are nonpoor. As nonpoor move from rural to urban areas, the urban-rural poverty gap widens. Nonetheless, rural-urban migration may indirectly promote poverty reduction, as in facilitating stronger rural-urban links. However, migration itself is not a major contributing factor. Most of the poverty reduction during the decade has happened within those areas.

Finally, table 2.7 also shows the power of a rural poverty reduction strategy for Tanzania. Declines in poverty in Dar es Salaam have had only a minor effect on national poverty rates because only 7.5 percent of the population lives there. The slight income growth for the rural poor had a large effect on overall poverty in Tanzania, accounting for one-half of the drop in the national poverty rate. The same circumstances apply to households engaged in farming and fishing, because they are a large share of the population and their income is low. However, the last section of table 2.7 shows that the movement of households out of agriculture has also played a strong role in poverty reduction and is likely to remain important in the future. Nevertheless, acceleration in national poverty reduction can be achieved only through an accelerated decline in poverty in rural areas.

The analyses in this section suggest that a successful poverty reduction strategy would include increases in rural income levels, an urban growth strategy, and facilitation of rural-urban migration.

Nonmonetary Poverty Measures

The measurement of poverty using consumption data can be imprecise, and it does not adequately capture other dimensions of poverty, such as insecurity and vulnerability. Therefore, analysis of nonmonetary indicators is helpful. Two types of analysis were performed:

- Analysis of food share and food security

- Analysis of change in reported assets and housing conditions.

Normally, if income is increasing, then households would purchase more nonfood items with the marginal income, whereas if poverty is going up, the food share would increase. Food share did go down among both the poor and the nonpoor during the period between the surveys (see table 2.8), suggesting increasing welfare, and the food share declined the most in Dar es Salaam, where poverty fell the most. Another important dimension is perceived food security. Unfortunately, such information is available

TABLE 2.8 Food Share by Strata and Poverty Status, 1991/92–2000/01

(percent)

Indicator	Food share of total household expenditures	
	1991/92	2000/01
Tanzania	74.7	**72.4**
Dar es Salaam	72.7	**58.7**
Other urban	70.3	**65.0**
Rural	75.5	**70.5**
Nonpoor	74.7	**67.9**
Poor	74.6	**70.8**

Source: Based on Household Budget Survey 1991/92 (National Bureau of Statistics 1993) and Household Budget Survey 2000/01 (National Bureau of Statistics 2002).
Note: **Bold** typeface indicates that the difference across years is significant at the 5 percent level.

only for 2000/01. Table 2.9 shows that perceived problems with satisfying food needs are highly correlated with actual poverty status.

Table 2.10 presents household asset holdings by quintiles in Tanzania across the years. In all areas and in all quintiles, data show some increase in assets, another indicator of increasing welfare. Only one asset (chair) in the poorest quintiles had a significant decrease. However, because some assets are held by very few households (for example. fishing nets), the increase is hard to interpret. But indices of consumer durables did go up, especially ownership of bicycles, radios, and stoves in all quintiles and ownership of motorcycles and televisions in the highest quintile. The quality of housing also improved (see table 2.11). When measured at the national level, the share of households without a foundation or without a durable roof went down substantially. Quintile analysis shows improvements across the spectrum. The disaggregation by regional strata suggests improvements, but outside of Dar es Salaam, the results are not significant.

In sum, the monetary and nonmonetary data are in broad agreement: welfare appears to have improved, but by a larger margin in Dar es Salaam than in the rest of Tanzania. We now look at the economic characteristics of households to learn more about how the growth process affected households.

Economic Characteristics of the Poor

Developing effective antipoverty programs requires going deeper into the economic characteristics of the poor. What is the ratio of dependents to earners? What are the human capital assets of earners in poor households? How do earners fare in the labor market? Beginning with the demographic analysis, earners in poor households clearly support more people than in higher-income households. Poor households have more children, and large households are a disproportionate share of the poor. Households that have four or more children have a 50 percent poverty rate, which is much higher than the national rate of 35 percent (table 2.12). The number of widowed heads of household has more than tripled, rising from 2.5 percent to 7.8 percent, and those households are also more likely to be poor (table 2.13). Female hardship has also increased (table 2.13), but it does not seem to be linked to poverty. Heads of households remain primarily uneducated: 37 percent have no education, and another 6 percent have adult education only. Less than 3 percent of the poor have any postprimary education,

TABLE 2.9 Households' Perceptions of Problems with Satisfying Food Needs in Relation to Actual Poverty Status, 2000/01

(percent)

Problems with satisfying food needs	Share below the poverty line
Never	26.3
Seldom	36.2
Sometimes	39.1
Often	47.2
Always	46.7

Source: Based on Household Budget Survey 2000/01 (National Bureau of Statistics 2002).

TABLE 2.10 Household Asset Holdings by Quintiles, 1991/92–2000/01

(percent)

Asset	Poorest 1991/92	Poorest 2000/01	2nd 1991/92	2nd 2000/01	3rd 1991/92	3rd 2000/01	4th 1991/92	4th 2000/01	Richest 1991/92	Richest 2000/01
Farming										
Fishing net	2.8	2.6	2.2	3.0	4.1	1.8	3.6	2.4	5.4	2.1
Livestock	42.0	52.0	47.7	47.8	47.4	46.5	49.9	42.1	42.2	34.7
Appliances										
Stove	15.2	**23.7**	16.7	**28.2**	21.5	**34.8**	27.9	**45.1**	34.4	**61.9**
Heater	24.2	20.9	18.9	24.5	18.6	22.9	18.5	23.0	18.0	24.4
Furniture										
Chair	82.6	**65.4**	83.4	**74.1**	83.9	81.4	86.4	81.8	87.7	86.1
Table	55.7	51.7	61.1	61.7	66.0	66.8	71.3	74.1	79.1	85.8
Transportation										
Bicycle	25.1	**38.1**	29.3	**41.6**	29.0	**46.5**	27.3	**42.2**	33.2	**42.5**
Motorcycle	1.8	0.3	0.1	**0.6**	1.0	0.5	2.2	1.2	1.2	**2.6**
Electronics										
Sewing machine	1.5	2.4	4.3	3.5	2.8	4.8	5.0	7.1	7.1	**16.1**
Radio	26.0	**40.8**	37.0	**50.4**	37.7	**55.9**	45.1	**61.3**	54.3	**74.8**
Telephone	0.1	0.2	0.4	0.2	0.5	0.8	0.6	**1.1**	1.6	**5.7**
Television	0.0	**0.4**	0.0	**0.5**	0.1	**1.8**	0.2	**3.2**	0.5	**10.1**

Source: Based on Household Budget Survey 1991/92 (National Bureau of Statistics 1993) and Household Budget Survey 2000/01 (National Bureau of Statistics 2002).
Note: **Bold** typeface signifies that the difference across years is significant at the 5 percent level.

TABLE 2.11 Housing Quality, 1991/92–2000/01

(percentage of population)

Construction	Tanzania		Dar es Salaam		Other urban areas		Rural areas	
	1991/92	2000/01	1991/92	2000/01	1991/92	2000/01	1991/92	2000/01
Foundation								
Concrete	18.3	**25.2**	64.3	**82.2**	34.1	41.2	13.8	18.3
Stones or other material	15.4	**18.2**	19.6	**9.3**	33.2	30.1	12.8	17.1
No foundation	65.7	**56.2**	16.1	**8.2**	32.6	28.4	72.8	64.3
Floor								
Earth	83.7	**77.3**	14.6	**7.3**	48.6	42.8	92.0	**88.1**
Concrete	14.7	**21.5**	84.0	**90.7**	49.9	56.3	6.3	**10.7**
Roof								
Durable	28.8	**38.2**	98.2	97.5	69.7	79.1	19.7	27.2
Nondurable	70.3	**61.2**	1.6	2.2	29.1	20.2	79.4	72.1

Source: Based on Household Budget Survey 1991/92 (National Bureau of Statistics 1993) and Household Budget Survey 2000/01 (National Bureau of Statistics 2002).
Note: **Bold** typeface signifies that the difference across years is significant at the 5 percent level.

TABLE 2.12 Poverty by Number of Children Age Five or Younger, 1991/92–2000/01

(percent)

	Poverty		Population share	
Age (years)	1991/92	2000/01	1991/92	2000/01
0	32.0	30.8	36.8	**32.9**
1	39.8	**32.3**	35.6	32.7
2	45.3	40.5	18.0	**23.2**
3	42.3	44.5	5.4	6.8
4 or more	53.4	50.1	4.2	4.4

Source: Based on Household Budget Survey 1991/92 (National Bureau of Statistics 1993) and Household Budget Survey 2000/01 (National Bureau of Statistics 2002).
Note: **Bold** typeface signifies that the difference across years is significant at the 5 percent level.

TABLE 2.13 Poverty by Civil Status of Head of Household, 1991/92–2000/01

(percent)

	Poverty		Population share	
Head of household	1991/92	2000/01	1991/92	2000/01
Never married	13.3	20.7	3.8	5.5
Married	40.2	36.3	87.6	**81.6**
Divorced	29.0	28.8	3.7	**5.1**
Widowed	37.3	40.0	2.5	**7.8**
Female	35.3	34.8	15.1	**24.4**

Source: Based on Household Budget Survey 1991/92 (National Bureau of Statistics 1993) and Household Budget Survey 2000/01 (National Bureau of Statistics 2002).
Note: **Bold** typeface signifies that the difference across years is significant at the 5 percent level.

but the share with some or complete primary education has risen during the past decade (table 2.14).

The economic activities of the very poor have remained virtually the same during the period, while those of the nonpoor have undergone a structural change. For approximately 80 percent of households in the lowest two quintiles, the head of household works in farming or fishing, as they did in 1991 (see table 2.15).[6] Meanwhile, the highest quintile showed a large shift into paid employment and self-employment and a shift away from unpaid nonagricultural family labor and agricultural labor. The middle and top quintiles register an increase in self-employment, and—especially in the top quintile—movements into paid employment. In Dar es Salaam, the heads of households have mainly moved out of paid employment and into self-employment, probably as a result of the government sector restructuring. In other urban areas, net paid employment[7] was constant, but the self-employed sector—most of such businesses are without employees—grew to be almost as large as the farming and fishing sector. That sector most likely absorbed much of the government and parastatal sector layoffs, as well as new entrants and those who left farming (10 percent of the urban heads of households outside of Dar es Salaam). However, without panel data drawn from surveying the same households, it is difficult to know how this transition really happened.

TABLE 2.14 Level of Completed Schooling of Head of Household by Quintile, 1991/92–2000/01

(percentage of heads of household)

Schooling	Poorest		2nd		3rd		4th		Richest	
	1991/92	2000/01	1991/92	2000/01	1991/92	2000/01	1991/92	2000/01	1991/92	2000/01
No primary	34.1	37.9	30.8	32.4	28.5	25.5	23.6	20.3	19.1	**12.0**
Some primary	51.3	52.1	52.9	56.4	54.1	**62.8**	57.2	63.8	59.5	61.4
Completed primary	3.8	2.0	3.8	2.9	4.2	2.6	4.2	2.4	6.0	3.4
Some secondary	0.7	0.3	1.0	1.3	0.8	1.2	2.1	2.0	3.3	3.8
Completed secondary	0.4	0.7	0.7	**2.0**	2.4	2.6	3.5	3.8	4.4	**8.4**
Post secondary	0.6	1.0	0.5	1.0	2.9	2.1	2.8	3.1	3.9	**9.0**
Adult education only	9.1	6.0	10.3	**4.0**	7.2	**3.2**	6.6	4.5	3.8	2.0

Source: Based on Household Budget Survey 1991/92 (National Bureau of Statistics 1993) and Household Budget Survey 2000/01 (National Bureau of Statistics 2002).
Note: **Bold** typeface signifies that the difference across years is significant at the 5 percent level.

TABLE 2.15 Employment of Head of Household by Quintile and Strata, 1991/92–2000/01

(percentage of heads of household employed)

Indicator	Farming and fishing		Paid employment		Self-employment		Family employment		No economic activity	
	1991/92	2000/01	1991/92	2000/01	1991/92	2000/01	1991/92	2000/01	1991/92	2000/01
Quintile										
Poorest	84.0	81.2	2.9	4.5	3.0	5.3	4.9	2.9	5.2	7.5
2nd	87.2	**77.8**	3.6	**7.0**	3.0	**8.3**	4.9	2.9	1.2	**4.8**
3rd	79.0	76.0	6.8	7.8	6.4	**9.5**	4.5	**2.2**	3.3	5.2
4th	73.5	69.0	9.4	**13.5**	8.0	11.7	6.2	**2.9**	3.2	4.4
Richest	66.1	**53.2**	11.9	**22.7**	9.0	**19.5**	9.5	**1.9**	3.6	3.3
Strata										
Dar es Salaam	3.9	6.8	65.0	**41.7**	28.2	**40.4**	1.6	**3.6**	1.2	**7.2**
Other urban areas	48.0	**34.8**	29.7	25.6	18.3	**31.2**	1.5	3.3	2.3	**4.6**
Rural areas	87.6	**83.4**	6.8	5.8	3.1	**5.1**	0.0	1.0	2.1	**3.8**
Tanzania	78.1	**72.1**	12.7	10.6	6.3	**10.8**	2.7	**1.4**	2.0	**4.1**

Source: Based on Household Budget Survey 1991/92 (National Bureau of Statistics 1993) and Household Budget Survey 2000/01 (National Bureau of Statistics 2002).
Note: **Bold** typeface signifies that the difference across years is significant at the 5 percent level.

Because we have no data on farming or self-employment income, we use the consumption per capita of the household as a proxy. Table 2.16 shows the change across the years in average household per capita consumption according to the sector in which the head of household is employed and the location. The differences are striking; the regional differences in poverty performance emerge again as a notable correlation with poverty reduction. In Dar es Salaam, where poverty fell, all types of households, except farming and fishing, had real consumption growth per capita, with the most growth occurring in the paid employment and self-employment households—more than 80 percent of all Dar es Salaam households. In those sectors, Dar es Salaam households began, on average, behind other urban areas, but during the decade, they not only caught up to but passed their counterparts elsewhere (tables 2.17 and 2.18). In Dar es Salaam during that period, the informal self-employment sector was not a stagnant poverty trap for most households.

In other urban areas, the picture is different. Households headed by someone in paid employment (about one-fourth of households) realized substantial gains, but these

TABLE 2.16 Change in Average Consumption per Adult Equivalent by Employment of Head of Household and by Strata, 1991/92 and 2000/01

(percentage change)

Employment	Tanzania	Dar es Salaam	Other urban areas	Rural areas
Farming and fishing	7.1	−6.3	7.8	7.3
Paid	28.2	60.0	17.8	19.2
Self-employed	18.3	64.5	7.2	5.7
Family	−19.2	17.6	−5.7	n.a.
No economic activity	15.9	25.5	44.4	7.3

Source: Based on Household Budget Survey 1991/92 (National Bureau of Statistics 1993) and Household Budget Survey 2000/01 (National Bureau of Statistics 2002).
Note: n.a. = not applicable, because family employment is mainly an urban category. Family employment comprises unpaid family helpers whose work is in nonagriculture and, for 1991/92, houseworkers in an urban area.

TABLE 2.17 Average Consumption per Adult Equivalent by Employment of Head of Household, 1990/91–2000/01

(constant Tanzanian shillings)

Employment	1990/91				2000/01			
	Tanzania	Dar es Salaam	Other urban areas	Rural areas	Tanzania	Dar es Salaam	Other urban areas	Rural areas
Farming and fishing	3,681	3,820	3,895	3,663	3,954	3,581	4,199	3,928
Paid	4,971	4,404	5,735	4,810	6,373	7,045	6,754	5,733
Self-employed	4,857	4,046	5,665	4,608	5,745	6,655	6,074	4,871
Family	4,964	4,420	5,220	n.a.	4,011	5,201	4,921	3,162
No economic activity	3,292	3,976	2,912	3,331	3,815	4,989	4,206	3,573

Source: Based on Household Budget Survey 1991/92 (National Bureau of Statistics 1993) and Household Budget Survey 2000/01 (National Bureau of Statistics 2002).
Note: n.a. = not applicable, because family employment is mainly an urban category. Family employment comprises unpaid family helpers whose work is in nonagriculture and, for 1991, houseworkers in an urban area.

TABLE 2.18 Index Number of Average Consumption per Adult Equivalent by Employment of Head of Household, 1991 Tanzania Basis

(constant Tanzanian shillings)

	1990/91				2000/01			
Employment	Tanzania	Dar es Salaam	Other urban areas	Rural areas	Tanzania	Dar es Salaam	Other urban areas	Rrual areas
Farming and fishing	1.0	1.0	1.1	1.0	1.1	1.0	1.1	1.1
Paid	1.0	0.9	1.2	1.0	1.3	1.4	1.4	1.2
Self-employed	1.0	0.8	1.2	0.9	1.2	1.4	1.3	1.0
Family	1.0	0.9	1.1	n.a.	0.8	1.0	1.0	0.6
No economic activity	1.0	1.2	0.9	1.0	1.2	1.5	1.3	1.1

Source: Based on Household Budget Survey 1991/92 (National Bureau of Statistics 1993) and Household Budget Survey 2000/01 (National Bureau of Statistics 2002).
Note: n.a. = not applicable, because family employment is mainly an urban category. Family employment comprises unpaid family helpers whose work is in nonagriculture and, for 1991, houseworkers in an urban area.

gains were only one-third of those received by similar households in Dar es Salaam. The fastest-growing and largest sector, self-employment households had a very small gain (on an annual basis, almost nothing). We are not surprised that the poverty reduction performance was much better in Dar es Salaam than in other urban areas. In other urban areas, the high inflow into the self-employment sector from agriculture and the low average consumption gains for that sector during the period suggest that the labor force shift was more likely caused by a push from other sectors than a pull and that the sector has a substantial low productivity and subsistence component. In Dar es Salaam, however, some pull elements into the self-employment sector may be present, given the income gains.

In rural areas, households did equal to or better than other urban areas in self-employment and in agriculture, whereas consumption in households headed by a self-employed person grew slower than in other urban areas. But because they started out behind the other sectors, even households in paid employment remain vulnerable to poverty, and those in the other sectors are highly vulnerable. Within all areas, the ratio of average household consumption in agriculture households compared with nonagricultural households widened, again highlighting the need for a rural poverty strategy.

If we consider the labor force as a whole, the shifts in employment patterns mirror those of heads of household, with some differences by gender (see table 2.19). Both genders moved out of agriculture, but women moved proportionately more. Nonetheless, women are still more likely to be employed in agriculture than men. Men still dominate the paid employment and self-employment sectors, but women were able to move into those sectors. The main difference with heads of households is that the whole labor force has a higher share working as family employment, which is to be expected.

Households normally have several earners and several sources of income. One way to get a snapshot of this is in table 2.20, which shows the sector of employment of the spouse compared with the sector of the head of household. In general, agricultural

TABLE 2.19 Share of Labor Force by Employment and Gender, 1991/92–2000/01

Employment	Share of all (as a % of total labor force)		Share of males (as a % of total labor force)		Share of females (as a % of total labor force)		Share of females (as a % of sectoral labor force)	
	1991/92	2000/01	1991/92	2000/01	1991/92	2000/01	1991/92	2000/01
Farming and fishing	81.3	**71.5**	77.5	**70.0**	84.8	**72.8**	55.0	55.1
Paid	7.9	**6.8**	12.7	**10.4**	3.6	3.8	24.2	**55.1**
Self-employed	5.5	**8.9**	7.4	**11.9**	3.7	**6.4**	36.0	38.7
Family	5.2	**12.8**	2.3	**7.9**	7.7	**17.1**	78.9	**71.9**
Total	100.0	100.0	100.0	100.0	100.0	100.0	n.a.	n.a.

Source: Based on Household Budget Survey 1991/92 (National Bureau of Statistics 1993) and Household Budget Survey 2000/01 (National Bureau of Statistics 2002).
Note: n.a. = not applicable. **Bold** typeface signifies that the difference across years is significant at the 5 percent level. Totals may not equal 100.0 because of rounding.

TABLE 2.20 Employment of Spouses Compared with That of Heads of Household, 1991/92–2000/01

(percent)

Employment of spouse	Employment of head of household					
	Farming and fishing		Paid		Self-employed	
	1991/92	2000/01	1991/92	2000/01	1991/92	2000/01
Farming and fishing	97.8	**94.1**	52.1	**41.7**	47.3	**39.3**
Paid	0.5	0.6	13.2	12.3	6.3	**3.3**
Self-employed	1.0	**2.3**	8.4	10.9	8.3	**18.4**
Family	0.5	**3.0**	26.3	**35.1**	37.9	39.0

Source: Based on Household Budget Survey 1991/92 (National Bureau of Statistics 1993) and Household Budget Survey 2000/01 (National Bureau of Statistics 2002).
Note: **Bold** typeface signifies that the difference across years is significant at the 5 percent level.

households have diversified, whereas nonagricultural households have moved the other way. The dominant trend in 1991 was for the spouse to work in agriculture while the head of household worked in a nonagricultural occupation. That situation has shifted as spouses have moved out of agriculture and into mostly nonagricultural family work—but also into self-employment if the head of household is self-employed. That shift may help explain the consumption gains of those households. Consistent with those trends, the number of households with a business has risen (table 2.21). But this trend, too, has left the bottom two quintiles behind. From the cross-section data, we cannot tell whether a household that added a business tended to move out of poverty or whether only those households not in poverty could afford to add a business.

In sum, where economic growth has occurred, the labor market has responded. In the self-employment sector, where supply equals demand, activity has increased, as well as incomes. Does the income growth represent simply an expansion because the demand for intermediate and final goods and services has changed, or is it explained by productivity increases (more capital, for example)? This analysis cannot answer those questions. However, we see clearly that earnings do not seem to have increased in areas with low growth and that policy needs to focus on those areas.

TABLE 2.21 Main Type of Business by Quintiles, 1991/92–2000/01

(percentage of households)

Type of business	Year	Poorest	2nd	3rd	4th	Richest
No business	1991/92	67.3	60.7	55.4	53.8	55.4
	2000/01	66.2	56.8	55.6	54.1	49.3
Agriculture	1991/92	20.9	21.7	30.4	27.2	25.5
	2000/01	15.4	22.2	**22.2**	20.9	22.3
Wholesale and retail	1991/92	9.6	13.7	11.2	16.1	13.8
	2000/01	6.4	8.5	8.9	13.3	16.8
Other	1991/92	2.3	3.9	3	2.9	5.3
	2000/01	**12.0**	**12.6**	**13.3**	**11.7**	**11.7**

Source: Based on Household Budget Survey 1991/92 (National Bureau of Statistics 1993) and Household Budget Survey 2000/01 (National Bureau of Statistics 2002).
Note: **Bold** typeface signifies that the difference across years is significant at the 5 percent level.

Explaining Household Consumption

Up to this point, we have relied primarily on bivariate analysis. We now turn to multivariate analysis to isolate the separate effects of independent variables on household consumption. The main advantage of such analysis is that it allows us to isolate the effect of a specific variable while holding all other (observable) factors constant. For example, households in Dar es Salaam are less likely to be poor than households in rural areas. Simultaneously, the level of education is also higher in Dar es Salaam than in rural areas (see table 2.22).

Regression analysis allows us to separate those two effects. Our regression analysis compares the determinants of the log of consumption per capita in rural areas and other urban areas. We regress log per adult-equivalent real consumption on a set of explanatory variables (compare with Datt and Joliffe 1999). The coefficients should be interpreted as the percentage change in per adult-equivalent real consumption resulting from a marginal change in the explanatory variable. We did three separate regressions by regional strata because, although most of the explanatory variables are significant in both regressions, the coefficients are different, and, overall, tests of significance confirmed a different structure at the 99 percent confidence level. The regression results are presented in table 2.23.

TABLE 2.22 Average Years of Education of Head of Household, 1991/92–2000/01

Location	1991/92	2000/01
Tanzania	4.0	**4.9**
Dar es Salaam	7.4	7.8
Other urban areas	5.8	**6.5**
Rural areas	3.5	**4.3**

Source: Based on Household Budget Survey 1991/92 (National Bureau of Statistics 1993) and Household Budget Survey 2000/01 (National Bureau of Statistics 2002).
Note: **Bold** typeface signifies that the difference across years is significant at the 5 percent level.

TABLE 2.23 Regression Results, Determinants of Consumption for Households, and Coefficients in Levels (Regional Dummies Included), 1991/92–2000/01

(log of household consumption expenditure per adult equivalent)

Indicator	Dar es Salaam		Other urban areas		Rural areas	
	1991/92	2000/01	1991/92	2000/01	1991/92	2000/01
Age of head of household	0.0	0.0	0.0	0.0	-0.0	0.0
Age of head of household squared	0.0	0.0	-0.0	0.0	0.0	0.0
Age of head of household missing	**-0.5**	0.0	-0.2	-0.2	-0.4	-0.2
Household members squared	**0.0**	**0.0**	**0.0**	**0.0**	**0.0**	**0.0**
Household members ages 0–9	-0.1	-0.1	-0.1	-0.1	-0.1	-0.1
Household members ages 10–14	-0.2	-0.2	-0.2	-0.2	-0.1	-0.1
Household members age 60 or above	-0.2	-0.1	-0.1	-0.1	-0.0	-0.1
Female household members ages 15–59	-0.2	-0.1	-0.2	-0.1	-0.1	-0.1
Male household members ages 15–59	-0.2	-0.2	-0.2	-0.1	-0.1	-0.1
Some primary education	-0.0	0.2	0.1	0.1	0.1	0.1
Completed primary education	-0.0	0.4	0.2	0.2	0.2	0.3
Some secondary education	0.0	0.3	0.1	0.3	0.2	0.4
Completed secondary education	0.0	0.4	0.3	0.4	0.2	0.5
Postsecondary education	0.2	0.6	0.3	0.5	0.2	0.6
Adult education only	-0.0	0.3	0.1	0.0	0.0	0.0
Paid employment	-0.0	0.1	0.0	0.1*	0.1	0.1
Self-employment	-0.0	0.1	0.1	0.1	0.1	0.1
Family employment	-0.1	0.0	-0.0	0.0	1.3	0.0
No employment	-0.1	0.0	-0.2	0.0	-0.1	-0.1
Constant	**9.4**	**8.9**	**9.1**	**8.8**	**8.9**	**8.8**
Number of observations	1,123	1,225	1,487	13,364	2,209	7,547
R squared	0.4	0.3	0.3	0.3	0.2	0.2

Source: Based on Household Budget Survey 1991/92 (National Bureau of Statistics 1993) and Household Budget Survey 2000/01 (National Bureau of Statistics 2002).
Note: Regional dummies are included. **Bold** typeface indicates that the difference across years is significant at the 5 percent level. The regressions include psu specific effects.

With respect to demographics, household composition affects consumption even though consumption is measured in per adult equivalents. The net effect of more household members is negative independent of age, but it is generally less negative in rural areas.[8] Furthermore, the negative effect of more adult male members is larger than the effect of more adult female members in all three areas in all years, although it seems stronger in Dar es Salaam. The age of the head of household has no effect, either in 1991/92 or in 2000/01.[9]

Education in general leads to significantly higher consumption in all areas compared with no schooling, which is the excluded category.[10] Furthermore, more education leads to even higher consumption, which is extremely positive given the recent policy of providing free primary schooling. However, returns may change if the level of education changes for the population in general. In 1991/92, the effects of schooling were higher in other urban areas and rural areas as compared with Dar es Salaam. That relation changed in 2000/01, though, when the effects were more comparable across areas and even higher in Dar es Salaam for primary schooling and postsecondary schooling.[11] In all areas, the marginal effects of schooling have risen during the decade, which is consistent with our findings on inequality.

The 1991/92 results on the influence of type of employment are puzzling because there are no significant differences in returns to different types of employment in Dar es Salaam, whereas self-employment leads to significantly higher consumption in other urban areas and in rural areas. Not surprisingly, paid employment increases consumption in rural areas. That pattern changes in 2000/01. Now, both paid employment and self-employment lead to significantly higher consumption, and the returns are almost twice as high in Dar es Salaam compared with other urban areas and rural areas. Furthermore, no employment reduces consumption in rural areas, and family employment increases consumption in other urban areas. No employment increases consumption in Dar es Salaam, but those households may depend on transfers. In general, this set of variables usually measures a range of nonobservable household characteristics that are related to income earning power, and thus they can be hard to interpret and should be viewed with some caution.

Overall, Dar es Salaam seems to have benefited from substantial increases in returns to education. The combination of higher levels of schooling in general and a much larger concentration of paid employees and self-employed workers in the capital area helps explain why Dar es Salaam fared much better in 2000/01 compared with other areas.

Conclusions

The household budget survey of 2000/01 showed only a modest reduction in poverty during the 1990s, reflecting the relatively poor growth performance during that period. Those poverty estimates do not yet capture the effect of high economic growth recorded since 2001, but poverty simulations suggest that they are likely to have had a significant effect on poverty. However, that effect can be confirmed only with the new household budget survey that was launched in 2006/07.

Nonetheless, even during the 1990s, poverty reduction occurred in some regions of Tanzania. The experience of those regions, especially Dar es Salaam, suggests that significant poverty reduction is possible. It also suggests that the reforms of the 1990s and the flow of foreign aid they triggered have, for the most part, benefited the better-educated, better-capitalized areas such as Dar es Salaam.

At the same time, that experience has also shown that when the private sector is able to create jobs, there is spillover to the nonwage sectors. In the language of the 1970s, growth did trickle down in Dar es Salaam, and it seems to have happened because of the economic links between the formal and informal sectors in terms of the demand for goods and services provided by the informal sector. Even though the growth process brought more inequality to Dar es Salaam, poverty reduction was not hampered. On the contrary, in other urban areas, where inequality was reduced only slightly, growth did not take place. So growth was more pro-poor in Dar es Salaam, despite the inequality increase. We do not argue that growth needs inequality or even that inequality is good. We simply point out that some increase in inequality can be tolerated along with growth. Tanzania's challenge will be to maintain the pace of growth and poverty reduction in Dar es Salaam and similar areas (for example, southern highlands), while adopting new strategies and measures to reach the rest of the country.

Notes

1. The seven geographic zones are coastal (Morogoro, Pwani, and Tanga), northern highlands (Arusha and Kilimanjaro), lake (Kagera, Kigoma, Mara, Mwanza, Rukwa, Shinyanga, and Tabora), central (Dodoma and Singida), southern highlands (Iringa, Mbeya, and Rukwa), south (Lindi, Mtwara, and Ruvuma), and Dar es Salaam.

2. The approach followed is the one developed by Datt and Walker (2002) and Datt and others (2003). That approach was used by Demombynes and Hoogeveen (2004) to investigate the pattern of growth in Tanzania during the 1990s.

3. In 1997, the Gini coefficient for Mozambique was 0.40. In 1999, the Gini coefficient for Uganda was 0.43. In 1997, the Gini coefficient for Kenya was 0.45 (World Bank 2005a).

4. The decompositions are implemented using Stephen P. Jenkins's Stata program, ineqdeco. Given the survey comparability problems discussed earlier, this analysis should be considered as only indicative.

5. The within-group estimate is calculated as the difference of 100 percent and the between-group estimate reported in table 2.4.

6. The survey records a decrease of farm activities in the middle quintile and an increase in "no activity." However, we suspect that those differences reflect a change in coding.

7. *Net paid employment* is government-private employment.

8. As consumption is measured as household consumption divided by household size and household size also appears on the right-hand side of the regression, the negative sign could very well be the result of a measurement error in household size.

9. A different model specification with age dummies did not give any economically and statistically significant effects either. We included in earlier estimated models a dummy for

female heads of households, for civil status variables, and for raising of a foster child, along with interaction terms between those dummies. The dummy for female heads of household was not significant despite the specification, and the same was true for civil status. But prevalence of a foster child was significantly positive, indicating that households with foster children are those that have the economic means to do so. However, given the endogeneity of that variable, we did not use it in the final results.

10. We include the type of schooling instead of just years of schooling to allow for nonlinear effects of education.

11. We reject the simple model with no variation in returns to education across areas and years.

3

Spatial Dimensions of Growth and Poverty Reduction

Philip Mpango

This chapter summarizes regional patterns of economic growth and poverty reduction in Tanzania, using regional gross domestic product (GDP) data, poverty measures, and other socioeconomic indicators for the period from 1992 to 2003. The main objectives are to highlight cross-regional[1] variations in incomes, to identify the most common barriers to economic growth, and to suggest regional policy options for improving economic growth performance.[2] Understanding the causes of the geographically uneven distribution of economic growth and the skewed income distribution is vital for at least two reasons. First, such understanding is considered to be the key for unlocking secrets of how to kindle growth of regions lagging economically and sustain growth in regions that are better off economically. As Krugman (1991) stated, if we want to understand differences in national growth rates, a good place to start is by examining differences in regional growth. Second, extreme economic gaps among different regions are potential flash points for social and political instability. Consequently, the challenge of advancing the kind of growth that creates benefits throughout society has figured prominently on the development agenda in many countries and continues to do so.

Overall Regional Income Patterns

Mainland Tanzania is characterized by highly uneven distribution of economic activity and incomes across its 21 administrative regions[3], with Dar es Salaam dominating all other regions. From 1992 to 2003, about 52 percent of the annual national GDP was produced in only six regions: Arusha, Dar es Salaam, Iringa, Mbeya, Mwanza, and Shinyanga (map 3.1). The Dar es Salaam region alone, which is home to less than 8 percent of Tanzania's population, contributes about 18 percent of Tanzania's GDP, equal to the combined contribution to national GDP by the bottom six regions (Pwani, Dodoma, Lindi, Kigoma, Mara, and Mtwara).[4]

In terms of ranking per capita GDP over time, the top five regions for the period from 1996 to 1999 were Dar es Salaam, Arusha, Rukwa, Iringa, and Ruvuma (figure 3.1a).

MAP 3.1 Main and Least Contributors to GDP, by Region

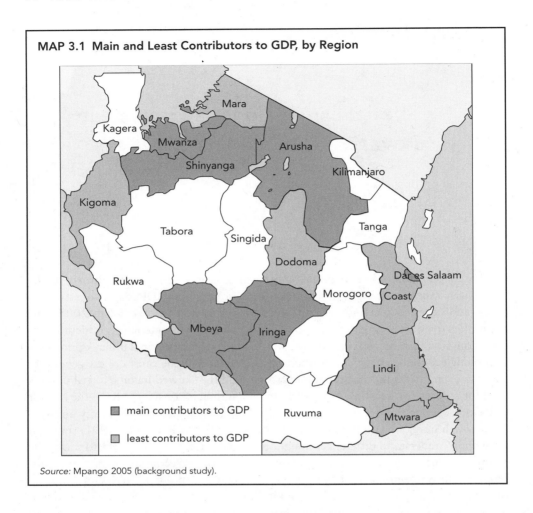

Source: Mpango 2005 (background study).

Those regions with the lowest GDP per capita were Kigoma, Dodoma, Kilimanjaro, Tanga, and Mara. However, the ranking changed during 2000 to 2003 (see figure 3.1b). The Mtwara and Mwanza regions replaced Rukwa and Ruvuma among the top five regions for per capita GDP. Similarly, the Coast, Tabora, and Kagera regions joined the ranks of those with the lowest GDP per capita, while the Mara, Kigoma, and Tanga regions made marginal gains. The reversals in the regional ranking of average GDP per capita reflect in part the new investment in mining, fishing, and related services around Lake Victoria; the improvement of the cashew nut industry in Mtwara; and the collapse of the coffee industry in Kagera, Kilimanjaro, and Ruvuma. See also box 3.1.

The dominance of Dar es Salaam is attributable to three major factors. First, Dar es Salaam is the de facto seat of government and therefore has the highest concentration of political power, resources, and related support and ancillary activities. Second, the city is Tanzania's major port and the commercial and financial capital, and therefore it is more connected to the global economy. As a port, it is the main conduit of export and import trade not only for Tanzania but also for the neighboring countries

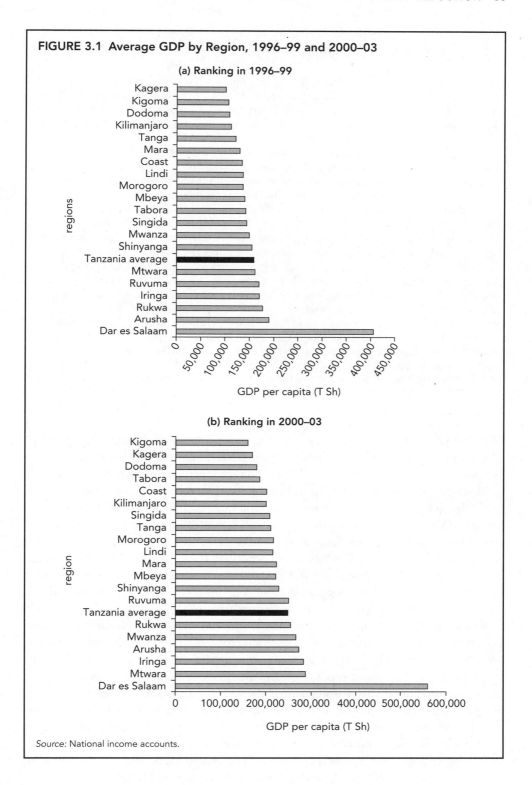

FIGURE 3.1 Average GDP by Region, 1996–99 and 2000–03

(a) Ranking in 1996–99

(b) Ranking in 2000–03

Source: National income accounts.

BOX 3.1 Regional Differences in Coping with External Shocks

In recent years, Tanzania suffered from declining international coffee prices. The price paid to growers of Arabica coffee in Tanzania declined from a peak of US$1.36 in 1997 to less than US$0.24 per pound in 2004 (see International Coffee Organization Web site, http://www.ico.org). However, the impact of this external shock on growth performance differed significantly across regions.

A study by Gresser and Tickell (2002) indicates that declining international coffee prices have had adverse consequences on smallholder coffee farmers in Kilimanjaro. These consequences include farmers exiting from growing coffee or turning to food crops and horticulture, as well as farmers migrating to towns and mining centers. Likewise, coffee traders gave up or closed their business. However, for some regions (such as Kilimanjaro, Mwanza, and Shinyanga), the decline in real incomes, caused by productivity decline for the major cash crops, was partly mitigated by substitution from coffee to other crops and new opportunities, by business and trading in other regions, and by disposal of assets. In addition, there was growth of other sources of income, particularly from new investments in mining, in fish processing, and in related services around Lake Victoria. In this regard, it seems plausible that the coffee-producing regions in the southern highlands zone did better than the northern highlands because the agricultural economy of the former is more diversified, with a wide range of agricultural sources of income (tea, pyrethrum, coffee, maize, potatoes, beans, paddy). In contrast, the northern highlands zone is dominated by coffee and has relatively fewer alternative crops. Therefore, a key message here is that the composition of production and the responses of the population to new challenges (including changes in relative prices) and opportunities have had a strong bearing on the relative growth performance of different regions.

---

of Burundi, Democratic Republic of Congo, Malawi, Rwanda, Uganda, and Zambia. Third, Dar es Salaam has the country's highest concentration of manufacturing and service industries and very little of traditional low-productivity agriculture.

In general, there are many reasons behind the observed spatial inequalities in Tanzania, including economic and noneconomic factors. Noneconomic factors relate mainly to historical reasons, especially colonial legacy as well as culture. For example, the colonial administration designated some regions, such as Kigoma, Mtwara, and Rukwa, as labor reserves. Following independence, some investments in human capital development, such as schools and hospitals, were directed to such regions. Also, because of differences in opportunities, some regions such as Kilimanjaro have developed a stronger entrepreneurial culture than others.

Regarding economic factors, variations in regional incomes in Tanzania are driven in part by the concentration of nonagricultural economic activities. The major contributors to national GDP by region also have the highest concentration of manufacturing; mining and quarrying; production and distribution of electricity, gas, and water; trade; tourism; and financial and business services. For instance, in addition to Dar es Salaam, other regions that are among the top five both in terms of contribution to national GDP and in terms of shares in manufacturing value added, number of industrial establishments, and employment are Mwanza and Shinyanga. The opposite is true of the poorer regions, where more than two-thirds of employed people earn a living from traditional low-productivity agriculture, livestock rearing, and fishing (see table 3.1).

TABLE 3.1 Distribution of Industrial Establishments, Workers, and Value Added, 2000 and 2004

(percent)

Region	Establishments[a]	Workers (2000)[b]	Workers (2004)[c]	Value added (2000)[d]	Value added (2004)[e]
Arusha	9.3	6.8	6.6	4.3	7.3
Coast	0.2	0.0	0.0	0.0	0.0
Dar es Salaam	43.4	25.9	33.5	41.6	59.0
Dodoma	0.2	0.2	0.2	0.6	0.3
Iringa	2.9	15.4	13.2	4.2	2.8
Kagera	4.8	1.8	1.8	2.6	1.8
Kigoma	0.4	0.2	0.2	0.3	0.1
Kilimanjaro	4.4	8.1	7.9	6.4	3.4
Lindi	1.0	0.1	0.1	0.6	0.1
Mara	2.7	0.8	0.1	4.4	0.0
Mbeya	3.2	3.6	3.4	3.3	6.1
Morogoro	2.9	14.3	11.6	4.3	2.9
Mtwara	0.6	0.1	0.1	0.1	0.0
Mwanza	7.2	5.0	6.8	9.2	2.2
Rukwa	0.2	0.1	0.1	0.1	0.0
Ruvuma	1.9	2.6	0.0	0.8	0.4
Shinyanga	2.9	2.9	2.9	6.0	0.9
Singida	0.4	0.1	0.1	0.2	0.6
Tabora	1.0	1.2	1.9	2.8	2.1
Tanga	10.7	10.2	9.5	8.3	9.9
Mainland Tanzania	100.0	100.0	100.0	100.0	100.0

Source: United Republic of Tanzania 2003a, 2004a.
Note: Totals may not equal 100.0 because of rounding.
a. The number of establishments was 525.
b. The number of workers in 2000 was 84,589.
c. The number of workers in 2004 was 89,826.
d. Value added in 2000 equaled T Sh 441,482 million.
e. Value added in 2004 equaled T Sh 701,057 million.

The importance of nonagricultural activities in regional economies is also clearly reflected in many other socioeconomic indicators. For example, 46 percent of electricity sold in mainland Tanzania is consumed in Dar es Salaam. The other major consumers of electricity—Arusha, Tanga, Kilimanjaro, Morogoro, Iringa, Mwanza, Mbeya, and Shinyanga (arranged in descending order of usage)—are also the major centers of industrial activity. By contrast, the poorer regions (Kigoma, Rukwa, Lindi, and Coast) together consume only 1.5 percent of the total quantity of electricity sold in the mainland. Analogously, the regional distribution of projects registered by the Tanzania Investment Centre from 1990 to June 2002 indicates that 58 percent of the total number of investment projects was for the Dar es Salaam region alone. Other regions that attracted a significant number of new projects were Arusha (11 percent), Mwanza (7 percent), and Tanga (4 percent). Most of the projects were in manufacturing (43 percent), agriculture and livestock development (7 percent), construction (7 percent), services (6 percent), and tourism (5 percent). Similarly, the revenue collection pattern also reveals that about 85 percent of total tax revenue comes from Dar es Salaam, although that figure also reflects Dar es Salaam's role as the main entry point for imports and the related customs payments. Other regions that are the main contributors to total tax revenue include Arusha (3.2 percent), Tanga (2.8 percent), Mwanza (2.4 percent), and Kilimanjaro (2.1 percent). Analogously, more than 50 percent of local government authorities' own revenue is collected by local government authorities in Arusha, Dar es Salaam, Kilimanjaro, Mbeya, and Mwanza. The pattern described above reflects the fact that concentration of secondary activities (manufacturing and so forth) tends to generate a wide range of supporting services as well as forward and backward links.

Climate and uneven natural resource endowments have also had a strong bearing on economic growth of different regions. That fact is perhaps most borne out by the recent growth of mining, concentrated around Arusha, Mbeya, Mwanza, and Shinyanga, and tourism, centered in Arusha, Kilimanjaro, Manyara, and Morogoro. Similarly, differences in agricultural production (crops grown, volume, farm productivity, and relative unit prices) have played an important role in shaping regional growth patterns in Tanzania. Basic agricultural statistics show marked regional differences in the crops cultivated, largely dictated by climatic conditions. For example, only three regions—Mara, Mwanza, and Shinyanga—produce about 88.6 percent of Tanzania's total annual yield of cotton. Analogously, Arusha, Kagera, Kilimanjaro, Mbeya, and Ruvuma together produce more than 90 percent of Tanzania's total yield of coffee. The Mtwara region alone accounts for two-thirds of the total national cashew nut production. Similarly, Arusha, Iringa, Mbeya, Rukwa, and Ruvuma are the main producers of legumes, maize, paddy, and wheat, just as Arusha, Dodoma, Mara, Mwanza, Shinyanga, Singida, and Tabora account for more than three-fourths of the total number of cattle, goats, and sheep in the country (figure 3.2). Significant variations also exist in individual crop-yield per hectare across regions and even within a particular region. In general, income levels are found to be extremely low in regions where smallholder agriculture and livestock keeping are the dominant economic activities, where the cultivated area for each crop and the average farm size are small, and where productivity is very low. Most of the regions that contribute least to national GDP also have very low productivity for all the major food crops compared with the regions that contribute more. Evidence also exists that major producers of traditional export crops have suffered extreme drops in real income in part because of a decline in world market prices, average farm size, and farm productivity or population pressure. However, for some regions, such as Mwanza, Shinyanga, and recently Mtwara, the decline in real incomes (mainly from export crops) was mitigated in part by the growth of other sources of income, particularly from new investments in mining, fish processing and related services, and the cashew nut industry.

The unequal contribution by regions to national income is also reflected in the poverty headcount ratios in the 1991/92 and 2000/01 household budget surveys. The ratios indicate that poverty is more severe in rural Tanzania than in urban areas. The data also suggest that during the 1990s, poverty fell in the southern highlands but increased in the northern highlands (see chapter 2 and table 3.2).

The observed regional income diversity in Tanzania also involves, at least in part, demographics. Generally, regions that lie at the bottom or top of the scale for GDP per

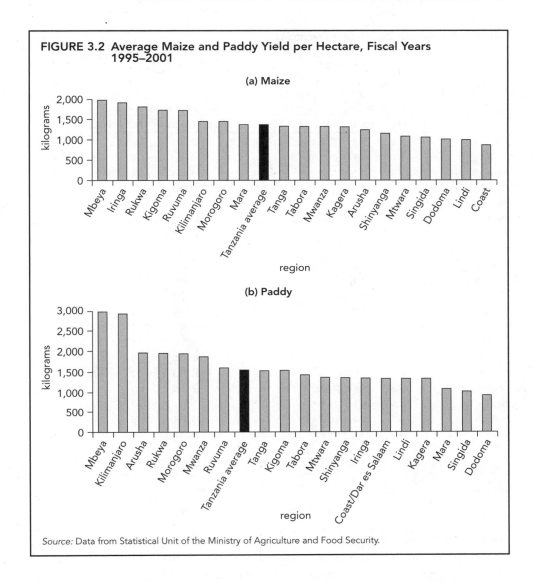

FIGURE 3.2 Average Maize and Paddy Yield per Hectare, Fiscal Years 1995–2001

Source: Data from Statistical Unit of the Ministry of Agriculture and Food Security.

capita also have the lowest or highest working age group, respectively. No clear relationship exists between the level of poverty in a region and the net migration flows between regions.

Regional growth patterns in Tanzania are influenced by changes in government policies, particularly those related to fiscal and trade regimes. A recent study using evidence from the 2000/01 household budget survey (Fan, Nyange, and Rao 2005) indicates that Tanzania can improve the effects of public expenditure on growth and poverty through better regional targeting. Specifically, investment in rural roads is found to have a larger effect on per capita incomes in the western, central, and southern areas of Tanzania and much less elsewhere. Data on actual expenditure by region for 1999/2000 to 2003/04 indicate that although recurrent expenditure (dominated by expenditure on social sectors) has been relatively more evenly distributed across the

TABLE 3.2 Regional Population Dynamics

Region	Population distribution (% of total population)		Population growth rate (%)		Net migration (no. people)	Population density (people per sq km)		Average household size (no. people)
	1988	2002	1978–88	1988–2002	1988 census	1988	2002	2002
Dodoma	5.5	5.1	2.4	2.3	−101,085	30	41	4.5
Arusha	6.0	3.8	3.8	4.0	141,724	20	35	4.5
Kilimanjaro	4.9	4.1	2.1	1.6	−124,383	83	104	4.6
Tanga	5.8	4.9	2.1	1.8	−52,168	48	61	4.6
Morogoro	5.6	5.2	2.6	2.6	30,437	17	25	4.6
Pwani	2.8	2.6	2.1	2.4	−103,912	20	27	4.4
Dar	6.0	7.4	4.8	4.3	500,621	977	1793	4.2
Lindi	2.9	2.4	2	1.4	−49,831	10	12	4.1
Mtwara	3.9	3.4	1.4	1.7	−98,689	53	68	3.8
Ruvuma	3.5	3.3	3.4	2.5	−15,219	12	18	4.8
Iringa	5.3	4.5	2.7	1.5	−120,198	21	26	4.3
Mbeya	6.5	6.2	3.1	2.4	46,999	25	34	4.2
Singida	3.5	3.2	2.5	2.3	−63,880	16	22	5.0
Tabora	4.6	5.1	2.4	3.6	66,370	14	23	5.9
Rukwa	3.1	3.4	4.3	3.6	38,305	10	17	5.1
Kigoma	3.8	5.0	2.8	4.8	−102,923	23	45	6.9
Shinyanga	7.8	8.4	2.9	3.3	6,763	35	55	6.3
Kagera	6.0	6.1	2.7	3.1	−5,980	47	72	5.2
Mwanza	8.3	8.8	2.6	3.2	−33,504	96	150	5.9
Mara	4.3	4.1	2.9	2.5	−39,878	50	70	5.5
Manyara	—	—	—	3.8	—	13	23	5.2
Mainland Tanzania	100.0	100.0	3	3.1	n.a.	26	38	4.9

Source: United Republic of Tanzania 2002a.
Note: — = not available; n.a. = not applicable.

regions (rightly so), development expenditure has been skewed and has been mainly in line with donor support preferences for the various regions. For example, although 11 regions out of 20 together claimed more than two-thirds of actual annual recurrent expenditure by region, more than 70 percent of annual regional development expenditure was spent in only 7 out of the 20 regions. The biggest beneficiary (Kagera) received about 27 percent annually, while the smallest beneficiary (Rukwa) received only 1 percent. Furthermore, with only a few exceptions (Dar es Salaam and Kilimanjaro), regions that received less than 2 percent each of total annual development expenditure also had the highest basic-needs poverty rates.

With regard to trade policy, one could argue that during the era of the control regime (1967–86), Dar es Salaam (and a few urban centers), as the headquarters of most of the parastatals, did benefit more from parastatal sector operations compared with peripheral regions with smaller branches. Restrictions also most likely forced private firms to locate in Dar es Salaam, where they could easily maneuver with the controls. By contrast, trade liberalization and removal of trade monopolies did create a window of opportunity for growth of other geographic zones, particularly in the southern highlands. That window is partly supported by the reemergence of an active private sector in crop and food grain marketing and distribution (for example, cashew nuts in the coastal zones), as well as new private investment in the tea sector, which is dominant in the southern highlands and is much less affected by a decline in world market prices compared with coffee, which is the main export crop of the northern zone.

The pattern of economic growth in Tanzania also reflects in part the differences in the level of human capital development (see table 3.3). The average levels of education and of general skills available in a region are critical because they are fundamental to private sector development. In particular, the level of human capital development dictates the capacity of individual regions to learn and adopt better land-use systems and new farming practices, to introduce new high-value crops, or to venture into other business opportunities as they emerge.

The general level of education is also paramount to the extent that it affects the quality of leadership in a region down to the village level. Indeed, though it is rather common to find village and district council chairpersons who are retired senior civil servants (permanent secretaries, teachers, and so forth) in the relatively well-to-do regions, finding them in the poorer regions is a quite rare occurrence. It is also interesting to note that the formation of effective and operational civic development forums has begun taking root in regions with a better human capital base (Iringa, Kilimanjaro,

TABLE 3.3 Selected Indexes of Human Capital Development, by Region

Region	Adult literacy rate (% age 15 and above)	Total net enrollment rate (2004)	Number of secondary schools (2004)	Mean monthly consumption per capita (T Sh thousand, 2000)	Life expectancy at birth (years, 1988)
Dar es Salaam	91	93.1	87	21.9	50
Arusha	78	91.9	107	10.3	57
Rukwa	68	87.9	33	6.7	45
Ruvuma	84	99.3	48	9.6	49
Iringa	81	99.1	82	11.2	45
Shinyanga	55	86.3	51	8.0	50
Mwanza	65	99.5	75	8.1	48
Singida	71	85.0	35	6.9	55
Mbeya	79	99.3	104	12.6	47
Tabora	65	68.2	41	10.4	53
Morogoro	72	81.9	58	10.0	46
Lindi	58	84.1	19	9.5	47
Coast	61	94.5	40	10.5	48
Mtwara	68	94.2	41	12.4	46
Mara	76	100.0	59	8.0	47
Kilimanjaro	85	100.0	160	11.2	59
Tanga	67	97.9	83	9.3	49
Dodoma	66	76.3	50	8.5	46
Kigoma	71	77.2	38	7.3	48
Kagera	64	86.8	70	9.0	45

Source: Ministry of Education and Culture 2004; United Republic of Tanzania 2003b.

Mbeya, and Ruvuma). These development forums are aimed at building consensus among stakeholders of a particular region on binding constraints and articulation of a shared strategy for faster progress. Similarly, the current drive in some regions to form community banks to deal with the problem of lack of financial capital is seen to be much stronger in regions that have, among other things, a better education base (Dar es Salaam, Kilimanjaro, and Mbeya). Basic education statistics and poverty indicators for Tanzania largely conform to the regional variations in incomes. Overall, Dar es Salaam, Kilimanjaro, Mbeya, Mwanza, and Ruvuma still rank as the top five regions in terms of human capital development, whereas Coast, Dodoma, Kigoma, Lindi, and Mtwara generally lie at the bottom of the spectrum.

Evidence shows the emergence of regional growth poles other than Dar es Salaam. Regional per capita incomes in Tanzania have tended to vary significantly over time. That variation is revealed in part by gaps between the top five and bottom five regions in terms of the average GDP per capita and the coefficients of variation of GDP per capita for the 20 regions of mainland Tanzania. For the period from 1980 to 2003, the coefficients of variation constructed for the 20 regions of Tanzania suggest that income differential relative to the national average has declined over the past two decades (figure 3.3). On average, although the per capita income of the top five regions doubled between 1992 and 2003, that of the bottom five regions increased slightly faster (two and one-half times). The apparent convergence of regional per capita incomes in Tanzania is driven by a combination of factors including sustained macroeconomic reforms, rural-urban migration, remittances, and the emergence of other regional growth poles—Arusha, Mbeya, Mwanza, and Shinyanga—because of new investments, particularly in mining, fish processing, transportation, tourism and related services, manufacturing, and high-value crops. Those new growth poles have generally recorded positive net migration in recent years.

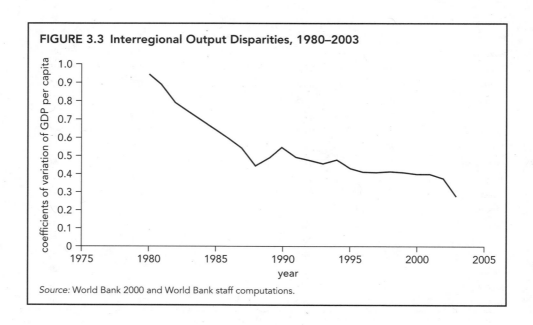

FIGURE 3.3 Interregional Output Disparities, 1980–2003

Source: World Bank 2000 and World Bank staff computations.

Implications for Regional Policy

This chapter has highlighted significant income disparities among the 21 administrative regions of Tanzania. It has also pointed to the most formidable obstacles to growth, some that are region specific and others that cut across regions. It is also quite apparent that the regions have different opportunities, some dictated in part by location and climate, natural resource endowments, and even economic history. An important question then follows: does regional policy have a role?

Given the substantial disparities in economic activities and incomes across the administrative regions of Tanzania and the fact that regional income convergence is far from inevitable, region-specific interventions that are based on geographically differentiated growth strategies must evolve:

- *Identifying and supporting growth opportunities that promise the greatest effect on national growth and poverty reduction.* An effective growth strategy must identify regional growth opportunities in order to provide adequate support through the provision of adequate infrastructure. That identification implies a process in which the various regions and districts compete for central government–funded infrastructure investments and other public expenditure measures that would facilitate the exploitation of growth opportunities. That identification also requires adequate capacity at the central level to evaluate projects and proposals from the various regions in order to allocate resources to those opportunities that have the highest expected economic returns or the largest effect on poverty.

- *Supporting measures by the local authorities.* Local revenue collection and business licensing requirements affect the local business environment. Strengthening the capacity and incentives of the local authorities to carry out their functions in a manner that supports economic growth would be important. In particular, those aspects should receive consideration in Tanzania's decentralization program and capacity-building efforts through the local government reform program, which to date primarily focuses on service delivery. In addition, local authorities are also in the best position to allocate locally available resources to expenditures that can contribute most to a district's economic development.

- *Sharing growth through social service provision.* Although different growth potentials of regions may lead to greater income disparities, public policy must reduce or prevent the emergence of disparities with regard to access to social services, such as education, health, and nutrition, or to water and sanitation.

Notes

1. Economic activity is unevenly distributed both across and within individual regions.
2. The concentration of economic activities around certain centers is also often associated with other costs, such as traffic congestion and pollution.

3. Until 2003, Mainland Tanzania was divided into 20 administrative regions: Arusha, Coast, Dar es Salaam, Dodoma, Iringa, Kagera, Kigoma, Kilimanjaro, Lindi, Mara, Mbeya, Morogoro, Mtwara, Mwanzan, Rukwa, Ruvuma, Shinyanga, Singida, Tabora, and Tanga. In 2003, Arusha was split into two regions: Arusha and Manyara. Zanzibar is divided into five regions: North Pemba, South Pemba, North Unguja, South Unguja, and Urban West. Most of the data used in this section refer to the 20 regions of Mainland Tanzania, combining Arusha and Manyara.

4. Regional GDP data for Tanzania could be overstating regional income disparities, in part because production in the regions that contribute little to national GDP is largely for subsistence and is not fully captured in market-based GDP numbers. The purchasing power of the shilling also tends to be higher in the poorer regions.

4

Outlook on Growth and Poverty Reduction

Robert J. Utz and Johannes Hoogeveen

This chapter assesses the likelihood that Tanzania will achieve and sustain high growth rates and reduce income poverty and other dimensions of poverty. We start by reviewing various scenarios for growth and poverty reduction to illustrate the relationship between economic growth and the achievement of Tanzania's objective of reaching middle-income status by 2025 and halving income poverty by 2010. We then assess Tanzania's growth targets against Tanzania's historical growth performance and also make a global comparison of growth performance. Policy-based growth projections indicate what growth rates seem feasible on the basis of the quality of Tanzania's policies and institutions. Growth accounting is used to estimate the input requirements of sustained high growth in terms of investment in both human and physical capital. This chapter also examines the implications of sustained high growth for structural transformation. The discussion of sectoral growth rates provides the basis for an assessment of whether macroeconomic growth projections are consistent with sectoral prospects for continued high economic growth.

Disaggregated poverty simulations are then used to project the effect of various growth scenarios on income poverty and inequality. Although the main focus is on income poverty, the chapter also reviews the prospects of reaching other National Strategy for Growth and Reduction of Poverty (NSGRP) and Millennium Development Goal (MDG) targets, such as reduction in hunger and improvements in education and health.

Growth Scenarios

We start the discussion with some simple illustrations of the effect of various growth rates on per capita income and poverty levels in Tanzania. The scenarios we consider are annual growth rates of real per capita gross domestic product (GDP) of 2 percent, 4 percent, 6 percent, and 8 percent. Figure 4.1 shows projections of per capita GDP as well as associated poverty rates for these growth scenarios. Tanzania's

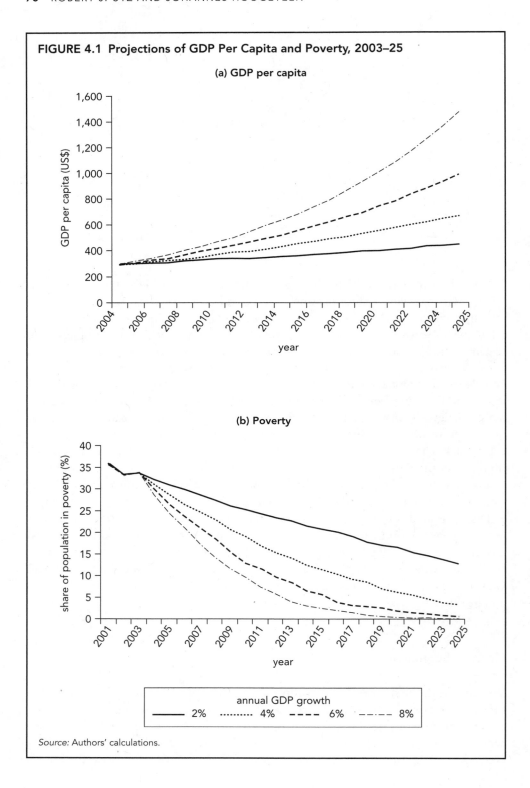

FIGURE 4.1 Projections of GDP Per Capita and Poverty, 2003–25

(a) GDP per capita

(b) Poverty

annual GDP growth
—— 2%   ········· 4%   – – – 6%   –·–·– 8%

Source: Authors' calculations.

TABLE 4.1 Projections of Per Capita GNI and Share of Population below Poverty Line, 2010–25

Year	Average annual real GNI growth rate			
	2%	4%	6%	8%
2010				
Percentage below poverty line	25	19	13	10
GDP per capita (US$)	372	418	468	524
2015				
Percentage below poverty line	21	11	<10	<10
GDP per capita (US$)	410	508	626	769
2020				
Percentage below poverty line	16	<10	<10	<10
GDP per capita (US$)	453	618	838	1,131
2025				
Percentage below poverty line	13	<10	<10	<10
GDP per capita (US$)	500	752	1,122	1,661

Source: Authors' calculations.

Development Vision (Vision 2025) aims for the country to reach middle-income status by 2025.[1] To reach the lower threshold for middle-income countries per capita—gross national income (GNI) of US$765—Tanzania's per capita income must grow by at least 4.1 percent annually. If per capita GNI were to grow at only 2 percent annually, it would increase from US$330 to US$500 by 2025. If it grew by 8 percent annually, GNI would reach US$1,661 (see table 4.1 and figure 4.1). The results of

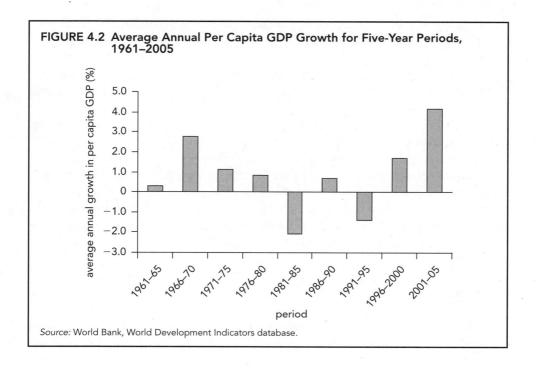

FIGURE 4.2 Average Annual Per Capita GDP Growth for Five-Year Periods, 1961–2005

Source: World Bank, World Development Indicators database.

these calculations are quite sobering: they imply that even with growth rates significantly higher than Tanzania has achieved in the past, the country will still be relatively poor in 20 years.

We now turn to the question of what effect various growth scenarios have on poverty. As shown in panel (b) of figure 4.1, with per capita GDP growth of 2 percent annually, poverty would decline to 25 percent by 2010 and to 21 percent by 2015. This growth rate would thus be insufficient to reach the NSGRP and the MDG targets of halving poverty by 2010 and 2015, respectively. However, a per capita growth rate of 4 percent, which would result in a decline in poverty to 19 percent by 2010 and to 11 percent by 2015, would be consistent with achieving Tanzania's poverty reduction targets. The projections of poverty levels need to be considered with a grain of salt, especially for estimates in the outer years and in cases in which poverty has declined significantly. Inequality is likely to increase with faster growth, and the income elasticity of poverty is likely to fall as poverty declines.

Review of Tanzania's Growth Prospects in Historical and International Contexts

It is informative to compare these growth scenarios with Tanzania's historical growth performance. Since independence, the average per capita growth rate has been a mere 0.7 percent; since the introduction of reforms in 1985, per capita growth has averaged 0.9 percent. The highest per capita growth rate that Tanzania has sustained over a five-year period was slightly higher than 4 percent (see figure 4.2). However, in most periods it was much lower.

International experience provides a more encouraging perspective on Tanzania's growth prospects. From 1994 to 2003, 9 countries were able to achieve an average growth rate of per capita GDP of 6 percent or more, 12 countries achieved rates between 4 and 6 percent, and 64 countries grew at rates between 2 and 4 percent (see figure 4.3). Thus, according to international experience, growth rates between 2 and 8 percent seem to be within the realm of the possible.

Our analysis of Tanzania's growth performance in chapter 1 suggests that the recent acceleration in economic growth may be largely driven by the demand-side stimulus that emanated from the sharp increase in government spending during that period. Without that demand-side stimulus, average growth in the medium term may revert to 4 to 5 percent annually (that is, the average growth rate of private sector expenditure during the past 15 years). However, with the consolidation of policy reforms, Tanzania may shift to a higher growth path. We review the potential effects of these policy reforms below using policy-based growth projections.

Policy-Based Projections

Policies and institutions are important determinants of growth. This section uses the estimated relationship between economic growth and various indicators of the

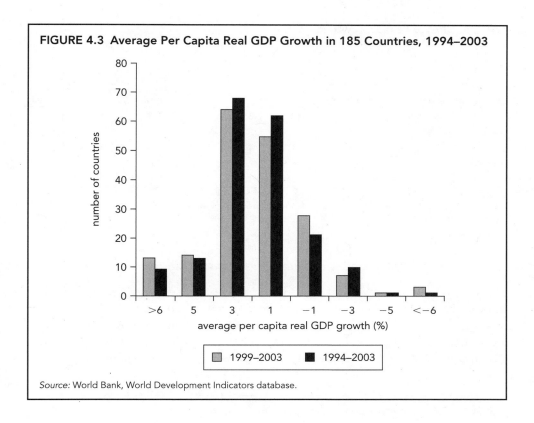

FIGURE 4.3 Average Per Capita Real GDP Growth in 185 Countries, 1994–2003

Source: World Bank, World Development Indicators database.

quality of policies and institutions to assess Tanzania's growth potential. Measures of the quality of policies and institutions are provided by four independent sources:

- World Bank's Country Policy and Institutional Assessment (CPIA)[2]

- *Institutional Investor* assessment[3]

- International Country Risk Guide (ICRG) assessment[4]

- Euromoney assessment.[5]

All suggest significant improvements between 1999 and 2006 (see table 4.2). According to the country ratings for 2006, the projections of per capita growth range between 3.8 and 5.0 percent, with an average for all four projections of 4.4 percent. If there are further improvements in institutions and policies, the projections suggest that per capita growth rates of more than 5 percent per year are even feasible.

Input-Based Projections

A complementary way to assess Tanzania's growth prospects is to use the growth accounting framework and look at the likely development of the immediate determinants of growth—human resources, physical capital, and total factor productivity.

TABLE 4.2 Policy-Based Growth Projections

(percent)

Source of projection	Rating 1999	Rating 2006	Per capita growth projections	
			Constant	Improve +0.5
CPIA	3.5	3.9	5.0	6.1
Euromoney	2.2	2.8	4.1	4.8
ICRG	3.8	4.1	4.6	5.1
Institutional	2.0	2.3	3.8	5.0
Average	2.8	3.3	4.4	5.3

Source: Authors' calculations.
Note: The ratings of the various sources have been standardized for comparability on a scale from 1 to 6, with 6 representing the highest achievement. *Improve +0.5* represents the case were the rating in 2004 to improve by 0.5 point.

Contribution of Increased Investment in Human Resources

The average number of years of education of the workforce is used as the basic indicator of the quality of human resources in an economy. According to Cohen and Soto (2001), in 2000 the average number of years of schooling in Tanzania (3.40) was higher than that in Uganda (3.22) but lower than that in Kenya (5.80) and far from that in South Africa (7.22) (figure 4.4). To assess possible progress in this indicator, it

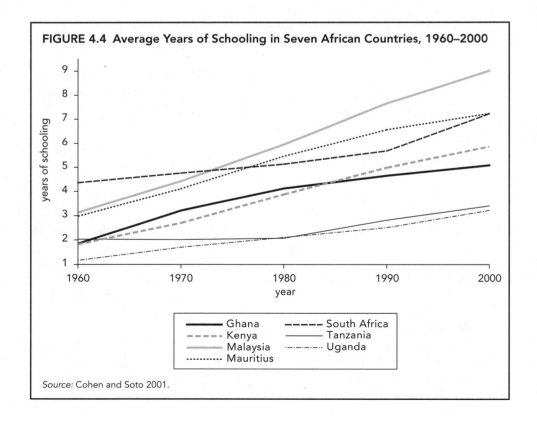

FIGURE 4.4 Average Years of Schooling in Seven African Countries, 1960–2000

Source: Cohen and Soto 2001.

is useful to look at the experience of other economies. Countries such as Malaysia have been able to increase average years of schooling by about 1.5 years per decade. Other countries that have also invested heavily in education, such as Mauritius and Kenya, have seen increases of about one year per decade. Ghana, Tanzania, and Uganda have seen much slower increases in average years of schooling. However, recent aggressive efforts to expand access to education, if sustained, are likely to result in a rapid increase in years of schooling over the coming decades.

In the following discussion, we look at the likely effect on economic growth of increases in schooling by 0.5, 1.0, and 1.5 years per decade. Such increases would result in contributions to economic growth of 0.8, 1.4, and 2.1 percentage points, respectively (table 4.3). In interpreting these results, it is important to recognize that number of years of schooling responds only gradually to increases in enrollment as more educated, younger cohorts replace less educated, older cohorts. Thus, even where a policy of universal primary education is in effect, the share of the population with no education will decline only gradually. Our scenario for low growth in years of schooling (0.5 per decade) assumes that universal primary education is not achieved and that increases in postprimary education are modest. The medium- and high-growth scenarios (1.0 and 1.5 years per decade, respectively) assume that universal primary enrollment is achieved and that there is also a substantial increase in postprimary education.

Contribution of Increases in Investment to Economic Growth

In the growth accounting framework, the relationship between growth and investment is more complex than in a simple incremental capital output ratio (ICOR) model. Changes in the stock of capital depend on the rate of capital depreciation, the share of GDP invested, and the level of GDP. For example, figure 4.5 illustrates that for a given growth rate of output (4 percent) and investment ratio (20 percent), the

TABLE 4.3 Effect of Additional Years of Schooling on Economic Growth

Highest level of education reached	1992	2001	2011 (low)	2011 (medium)	2011 (high)
None (% of population)	24.9	25.2	20	15	15
Adult only (% of population)	3.3	2.1	2	2	2
Primary 1–4 (% of population)	15.2	11.9	11	11	8
Primary 5–8 (% of population)	50.7	54.6	58	58	55
Forms 1–4 (% of population)	3.9	4.6	6	9	11
Forms 5–6 (% of population)	0.3	1.4	2	3	5
Diploma or university (% of population)	0.2	0.4	1	2	4
Average years of education	3.8	4.2	4.7	5.2	5.7
Contribution to economic growth (percentage points)	n.a.	0.7	0.8	1.4	2.1

Source: Years of schooling are calculated based on Household Budget Survey figures and differ from data by Cohen and Soto (2001) because of different methodology.
Note: n.a. = not applicable.

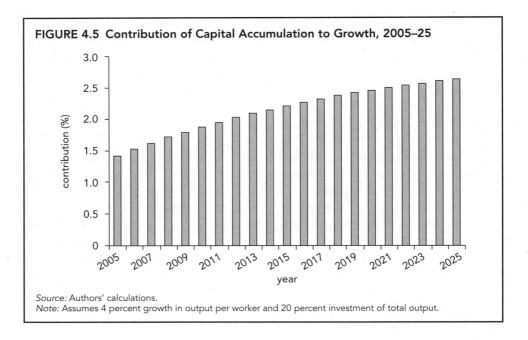

FIGURE 4.5 Contribution of Capital Accumulation to Growth, 2005–25

Source: Authors' calculations.
Note: Assumes 4 percent growth in output per worker and 20 percent investment of total output.

contribution of investment to GDP growth increases over time. This result occurs because with increasing GDP the real amount of investment increases, even with a constant investment ratio.

Table 4.4 shows the projected contribution of investment to growth for various combinations of overall growth rates and investment ratios. The higher the investment ratio and the growth rate are, the higher is the contribution of investment to growth. For example, if output per worker is stagnant and the investment ratio is 18 percent, the contribution of investment to growth is 0.3 percent. In a high-growth, high-investment scenario, the average contribution could be 2.7 percent. Of course, those projections need to be considered carefully because investment spending does not automatically translate into an equivalent amount of productive capital. The composition of total investment (the mix of private and public investment) and the share of public investment used for directly productive purposes (such as infrastructure) are important factors that affect the relationship between investment and its contribution to economic growth.

TABLE 4.4 Contribution of Investment to Growth: Average over 10 Years for 0, 2, 4, and 6 Percent Growth Rates

Growth rate	Investment as share of GDP			
	16%	18%	20%	22%
0	−0.1	0.3	0.8	1.2
2	0.3	0.8	1.2	1.6
4	0.7	1.2	1.7	2.1
6	1.2	1.7	2.2	2.7

Source: Authors' calculations.

Contribution of Total Factor Productivity to Economic Growth

Enhancing factor productivity refers to obtaining more output from a given amount of resources, whether human or physical capital. In the long run, there are essentially two types of constraints on productivity:

- Policy-imposed constraints and distortions

- Knowledge constraints.

In the short run, productivity can also be constrained by demand, leading to under-utilization of resources. However, in the absence of other constraints, either (a) such demand constraints would be temporary or (b) the economy would adjust appropriately.

Cross-country studies on factor productivity provide an indication of possible productivity growth rates for Tanzania in the long run. Some studies that look at the experience of Southeast Asian countries indicate that about half of such countries' rapid growth is attributable to productivity gains. More conservative estimates (Collins and Bosworth 1996) nonetheless attribute between 0.8 and 2.0 percentage points of East Asian countries' growth of output per capita to increases in total factor productivity (table 4.5). In assessing Tanzania's growth potential, it appears clearly possible that about 1.0 percentage point of growth per worker could come from productivity gains. In the immediate future, the contribution of productivity gains to output growth can be expected to be even higher, given the potential for more productive use of the existing capital stock.

Assessment of Growth Potential Based on Projected Factor Accumulation and Productivity Increases

This section aggregates the individual projections of the potential contribution of physical capital accumulation, education, and total factor productivity to total growth. We present three scenarios, using the lower and upper estimates of the contribution of each factor as well as an intermediate estimate (see table 4.6).

The resulting aggregate output projections suggest that the policy-based projections of 4.4 to 5.3 percent (average annual growth) seem to be achievable, although the input requirements—in terms of investment, education, and factor productivity—are quite demanding. In interpreting the results shown in table 4.6, it is important to note that even the low-growth scenario requires maintaining the performance of the period from 1995 to 2004. Any reversals could result in much lower growth.

TABLE 4.5 Growth and Total Factor Productivity in Selected East Asian Countries, 1960–94

(percentage points per year)

Indicator	Indonesia	Korea, Rep. of	Malaysia	Thailand	Taiwan, China
Growth of output per worker	3.4	5.7	5.7	5.0	5.8
Contribution of total factor productivity	0.8	1.5	1.5	1.8	2.0

Source: Collins and Bosworth 1996.

TABLE 4.6 Overall Input-Based Projections

(percentage points)

Factor of production	Contribution of factor of production		
	Low	Medium	High
Physical capital	0.3	1.2	2.7
Education	0.8	1.4	2.1
Total factor productivity	0.5	1.0	1.5
Total	1.6	3.6	6.3

Source: Authors' calculations.
Note: Low = investment-to-output ratio of 16 percent at 2 percent output growth, increase in average years of schooling by 0.5 year. Medium = investment-to-output ratio of 18 percent at 4 percent output growth, increase in average years of schooling by 1.0 year. High = investment-to-output ratio of 22 percent at 6 percent output growth, increase in average years of schooling by 1.5 years.

Sectoral Projections

Development and economic growth are characterized by structural transformation of the economy. The share of agriculture typically declines, while that of industry and services increases. Table 4.7 shows the changes in the composition of GDP for a number of countries, illustrating the potential magnitude of transformation possible over a 20-year period. Fast-growing countries such as Ghana, India, Indonesia, and Thailand experienced relatively rapid structural transformation, while slow-growing economies such as Kenya and Tanzania experienced a slower pace of structural transformation.

For Tanzania, we examine three scenarios. The baseline scenario projects current sectoral growth rates. We compare this scenario with one that has a higher aggregate growth and faster structural transformation and with one that has lower growth and limited structural transformation (table 4.8).

Under the baseline scenario, the share of agriculture in GDP drops to 34 percent by 2025, while the shares of industry and services increase to 32 percent and 33 percent, respectively. Comparing these sectoral projections with international experience suggests that they are consistent with the pattern of structural transformation observed in other economies. However, it seems likely that industry and services will grow at similar rates, which would imply a slightly higher share of services and a slightly lower share of industry in GDP by 2025.

TABLE 4.7 Structural Transformation, Selected Countries, 1980–98

(percent)

Country	Share in GDP							
	Agriculture		Industry		Manufacturing		Services	
	1980	1998	1980	1998	1980	1998	1980	1998
Ghana	58	37	12	25	8	8	30	38
India	38	25	24	30	16	19	39	45
Indonesia	24	16	42	43	13	26	34	41
Kenya	33	29	21	16	13	10	47	55
Tanzania	**45**	**46**	**18**	**14**	**12**	**7**	**37**	**40**
Thailand	23	11	29	40	22	29	48	49

Source: World Bank 2000.

TABLE 4.8 Scenarios for Economic Growth and Structural Transformation

(percent)

Sector	Share in GDP 2005	Slow growth		Medium growth (baseline)		High growth	
		Average real growth rate 2006–25	Share in GDP 2025	Average real growth rate 2006–25	Share in GDP 2025	Average real growth rate 2006–25	Share in GDP 2025
Agriculture	45.6	3.3	40	4.8	34	5.0	26
Industry	19.7	4.8	23	9.0	32	10.7	32
Services	34.8	4.4	37	6.1	33	9.0	42
Total	100.0	4.0	100	6.3	100	8.0	100

Source: Authors' calculations.

One of the key characteristics of structural transformation is that the industry and service sectors have to grow faster than the agriculture sector. The underlying process starts with an agricultural surplus, which is invested in the industry and service sectors; that higher productivity in agriculture allows the movement of labor from agriculture to other sectors.

Reaching the MDG and NSGRP Targets

It will be challenging for Tanzania to meet many of the various MDGs, and yet there is room for cautious optimism in some areas (see table 4.9). Preliminary results from the 2004 Demographic and Health Survey (DHS) (National Bureau of Statistics and ORC Macro 2005) suggest that considerable progress was made in the reduction of malnutrition and child mortality. Policy simulations show that the income poverty and hunger MDGs may be attainable if Tanzania is able to continue with its episode of relatively high growth and with its improvements in the social sector.

Consumption Poverty

Will economic growth be sufficient to attain the MDG of reducing poverty by half by 2015 (or the more ambitious NSGRP date of 2010)? The likely path of poverty reduction can be determined by applying GDP growth rates to unit-record household consumption data taken from the Household Budget Survey (HBS). The growth rates are taken from the medium-growth projections presented in table 4.10 but have been adapted. They reflect the inability of the HBS to identify, without major assumptions, a household's sector of employment (beyond a rural-urban breakdown). Growth projections for agriculture, industry, and services were therefore adjusted to reflect a rural-urban breakdown.

To this end and under the premise that agricultural production in urban areas is small, the urban growth rate is taken to be the average growth rate of the industrial and service sectors. Because rural income is generated from activities in agriculture as well as

TABLE 4.9 MDG Baseline, Most Recent Estimate, and Target

Millennium Development Goal	Baseline (%)	Most recent estimate (%)	Target (%)	Year of baseline	Most recent year
Goal 1: Eradicate extreme poverty and hunger					
Reduce extreme poverty by half:					
National poverty line	38.6	35.6	19.3	1991	2000
Dollar a day poverty line	61.1	57.5	30.6	1991	2000
Reduce hunger by half	29	22	14.5	1991	2004
Goal 2: Achieve universal primary education					
Net enrollment in primary school	51	91	100	1990	2004
Goal 3: Promote gender equality and empower women					
Equal girls' enrollment in primary school	1.01	0.99	1	1990	2004
Equal girls' enrollment in secondary school	0.70	0.81	1	1990	2000
Goal 4: Reduce child mortality					
Reduce mortality of children under					
five years by two-thirds	141	112	47	1991	2004
Goal 5: Improve maternal health					
Reduce maternal mortality by three-fourths[a]	529	578	132	1996	2004
Goal 6: Combat HIV/AIDS, malaria, and other diseases					
Halt and reverse spread of AIDS	n.a.	7.0			2003
Halt and reverse spread of malaria	21	36		1999	2004
Goal 7: Ensure environmental sustainability					
Halve proportion without improved drinking					
water in urban areas	13	10	7	1991	2000
Halve proportion without improved drinking					
water in rural areas	65	54	33	1991	2000
Halve proportion without sanitation in					
urban areas	2	4	1	1991	2000
Halve proportion without sanitation in					
rural areas	9	8	5	1991	2000

Source: MDG table references.
a. Maternal mortality is a so-called low-frequency event. Low-frequency events are difficult to measure accurately in surveys like the Demographic and Health Survey, which serve as sources for these estimates, as few cases of maternal mortality are registered. Consequently maternal mortality rates are associated with large confidence intervals, and the observed maternal mortality rates of 529 in 1996 and 578 in 2004 are statistically not different.

activities in industry and services, the rural growth rate is determined as the residual calculated from overall GDP growth, after allowing for the urban growth rate. The shares of the contribution of each of the rural-urban sectors to GDP are from the HBS, according to which 75 percent of consumption takes place in rural areas and 25 percent in urban ones. This approach results in rural growth rates that are substantially higher than the growth rates for agriculture alone. Compare, for instance, in the medium- and high-growth scenarios, the agricultural growth rates of 3.7 percent and 5.0 percent with the rural growth rates of 5.0 percent and 7.4 percent. Per capita growth rates are calculated by deducting the population growth rate of 2.9 percent—this is the population growth observed between the 1988 and 2002 censuses, drawn from the respective sector GDP growth rates.

TABLE 4.10 Scenarios for Economic Growth

(percent)

Sector	Share in GDP	Average real growth rate		
		Low growth	Medium growth	High growth
Agriculture	46.8	3.3	3.7	5.0
Industry	18.5	4.8	7.8	10.9
Services	34.8	4.4	5.7	8.9
Total		4.0	5.4	8.0
Rural	74.6	3.8	5.0	7.4
Urban	26.4	4.6	6.5	9.7
Total		4.0	5.4	8.0

Source: Author's calculations.
Note: The share in GDP for agriculture, industry, and services is for 2003. The share in rural and urban GDP is from the 2000/01 HBS and was calculated as the rural and urban share in total consumption.

Figure 4.6 presents poverty simulations for the medium- and low-growth scenarios. For the medium-growth case, the figure also presents scenarios in which inequality increases over and above any increases associated with the differential rural and urban growth rates. The horizontal line in figure 4.6 reflects the MDG and NSGRP objectives.

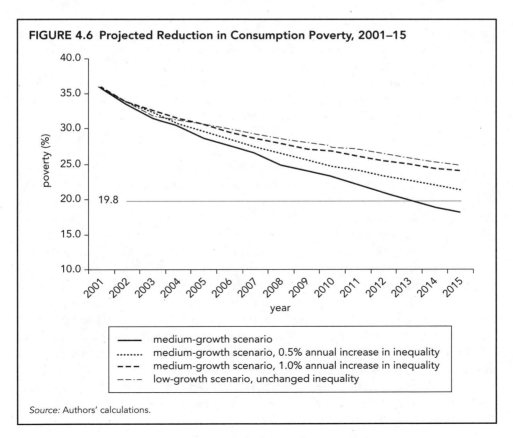

FIGURE 4.6 Projected Reduction in Consumption Poverty, 2001–15

——— medium-growth scenario
········ medium-growth scenario, 0.5% annual increase in inequality
– – – medium-growth scenario, 1.0% annual increase in inequality
—··— low-growth scenario, unchanged inequality

Source: Authors' calculations.

According to the medium-growth scenario (the solid line in bold), the NSGRP objective of 19.8 percent poverty incidence by 2010 will not be met. Yet the MDG objective of attaining the same level of poverty five years later, by 2015, is attainable.

The baseline scenario incorporates differential rural-urban growth rates, leading to a worsening of inequality. The Gini coefficient increases from 0.337 in 2001 to 0.352 in 2015. If one assumes in addition that inequality increases further, not only the NSGRP target but also the MDG target will be missed. This is illustrated by two lines in the middle of figure 4.6; in them an autonomous increase in inequality of 0.5 percent and 1.0 percent per year, respectively, is added to the medium-growth scenario. Under these scenarios, inequality rises to 0.377 and 0.402, respectively, by 2015. This result is high—at least from the current perspective—but not unimaginable. For instance, in Uganda inequality was 0.429 in 2000/01.

Even in the absence of additional increases in inequality, the NSGRP and MDG poverty reduction targets will be missed under the low-growth scenario (represented by the top line), underscoring the need for at least medium growth if the objective is to attain at least the MDG poverty reduction target by 2015. The NSGRP target of reducing poverty by half by 2010 can be attained only under a high-growth scenario. Under that scenario, poverty would be reduced to 16 percent by 2010.

The projections are sensitive to changes in rural growth. Because the majority of the poor live in rural areas, the national poverty incidence is driven by rural poverty. A small change in rural growth therefore leads to a substantial change in national poverty. Figure 4.7 illustrates what would happen to the medium-growth scenario if the composition of growth were different. It presents two scenarios: one in which rural growth is 1 percentage point lower (4.0 percent), and another in which it is 1 percentage point higher (6.0 percent). The overall GDP growth rate is maintained. For these scenarios to occur, urban growth must be 9.5 percent or 3.5 percent, respectively. Under the scenario with lower rural growth, poverty declines by only approximately 1 percentage point a year. In the higher rural growth scenario, the decline is much larger—almost 2 percentage points per year.

This analysis illustrates the sensitivity of poverty reduction to growth in rural areas. It also illustrates the sensitivity of these projections to modeling assumptions. For instance, by taking GDP growth as a proxy for consumption growth, one ignores that the two may not move in parallel. In the face of high-income growth, households might change their propensity to save. And even if the propensity to save remains constant, GDP increases may not translate into income increases. GDP is measured in constant prices—it is an index of the quantity produced—but real income is a composite of quantity and prices. When relative prices change, as is the case when terms of trade change, one may observe GDP increases but no associated income increases (Wuyts 2005). Likewise, if the relative purchasing power between rural and urban areas changes because relative prices of agricultural products fall compared with prices of goods and services from urban areas, then increased rural GDP may not translate into increased rural income.

Other changes may affect the pattern of poverty reduction as well. Migration from rural to urban areas is likely to accelerate poverty reduction, just as increases in

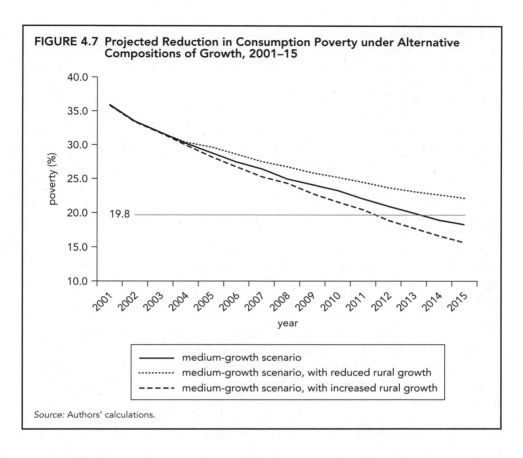

FIGURE 4.7 Projected Reduction in Consumption Poverty under Alternative Compositions of Growth, 2001–15

Source: Authors' calculations.

population growth rates diminish it. Despite these various uncertainties, what is very clear from these simulations is that it will be difficult to attain the NSGRP and MDG targets for poverty reduction and that enhanced rural income growth is a prerequisite to achieving those objectives.

Malnutrition

Progress in poverty reduction is typically not only expressed by the reduction of the fraction of people whose consumption falls below the poverty line, but also measured by the reduction in the number of malnourished people. The reason is that consumption poverty and malnutrition are quite distinct aspects of human welfare that may well respond differently to changes in income growth. Hence, the MDG for poverty and hunger reduction aims not only at reducing consumption poverty by 50 percent but also at reducing malnutrition, particularly the proportion of underweight children under five years of age. Underweight is a composite indicator for malnutrition, and it generalizes stunting (low height for age) and wasting (low weight for age). The under-five malnutrition rate, in terms of weight for age, in 1991/92 was 29.0 percent, so the MDG objective for Tanzania is 14.5 percent by 2015.

The NSGRP also explicitly aims at reducing the prevalence of malnutrition, taking as its measurable outcome the reduction in stunting among children under five from 43.8 percent in 1990 to 20.0 percent in 2010. In this section, the focus is on attaining the MDG on hunger reduction.

Income growth is clearly important for reducing malnutrition. Greater incomes at the household level allow families to spend more on food, clean water, hygiene, and preventive and curative health care. Greater incomes allow them to have more diversified diets and to obtain more effective child care arrangements. At the community level, greater income eventually leads to better access to and higher quality health care, improved water and sanitation systems, and greater access to information. Higher incomes also mean that the government can collect more revenues to spend on nutrition-improving programs. It seems therefore reasonable to expect that income growth contributes to the reduction of malnutrition.

For the malnutrition simulations, the focus is on the MDG objective. It is assumed that the malnutrition elasticities of real per capita income are 0.51 in the optimistic scenario and 0.30 in the conservative scenario (Mkenda 2004). These elasticities are determined on the basis of results reported by Haddad and others (2003) from their cross-country study. Haddad and others' (2003) findings are in the range of elasticities of demand for nutrients calculated by Abdulai and Aubert (2004a, 2004b) using HBS data collected from two regions in Tanzania in 1998 and 1999.

For income growth, the growth scenarios from the previous section are followed— that is, per capita GDP growth of 1.1 percent per year in the low-growth scenario, 2.5 percent in the medium-growth scenario, and 5.1 percent in the high-growth scenario. Figure 4.8 clearly shows that an optimistic 5.1 percent growth rate of GDP per capita and a malnutrition elasticity of per capita income of 0.51 (also optimistic) would reduce the prevalence of malnutrition from 22 percent in 1999 to about 17 percent in 2015. A simulation that uses the medium-growth scenario and the elasticity of 0.30 reduces malnutrition from 22 percent in 1999 to 20 percent in 2015, a rather marginal decrease. This scenario seems to be more realistic, if a bit conservative, and suggests that income growth alone cannot resolve the malnutrition problem in Tanzania. Furthermore, the simulation did not take into account the effect of HIV/AIDS (human immunodeficiency virus/acquired immune deficiency syndrome). The disease is likely to increase malnutrition because of the increase in the number of orphans and the decrease in the effective household labor force.

The simulations suggest that income growth alone is not sufficient to attain the MDG on hunger reduction. However, the drop in the prevalence of malnutrition between 1999 and 2004 from 29 percent to 22 percent (National Bureau of Statistics and ORC Macro 2005) shows that large declines in the prevalence of malnutrition can be attained in a relatively short period. The observed decline could be the result of much higher income-nutrition elasticities than the ones used here, but this explanation seems unrealistic. To attribute the observed decline in nutrition to income growth alone would require an elasticity of 2.1. It is more plausible that the decline is the result of a combination of income growth and nonincome factors such as more effective management of malaria, improved breastfeeding, and vitamin A supplementation. Between 1999 and 2004, the use of mosquito nets increased from 21 percent to 36 percent,

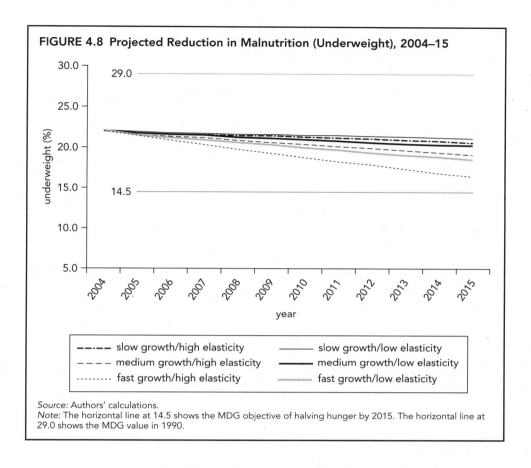

FIGURE 4.8 Projected Reduction in Malnutrition (Underweight), 2004–15

Source: Authors' calculations.
Note: The horizontal line at 14.5 shows the MDG objective of halving hunger by 2015. The horizontal line at 29.0 shows the MDG value in 1990.

vitamin A supplementation went from 14 percent to 46 percent,[6] and the proportion of children who are exclusively breastfed increased from 58 percent to 70 percent. At an average GDP growth rate of 5.4 percent and an income-nutrition elasticity of 0.51, about one-third of the decline in the prevalence of malnutrition between 1999 and 2004 can be attributed to income growth and the remainder to nonincome factors.

A study carried out by Alderman, Hoogeveen, and Rossi (2006) for the Kagera region also concludes that income growth in combination with nutrition interventions is required to attain the MDGs. In this study, the effects of the availability of community-based nutrition interventions (a child feeding program) are measured after controlling for common determinants of nutritional status such as community factors, individual and household characteristics (including log per capita consumption), and possible endogenous factors of program placement (such as mean log per capita consumption/income of the village, nutritional status of parents, major disaster in the preceding 10 years, and the like). Results of the study show that both income growth and the availability of a nutrition program significantly improve the nutritional status of children by reducing stunting and underweight (table 4.11).

The projections carried out by Alderman, Hoogeveen, and Rossi (2006) show that it is feasible to achieve the MDG on consumption poverty in Kagera (as it is nation-

TABLE 4.11 Reduction in Malnutrition in Kagera

(percent)

Per capita income growth	Reduction in consumption poverty	Reduction in malnutrition		
		No additional interventions	Interventions in 50% of communities	Interventions in all communities
Underweight				
1.3	44.1	6.8	37.0	57.6
3.1	66.6	13.3	42.0	61.5
5.0	84.1	19.5	46.7	65.1
Stunting				
1.3	44.1	5.3	44.4	70.3
3.1	66.6	8.7	48.1	73.2
5.0	84.1	13.9	51.0	75.2

Source: Alderman, Hoogeveen, and Rossi 2006.
Note: The simulations were done taking 1993 as the base year. Because the per capita income growth rate between 1993 and 2003 is known—0.7 percent per year—the effective growth rates required to attain the 1993–2015 mean growth rates of 1 percent, 2 percent, and 3 percent for the 2003–15 period are, respectively, 1.3 percent, 3.1 percent, and 5.0 percent. Shaded cells indicate that the MDG and NSGRP objectives are attained (that is, there is a 50 percent reduction).

ally) and that the MDG on nutrition cannot be achieved even under the highest income growth scenario. Only when nutrition interventions are available in the majority of villages will it be possible to achieve the MDG on nutrition. Considering the difficulty of covering all communities in the short term, the only solution for meeting the MDG target is to focus on per capita income growth while initiating or expanding nutrition interventions.

This analysis raises the question of whether further declines in the prevalence of malnutrition—beyond those attributable to income growth—can be expected and whether the MDG on hunger reduction is attainable. There seems scope for a positive response as long as nutrition interventions accompany income growth. Despite the noted improvements, only 36 percent of children under five slept under a mosquito net in 2004, vitamin A supplementation can be further expanded, and 30 percent of babies younger than two months are not exclusively breastfed. Given these data, there certainly seems to be scope for further improvements. Furthermore, the evidence from Kagera suggests that community-based nutrition interventions have considerable potential. Provided that an additional effort in nutrition-related interventions is made, the MDG on hunger reduction seems attainable.

Other MDGs

Progress toward attaining the MDG on universal primary education has been impressive. As soon as universal primary education was introduced in 2001, net enrollment rates jumped and are now close (91 percent) to the target of 100 percent enrollment.

Close to complete enrollment also implies gender equality in education. In primary education, such inequalities are small (table 4.9), but in secondary education, gender inequalities persist. These inequalities may be on the way out: in 2004, the girl-boy ratio in form I was 0.98, while it was 0.55 in form IV. However, further monitoring is needed. Other non-MDG indicators, such as the woman-man prevalence of HIV/AIDS (of 1.22), show that gender inequality persists.

Another encouraging fact is the observed reduction in child mortality from 141 per 1,000 in 1991 to 112 in 2004. This drop occurs after stagnancy in child mortality rates during the 1990s (it was 137 in 1996 and 147 in 1999) and appears to be a reflection of improved malaria management (improved treatment as well as increased use of bednets) and stronger health systems in general. The MDG target of 47 deaths per 1,000 is ambitious, however, and meeting this objective will remain a challenge.

With respect to the reduction of maternal mortality, no progress has been made. The data in table 4.9 even suggest an increase in maternal mortality rates, but the difference is not statistically significant. The lack of progress is reason for concern because the MDG is ambitious (a 75 percent reduction) and maternal mortality rates are high (578 per 100,000 births).

A recent blood sample survey suggests that the prevalence rate of HIV/AIDS is 7 percent, which is less than was expected on the basis of tests performed on blood donors. There is much variation in infection rates by age group, gender, and location. Women (7.7 percent) are more affected than men (6.3 percent). Prevalence is 5.2 percent in the 20 to 24 age cohort but more than double that (10.9 percent) in the 30 to 44 age cohort. Prevalence rates vary from a low of 2.0 percent in Manyara and Kigoma to a high of 13.5 percent in Mbeya and Iringa.

Finally, some limited progress was made in improving access to drinking water, mainly because of increased access to protected wells and springs. Still, some 54 percent of all rural households do not have access to improved drinking water, and much needs to be done to attain the MDG objective of 33 percent. As far as sanitation is concerned, almost all urban (96 percent) and rural (92 percent) households have access to a toilet. In urban areas, one observes an increase in the fraction of households without a toilet from 2 percent in 1991 to 4 percent in 2000, possibly as a result of rapid urbanization.

Conclusions

Our analysis of Tanzania's historical growth performance suggests caution as to the likelihood that recent high growth rates can be sustained or even further increased. To the extent that the demand-side stimulus emanating from increasing government spending disappears, growth may revert to the range of 4 to 5 percent per year, unless there is a marked improvement in Tanzania's international competitiveness and ability to diversify its economy. Policy-based growth projections provide a more optimistic picture and suggest that a per capita growth rate of about 4 percent should be sustainable in the medium term, given Tanzania's current economic policies and institutions. Further improvements in policies and institutions are necessary to scale up economic growth to the level of about 8 percent targeted in the NSGRP. On the input side, achieving these growth rates requires continued investment in human resources with greater concentration on secondary and tertiary education, building on the significant achievements in recent years in expanding access to primary education. Sustaining higher growth also requires scaled-up private sector investment and complementary investment in infrastructure. Although in the past gains in productivity have been primarily reform driven, in the future gains in productivity must come more often from innovation and technological change.

Progress in reducing poverty depends critically on the pattern of economic growth. Because poverty is concentrated in rural areas, a growth strategy needs to focus on rural growth (although urban growth also is important), both by reducing urban poverty and by providing opportunities for rural populations through migration. Achieving the NSGRP target of halving poverty by 2010 requires a rural growth rate of at least 4.5 percent per year and an urban growth rate of about 10 percent.

Hunger is another important dimension of poverty. Economic growth alone is likely to be insufficient to reach the NSGRP and MDG targets for reducing malnutrition. Additional interventions, such as micronutrient programs and community-based interventions, are necessary.

Notes

1. Middle-income economies are those with a gross national income per capita of more than US$765 but less than US$9,386.

2. The CPIA is based on Bank economists' and sector specialists' ratings of 20 items in four areas: management of inflation and current accounts, structural policies, policies for social inclusion and equity, and public sector management and institutions.

3. *Institutional Investor* credit ratings are based on a survey of leading international bankers, who are asked to rate each country on a scale of 0 to 100 (in which 100 represents maximum creditworthiness). *Institutional Investor* averages these ratings, attaching greater weights to respondents with greater worldwide exposure and more sophisticated country analysis systems.

4. The ICRG compiles monthly data on 13 political, 6 financial, and 5 economic risk factors to calculate risk indexes in each of these categories, as well as a composite risk index. Political risk assessment scores are based on subjective staff analysis of available information. Economic risk assessment scores are based on objective analysis of quantitative data. Financial risk assessment scores are based on analysis of a mix of quantitative and qualitative information. The political risk measure is given twice the weight of the financial and economic risk measures.

5. Euromoney country risk scores are based on the weighted average of quantitative indicators in nine categories: political risk (25 percent), economic performance (25 percent), debt indicators (10 percent), debt in default or rescheduled (10 percent), credit ratings (10 percent), access to bank finance (5 percent), access to short-term finance (5 percent), access to capital markets (5 percent), and discount on forfeiting (5 percent). For items for which no data are available, the rating is 0. This method might introduce a downward bias for countries such as Tanzania, for which data availability is often poor.

6. A nationally representative survey carried out by the Tanzania Food and Nutrition Center in July 2004 and implemented immediately after the vitamin A supplementation campaign shows that vitamin A coverage for children between 6 and 59 months is 85 percent (TFNC 2004b).

PART II
Sectoral Perspectives on Growth

5
Agricultural Productivity and Shared Growth

Henry Gordon

At an average annual rate of 3.5 percent, Tanzania's agricultural growth exceeds the Sub-Saharan African average of 3.3 percent.[1] Sub-Saharan Africa's average growth rate, although lower than the growth rates targeted by many African countries, exceeded growth in other regions of the developing world between 1990 and 2003 (figure 5.1). However, with a population growth rate of 2.9 percent during the 1990s, agricultural growth was insufficient to make a significant difference in per capita incomes and rural poverty.

Growth in Tanzania's agricultural gross domestic product (GDP) accelerated over the period, reaching an average rate of 4 percent for 1996 to 2003. Sectoral performance showed variation around the average, but the variation was considerably less in Tanzania than in many of its neighbors, indicating a somewhat greater degree of protection against severe shocks. The growth was accompanied by structural and policy changes that created new opportunities for producers and brought benefits to consumers. For example, Tanzanian grain and horticultural producers participate in regional markets to a much greater extent than in the past, when barriers to trade were higher. Because of its growth and its increased openness to trade, Tanzania was able to manage recent variability in weather with minimal assistance, avoiding the severe food shocks that adversely affected its neighbors.

Agriculture has been a substantial contributor to overall national growth. Table 5.1 shows that between 1995 and 2003, primary agriculture directly accounted for 37 percent of the country's very strong annual growth in GDP.[2] Agriculture's contribution to growth is high even though it is not the fastest-growing sector. Why? Because its share in the economy is large, and unlike tourism and the mineral sectors, it has a relatively low share of intermediate inputs in gross value. Moreover, primary agriculture contributes indirectly to growth in other sectors by stimulating demand for supplies of goods and services to farmers (agricultural transport, storage, and marketing, as well as consumer goods); by providing raw materials to processors; and by providing urban workers with food at affordable prices. Food takes a high share of urban household budgets, ranging from 58 percent in Dar es Salaam to 65 percent in other towns. Some but not all of those secondary effects of farm growth are captured in the contribution of

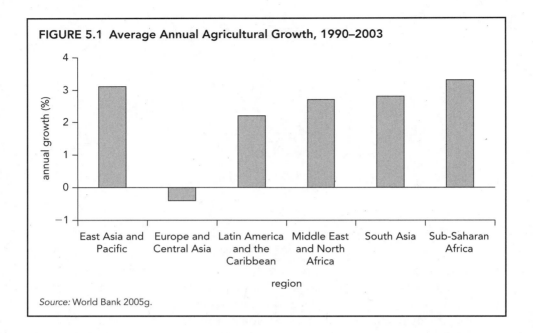

FIGURE 5.1 Average Annual Agricultural Growth, 1990–2003

Source: World Bank 2005g.

TABLE 5.1 Sectoral and Subsectoral Contributions to GDP Growth, 1995–2003

(percent)

National accounts components	Subcomponents	Annual growth	Share of GDP	Contribution to GDP growth
Manufacturing and services	Nonagricultural manufacturing and services	5.8	32	39
	Agribusiness[a]	5.8	19	23
Primary agriculture	Crops	3.8	36	28
	Livestock	3.3	6	4
	Forestry and hunting	3.1	3	2
	Fishing	5.1	3	3
Total[a]			100	100

Source: Author's computations from national accounts data with agribusiness shares taken from Jaffee and others 2003.
a. Numbers do not add because of rounding.

agribusiness to GDP growth, estimated at 23 percent.[3] Together, primary agriculture and agribusiness contributed roughly 60 percent to Tanzania's growth in GDP between 1995 and 2003.

The positive performance of agriculture, particularly in the latter part of the period, is all the more remarkable because it was achieved when global prices for major export commodities (coffee, cotton, cashews, tea, and tobacco) were low and when the appreciation of the shilling was depressing producers' incentives.

Despite the positive performance overall, Tanzania's recent agricultural growth is not sufficient to meet the ambitious goals embodied in the national poverty reduction

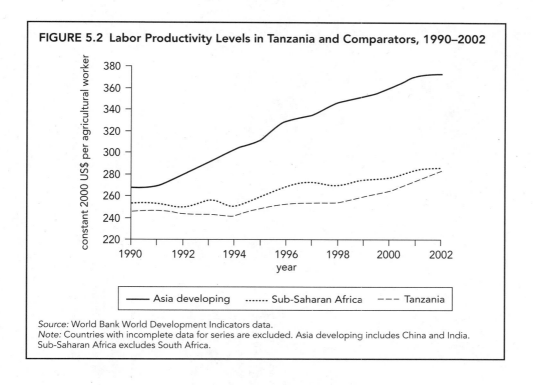

FIGURE 5.2 Labor Productivity Levels in Tanzania and Comparators, 1990–2002

Source: World Bank World Development Indicators data.
Note: Countries with incomplete data for series are excluded. Asia developing includes China and India.
Sub-Saharan Africa excludes South Africa.

strategy. The strategy sets a target of sustained agricultural growth of 5 percent per year.[4] Achieving this target requires a growth process that is quantitatively faster and qualitatively different from that of the late 1990s, even though that period was relatively successful. As in much of Africa, growth in Tanzania has depended on expanding the area cultivated, but labor productivity increases have been insufficient to support faster growth and poverty reduction. As shown in figure 5.2, labor productivity in Africa has trended up only since 1994, with Tanzania's average level below that of the Sub-Saharan Africa average. Tanzania's 1.1 percent per year increase between 1990 and 2003 was lower than that recorded by some of its immediate neighbors, such as Malawi (5.5 percent), Mozambique (2.3 percent), or Uganda (1.8 percent), as illustrated in figure 5.3.

At 1.1 percent, Tanzania's labor productivity growth falls far short of the level needed to reduce rural poverty. Given the country's 2.3 percent annual increase in its agricultural labor force, labor productivity must grow at least 2.7 percent per year to reach a rate of 5.0 percent annual growth in agriculture.[5] As figure 5.3 shows, such increases are rare among the country's regional neighbors.[6]

Tanzania's experience and its strategy for agricultural growth should be seen more broadly in light of global experience. Countries that have achieved sustained agricultural growth have done so by generating and adopting technological change, resulting in increased joint productivity of land, labor, and capital (total factor productivity). Whether the pattern of technological change has been labor saving or land saving has depended on which factor is relatively scarcer.[7] Countries with abundant land or

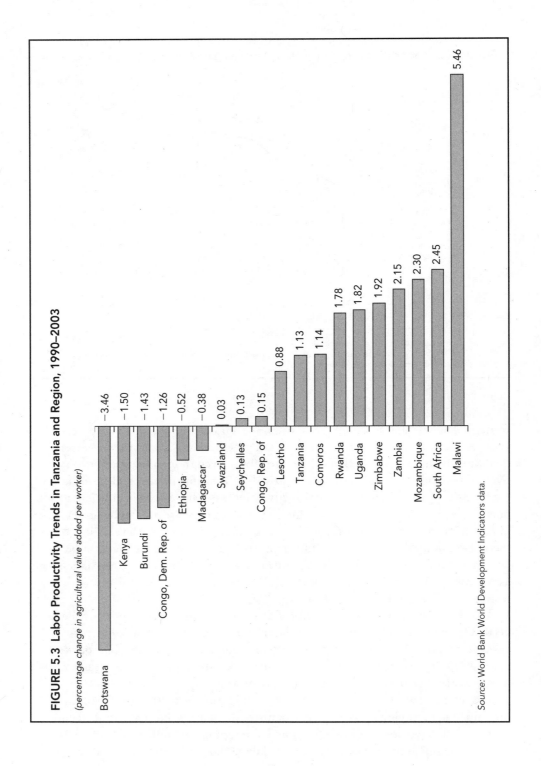

FIGURE 5.3 Labor Productivity Trends in Tanzania and Region, 1990–2003

(percentage change in agricultural value added per worker)

Botswana	−3.46
Kenya	−1.50
Burundi	−1.43
Congo, Dem. Rep. of	−1.26
Ethiopia	−0.52
Madagascar	−0.38
Swaziland	0.03
Seychelles	0.13
Congo, Rep. of	0.15
Lesotho	0.88
Tanzania	1.13
Comoros	1.14
Rwanda	1.78
Uganda	1.82
Zimbabwe	1.92
Zambia	2.15
Mozambique	2.30
South Africa	2.45
Malawi	5.46

Source: World Bank World Development Indicators data.

rapid expansion of off-farm work have expanded the area cultivated per worker by adopting labor-saving technologies, typically involving improved machines, implements, and animal power. Given the relative abundance of land in Tanzania, a sectoral growth strategy reliant on expansion of area could be considered consistent with the resource endowment. It would follow the historic path of other land-rich countries, such as Argentina, Australia, Canada, the Russian Federation, and the United States. In those countries, labor productivity rose sharply as additional land was brought into cultivation. Growth in those countries was accompanied by marked structural change in farming and by rapid technological change, largely in mechanical technology, that reduced labor requirements in agriculture.

Although several African countries have an endowment of land sufficient to follow this course, few have done so successfully, at least on a widespread basis. In some cases, the property rights regime constrained access to land; in others, mechanical or animal draft innovations were limited by poor access to output markets, too limited a range of appropriate and affordable technologies for farmers' conditions, and thin or nonexistent markets for long-term credit and for nonbank financial services such as leasing.

A second path involves adopting technologies that increase the productivity of land. Yield increases in crops were the defining characteristic of the Green Revolution in land-scarce Asia, transforming the rural sectors between the 1960s and the 1990s. Those increases were preceded by hundreds of years of investment in irrigation. The investment in irrigation complemented the new biological technologies and reduced the risks associated with their adoption, while creating a homogeneous production environment more amenable to accepting "broad spectrum" seed packages. New breeds of livestock and more efficient feeding regimes correspondingly increased the yield of meat and milk per unit of land devoted to fodder. In Tanzania, as elsewhere in Africa, increases in the productivity of land on the scale of the Asian Green Revolution have been elusive, although some progress has been achieved in the uptake of improved varieties of maize, beans, and cassava.

In either of the growth paths described above, the productivity of scarce factors increases, raising the returns to and the value of those factors. A dynamic process of adjustment starts whereby rural households invest in education, implements, technology, and land. Farm size and structure change in response to economic signals.

The agricultural growth process in the 1990s, with its modest increases in labor productivity and stagnant yields of most crops, derived largely from area expansion.[8] Data from the 2002/03 agricultural sample survey suggest that between 1998/99 and 2002/03 there has been no further expansion of arable land under cultivation. Examples of labor-saving innovation exist—for example, land expansion through increased use of animal traction in the land-abundant Rukwa region. However, a significant portion of agricultural growth involved keeping up with population growth by expanding cultivated area using existing production methods. Had this growth path not been an option, food security would have declined as the labor force expanded, rather than holding its own or improving modestly. But for the sector as a whole, a more widespread pattern of technological change is necessary, one that is adapted to regionally varied factor endowments and to Tanzania's extraordinarily diverse production environments. Moreover, land expansion using existing techniques carries environmental costs as forests and wildlife areas are encroached on, as increasingly marginal land comes into cultivation, and as fish stocks are depleted.

Tanzania's agricultural growth path needs to combine features of the land-intensive and labor-intensive models that conserve the resource base and thus, of necessity, will differ from the experience of the 1990s. Because of the diversity of Tanzania's endowments and agroclimatic conditions, growth paths deriving from better cultivation of larger tracts will be optimal in more land-abundant parts of the country such as the southern highlands, whereas those associated with high yields and intensive cultivation will suit such areas as Morogoro and Kilimanjaro. Where an increase in area per worker is possible (for example, in relatively land-abundant areas such as Rukwa or where growing urban centers draw workers away from farms), yield increases will be less necessary. The converse applies to areas where land and off-farm jobs are scarce. This situation exists because of an adding-up requirement: the change in labor productivity must equal the change in land productivity plus the change in area per worker. Table 5.2 illustrates the trade-off, showing different combinations of change in land per worker and change in land productivity that are required to meet a 2.7 percent rate of increase in agricultural labor productivity.

Agriculture's value added can grow not only through expansion of cultivated area or increases in yield but also through changes in the composition of output that shift production out of activities with low or negative value added into existing or new activities with higher profitability. Such a process underpinned Kenya's successful smallholder-based growth in the 1970s and 1980s. Table 5.3 shows that such a process is beginning in Tanzania, as production has shifted to nontraditional exports and import-competing commodities.

A significant portion of the contribution of nontraditional exports to sectoral growth derives from maize (a regional export) and pulses. These products are classified as nontraditional exports simply because in the past they were produced largely for home consumption and trade was of low volume and informal. The performance of maize is particularly notable, because the decision to open the borders to trade in maize was

TABLE 5.2 Labor Productivity Growth: Contributing Factors

(percent)

Target yearly increase in agricultural labor productivity	Assumption regarding annual change in land cultivated per agricultural worker	Required annual increase in land productivity
2.7	0	2.7
	(no future growth in area per worker)	
	1.1	1.6
	(future area/worker growth same as in past)	
	1.7	1.0
	(future area/worker growth higher than in past because of labor-saving innovations)	

Source: Author's calculations.

TABLE 5.3 Contributions of Subsectors to 5.3 Percent Growth in Agricultural Gross Value of Production, 1995/96–2002/03

(percent)

Subsector	Growth rate	Share of agricultural gross value of production	Growth contribution
Crops	5.5	87	4.8
Livestock	4.2	13	0.6
Total		100	5.3
Traditional exports	−6.9	7	−0.5
Nontraditional exports	7.5	40	3.0
Importables	6.5	26	1.7
Nontradables	4.1	26	1.1
Total		100	5.3

Source: United Republic of Tanzania 2004a.
Note: Numbers may not sum because of rounding. Some readers will note that the 5.3 percent rate of growth in this table differs from the 4 percent rate cited in chapter 1. Here the figure is based on a different sectoral aggregate, the gross value of production. The rate in chapter 1, which is the more widely cited agricultural growth statistic, is based on the growth rate of agricultural GDP, which nets out purchased inputs and covers a broader array of products than does gross value of production.

very controversial, potentially exposing the country to vulnerability in a commodity important to domestic food security. The growth in exports of maize has not brought about domestic shortages, because supply has grown commensurately. Production of fish from Lake Victoria is not included in the aggregate, but its inclusion would increase further the contribution of nontraditional exports to sectoral growth. One nontraditional export crop, pyrethrum, had an impressive annual growth trend of 23 percent over the period from 1995/96 to 2002/03, but because of its low share in the total value of agricultural production, its contribution (measured in the table as rate of growth times share in gross value of production) was small.

Import-competing commodities with high income elasticities constituted a surprisingly high share of sectoral growth,[9] accounting for almost one-third. Examples of commodities with strong performance include rice and livestock products (milk and dairy—especially yogurt and poultry). This finding illustrates the need for an approach to supporting agricultural growth that recognizes the diversity of the sector. Maize is clearly a dominant crop, accounting for more than 30 percent of the gross value of agriculture production, and it is singularly important for food security. Yet no single commodity or group of commodities can be preselected as the one that will deliver the desired sectoral performance. Traditional export crops must not be forgotten. Although not performing well in recent years because of low global prices (particularly for coffee, cotton, and cashews), traditional crops have shown signs of revival since 2003 (particularly cotton and tobacco). This recovery may be due in part to the recent depreciation of the shilling in real terms. Finally, nontradables (bananas, potatoes) appear to have a robust domestic market.

Assessment of the sources of Tanzania's agricultural growth since 1990 thus leads to the conclusion that although aggregate growth is commendable by regional and even global standards, that growth has been of a magnitude and nature insufficient to meet the country's objectives for the future. Agriculture has not led national growth, even though the sectoral endowment is quite favorable. Past growth derived in large part from expanding the area under cultivation to meet growing domestic and regional food demand. What technological change occurred has not been sufficiently widespread to induce higher sectorwide incomes. Improved opportunities for trade, particularly in cereals, have led to some increase in food security and some shift of area away from products for household consumption toward products destined for markets. This change in the composition of output represents an important target of opportunity for the future. But income per worker has not yet increased appreciably, and the gap in incomes between farming families and those in more dynamic sectors has widened.

The lessons of the agricultural growth experience of the recent past have important implications for the future. Expansion of cultivated area is likely to remain important, but it cannot be the sole source of growth, because land and labor endowments vary considerably between and within regions. Research and marketing strategies need to be more location specific, and the decentralization of research and public administration is beginning to support this shift. Future expansion of area cultivated must be accompanied by greater investment in land improvements for both existing and newly cultivated area. In areas with higher population densities and adequate market access, more emphasis needs to be put on generating and adopting technologies that increase land productivity. Shifts in the composition of output toward products with higher value added will be important to drive growth—in some cases, the most important shifts. These shifts will depend heavily on improving the outreach of agricultural markets, as well as the capacity of farmers to coordinate among themselves to expand their marketing options and take advantage of economies of scale in transport and storage.

The imperatives of the growth process determine the priorities for public support. Improvements in land require attention to land tenure issues and mobility of land through functioning factor (especially land and labor) markets. Accelerated adoption of technology requires public investments in its generation and dissemination through support for effective agricultural research and advisory services, as well as publicprivate cost sharing for early phases of adoption. Shifts in the composition of output require well-functioning markets and declining transaction costs. Costs of transportation and communications are important, but so is the quality of the business environment in rural areas, which either attracts or repels competitive enterprises that can interact profitably with primary producers.

To achieve ambitious sectoral targets for growth, the government needs to persevere with policy reforms started in the 1990s and complete the unfinished agenda without regression or reversals. In addition, it is critical that the government rebalance public expenditure to align with its objective of broad-based growth. Continued technological and financial assistance from development partners will be needed, as will reductions in industrial countries' farm subsidies, which distort international agricultural markets. The private sector must seize new opportunities opened in agricultural production, trade, processing, and input supply and, in most cases, can be counted on to do so if the business and regulatory environment improves.

These requirements underscore two enduring themes of Tanzanian agriculture that provide a strong basis for future growth. First, farmers are a diverse group, not limited to the stereotypical image of the peasant household with hoe technology, providing its members with food and a small commercial surplus. Rather, a range of households operate in diverse farming systems, with varying degrees of market involvement. Second, Tanzanian farmers—wherever they lie on the continuum between subsistence and commercial orientation—have continually proven themselves resourceful, market oriented, and eager to respond to market opportunities.

A successful tripartite partnership between the government, the development partners, and the private sector can nurture a growth process that is more protective of the natural resource base than in the past and more effective in increasing labor productivity, the key indicator of improved farm incomes and poverty reduction. Government policy actions and decisions on institutional reform and public expenditure set the context in which the agricultural sector can grow to meet the high national expectations—or fall substantially short. Given the stated goal for sustained sectoral growth of 5 percent per year, only an ambitious agenda of reforms and well-chosen public expenditure can be expected to succeed. More limited actions require amendment of the growth and poverty reduction targets or entail recognition from the outset that they will not be met.

Removing Constraints on Agricultural Growth

Although microlevel studies repeatedly emphasize the financial and economic profitability of farming in Tanzania, as well as the benefits associated with technology adoption, the agricultural sector appears to be far from a productivity take-off. Yet there are signs of real progress in the forms of market- and farm-level innovation and emerging institutions that can provide a foundation for accelerated productivity. The analysis of sources of growth has documented some of the more visible factors. The tremendous responsiveness of Tanzanian farmers to changing market conditions has accounted, in part, for the good agricultural growth record recently, in the face of highly unfavorable prices for traditional exports.

Owing to the many farm- and market-level constraints on smallholder producers, there is a vital, positive role for national government and local institutions in enabling agricultural growth and rural poverty reduction. Removal of constraints on agricultural marketing, processing, and farm productivity requires focus on the following:

- Improved implementation of land tenure and reforms

- Expansion of agricultural research effort, continued research and extension focus on client responsiveness and engagement of farmers in the research process, and strong emphasis on sustainable use of land and water resources

- Irrigation improvements

- Support for improved functioning of output and input markets and for associated rural services, including finance.

Management of Land for Agricultural Growth

As shown in table 5.4, Tanzania is a large country, primarily rural, with only a modest proportion of land currently used for agriculture. Although land appears to be ample, rural areas suffer from a frequency of disputes over land and insecurity of tenure that one would expect to see only in a country with a higher density of settlement and, hence, greater competition for land. These circumstances derive in part from the colonial legacy of land administration, in part from the disruptions of the villagization campaign of the 1970s, and in part from the subsequent delay in adjusting land policy and administration to the needs of a changing market economy. Factors limiting the mobility of farm families from areas of greater to lower population density may also be important.

To address the growing problems, the country passed the national land policy of 1995. The policy provides more expeditious access, enhanced security of tenure, and better management of land as a natural resource. Implementation of the policy is defined under three main pieces of legislation: the Land Act, No. 4 of 1999; the Village Land Act, No. 5 of 1999; and the Land Disputes Courts Act, No. 2 of 2002. Commonly referred to as the new land laws of mainland Tanzania, these laws replace the Land Ordinance of 1953. Given the large-scale movement of people under the villagization program and the separation of households from their traditional lands, the current law recognizes that land rights are confirmed through long-term occupancy, use, and development of the land.

A plan of actions and investments to implement the laws was drawn up in 2005.[10] Under the laws, all land is state property under the trusteeship of the president. It is allocated for use under varying forms of tenure, foremost of which is the 99-year

TABLE 5.4 Land Use and Potential for Agricultural Land Expansion, Mid-1990s

Land use	Hectares (million)	Share of total land area (%)
Urban	0.065	0.1
Rural protected land		
Protected forest/woodland	13.838	15.0
Other protected (wildlife, national park)	13.291	14.0
Agricultural land currently used (10.8 million hectares)		
Temporary crops	3.700	4.0
Pasture	6.150	6.5
Permanent crops	0.950	1.5
Rural unprotected land—available but not used		
Unprotected forest/woodland	26.321	28.0
Suitable for cropping but unused	7.000	7.0
Grassland/bushland not suitable for cropping; may be suitable		
for grazing[a] (may include some water area)	23.221	25.0
Total land area	94.536	100.0

Source: FAO and World Bank 2001.
a. As much as 25 percent of potentially suitable pasture land is affected by the tsetse fly and cannot be used for cattle at present.

leasehold. The plan identifies separate actions for the three main categories of land: village land, urban land, and reserve land.

For village land, attention is focused on clarifying village boundaries to reduce conflicts over encroachment, surveying and demarcating plots within the village, distributing certificates of customary rights of occupancy, establishing village land councils, and introducing formal working links and vertical-horizontal reporting relationships between community-based organizations (CBOs), nongovernmental organizations (NGOs), and district land offices. The program also seeks to set upper and lower limits on plot sizes, to prevent excessive fragmentation or concentration of village land holdings.

The plan of action in the reserve lands aims at clarifying and demarcating boundaries of conservation areas, game reserves, and national parks to resolve concerns of adjoining villages. Land rights for pastoral and nomadic peoples remain controversial; the strategic plan for land states simply that nomadic livelihoods are not consistent with sustainable and undisputed land rights. For all categories of land, the program outlines a process of documentation, public education, staffing, and capacity building to provide adequate attestation of land rights and resolution of disputes.

The program emphasizes affirmation of existing land rights and reduction of conflict. This emphasis emerged from broad consultation with stakeholders leading up to the formulation of the policy and legislation, and it clearly responds to immediate needs. The framework supports transactions in rural land, in particular by clarifying boundaries to prevent disputes that would otherwise stymie transactions. Little emphasis is accorded to detailed planning for the increased volume of transactions that can be expected as the agricultural economy becomes more dynamic.

Although it calls for setting limits on the upper and lower sizes of holdings, the program does not address the practical details associated with limits. Will limits be uniform, or will they vary by locality? According to what criteria will they be set? How will they be enforced? Upper limits on the size of holdings have been difficult to enforce. Where lower limits have been enforced, as in the restrictions on subdivision in South Africa under apartheid, they have had negative economic and social effects and have been difficult to reverse, even after a change in the political order that imposed them. In Tanzania, the proposed restrictions on subdivision are intended to prevent trapping people on small and diminishing plots in an environment where land is relatively abundant. Yet because land is abundant, legal restrictions on plot size may not be necessary if land markets can be made fluid enough and if resources can be made available to facilitate voluntary migration.

The program recognizes that some aspirants will not be able to get land in their own localities if lower limits on plot sizes are introduced. It thus recommends establishment of a voluntary resettlement program to accommodate those demands. Such a program could be regarded as a homesteading program, open to any interested and qualified participant seeking to move where land is available for agricultural production. The program could be designed as a public-private partnership in which the public sector makes land available; provides a right to conditional use for an initial period; assists with costs of relocation; provides infrastructure to meet defined minimal standards (roads, water, public services if not already offered); and leverages resources that the participant invests according to a formula for matching grants. Participants could bring their investment as their share of the matching grant and commit to working the land for a period of time, after which the right to conditional use would be converted to a 99-year leasehold and would be recorded as such.

The land program document refers broadly to a national village resettlement scheme without further elaborating on the scheme's design. Such a program could successfully draw on experience in Africa and in Latin America and would benefit from the other activities foreseen under the land program. Those activities will assist in clarifying which lands could be brought into the program on the supply side without compromising commitments to reserves or the rights of current users. Facilitating the mobility of land through transactions could forestall the need to set legal restrictions on plot size and simultaneously serve the growth agenda.

Technological Change to Foster Growth: Generation, Dissemination, and Adoption

Given the sustained rapid growth of the population, the limited creation of employment outside agriculture, and the rapid increase in area farmed per worker (through outmigration or increased off-farm rural employment), it will be a challenge to achieve more rapid growth in labor productivity. Sustained increases in labor productivity and rural incomes therefore depend on more rapid technological change that is either labor saving or land conserving, depending on local endowments and marketing options.

A successful dynamic of technological change in the smallholder sector starts with increased productivity in the products that farm households produce for their own consumption. Often a distinction is drawn between food crops and cash crops, but this distinction is no longer helpful because most food crops now serve a cash crop function. Maize and cassava are often considered food crops, as opposed to cash crops such as cotton and coffee. Yet maize and cassava have considerable importance as cash crops because market demand exists for them in raw and processed forms.

As producers realize productivity gains in products for their own consumption, they can sequentially reduce the area devoted to that consumption and increase the area devoted to products for markets. This shift may mean simply marketing more of the same product or taking advantage of opportunities to shift into products with higher profitability. Increased productivity allows smallholders to move incrementally from subsistence to commercial farming.

Higher profitability translates into higher earnings, with increased savings, investment in land improvement, and ability to finance inputs for profitable production in the next season. Demand for locally produced nonfarm goods and services also increases—for tin roofs, pumps for water management, implements for conservation tillage, and other items. The initial increase in productivity thus multiplies to support greater dynamism in agriculture and local rural growth.

Three elements must be present in the technology system to trigger the initial round of increased productivity:

- Researchers must have developed new varieties and production techniques that are profitable under the conditions that smallholders face.

- Producers must have information about the availability of the varieties and guidance on how to use them.

- Money must be available to cover the costs of early adoption of the new varieties.

All three elements—the varieties, the knowledge, and the financing—must be linked in a way that provides access for smallholders.

Tanzania has invested in elements of the technology system with some success. Indeed, past investments in research and extension explain part of the recent good performance of the sector. During the early 1990s, agricultural services consisted primarily of centralized, supply-driven public services through the then Ministry of Agriculture and Cooperatives (MAC).[11] Crop and livestock services were integrated and organized around three main domains: research, training, and extension. Technical services were handled separately.

As the 1990s progressed, shortcomings in the technology system became clear, and adjustments were made in particular aspects. The technology transfer model inherent in the Training and Visitation extension system was found to be unsustainable because of the high costs of service delivery. Extension approaches barely took into account the concerns, needs, and involvement of farmers. As a result, the majority of the farmers either did not access the services or, if they did, often found them irrelevant. Decentralization of research was initiated in the early 1990s with the establishment of seven agricultural research zones. The *farming systems approach* was adopted in research operations to strengthen the link between researchers and farmers. That approach was followed by the introduction of the *client-oriented research management approach* in selected zones. Research for coffee, tobacco, and tea was privatized and funded largely by a combination of direct donor support and a cess on producers. In 2000, the former MAC was divided into three ministries: the Ministry of Agriculture and Food Security (MAFS), the Ministry of Water and Livestock Development (MWLD), and the Ministry of Cooperatives and Marketing (MCM). This division fragmented some of the research efforts and introduced new requirements for coordination (for example, livestock and crops for integrated farming systems were handled by different ministries, as were crops and investments in irrigation schemes). In 2005, the three ministries were consolidated into two, namely, the Ministry for Agriculture, Food Security, and Cooperatives (MAFSC) and the Ministry for Livestock Development (MLD).

Research undertaken in the 1990s addressed varietal improvements in the crop sector, new breeds in livestock, pest and disease management, improved management of soil fertility, and reduction of postharvest losses. A summary of selected achievements appears in table 5.5.

These and other research results were produced by the National Agricultural Research System (NARS), which comprises various public organizations—namely, the Department of Research and Development (DRD), the Tropical Pesticides Research Institute, several universities, and the Tanzania Forestry Research Institute—along with private sector organizations, which include crop research institutes for tobacco, coffee, and tea. The DRD of the Ministry of Agriculture, Food Security, and Cooperatives is the lead institution of NARS. It is tasked with the public role of conducting, coordinating, and directing agricultural research in the country. The DRD operates a network of more than 50 research institutes and associated centers and substations, which

TABLE 5.5 Inventory of Technologies Coming Out of the Research System in the 1990s

Innovation	Existing or pipeline technologies
Maize varietal improvement	Maize gray leaf spot–tolerant and high-yielding varieties (UH 615, UH 6303) have been developed and adopted widely in high-altitude areas with severe crop loss.
Cassava	Cassava mosaic disease–tolerant clones have been developed. Cassava mealy bug reduces yield by 80–100%.
Cassava postharvest losses	Improved processing equipment has been tested and recommended and is now available.
Bean disease resistance	Improved varieties Uyole 94, Uyole 96, Uyole 98, and Kabanima are high yielding and tolerate diseases.
Bean multiplication	Bean Improvement Program supports seed multiplication.
Bean maggot control	Combination of integrated pest management and cultivation techniques reduces population of maggots and magnitude of loss.
Tomato seed development	Tanya and Tengeru 97 tomato varieties increase yields and incomes and reduce dependence on imported seeds.
Cashew disease	Plant protection agents (sulfur, organic fungicide Anvil, Bayfidan, and Topas) reduce powdery mildew disease; 20 clonal varieties have been identified as potentially high yielding and tolerant of diseases and pests.
Banana pests	Nematodes and weevils are managed through application of plant protection agents, varietal improvements, and cultural practices.
Deforestation in tobacco areas	Varieties suitable for fuelwood and enhancement of soil fertility have been developed and introduced through agroforestry.
Cattle breeds	Dual-purpose Mpwapwa cattle have been introduced in pilot villages, and milk production increased from 1–2 liters/day to 5–7 liters/day under farmer management.
Goat breeds	Dual-purpose goats with live weights of up to 45 kg and milk yields of 1.5 liters/day have been introduced.
Newcastle disease for chickens	Thermostable vaccine (I-2) is available for control in rural areas.
Rice variety	Popular aromatic variety has been developed.

Source: World Bank 2004e.

cover the main areas of crops and livestock research in the country. The main research effort comes from seven zonal research and development centers (ZRDCs), each comprising a lead station and associated centers and substations. The ZRDCs are located in the seven agroecological zones and are responsible for both applied and location-specific adaptive research and training. There are also a few institutes that are not under the zonal research setup and that undertake specialized research work. They include the Animal Diseases Research Institute in Temeke, Dar es Salaam, and the Tsetse and Trypanosomiasis Research Institute in Tanga. These institutes have a national mandate and are responsible for the design and evaluation of nationwide research programs in collaboration with the zonal centers.

Throughout much of the 1990s, with the support of several development partners, including the World Bank, Tanzania's agricultural extension program followed the traditional and centralized model of training and visitation. By the end of the 1990s, evidence emerged that the cost of the program was high and unsustainable and that its effectiveness was limited. At the same time, commitments to decentralize service delivery under the local government reform program made the traditional administrative framework for extension untenable. In December 2000, a new approach to extension was developed under the *Vision and Strategy Outline to Year 2010* (MAFS 2001). It involved an incremental shift to an extension service that is responsive to clients, pluralistic in the delivery of services, cost-effective, and sensitive to the gender mix in Tanzania's agricultural sector.

Several pilot activities helped to make the vision a reality. The pilot initiatives were designed to test modalities for training, delivery of technical advice, and strengthening of support for marketing and economic decision making, as well as to provide technical expertise. The period from 2000 to 2005 was a challenging one for the extension service, as staff at national and district levels sorted out the implications of decentralization and pilot efforts in alternative modalities of service delivery were designed and implemented. Despite some institutional confusion and scarcity of resources because of mismatches between the fiscal and the administrative decentralization, extension continued to function and, together with the research establishment, contributed to the growth in output over this period.

Farmer organizations, together with research and extension services, are key contributors to the technology system. MVIWATA (Mtandao wa Vikundi vya Wakulima Tanzania), the country's main farmer group network, has built an impressive organization up to the national level. Since its formation in 1993, MVIWATA has expanded to cover 120 local networks with some 1,000 affiliated groups in more than 80 districts (representing some 50,000 to 70,000 households). A number of other groups operate at the community level, either independently or with NGOs. They have played an active role in the generation and transfer of technology.[12] Farmer groups improve access to technology (for example, through experiential learning, as in farmer research groups and farmer field school groups); to funding (for example, through credit and savings groups); to crop processing and marketing (through commodity marketing groups); to livestock production (through dairy or poultry groups); to gender-based activities; and to member support in case of need (through indigenous and traditional, religious, and culturally based groups).

The contribution of agricultural research, extension, and empowerment of farmers in the 1990s and early 2000s was positive but also limited by several factors. Services generally focused on increasing production through short-term technical packages, without paying sufficient attention to farmers' circumstances, markets, and sustainability. Despite various attempts to strengthen them, the links between research, extension, and training were weak, and collaboration between public and private partners was limited. Disproportionate emphasis was placed on generating and disseminating technology, and less on empowering farmers (in terms of both skills and finance) to adopt the technology. As a consequence of weak links in the system, research did not always focus on technologies that had the greatest potential effect on production systems. Technical breakthroughs did not yield good economic returns. And promising technologies remained on the shelf because of lack of knowledge or financing for adoption. Ruptured links in the technology chain reduced returns to investments in each of the elements. Moreover, the system was underfinanced—but given the somewhat depressed returns resulting from the institutional deficiencies, underfinancing was an appropriate response.

Under the Agricultural Sector Development Programme (ASDP), a major reform of the institutional structure of the agricultural technology system has been designed and is being implemented. The reform embodies the following guiding principles:

- *Client and farmer empowerment.* Through knowledge, control of funds, influence on organizations, and institutional change, farmers acquire the capacity to analyze their constraints and identify opportunities, articulate their needs, exchange knowledge, access the services they need, become active partners, improve their bargaining power, and have final jurisdiction over the disposition of funds provided to ensure that they receive the services they need and demand. Farmers' organizations and CBOs and networks are promoted and strengthened to become key development partners.

- *Demand-driven and market-led technology development and adaptation.* Farmers select, test, compare, and adapt appropriate technological, service, and market options.

- *Pluralism of providers of services and approaches.* Diverse methodologies, processes, and funding, as well as service providers, are supported. Public funding for the system remains important, but services can be provided by public extension workers, NGOs, and private advisers.

- *Subsidiarity.* A constructive division of labor between the national, district, and local levels is maintained. At the national level, the extension service feeds knowledge into the system through provision of training, identification of new approaches and technologies, and preparation of materials. Service standards are also defined and enforced at the national level. At the local level, organizations contract the most suitable service providers, both public and private.

- *Focus on economics and natural resource management, HIV/AIDS and malaria, and technical solutions.* Agricultural service providers assist in issues related to economic decision making and management of soil, forests, and water.

- *Transparency and accountability.* Accountability is built in through performance contracts, performance monitoring, and the ability of farmers to choose their providers. Farmers' feedback on services is integrated into the periodic evaluation of service providers.

The reforms in the system operate at the village and ward levels, the district level, the zonal level (through the zonal agricultural research stations), and the national level (through the line ministries). Financing is made available at each level, as, for example, through the competitive Zonal Agricultural Research and Development Funds.

At the village level, farmers are encouraged to organize into voluntary groups and are empowered to articulate demand for—and control over—agricultural services. The interventions build on successful grassroots, bottom-up initiatives and operations, such as MVIWATA groups, farmer field school groups, and the like. Farmer groups will continue to access public services, while also contracting more private service providers.

At the ward level, a Ward Farmer Forum will be established to aggregate, prioritize, and present demands for services. The ward extension team will typically comprise one to three government extension staff members based at the ward or village level, as appropriate, depending on the degree of coverage of private and NGO services. The extension staff will be trained to facilitate agricultural development, both providing services directly according to their expertise and assisting groups in accessing other services as needed.

At the district level, each district council and administration develops a District Agricultural Development Plan (DADP), to be funded in part through a conditional grant called the District Agricultural Development Grant (DADG). The grant will pay for locally financed services, for investment in local infrastructure of high priority (such as roads and bridges to improve marketing), and for cost sharing for adoption of new technologies. The staffing of the District Agricultural Sector Office will be revised to reflect the new functions. The role of the DADGs is very promising because it brings together the administrative and fiscal architecture of the local government reform and institutional reforms in agricultural services.

At the national level, the agricultural sector line ministries are responsible for policy, regulatory, and planning functions. In the institutional restructuring to support agricultural services and investment at the district level under the ASDP, the fragmentation of the line ministries at the national level is difficult to justify (because core elements of their previous responsibilities have shifted to the district levels) and is costly.

Irrigation to Raise Productivity and Incomes

Tanzania is well endowed with water, both on the surface and below it, but the country suffers, nevertheless, from water shortages because of insufficient capacity to store and access water. Cumulatively, the lakes, wetlands, and aquifers provide huge natural storage capacity. The country also has 2.7 million hectares of wetlands (in Usangu and Malagarasi). Total renewable water resources are estimated at about 80 cubic kilometers per year, of which 30 cubic kilometers per year is groundwater (FAO 2004). Several hydrological studies indicate locations where water tables are shallow and water yield is potentially quite significant (JICA 2002). Some of the areas with high groundwater potential include the following:

- Makutupora in the Dodoma region and Ruvu basin in the Coast region
- Sanya-Hale plain in the Pangani basin
- Arusha and the Karoo sandstone in the Tanga region
- Fault zones around Kilimanjaro
- Parts of Morogoro, Iringa, Mbeya, Mtwara, and Lindi.

The National Irrigation Master Plan confirms that abundant groundwater is available in several regions—for example, in the volcanic areas of northern and southern Tanzania as well as in the sedimentary coastal basins (JICA 2002).

Tanzania's ample water is matched by ample land suitable for irrigation. Of the 44 million hectares suitable for agricultural production, only 10 million are under cultivation and only 200,000 are irrigated. This fraction represents a mere 2 percent of the cultivated area in the country. It is estimated that up to 2 million hectares could be irrigated. Approximately three-fourths of the area currently irrigated is farmed by smallholders in about 600 small-scale irrigation schemes, usually using diversions and furrows in one of the nine major river basins. Very little irrigation is drawn from groundwater; this lack of activity is a promising area for future development, with direct and affordable benefits to the poor. Rice is by far the most important crop irrigated in Tanzania, but sugarcane is also irrigated.

Irrigation is constrained by the affordability of the investments required and by the profitability of their use. Even the relatively modest implements needed for localized access to groundwater are more expensive in Tanzania than in, for example, India—by a factor of about three (FAO 1997). Researchers from the United Kingdom's Cranfield University found, "In Africa, the cost of a borehole drilled by a truck-mounted rig can be extremely high, costing as much as 10 to 20 times the cost of the drilling and pump in Asia. High unit costs mean that too few wells are drilled and communities and farmers remain dependent on international aid programs for this form of infrastructure development" (Carter 1999). And to compound the adverse impact of high initial costs, producers face difficulties in accessing high-yielding varieties and moving products to market. Irrigation and agricultural productivity are clearly intimately linked, and neither can advance substantially independently from the other.

A suitably designed groundwater irrigation system could reduce reliance on large bodies of water, including rivers and lakes, and could promote more sustainable use of locally sourced and managed irrigation systems. Surface water available varies with rainfall, so open wells and borehole tubewells can be constructed to spread the availability of water throughout the growing season. Compared with large surface irrigation schemes—the design of which is driven by topography and hydraulics—groundwater development is often much more amenable to poverty targeting and is generally less capital intensive.

Groundwater irrigation can complement irrigation using surface water. Integrating groundwater extraction with rainwater harvesting and watershed management, along with efficient water distribution systems, leads to reliable, cost-effective irrigation systems.

Groundwater can be extracted and distributed in three ways:

- *Open wells.* Over a broad part of the country groundwater development has concentrated mainly on shallow open wells for domestic purposes. The Ministry of Agriculture estimated in 1996/97 that the cost of digging a well is about US$3,000.

- *Borehole tubewells.* Shallow tubewells can be drilled by hand with simple tools similar to soil augers, by power rotary drilling, or by a drilling method. Drilling a borehole, along with installing pumps and pipes, costs up to US$8,000 in Tanzania.

- *Rainwater harvesting*. Rainwater harvesting, which has received greater
  in recent years, refers to the small-scale concentration, collection, storag
  of rainwater runoff for both domestic and agricultural use. Rainwater r
  be stored behind bunds or in tanks. In areas with vast terrain and gentle slope, it is
  possible to construct small and medium tanks to collect and store water during
  heavy rains for supplemental irrigation during the rainy season and full irrigation
  during the dry season. These tanks can also help recharge aquifers, which feed into
  open wells or tubewells. The average cost of a tank to store about 30,000 cubic me-
  ters of water is about US$4,000; that tank will irrigate about 2.5 hectares of paddy
  or 5.0 hectares of fruits and vegetables.

These costs are very high. In South Asia, rapid groundwater development has supported a booming pump industry, which is characterized by both economies of scale
and intense competition. As a result, South Asia's rural poor have benefited from low
costs for drilling and pumps. In Tanzania, however, pump irrigation development is
limited and the costs of drilling and pumping equipment are beyond the reach of smallholders. In Nigeria, by contrast, technical innovations reduced the cost of constructing shallow tubewells by about two-thirds between 1983 and 1990, with a commen-
surate increase in activity.

Tubewells and open wells are easy to manage and can irrigate up to 5 hectares. The
maintenance of the pump or well is local, and farmers have a direct stake in its upkeep
and usage. Individuals or groups of farmers can invest on their own initiative. Efficient
distribution methods such as hand or treadle pumps and drip irrigation can lift and
distribute water. Because pumping water, whether it is done manually or with electricity, involves direct costs to farmers, the expense encourages efficient use.

To promote the expansion of smallholder irrigation, poor farmers must have access
to cost-effective irrigation technologies that provide a rapid return on investment.
They must also have a reliable supply of improved crop varieties and other inputs, as
well as land tenure rights and markets to absorb increased production. Public and
private investments in the assessment of the supply and quality of groundwater, in the
regulation of groundwater extraction, and in technical support to farmers are needed
to enable groundwater irrigation—and thereby help reduce poverty. These efforts may
require institutional interventions to provide technical know-how, support agriculture research and extension, improve land tenure, and develop markets and infrastructure (table 5.6).

If smallholder groundwater irrigation is to be sustainable, watersheds must be well
managed to ensure adequate recharge. Groundwater recharge may also involve large
areas and several communities.

Access to land and security of tenure remain important constraints on the expansion of irrigation. The efforts noted above to implement land laws, enhance tenure, and
reduce conflicts over land all support the expansion of irrigated area. Expanding the
area irrigated before clarifying the tenure issues that now spawn conflict will increase
the level of conflict along with the value of the underlying asset.

In view of the importance attached to irrigation, the MAC formulated and
adopted the National Irrigation Development Plan in 1994, with support from

TABLE 5.6 Institutional Framework for Sustainable Development of Smallholder Irrigation Systems

Required conditions	Targets
Technical self-reliance	Capacity of Irrigation Department staff, local government authorities staff, and extension workers
	Farmers knowledgeable about water management and operations and maintenance
	Appropriate choice of technology
	Attention to environmental issues
Financial self-reliance	Rationalization of tax regime for small farmers
	Better access to financial services, especially savings
	Private firms active in supplying equipment and implements
Institutional and organizational support	Clarity on roles and responsibilities of public servants at district and national levels
	Strengthening and reform of Irrigation Section, zonal irrigation units, and local government authorities
	Legal attention to land tenure, water rights, and ownership of and responsibility for irrigation infrastructure
	Improved access to advisory services
	Capacity to collect water fees and pay operations and maintenance cost
	Investment climate to support growing constellation of small firms manufacturing equipment and providing services

Source: ASDP Working Group 2 2004.

several development partners. The plan recognizes the deficiencies of past interventions and assigns highest priority to rehabilitation of and low-cost improvements to existing schemes and traditional water harvesting systems. The plan stresses (a) according the highest priority to the rehabilitation or upgrading of existing irrigation schemes; (b) upgrading traditional water harvesting technology where more intensive irrigation is not possible; and (c) investing in new smallholder schemes in those regions where conditions are appropriate and traditional schemes do not exist.

The institutional support for smallholder irrigation development in Tanzania involves key ministries, district authorities, agencies, and CBOs. MAC support for smallholder irrigation is provided through zonal irrigation units of the Irrigation Department, and through a limited number of irrigation technicians and agricultural extension staff members in the districts. The units have limited planning, designing, and supervision capacity. The Irrigation Department is expected to provide coordination and policy guidance through its headquarters, as well as specialized technical services on site selection, survey and design of irrigation infrastructure, and supervision of scheme construction. The MWLD is responsible for collecting and analyzing hydrological data for the development of water resources and for the issuance of water rights. However, its capacity to fulfill these functions at the district level is extremely limited. Private sector involvement is expected to increase gradually and to concentrate on infrastructure construction by contractors and artisans and capacity building of water user associations (WUAs) by specialized training institutions and NGOs.

The new water policy, formulated in 2002, is among the most advanced on the continent, linking the various subsectors that use water (such as domestic supply, irrigation, hydropower, and environment) with water resources management. A new water sector development strategy, along with legislation and an institutional framework, is being finalized.

Policy reforms in several key areas are needed to underpin the expansion of irrigation. Administrative regulations and restrictions on marketing and trading irrigation equipment should be simplified or removed. Procedures for importing irrigation equipment—drilling machines, pumps, and so forth—should be simplified (by reducing the import duty, providing an import subsidy, and so on). Instruments such as microfinance lending, matching grants, and joint ventures should include among allowable projects the smallholder groundwater irrigation projects. To support the pursuit of additional financing, the development partners and the government could join forces with NGOs such as International Development Enterprises to enhance the supply of low-cost irrigation equipment (for example, treadle pumps and drip irrigation). Finally, actions that affect the profitability of irrigated agriculture, such as the ongoing adjustment in the real exchange rate, continued liberalization of trade, and reforms of crop boards, will also accelerate the expansion of the area irrigated.

Irrigation presents a good array of opportunities for partnerships between the public and private sectors. Open well or tubewell investments are a private good that should be the responsibility of the beneficiaries of the investment. The public sector role should generally be limited to establishing a conducive policy and an institutional environment for investment. Direct subsidies for tubewell drilling and operation are best avoided unless there is a compelling poverty reduction argument for the subsidies. One-off matching grants may be useful in situations of great poverty and poorly functioning financial markets. Sharing investment costs between the private and public sectors through public-private partnerships would reduce the often heavy burden on the public budget. Models for private investment include direct investment in production (including investments by smallholder farmers), provision of irrigation services (including operation and maintenance of infrastructure), leasing of irrigation technologies, and infrastructure development.

Water management can best be structured when governments are responsible for the main infrastructure and farmers are responsible for management and oversight through local bodies, such as WUAs and distribution boards. In areas where groundwater irrigation predominates, WUAs are valuable for organizing hardware and infrastructure maintenance. WUAs could hold community water rights and oversee water use among their members. Aquifer management organizations under the umbrella of the river basin committee or authority can complement effective local organizations for managing groundwater.

Many WUAs in Tanzania are comparatively new and still weak. Such associations require significant investments in capacity strengthening and in defining roles and responsibilities. Transfer of irrigation management responsibility from the government to WUAs can be done effectively only when accompanied by sufficient support for capacity building.

WUAs provide the mechanism for registering the demands and rights of all users in a particular catchment. Under the new water policy, they are legally constituted bodies, drawing their membership from the water users in a particular locality. They link with individual users and with irrigation organizations that represent their members. The role of catchment water user organizations is to manage the allocation of water resources at the local level and the equitable allocation of these resources during droughts. They also assist in resolving local disputes. In areas where WUAs have been formed, they have been extremely useful in finding solutions to water management issues.

Agricultural Marketing and Producer Prices

Agricultural marketing and intermediary costs have decreased over time as policy reforms during the 1990s reduced price interventions and eliminated monopoly purchases by government bodies, allowing greater scope for private sector trade and investment.

Traditional Export Crops

Despite the increase in market entry and the investment associated with reforms, real producer prices for traditional export crops did not increase significantly from the prereform and early reform period (1987–94) to the period of most rapid reform (1995–2002). The recent crop board study, which identified the various factors influencing producer prices, nonetheless documented a reform-induced increase in the producer's share of the world price, ranging from 21 percent to 26 percent for the four largest traditional export crops (coffee, cotton, tobacco, and tea). The reason producer price levels did not increase is that this gain was offset by a 26 percent appreciation in the real exchange rate and reinforced in some cases (tea and cotton) by smaller reductions in the real world price. Sectoral policies thus had a significant positive effect on producer incentives, offsetting the negative effect of real exchange rate movements. The reforms changed the institutional environment in the marketing of traditional export crops, leading to an influx of private traders, increased direct payment of cash to producers, and in some cases (cotton and coffee) a significant increase in private investment at the processor level. The chief negative effect was a disruption of input supply and financing.

Overall, the reforms helped producers cope with a challenging external environment. A World Bank–supported survey in December 2004 analyzed the cost elements in marketing four traditional export crops: coffee, cotton, tea, and cashews. Figure 5.4 shows that despite the improvement in the producer's share of the border price, which implies a narrowing of margins, marketing margins remain significant relative to final prices, accounting for 30 to 50 percent of the border value. The results point toward a variety of costs that might be reduced even further through improved public investment, policies, and public-private sector collaboration. Although the motivating hypothesis of the survey was that high transport costs drive a significant wedge between producers and the border, the survey found great variability across crops and locations. Because cost structures vary, so do the specific remedies for high or unstable marketing margins, and so will the role of public and private bodies in relieving constraints. A variety of crops were analyzed, with farm-to-border marketing chains assessed for

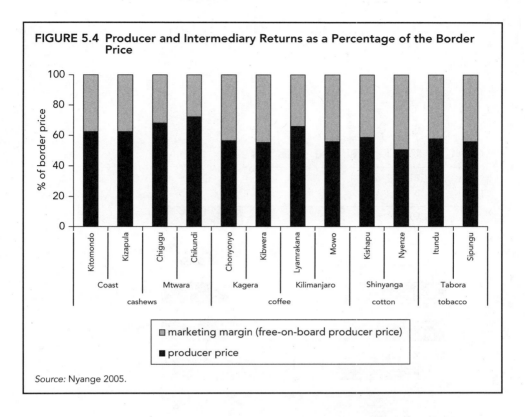

FIGURE 5.4 **Producer and Intermediary Returns as a Percentage of the Border Price**

Source: Nyange 2005.

cashews (in Mtwara and Coast), coffee (in Kagera and Kilimanjaro), cotton (in Shinyanga), and tobacco (in Tabora).

Reducing the large margins between the farm and the border will have a large positive effect at the farm level when markets are reasonably competitive, passing the savings through to farmers. Similarly, an increase in the border price has a potentially large positive effect on producers, because a given change in the border price represents a much larger percentage change in the farm price.

The components of marketing margins vary across crops and locations (figure 5.5). Large items can include taxes and fees, the trader's margin (trading revenue minus out-of-pocket costs), the processor's margin, transport, finance, or packaging materials. Is there scope for reduction in these items? In some cases, perhaps not: for example, packaging material costs may simply reflect the full import cost of the required materials. But for other items, it may be possible to reduce costs through public sector investments (in transport or in power and water, which are particularly important for processing) or policy (tax and regulatory). Clearly, the public sector role in improving prices for farmers through cost-reducing measures, as well as the scope for such reductions, depends on local conditions and the specific crop under discussion. In many cases, the specific remedy requires knowledge of the local cost constraint and of trade-offs between the removal of the constraint and other objectives (such as tax revenue needs). Thus, district-level growth strategies play an important role in identifying market-level constraints on growth and possible solutions. In some cases, local

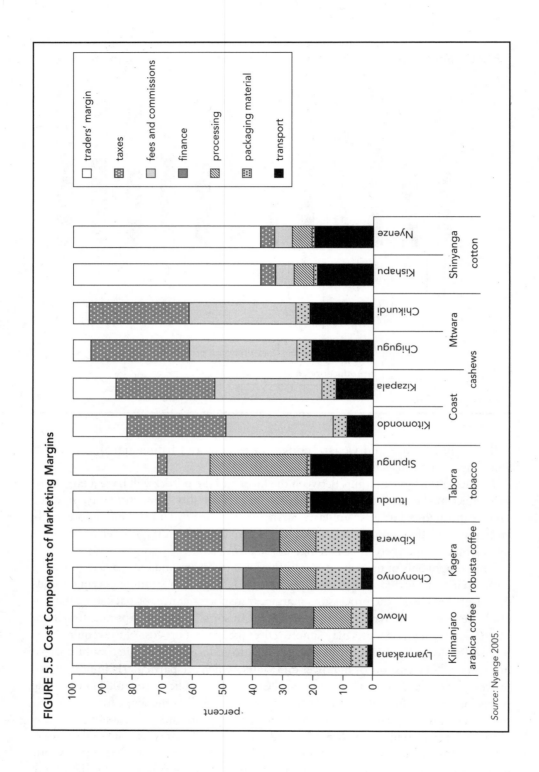

FIGURE 5.5 Cost Components of Marketing Margins

Source: Nyange 2005.

bodies can address the problems on their own. But in many others, they need to collaborate with outside service providers and work with national or regional bodies.

The importance of large trading margins in some marketing chains requires special comment. Large margins, especially important for cotton and tobacco, do not represent traders' profits. They represent the traders' revenue net of out-of-pocket costs, but they do not subtract the costs of risk; the costs of time spent on coordinating, searching for, and collecting market information; and, more generally, transaction costs. Those other costs, which are likely to be significant, must be accounted for in order to assess the profits and rates of return to traders.

Public decisions or actions may be necessary to reduce transaction costs. Such a reduction could occur through some combination of better market information, improved transport and communications, and better enforcement of contracts. Rural law and order is a factor as well.[13] Here too, knowledge of the local business environment and the constraints on rural trade and investment are required. District growth strategies rooted in local consultations with farmers, processors, and traders are an important instrument for identifying constraints and strategies to remove them.

Transport costs were hypothesized in this study to be the most important cost element, but it is clear that although they are significant in some cases and require attention (as for tobacco, cashews, and cotton), they are not the primary cost factor. For cashews, transport costs assume more importance in Mtwara than in Coast, but field visits in Lindi and Mtwara indicated that processing improvements that enable the export of value-adding cashew kernels are likely to be important as well. The importance of such innovations is not reflected in the current cashew marketing chain, because most exports are of raw nuts. But improved processing, packaging, and handling and expanded end uses are important avenues for increasing producer returns in the future.

Producer margins (figure 5.6) are also crucially affected by labor costs. Producer margins are sometimes very high, but as with traders there may be nonpecuniary marketing costs that are hard to observe (for example, the search for a buyer). Furthermore, discussion with the survey organizer indicated that because the farmer typically travels a considerable distance to sell at market, transport costs between farm and market are an important unaccounted-for component of the producer's margin. In that sense, the main hypothesis of this study regarding the importance of transport costs is valid, but for farm-to-market transport rather than for transport from district markets to the border.

Sustained 5 percent growth is feasible but will require renewed and increased attention to the reform agenda and to the public sector's role in supporting traditional export crops. Exports are likely to diversify, and the relative importance of the present "big five" may decline, but traditional exports could be important future contributors to growth and smallholder income. The challenge is to raise productivity in the face of increasingly demanding international markets.

What must be done? For coffee, potential exists to meet the increased demand for lower-quality robusta as well as specialty coffees. Getting ahead in international cotton markets requires cotton of consistently good quality, high yields, and high ginning ratios. For cashews, improved farm productivity, product quality, and value addition

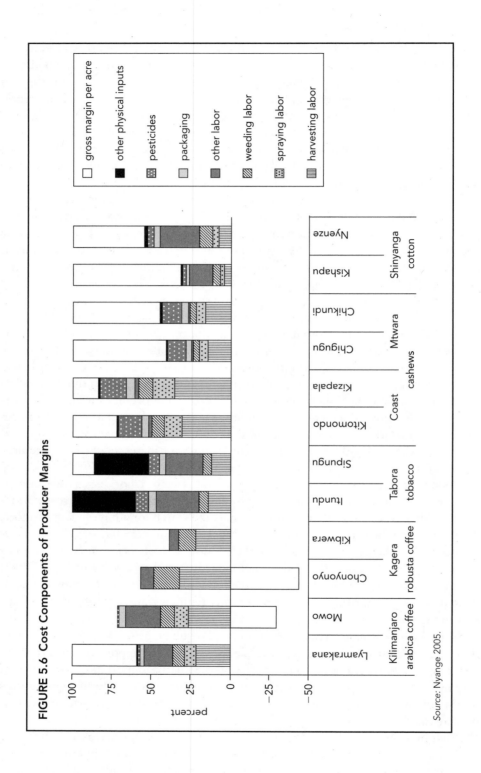

FIGURE 5.6 Cost Components of Producer Margins

Source: Nyange 2005.

at the processor level are central to improving market share. Furthermore, as local processing capacity grows, more cashews will be sold into the competitive and remunerative global market for kernels, rather than the more restricted market for unprocessed nuts, as at present. Improving tea exports requires a continued focus on quality in order to capture the significant price premiums for higher-quality tea.

New acts passed in 2000 and 2001 for coffee and cotton enhanced the regulatory and discretionary powers of crop boards. The new acts responded to concerns that traditional exports had weakened during the final years of the 1990s and reflected a desire to take strong measures to set things back on course. Crop boards were empowered to inspect, monitor, register, regulate, and license varieties, producers, traders, grades, standards, processors, storage facilities, and exporters. The tea industry was not subject to further regulation. New regulatory measures for cashews were introduced under the Cashew Act of 1994, its amendments in 1997, and related regulations of 1996.

The additional regulatory powers were introduced largely to address a perceived need to enhance competition, promote fair trade, improve quality, and augment value. In pursuit of those objectives, crop boards have applied buying rules; introduced a "one-license rule" to maintain the integrity of the coffee auction; announced indicative prices for cashew, tea, and cotton; and required that growers be registered. The Cashew Board applied resources from the development fund to revive processing factories in an effort to improve access to global markets for kernels. The factories subsequently closed because they were not viable in the specific circumstances of the investments.

Vertically integrated firms that were engaged in purchasing, processing, and exporting emerged following liberalization. Firms specializing only in purchasing primary products have limited scope to manage risks and access capital through prefinancing. Yet regulations that require traders to give a two-week notice of any downward changes in price weaken their ability to manage risks. Vertical integration can be understood, therefore, as an institutional response to conditions in the markets. The one-license rule, which was introduced to enhance competition and maintain the integrity of coffee auctions, has served, perversely, to reduce competition. Because coffee buyers cannot export, the number of coffee buyers has declined. More than 50 percent of coffee transactions took place with only one buyer in the market during the 2004 season.

Producer organizations have also emerged and grown since the passage of the acts. They include farmer groups, cooperative societies not affiliated with the cooperative unions, cashew groups, and tea associations. Most important among them are groups of coffee producers, which were initiated by private companies and NGOs to bring together smallholders. These groups empower producers, but they need technical and organizational support, either from public or private advisers or from contractual arrangements with vertically integrated firms. Farmers in groups are better able than individual farmers to access and understand information about prices, technology, and risks and to participate directly in markets.

Information and institutional arrangements that help farmers process information are particularly important, given the widespread suspicion of traders and the history of stable panterritorial prices under the previous marketing regime. Many producers perceive the normal fluctuations of prices inherent in open market economies as attributable to the machinations of traders or others acting to manipulate markets. Information about the movement of prices over space and time is particularly important because producers are still gaining experience with regard to expectations of price behavior. The management of price movements and expectations was among the original functions assigned to the crop boards, and the growth of producer organizations allows other entities to take on this role.

Price setting (in various forms) that seeks to inform producers of prices that they should expect has not helped them understand price movements or make informed decisions. Producers seem to have little access to information on the global price movements that ultimately determine their opportunities. A systematic effort to make market intelligence available to producers and to assist producer groups in marketing would be a constructive step toward integrating Tanzanian producers into global markets.

Restrictive regulations, particularly in the coffee sector, have prevented organizations from evolving to meet the needs of changing conditions in the market. For example, coffee exporters cannot make investments upstream in central pulperies or buy unprocessed cherries from growers to improve quality and cater to niche markets. Such restrictions also have hampered investments that are necessary to improve quality. In addition, the cost of entry into crop buying is high, resulting from regulations and the tendency to use buyers to collect taxes—a cashew buyer must deposit cesses, levies, and taxes on 100 tons before getting a buying permit. This high cost prevents potential buyers who have limited resources from entering the market. Removing restrictive regulations and reducing the costs of entry will encourage more agents to enter markets and new forms of exchanges to emerge, thus enhancing competition. The role that producer organizations can play in countering the monopsony power of traders and the potential to enhance competition by facilitating their development—rather than restricting the scope of activities of traders—are still not adequately recognized.

Quality management remains a key issue that institutions seeking to improve marketing opportunities must address. Although quality is specific to the products and even to individual lots, it also has an element of public good through its link with reputation. When a country's coffee or cashews are known to be of higher-than-average quality, international agents seeking high-quality specialty and niche products are more likely to invest in the country than if their quality is perceived to be low. Investment in quality can thus lead to higher unit values and to improved prospects for growth. Regulations on grading and quality premiums have been introduced under the assumption that the individual actions of firms may damage reputations or that the firms may not act in ways that build or maintain reputations. This assumption is based on the perceived decline in quality following liberalization.

The quality of cotton lint appears to have begun a long decline before liberalization; the decline in premiums for cleanliness began in the 1980s. More recent evidence is not conclusive. The quality of cotton exports to Europe appears to have declined marginally, but that decline may be a response to the demand for cotton for a broader range of purposes. The quality of coffee does not appear to have declined. An examination of the class of mild arabica coffees produced in the north zone and sold at the Moshi auction for four years before and four years after liberalization suggests that coffee quality in terms of class alone remained roughly constant, with estates producing higher-quality coffee than other producers. For more recent years, available information suggests that it is primarily estates that produce coffee falling into the top five classes and that the proportion of their coffee that is of highest quality varies considerably from year to year. Fewer concerns exist about tea and cashew quality. In the case of cashews, the concern is largely about producers not being compensated for quality rather than any decline in quality. And in tea, the quality has improved.

There has been a decline in grading practices. For coffee, the extent of adoption of improved grading practices is mixed. Exporters who established large buying operations indicated that it was difficult to enforce grading because they bought coffee through agents. For cashew nuts, proper grading to assess kernel outturn requires cutting tests, which are rarely done. Traders seem to rely more on regional differences in outturn rates, mixing nuts from different regions to achieve the quality required by importers. For tea, some factories insist that at least 80 percent of tea leaves have two leaves and a bud. The requirement that tea leaves be processed within four hours is apparently rarely followed, but the situation has improved since privatization.

Whether quality problems exist in a sector depends on the unique aspects of the crop, the nature of the commodity market, and the industry structure. For each of the crops, cultivation and processing practices have clear and measurable effects on quality, but relative effects may differ, with implications for when quality differentiation should take place. For coffee and cotton, producers' practices largely determine quality, with secondary processing having marginal effects. Any loss of incentives for producers would have serious consequences for quality, because damage by producers is irreversible. Secondary processing has a greater effect on the quality of tea and cashews (kernels), although the source and quality of green tea leaves are major determinants of tea quality. Reputation for cotton may be associated with the country as a whole, whereas for coffee, it may be associated with an agroclimatic niche; for cashews, with processors; and for tea, with individual factories. Finally, excess processing capacity may be an important factor in making firms bid up the price of poorer grades of products.

The current institutional structure in the cotton sector is such that it is not feasible for one or more firms to offer a premium for quality and thereby enhance the quality of their exports. The growth in processing capacity may have led to a situation in which the processing of large quantities of low-quality cotton is superior to other processing alternatives. There are clear indications that this situation does not exist in other sectors, although one sees multiple strategies in operation in coffee. The presence of farmer groups that can directly capture quality premiums in the market also ensures that quality differentiation does not disappear. The incentive structures and strategies of some firms suggest that the private sector markets Tanzanian coffee, cashews, and tea in ways that enhance reputation.

Regulating grading practices has not been effective, because it is difficult to enforce and may be counterproductive when done without understanding the level of quality differentiation that markets are likely to support. A better strategy would be to pilot market activities that support a greater level of quality differentiation and to reduce constraints on coordination among buyers that may prevent them from dealing effectively with quality issues. Examining ways to create more distinct levels of quality would help further this process.

Access to and use of inputs affect the costs of production and the quality of products. Plant protection is critical for coffee, cotton, and cashews. Application of inorganic nutrients is widely practiced only in tea production, and even there levels of application may not be optimal. Surveys of coffee and cotton producers indicate that only about 13 percent of the growers use inorganic fertilizers. The use of pesticides is somewhat higher but perhaps not high enough, considering the level of incidence of disease in coffee. Among producers of the four crops, only smallholder tea producers have significant access to credit. Cashew producers often can obtain credit for fumigation. Smallholders producing cotton and coffee report little or no access to credit.

Although access to credit is recognized as an important contributor to successful outcomes, the crop boards have appropriately refrained from getting involved directly in the provision of credit. A number of emerging innovations show promise in improving the supply of inputs. Groups of coffee farmers and independent societies are exercising strong voluntary control over members to produce high-quality coffee; to market collectively; and, in turn, to gain access to credit markets. Contract farming in cotton allows the ginner to offer credit and extension services to individuals who can offer collateral. Agents familiar with borrowers are employed to recover credit (say, for cotton) and, hence, serve to inculcate a culture of discipline in repayment. Outgrowers producing tea under contract to processors receive credit as part of the contractual relationship. The coffee vouchers and cotton passbooks are each prepayment schemes under which a portion of the growers' sale is retained for inputs for the following season; however, these schemes are reported to be problematic for a number of reasons.

In an environment in which contract enforcement is difficult, the innovative credit arrangements that have developed involve self-selected groups that are capable of exercising control over their members or personal relationships and the social capital that may exist in communities. In most cases, the private sector has organized producers and developed relationships that are informal but effective to give them access to information and inputs and to gain greater control over supplies and quality. Vertically integrated firms that can better manage risks and gain access to resources at reasonable costs appear to have incentives to enter into contract farming arrangements. They need flexibility to fashion relationships and make exchanges in ways that may not be feasible under many of the current crop acts, as noted earlier.

The crop acts authorize the establishment of industry development and input funds, supported by contributions from producers, to organize supply of inputs and undertake development activities deemed necessary. Cotton and cashew boards have operationalized them. The funds are managed by trustees, who are less accountable to stakeholders than are the boards. The funds are also centralized. Some of the programs (such as passbooks) were introduced recently and are therefore difficult to evaluate, but problems associated with centralized decision making and organization of supplies are apparent. The programs would benefit from greater responsiveness to the needs of producers and from stronger participation by traders and private input suppliers.

Research remains underfunded and not fully able to meet the needs of the sectors, particularly with regard to developing suitable varieties and organizing the supply of planting materials. Industry support to privatized coffee and tea research institutes is not adequate to fulfill their mandates. Planting material is supplied at subsidized prices in all cases. The acts give boards the authority to control the import of varieties in order to safeguard product quality and reduce the chance of disease or pest outbreaks, but the boards and partners in the private sector have not succeeded in identifying successful strategies for ensuring the commercial supply of plant material. Scarce resources that go into extension for these commodities are used mostly for regulatory rather than advisory purposes.

These findings have significant implications for regulations and for the activities of boards. Since these recommendations were put forward, the government of Tanzania has been moving toward greater specifics on the reform timetable. However, to date much of the government's reform emphasis has been on financing issues rather than on clearer delineation of public and private sector functions. More specifics are needed on redefinition of board functions; measures to increase accountability; and reduction in the number, cost, and scope of licensing requirements. These issues need to be clarified and agreed on before amendment of the boards' respective acts.

Nontraditional Agricultural Exports

Past agricultural growth was maintained in part because farmers substituted other production activities for traditional export crops. The export of nontraditional products, including horticultural products, maize, rice, and beans, has played an important role. The contribution of these products to Tanzanian exports is undervalued because a significant portion occurs as informal cross-border trade. Greater attention to the development of these regional exports would heighten appreciation of their income-raising and stabilizing roles, while increasing the benefits that flow to smallholder farmers, who are actively engaged in this trade not only as producers but frequently as traders. Fortunately, a base of donor support in these areas has facilitated expansion of the trade. This support, along with strategic infrastructure planning and research system support from local government, will be essential to future development.

Tanzania's horticultural and floricultural exports consist of a broad-based but small trade with Europe, as well as a growing trade with neighboring countries—especially Kenya—in onions, tomatoes, potatoes, and oranges. A background study (Sergeant 2004) on horticulture for the recent *Tanzania Diagnostic Trade Integration Study* (World Bank 2005f) calculates that in 2004/05 officially recorded exports to Europe totaled US$24.4 million. The exported items included cut roses, flower cuttings, bean seeds, and fresh fruits and vegetables. Unofficial exports to Kenya of oranges, onions, and tomatoes are estimated at US$37 million over the same period.

Horticulture can reduce poverty through existing links with small farmers or potential links through the expansion of outgrower schemes. Seasonal employment in larger production facilities oriented to the European market is also significant. It is estimated that more than 7,000 workers, mainly women, work seasonally in vegetable packing operations, floriculture greenhouses, and bean seed preparation units. The informal trade with Kenya has even more direct links to small, resource-poor farmers, many of whom are actively engaged in trading (box 5.1).

BOX 5.1 Organization of the Marketing Chain for Oranges and Onions

Orange Marketing and Competitiveness

Most of the oranges imported into Kenya originate from Tanga and Morogoro. Tanzania's competitiveness in Kenyan markets is due in part to the absence of greening disease, a problem that affects Kenya's higher-elevation growers. In addition, Kenyan producers face tighter land constraints, and orange production competes with more profitable export crops.

Government provision of new planting material in the Muheza district, in the Tanga region, helped establish significant orange production in the 1970s. More recently, the Development Alternative Inc. Private Enterprise Support Activities project has helped farmers form marketing associations that streamline the marketing chain, with farmer associations now selling straight to Nairobi-based traders. Over time, farm-gate prices have almost doubled as farmers' marketing options have increased, and the bargaining power of local traders has declined. The project continues to document and assess the effect of taxes and fees levied during transport to the border, which appear to be a continuing constraint on the trade.

The Marketing Chain for Onions

Tanzanian exports now account for a significant portion of the Kenyan onion market. Tanzania exports throughout the year, mainly from Mang'ola in the Arusha region. The marketing chain includes rural brokers who, for a fee, introduce wholesale traders to farmers who have onions for sale. The trader buys the crop from the farmer, packs it, and hires transport to the Arusha market, where the produce is unloaded and sold by the wholesaler. Some efficiencies could perhaps be achieved by having the Nairobi trader work directly with the Tanzanian trader who buys from the farmer, rather than through the Arusha market. This approach would save handling costs, market fees, and the wholesaler's margin and would allow a greater portion of the sales price to be returned to the farmer. Reducing the number of times that onions are handled would also improve quality further. During interviews, traders stated that there was a law or rule that all produce destined for Nairobi had to be traded through the Arusha market. This information needs verification.

The Mang'ola onion producers have not yet received support from a donor-funded project, but their competitiveness is based on both their proximity to Nairobi and their higher yields, which are probably due to a lower incidence of fungal diseases in Tanzania's drier production areas. Tanzanian producers also have a quality edge in the Nairobi market: farmers grade the onions, and the better ones are exported. Farmers and traders note that their competitive position could be improved further by improvements in onion seed quality and an increase in the range of seed varieties.

Source: Sergeant 2004.

Future potential for export growth varies by commodity. The regional horticultural trade with Kenya is based on a true comparative advantage; however, it could be threatened if Kenyan orange and onion production shifted to more suitable areas. The challenge for the Tanzanian industry is to strengthen its competitive position. The government and donors have taken specific actions to facilitate orange production and marketing, whereas the onion trade has emerged more spontaneously. But both appear to have been helped by the general regulatory environment and infrastructure planning in northern Tanzania. As the *Tanzania Diagnostic Trade Integration Study* (World Bank 2005f, Vol. 2, 36) noted, "Improved infrastructure and fewer regulations in Tanzania may be one key reason that it is able to export more successfully to Kenya than Kenya is to Tanzania. Unlike Kenya, Tanzania has continued to tarmac roads to its border posts. Tanzanian authorities have made issuance of trade permits administratively easy and cheap . . . whereas in Kenya, procedures for issuing permits and import brokerage are complex and only known traders can clear goods." Box 5.1 indicates that future efficiencies are possible, but they depend on continued efforts—some of which would benefit from government attention, including infrastructure and support for farmer marketing initiatives, as well as reducing constraints on output and input access.

Concerning exports bound for Europe, demand prospects are good, but Tanzania's future competitive position depends on continued reform of the regulatory environment and upgrading of infrastructure, along with continued diversification into production of seeds and cutting materials for export.[14] Interestingly, market participants do not list access to finance as a significant constraint. Specific steps to improve competitiveness include improving customs efficiency (that is, more speedy recovery of value added tax payments for exporters and payment of duty drawback); increasing access to air freight capacity from Kilimanjaro International Airport; improving the supply of skilled middle managers and supervisors; and establishing an open regulatory environment for seeds, equipment, and other inputs. Some agrochemical products used and approved in Kenya cannot be imported because they are not approved in Tanzania, thus putting Tanzania at a disadvantage because it cannot always use the safest, most effective, or cheapest agrochemical inputs.

Horticulture is not the only nontraditional export that requires increased attention. Over the past decade, cross-border trade in staple foods between the countries of eastern and southern Africa, with Tanzania as a crucial balance wheel, has become an increasingly important base of food security for regional consumers and source of income for smallholding producers. The Regional Agricultural Trade Intelligence Network, a donor-funded project that monitors informal cross-border flows, reports that in 2004 Kenya imported 88,000 metric tons of maize and 18,000 metric tons of rice from Tanzania, while importing 75,000 metric tons of maize and 53,000 metric tons of beans from Uganda. The Democratic Republic of Congo is another important destination for Tanzania's exports. The Central Bank of Uganda now considers its own unofficial cross-border exports sufficiently important that it has established a bimonthly monitoring system at dozens of border crossing points. Recent discussions within the newly formed East Africa Community on common grain grading standards also attest to the trade's current importance to the three members.

Critical factors behind the East Africa flows are the trade and marketing reforms of the late 1980s and 1990s and the movement of Kenya into a position of long-term structural deficit in maize and other grains. The entry of the major surplus producer, South Africa, into Kenyan markets is likely if and when Kenya reduces its 35 percent import tariff on maize. Reform of Kenya's National Cereals and Produce Board would also have important repercussions for regional production and storage. This policy instability, along with the market instability associated with poor infrastructure, contracting mechanisms, and information systems, makes for a volatile market. The long-term viability of this market will depend on focused efforts to improve regional infrastructure and information systems, along with efforts to improve the transmission of prices and information back to Tanzania's smallholding maize producers.

A particular problem is the virtual absence of information and analysis on grain storage systems and behavior. Africa's seasonal grain price instability is the highest in the world, and Tanzania's price instability is also considerable, often moving from export to import parity levels within a season. This instability is undoubtedly a factor behind recent efforts to expand the ambit of the strategic grain reserve, but a coherent program for reducing the source of instability is lacking. Doing so depends on establishing a better information base about the entities that store grain, their decision-making framework, the accuracy of the information on which they make decisions, and so on. Assessment of grain marketing performance in a regional context and the development of a coherent policy framework based on this assessment are essential.

Public Expenditures to Support Agricultural Growth

Competent management of public expenditure to support agricultural growth is critical for achieving Tanzania's strategic economic objectives. Most agricultural activity is the business of the private sector. Nonetheless, private agents—from the most modest smallholders to medium- and large-scale commercial producers, to traders and processors—rely on publicly supported goods and services not adequately supplied by the private sector. Decisions on public spending for recurrent costs and investment to support agricultural growth, along with definition of national and local institutions' roles and priority activities, are the most important issues the government must tackle in pursuit of its strategic objectives.

Balance, Efficiency, and Timing of Agriculture-Related Expenditures

Although the management of public expenditure is important for all developing countries, those like Tanzania face a special macroeconomic challenge because of the large flows of assistance from development partners. Large inflows can help in meeting key objectives for reducing poverty, but even with careful management, the flows will have real exchange rate effects that encourage the country to import more and export less. These effects will be more pronounced as more assistance is channeled to nontradable services and activities with high domestic content and low import content. Increased spending on labor-intensive activities in the social sectors tends to have a relatively large effect on the real exchange rate in the short run, but they are also the activities that over the longer run will enhance growth and ensure sustainability. Investments in education (particularly for girls), in primary health care, in control of malaria and HIV/AIDS, and in clean water are clearly important for growth and for poverty reduction. But difficult trade-offs must be faced when the financing for these activities brings changes in the real exchange rate that lower prices for the grain, coffee, cotton, meat, skins, and other products on which the incomes of the rural poor depend.

Management of the trade-offs requires attention to three dimensions of the decision process on public expenditure: balance, efficiency, and timing. Expenditures must be sufficiently balanced so that as the real exchange rate shifts, competitiveness in the tradable sectors increases through reduced costs of transportation, more reliable and efficient provision of power and water, generation and dissemination of improved technologies, and better public services. Economies can improve social indicators and rural growth as long as investments that enhance competitiveness accompany investments in health and education.

Efficiency of expenditure requires that the public sector confine itself to activities that are genuinely public in nature and that it allow and encourage the private sector to expand into the private sector's appropriate domain. Public goods and services are those that will be undersupplied by the private sector even under circumstances in which the private sector is mature, well developed, and operating with a full array of markets. Classically defined public goods and services are those with environmental externalities or poorly defined property rights (air quality and biodiversity) and those for which nonpaying beneficiaries cannot be excluded at reasonable costs (much agricultural research, primary education, basic health care and prevention of disease, and roads). The array of public goods and services that governments must provide to support growth in developing countries is so large and costly—and the resources for providing them are so constrained—that efficiency is a fairly obvious requirement. Yet it is often not achieved in practice. Finally, the timing of expenditures is closely linked to balance. Investments in the social sectors and competitiveness must be timed to complement each other. When they do, a healthier and better-educated labor force has new economic opportunities, and more prosperous rural households are better able to undertake measures on their own to sustain the health and creativity of their members.

Managing public expenditure to achieve balance, efficiency, and timeliness is challenging, and no technical algorithm exists to guide the process. Even if the technical knowledge existed, it is not obvious that it would be applied, because decisions on public expenditure are profoundly political. The budget is allocated in negotiations between ministries, implemented by the civil service, monitored through the public expenditure review process, and evaluated ultimately by voters through relations with their parliamentary representatives. Development partners take an active interest in providing information to underpin the process, in helping clarify options and trade-offs, and in monitoring outcomes.

In the imprecise process of allocating public expenditure, the lessons of the past can be very informative. In the period of the 1980s leading up to the reforms of the 1990s, public expenditures for agriculture were quite substantial, but they failed the test of efficiency, and much of the money was spent on direct production on state farms, marketing through parastatal boards, and input subsidies. Research received support, but scientists or public servants determined the priorities for research without much input from producers. Agriculture's share of the economy at the time was even greater than at present, and other sectors could not balance the slow growth in agriculture. The costly and inefficient public expenditure for agriculture could not be sustained at the observed rates of sectoral growth, and the poor performance of agriculture was a key determinant in the decision to undertake fundamental reforms in the 1990s.

The reforms of the 1990s attracted the support of development partners at a time when priorities in the development community were shifting toward investments in the social sectors. Because of a shift in priorities and because expenditure on agriculture under the previous economic order had yielded disappointing results, the budgetary share of agriculture declined markedly. The drop in spending included areas that should have been cut or eliminated because the private sector could do them better (such as production on state farms and marketing), but it also included investments in agricultural research and extension.

During the 1990s, the agricultural sector adjusted well to the reforms and shift in expenditure. Until 1997, global prices for the key export commodities were quite strong, and Tanzania's liberalization provided producers with greater access to world markets at a propitious time. As reforms in marketing proceeded, producers received a high share of border prices, and the liberalization improved incentives.

At the same time that sectoral reforms assisted producers, movements in the real exchange rate associated with the shift in patterns of public expenditure acted against them. The increase in the real value of the shilling of about 40 percent between 1996 and 2001 compounded a weakening of global prices for Tanzania's chief agricultural exports over the same period. The increased efficiency in the marketing system associated with the liberalization and the rising share of border prices passed back to producers insulated rural households somewhat from what would otherwise have been a severe shock. Sectoral reforms largely offset the adverse impacts of movements in the exchange rate and global prices.

Between 2001 and 2003, the real value of the shilling adjusted back toward the level it held before the appreciation of the mid-1990s. Realignment of the exchange rate improves competitiveness and assists agricultural producers and exporters. The current attention to the performance of the crop boards and proposed changes in the regulatory environment for coffee, cotton, and cashews will, if implemented, replicate some of the benefits of the reforms of the 1990s. But exchange rate pressures can be expected to remain, and regulatory reforms deliver mostly one-time benefits, albeit over a period of time. Continuous public investment to enhance competitiveness will be needed to position the agricultural sector for dynamic adjustment in a growing economy with a strong currency.

Agricultural Policy Framework and Public Expenditure

The government, with the support of development partners, developed the Agricultural Sector Development Strategy (ASDS) and adopted it in 2003 to enhance sectoral growth and competitiveness. The objective of the ASDS is to achieve a sustained agricultural growth rate of 5 percent per year, primarily through transformation from subsistence to commercial agriculture. The private sector is to lead the transformation. The government has committed to improve the enabling environment through policy and institutional reforms and appropriate public expenditure. Development partners have been asked to harmonize their assistance with agricultural growth and to provide it in support of implementation of the ASDS. Core features of the strategy are to strengthen the policy and regulatory framework at the national and local levels, to provide efficient and relevant public services, to support public-private partnerships across all levels of the sector, and to support formulation and implementation of DADPs as the comprehensive tool for agricultural development at the district level.

The ASDP framework and process document is an operational response to the ASDS. The ASDP identifies five key operational components as a focus for implementation at both the national level, including zones, and the district level through DADPs: (a) policy, regulatory, and institutional arrangements; (b) agricultural services (research, advisory and technical services, and training); (c) physical investment; (d) private sector development, market development, and agricultural finance; and (e) crosscutting issues, such as gender rights.

The ASDP framework and process document estimated five-year projections of public expenditures needed for implementation. A 20 percent annual increase in development expenditures was projected over the five-year period, with an emphasis on research, extension, the policy and regulatory environment, and marketing and institutional support. This emphasis is consistent with that of the ASDP on commercializing agriculture and on decentralizing support through districts (through DADPs) (table 5.7). The specific proposals imply that research and extension, marketing and finance,

TABLE 5.7 Proposed Growth in Development Expenditures for ASDP, 2002/03

Area of intervention	Amount of expenditure (T Sh million)	Current share of total cost (%)	Annual increase (%)
Technical area			
Research	6,527	15	20
Extension and advisory services	9,404	22	20
Livestock production	792	2	10
Crop production	5,164	12	10
Irrigation	6,919	16	10
Marketing and finance	7,996	19	30
Policy and regulatory work	1,805	4	40
Food security	488	1	10
Institutional support	3,749	9	30
Training institutions	97	—	10
Total	42,940	100	20

Area of intervention	Amount of expenditure (T Sh million)	Current share of total cost (%)	Target by year 5 of implementation (%)
National vs. district			
National level	19,900	61	25
District level	31,600	39	75
Recurrent vs. development			
Total recurrent	41,300	45	33
Total development	51,500	55	67

Source: United Republic of Tanzania 2002b.
Note: — = not available.

policy and regulatory work, and institutional support become a larger share of the agriculture budget over time. In addition, 75 percent of public resources for the sector are envisaged to be channeled through districts.

According to the projected financing for the ASDP, the budget for 2005/06 should be allocating T Sh 72 billion to ASDP priority areas. That amount is expected to rise to T Sh 104.5 billion by 2007/08. Because the categories in which the budget lines are reported do not correspond directly to those of the ASDP, it is difficult to assess the degree to which the 2005/06 budget shown in table 5.8 accords with the planning underlying the ASDP. The amounts allocated to the MAFS, MCM, and MWLD for households without rural water supply in 2005/06 appear to be approximately T Sh 115 billion. If the agricultural allocation under the President's Office–Regional Administration and Local Government (PORALG) is included, the total increases to T Sh 121 billion. The government appears able to spend fully enough to finance the ASDP, because current expenditures are already more than the amounts required to support the core activities.

Present Expenditure Patterns

The share of spending on agriculture[15] in total government expenditure has fluctuated widely over the past decade, between 1.5 percent in 1995/96 and 5.5 percent in 2000/01 and reaching 3.7 percent in 2005/06. Nine ministries hold votes on categories of expenditure directly relevant to agricultural performance. As shown in table 5.8, the MAFS holds the largest budget, at just over US$93 million.

The spending displayed in table 5.9 raises a number of questions, some of which will be elucidated in a detailed public expenditure review focusing on agriculture. With the government's commitment to the ASDP, the correspondence between the budget categories for agriculture and the program categories within ASDP should be clear and straightforward, so that the degree of consistency is readily apparent. At present, this is not the case. Allocations to forestry and fisheries fall outside the ASDP as defined, although inside the broad category of agriculture as it appears in governmental aggregates. Discrepancies in categories for this reason are readily understandable. But even within agriculture, narrowly defined, the alignment of the budget with

TABLE 5.8 2005/06 Budget Proposals

Line ministry	Votes	T Sh (million)	US$ (million)	Share in total (%)
Ministry of Agriculture and Food Security	43	102,414	93.1	40
Ministry of Water and Livestock Development	49	45,961	41.8	18
Ministry of Works	47	44,010	40.0	17
Ministry of Natural Resources and Tourism	69	38,059	34.6	15
Prime Minister's Office	37	8,335	7.6	3
Ministry of Cooperatives and Marketing	24	5,974	5.4	2
President's Office–Regional Administration and Local Government	56	6,321	5.7	2
Ministry of Energy and Mining	58	89	0.1	0
Ministry of Lands, Housing, and Settlement Development	48	3,284	3.0	1

Source: United Republic of Tanzania 2005a.

TABLE 5.9 Budget Ceilings for Rural Development and Agriculture in Line Ministries, 2005/06

Ministry/indicator	T Sh (million)	US$ (million)	Ministry total (%)
Ministry of Agriculture and Food Security			
Total budget	102,414	93.1	488
Increased crop production through improved technology	14,135	12.9	67
Input subsidies on selected food crops	7	0.0	0
Increased crop production through improved technology	621	0.6	3
Strategic grain reserves	543	0.5	3
Irrigation	9,712	8.8	46
Harmonized agricultural taxes to support export crop efficiency	0.0	0.0	0
Ministry of Water and Livestock Development			
Total budget for rural water and livestock activities	45,961	41.8	100
Rural water supply	38,530	35.0	84
Animal production	2,639	2.4	6
Veterinary services	2,465	2.2	5
Livestock research and training institutes	2,327	2.1	5
Ministry of Cooperatives and Marketing			
Total budget	5,974	5.4	197
Support to cooperatives	2,001	1.8	66
Community credit (savings and credit cooperatives, revolving funds)	545	0.5	18
Marketing development	1,333	1.2	44
Identification of markets, promotion of value-adding products (Policy and Planning, 30%; Marketing Development, 70%)	1,260	1.1	42
Ministry of Natural Resources and Tourism			
Total budget for forestry and fisheries activities	38,059	34.6	100
Forestry and beekeeping activities	20,985	19.1	55
Fisheries activities	15,240	13.9	40
Land management in wildlife reserves	1100	1.0	3
Agricultural research and extension	634	0.6	2
Rural small and medium-size enterprises	100	0.1	0.3
Ministry of Works			
Total for rural roads activities	44,010	40.0	100
Rural roads construction, maintenance, and community roads	21,979	20.0	50
Ministry of Energy and Mining			
Total for rural energy activities	89	0.08	100
Rural energy	89	0.08	100
Ministry of Lands, Housing, and Settlement Development			
Total for land management activities	3,284	3.0	100
District land tribunals—34 functioning by July 2007	746	0.68	23
Prime Minister's Office			
Total for rural food security, finance, and disaster planning	8,335	7.6	100
Rural financial services	3,030	2.75	36
Coordination of Agricultural Marketing Services Development Program	4,638	4.22	56
President's Office–Regional Administration and Local Government			
Total budget	126,412	114.9	100
Budget to strengthen, extend, and monitor resource allocation formula ensuring equity among local authorities	91,901	83.5	73

Source: United Republic of Tanzania 2005a.

the ASDP priorities is difficult to discern. If the government is allocating significant resources to agricultural expenditures that are not part of the ASDP, what does this spending imply about the degree of commitment to the program and the extent to which development partners should support it?

The budgetary lines for the MAFS under crop development include support to research and extension accounting for about 16 percent of expenditure of the MAFS. The allocation represents an increase relative to historic levels and is consistent with the commitment to support for generation and dissemination of technology under the ASDP. But even with this substantial increase in spending on research and extension, Tanzania's investment remains low by international standards. Space must be made for rising allocations to research and extension in the future. This consideration, in turn, suggests that less critical or productive expenditures should include sunset clauses that will allow them to be phased out over time.

Among the items that should be phased out is the allocation to input subsidies. Most of this allocation goes to fertilizer subsidies, and the amount has increased from T Sh 2 billion in 2003/04 to T Sh 7 billion in 2004/05 and T Sh 14 billion in 2005/06. The Medium-Term Expenditure Framework guidelines suggest that, over the medium term, the government will focus on minimizing the costs of production through subsidies on the price of inputs. Thus, the fertilizer subsidies should be seen as part of the expenditure in pursuit of competitiveness; however, the record of experience globally shows that they do not pass the tests for efficiency of expenditure. Moreover, resorting to input subsidies to increase competitiveness is not consistent with the strategic directions underlying the ASDS.

The profitability of fertilizer use varies widely. In some areas, the subsidies can be phased out only at great hardship to the former beneficiaries. Subsidies are difficult to target, and benefits are modest even for the recipients. Often, the least needy farmers capture the benefits. Administrative costs (including rent seeking) often outweigh the benefits. Subsidized fertilizer has often arrived too late to be effective and has often been of the wrong type. In 2003/04, the fertilizer subsidy to farmers was relatively small, ranging from T Sh 950 per bag for fertilizer destined for Makambako depots to T Sh 2000 per bag for consignments going to Songea depots. The reduction in the retail price of fertilizer was only 8 to 10 percent. In addition, fertilizer prices per bag ranged from T Sh 13,000 to T Sh 14,000, depending on the type of fertilizer, an amount that was not significantly different from the 2002/03 prices. Delays in delivery of the subsidized fertilizer caused panic among farmers. As demand grew, rent-seeking behavior emerged, and in some parts of the southern highlands, fertilizer prices reached T Sh 18,000 per bag.

Subsidies are expensive to administer. Reimbursement of transport costs by the government is reported to be time consuming. Transporters were required in 2003/04 to produce four sets of copies of notary-certified cash sale receipts before submitting reimbursement claims to the MAFS. Importers were concerned about the frequent changes in procedures, which caused more than three months of delay in reimbursement. The slow reimbursements led to exchange rate losses for importers (the Tanzanian shilling depreciated from T Sh 1,050 to T Sh 1,120 against the U.S. dollar at import between December 2003 and March 2004, the date of refund).

Subsidies crowd out the private sector. Even when programs are implemented through the private sector, they tend to send the signal that the government's behavior may be unpredictable and, hence, increase the risk associated with a change in policies. Under those circumstances, private input suppliers who could enter the market are reluctant to do so. Intervention affects the expectations of farmers. Programs have continued to perpetuate dependency and result in future demands for assistance. Assuming that intervention will be forthcoming, farmers underinvest in strategies to cope with risk.

Subsidized fertilizer displaces more sustainable and profitable land-use practices. Fallowing and the use of organic matter become less attractive when free or subsidized fertilizer is available. Other technologies, such as minimum tillage and conservation farming or low-input agroforestry, are in some cases superior alternatives.

Fertilizer subsidies played a significant role during the early years of the Green Revolution in India, although they also left a legacy of costly and inefficient public intervention that has been politically difficult to divest. But India's subsidized fertilizer was applied to fields well watered by subsidized irrigation. Africa has lower levels of irrigation and correspondingly higher production risk associated with input use, lower levels of rural literacy, generally weaker research and extension systems, lower population densities, less infrastructure, and fewer well-developed institutions for credit and contract enforcement than India had at the time. Subsidies in India were preceded by public investment in infrastructure (roads and irrigation) and in research and extension.

The steeply rising expenditures on fertilizer subsidies in Tanzania could be more productively spent on irrigation, research, extension, roads, and rural infrastructure. Rather than spending to subsidize one input, the government would be well advised to spend to increase productivity and earnings so that farmers can afford to purchase an appropriate array of inputs, including fertilizer, plant protection agents, seeds and seedlings, tools, draught power, breeding stock, improved feeds, and veterinary medicines. Alternative approaches to increasing productivity and profitability are consistent with the ASDP, and fertilizer subsidies are not.

Spending on irrigation is very small. The MWLD manages a substantial budget and allocates significant amounts to rural water supply—but for human use, not for production. The comprehensive water strategy under preparation may provide some guidance on how much spending on irrigation would be appropriate, but current levels are clearly too low. The disproportion is all the more evident in that underallocation to irrigation falls within the same budget vote as overallocation to fertilizer subsidies—when increased investment in water management would reduce the need for subsidized inputs by raising returns to their application.

The management of the strategic grain reserve will be evaluated under the enhanced public expenditure review that is under way. The costs have risen over recent years, for reasons that are not well understood, at the same time that Tanzania has experienced a reduction in the volatility of food production and regional grain markets have become more active. The costs to hold and rotate a modest stock should be low, and significant savings may be available through different approaches to the strategic grain reserve.

Spending on the livestock sector is small in absolute numbers, relative to the legitimate public agenda for livestock, and relative to the potential contribution of the subsector. Tanzania has the second-largest herd of cattle in Africa, and substantial numbers of sheep and goats. Ready availability of poultry feed and a suitable climate can support the growth of poultry products for local markets and for export. Demand for meat is rising globally, particularly in Asian and Middle Eastern markets accessible to Tanzania. Opportunities in global poultry markets are likely to increase as the intensive production regimes in Asia are forced to adjust to concerns about avian flu.

Legitimate public expenditures that would support growth in the livestock sector include research on breeds and improved feeds; pasture and rangeland management; training of veterinarians, paraveterinarians, and farmers to improve animal health and quality; investment in reliable power and water supply to attract private meat processors and packers; disease control; and assistance in meeting sanitary and phytosanitary standards.

The adequacy of spending on rural roads and energy should be judged against the cost of meeting standards of service over a five-year horizon. For example, the 5 percent growth target for agriculture implies that targets must be set for the density of all-weather roads, so that farmers can reach markets at a lower cost. The adequacy of the present allocation should be judged against the annualized costing to meet the target.

Forestry is well funded, as is appropriate for a country with as rich an endowment as Tanzania has. But the allocation to and effectiveness of the use of public money for forestry should be assessed in conjunction with the targets for establishing the mandated Forest Service and its performance, as well as the increased constructive role of the private sector that is envisaged. In forestry, public and private contributions can combine for effective management, and Tanzania's experience can be enhanced on both counts.

An assessment of the allocation of public spending on agriculture for 2005/06 according to criteria of balance, efficiency, and timeliness thus suggests several conclusions that can be checked further in the pending public expenditure review. Spending on agriculture is increasing, and this trend is a positive indication of the willingness to rebalance the budget in favor of competitiveness. At the same time, the efficiency of expenditure in the current allocation, relative to the goals for growth and competitiveness, appears low. Too little is spent on research, extension, irrigation, livestock services, roads, land administration, and energy. Too much is spent on input subsidies and probably on the strategic grain reserve. Crop development warrants careful evaluation, because this category of spending is quite large and opaque. The consistency of expenditures with the commitments underlying the ASDP is not readily apparent in the budget.

The alignment of expenditures around core and complementary categories to support the ASDP would contribute to efficiency. The core elements would be those currently included under the MAFSC mandate, as well as livestock under the MLD. Activities supported under these mandates currently take place at the national and local levels, and spending at the local level will increasingly be channeled through the PORALG. As local governments increase in capacity and as the DADG becomes operational, the major distinction in managing public support for agricultural development will not be along ministerial lines, but rather according to subsidiarity. That is, the national-level institutions will undertake activities with national implications, and districts and local institutions will take responsibility for the local activities. By 2007/08 three-fourths of expenditures to support the ASDP are expected to flow through district governments.

As participants in the political process become more familiar with the ASDP and the implications for the organization of public support, a reconfiguration of responsibility at the national level may be appropriate and feasible. Such a reconfiguration would imply mergers of the departments and entities that are at present responsible for elements of the ASDP at the national level into one ministry. That ministry would coordinate closely with the ministries responsible for complementary activities (roads, energy, and water), particularly at the planning stage.

Such a reconfiguration of responsibility at the national level and improved coordination with both local and complementary counterparts would facilitate adequate funding of exciting elements of the ASDP agenda, such as the following:

- *Share costs of adopting improved technologies, rather than subsidizing a single input.* Tanzania is already using a public-private cost-sharing mechanism (through a matching grant) for adopting new technology under the Participatory Agricultural Development and Empowerment Project within the ASDP. The selected technology is one that is profitable in the longer run, and the matching grant makes fertilizer, seeds, seedlings, plant protection agents, implements, and any other needed inputs affordable during the period of adoption (in most cases, two years). Inputs are purchased from the private sector, and farmers save increased earnings while receiving the matching grant so that they can continue to purchase inputs on their own. This approach can be scaled up through the DADPs.

- *Continue reform of taxes.* The government has already undertaken a number of commendable reforms to improve the tax regime for agriculture, including setting limits on local taxes for traded agricultural commodities and reducing customs fees and value added tax. Enforcement of those measures should be pursued and their effects monitored, because they can improve profitability if well implemented. The value added tax on port charges and transport costs adds to the cost of fertilizer and could be reevaluated.

- *Reduce cumbersome importation procedures for fertilizer.* Such procedures include double inspection of consignments, preshipment inspection by Cotecna at 1.2 percent of the free-on-board price, and the Tanzania Bureau of Standards (TBS) quality inspection at 0.25 percent of the cost, insurance, and freight price. Any delay by the TBS means port charges accumulate, thereby increasing the cost of fertilizers to farmers. In addition, importers are required to produce certificates of quality from manufacturers. Abolishing inspection requirements and retaining the certificate of quality from manufacturers, together with spot-checks by the TBS, would significantly reduce the cost of fertilizers to farmers.

- *Improve the road network.* As much as 40 percent of the cost of grains in the major urban markets is attributed to transportation costs. Reducing this cost would increase farm profitability.

- *Develop and disseminate more profitable technologies.* This effort includes ensuring that agricultural research and extension focuses on developing more profitable technologies and varieties more responsive to the application of inputs. It also means ensuring that farmers have access to information and recommendations specific to the technologies (rather than blanket prescriptions) and that profitability is part of the calculus in deciding which technologies are recommended.

- *Ensure consistency in the policy environment.* The costs of inputs decline as the volume of transactions increases. The number of private input dealers and distributors is more likely to expand when the policy environment is consistent and the government stays away from direct intervention.

- *Improve the opportunities for viable systems to finance technology and inputs.* Vertically integrated private systems of extension, credit, and inputs linked to output markets (as for tobacco) are functioning in some areas. They can be encouraged by reducing inefficiencies in the banking systems (reducing interest on borrowing), strengthening institutions for contract enforcement, improving taxation (as noted above), and improving the flow of information. For example, small farmers in Msowero and Sonjo villages were assisted under the PASS (Private Agricultural Sector Support) program—supported by DANIDA (the Danish International Development Agency)—in forming groups and accessing loans that were repayable over a three-year period. Initial reports on the program are positive.

- *Reduce risks.* Periodic weather shocks and external price shifts, together with household-level production risk, significantly affect technology adoption, profitability, and incomes. New methods to manage external shocks, such as weather insurance, forward contracts, and options for price risk, are being piloted and should be evaluated carefully to determine the scope for scaling them up.

- *Improve market access and product quality.* Investment in, awareness of, and compliance with sanitary and phytosanitary standards for high-value products and stronger linkage of groups of smallholders with supermarket chains will improve marketability and profitability. The public sector can play a very constructive role here, even though the market transactions are between private parties. For example, through an agreement with TechnoServe, the U.S. Agency for International Development (USAID) has helped coffee growers respond to October 2003 changes in the policy regime, whereby Tanzanian premium coffee producers and specialty roasters can export high-quality coffee directly. This change in the marketing regulations (the contribution of the public sector) creates new opportunities for Tanzanian farmers to supply roasters with specialty coffee for premium prices. TechnoServe's conservative estimate is that farmers' incomes will be boosted by US$20 million over the next 10 years as a result of the combined effect of direct export of premium coffee and a new value added tax reclamation policy.

Concerted pursuit of those steps and others through adequate funding of activities under the ASDP will provide a reasonable likelihood that the growth targets can be met. Five percent annual growth is ambitious but not impossible. Meeting this target, however, requires moving ahead decisively on the agendas of policy reform and alignment of public expenditure. Half-measures and compromises to accommodate special interests require sober reassessment of the growth targets or admission from the outset that they will not be met.

Notes

1. The sectoral aggregate measured in the World Bank Development Data Platform dataset used for this calculation is agricultural value added (gross value of agricultural production minus purchased intermediate inputs). The Tanzanian agricultural value added measure includes fisheries and forestry or hunting, in addition to crop and livestock production. The average rate of increase measured here is the average of year-to-year changes during the period in question.

2. *Primary agriculture*, as defined in the national accounts, includes crops, livestock, forestry, and fisheries.

3. The full effects of farm growth on the economy as a whole are capture in intersectoral growth multiplier models, such as the one implemented by Mahamba and Levin (2005) for this Country Economic Memorandum. Mahamba and Levin's analysis indicates substantial farm growth multipliers that exceed those from nonfarm growth.

4. Tanzania's second poverty reduction strategy (MKUKUTA) sets an even more ambitious target of increasing agricultural growth to 10 percent by 2010.

5. This calculation is based on an adding-up requirement: sector growth must equal the sum of labor force growth and labor productivity growth. The 2.7 percent labor productivity growth requirement is simply the difference between the target sector growth of 5.0 percent per year and the labor force growth of 2.3 percent per year.

6. Uncertainties in data for Malawi came to light during the food crisis of 2001 and 2002 and may be affecting the historic averages.

7. Total factor productivity, the productivity associated with improved use of all factors (land, labor, capital) together but not attributable to any one factor, should increase in either case.

8. A subsequent section deals with successes in the agricultural research system over the past decade. Many of the successes involved generating higher-yielding seed varieties. The key point here is that progress has been made in the recent past but has not been sufficient to induce the desired growth. This point argues for greater support for research, as discussed in the section on public expenditures.

9. From table 5.3, this number is computed by dividing the growth contribution of importables, 1.7 percent, by the agricultural gross value of production rate of 5.3 percent.

10. The SPILL (Strategic Plan for Implementation of Land Legislation) of 2005.

11. The discussion of the historical experience with agricultural services is drawn from the program document for the Agricultural Sector Development Programme, developed by Task Force 3 of the Agricultural Sector Development Programme formulation team.

12. For example, Mogabiri Extension Micro-Project in Tarime district, Eastern Zone Client-Oriented Research and Extension Project in Kilosa and Muheza districts, and the farmer field schools in Morogoro, Bukoba, and Muleba districts.

13. In Mtwara region, for instance, traders must carry cash from Mtwara town to collection areas. Robbery and injury are ever-present threats that impose costs on marketing agents.

14. One of the keys to the success of diversification in the cuttings and seed propagation industry has been the involvement of Dutch partners, who provide plant material on the condition that all the output is sold back to them for retailing. Diversification efforts have been helped by the provision of grants from the Program for Cooperation with Emerging Markets to at least four of the companies. Enza Zaden and Q-SEM Ltd. have been established to produce hybrid seed. These companies have invested on the basis of cheaper labor (compared with Europe) and the climate, which allows all-year production with no heating costs. As with the cuttings industry, a viable cut flower sector gave these investors confidence that sufficient skills and services were available to establish a higher-value floricultural industry. Freight is not an issue, because the output from these companies is only a few kilograms of high-value seed that can be exported by courier.

15. That is, spending on agriculture, forestry, fishing, and hunting services and affairs.

6

Fostering Growth, Export Competitiveness, and Employment in the Manufacturing Sector

Vandana Chandra, Pooja Kacker, and Ying Li

Tanzania's manufacturing sector is still small and contributes only about 8 percent to gross domestic product (GDP). However, in recent years, the sector has experienced fast growth, and exports of manufactured goods have also recovered (figure 6.1). The analysis of panel enterprise surveys covering 1992 to 2000 by Harding, Söderbom, and Teal (2002) suggests that, in general, output, employment, and the capital stock declined during that period. The authors also document large rates of turnover of firms in Tanzanian manufacturing, with new firms having higher productivity levels than older incumbent firms. They conclude that reforms, including introduction of a market-based foreign exchange system, liberalization of trade policy, privatization of state-owned enterprises, and fiscal policy reform, have promoted a more effective production structure through a reallocation of capital and labor into more productive plants. Harding, Söderbom, and Teal (2002) suggest that such a structure should provide the basis for improved growth potential, which seems to have materialized in recent years with growth rates of around 8 percent in the manufacturing sector.

Production is concentrated in three types of firms: (a) agroprocessing and food and beverage production (fish processing, beer, spirits, and cigarettes), which are nontraditional natural resource–based activities; (b) textiles and other light industry such as furniture; and (c) heavy industry–producing metals (aluminum and iron sheets), cement, paints, and plastics. Recent growth has occurred mostly in consumer goods, such as food products and beer, edible oils, textiles and garments, and metals, because they have attracted new investment. Growth in industries such as wood and paper, furniture, and construction has declined. Other signs of progress are described by increased industrial capacity use.

In 2001, manufacturing's contribution to total employment was 245,000, or 1.5 percent of all employees. Manufacturing accounted for about one-third of nonagricultural

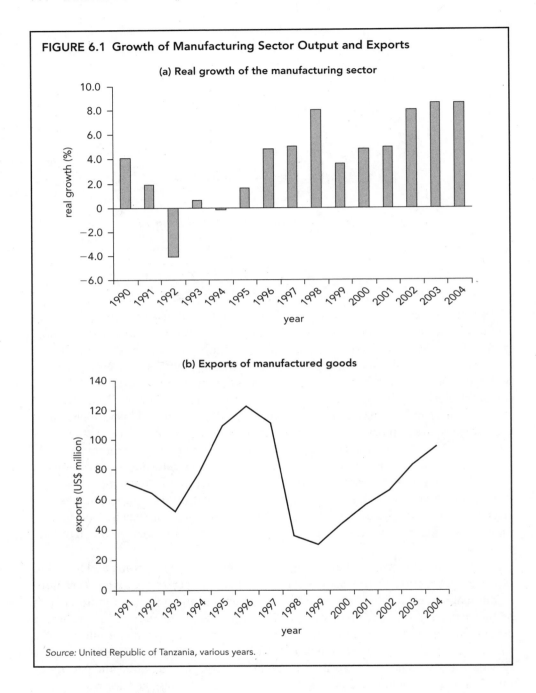

FIGURE 6.1 Growth of Manufacturing Sector Output and Exports

(a) Real growth of the manufacturing sector

(b) Exports of manufactured goods

Source: United Republic of Tanzania, various years.

private employment (industry and services). Although small at present, the sector has the potential to create better-paying jobs relative to those in agriculture. Incomes of workers in agriculture typically fall below the poverty line. Labor demand in 2001 in manufacturing reflected the sector's need for workers with technical skills. Manufacturing employed 34 percent of all workers with craft and related skills, 32 percent of all machine and plant operators, and 11 percent of all clerks. The manufacture of labor-intensive goods such as textiles, garments, furniture, and nonmetallic products occurs in both the formal and the informal sectors. Between 2000 and 2002, large firms contributed the most to employment growth in manufacturing. However, employment growth was not even across sectors. Agroindustry and chemicals experienced job cuts; in contrast, employment in metals and plastics grew significantly. For policy makers interested in sustained poverty reduction, creating good jobs through growth in manufacturing has clear advantages.

Tanzania needs a vibrant manufacturing sector today for several reasons. Historically, worldwide manufacturing has been the foundation for a modern economy. A growing manufacturing sector triggers the development of ancillary activities and better-paying jobs. A large manufacturing sector can enable export diversification that is necessary to reduce Tanzania's vulnerability to external shocks. It can smooth incomes at the household level through the creation of nonfarm jobs that are more stable and provide higher incomes. On average, the monthly income in 2001 from a manufacturing job was T Sh 103,407, compared to T Sh 76,277 in mining, T Sh 49,693 in construction, T Sh 31,301 in trade, and only T Sh 15,234 in agriculture, which is at present the largest source of livelihood for Tanzanians.

This chapter analyzes the results of a recent enterprise survey to identify the determinants of enterprise growth, investment, exports, and employment. The objective is to identify what more needs to be done to unleash Tanzania's manufacturing potential in order to achieve its vision of a modern economy.

Determinants of Manufacturing Sector Growth

The 2003 survey of Tanzanian firms (World Bank 2004c) covers the period from 2000 to 2002 and consists of a sample of 276 manufacturing firms in eight sectors— including food and agroindustry; chemicals and paints; construction materials; metals; furniture and wood products; paper, printing, and publishing; plastics; and textiles, garments, and leather products. The sample can also be disaggregated by firm size as measured by the number of employees: 6.1 percent of the firms are micro (1 to 5 employees); 41.3 percent are small (6 to 29 employees); 27.5 percent are medium (30 to 99 employees); and 25.3 percent are large (100 plus employees).

Of the surveyed firms, 72 percent are located either in the capital (39 percent) or in other urban areas (33 percent). Most of the firms in the larger urban centers are engaged in heavy manufacturing, such as the manufacture of plastics, construction materials, chemicals and paints, and metals. More labor-intensive industries are located mostly in smaller towns with populations of 1 million or less. About 72 percent of the food and agroindustries, 66 percent of the furniture and wood products industries, and 65 percent of the textiles and garments industries are located outside the larger cities.

The average age of a manufacturing firm is about 13 years. Except for 2 percent that are publicly held and 1 percent that are government owned, the remaining firms are privately owned. Only 16 percent of all firms were previously state owned. Of those, 75 percent, or 33 firms, were privatized as follows: 12 in 1996 when the government accelerated the privatization process, 13 in 1997–98, and 8 in 1999. Moreover, 20 percent of Tanzania's manufacturing firms have some degree of foreign ownership; the average share of foreign equity is 72 percent. About 5 percent of all firms are 100 percent foreign owned. The majority of the firms' shareholders are Tanzanian nationals (60 percent). The share of non-African nationals is 14 percent; the share of Kenyans, Ugandans, and other African nationals is between 2 and 3 percent each. The ethnicity of the principal owners is predominantly African (44 percent), followed by Asian (26 percent), European (6 percent), and Lebanese (4 percent).

Start-up capital for about 72 percent of the firms came from the owner's personal savings or internal business funds from some other source. Bank loans, equity or sale of stock, and family and friends play a small role in financing start-up capital. Money lenders and informal sources are also less important. These findings are quite similar to those of Harding, Söderbom and Teal (2002).

When the links between private investment and growth were examined at the microlevel using firm survey data for 2000 to 2002, a positive association between private investment and growth in manufacturing surfaced. That association is encouraging and underscores the necessity of policies that can boost private investment for faster growth in the sector. Empirical microeconomic analysis is used to identify the main constraints to investment, growth, and employment in Tanzania's manufacturing sector.

During 2000 to 2005, aggregate growth in GDP was 6 percent per year; in manufacturing, it was about 7 percent. In 2002, growth in manufacturing was 8 percent. Firm survey data for value added in manufacturing are unreliable, but trends in sales growth from 2001 to 2002 are consistent with aggregate growth trends. Firm sales grew at 9 percent in 2001 and at 11 percent in 2002 in nominal terms. The variance in sales growth was large.

Between 2000 and 2002, growth in sales increased in correspondence with firm size as measured by the number of employees. Large firms and exporters outperformed smaller firms with sales growth rates of about 19 percent in 2002. In contrast, sales in micro firms grew at only 2 percent. Growth across manufacturing subsectors was not uniform. The fastest-growing subsectors were metals (21 percent), agroindustry (18 percent), plastics (17 percent), and textiles and garments (16 percent). Furniture sales grew at only 3 percent. Faster growth in metals and machinery was related to higher growth in construction, mining, and quarrying in 2002 to 2003.

Besides macroeconomic stability, what are the main determinants of manufacturing growth in Tanzania? Empirically, for the period from 2000 to 2002, the key factors driving manufacturing growth in Tanzania, measured by growth in sales, included the following characteristics of a firm:

- Age

- Size

- Rate of investment growth

- Share of sales exported

- Use of newer technologies.

In general, a firm's sector or location (large cities or smaller towns) did not affect growth. Similarly, a firm's other characteristics, such as the nationality or ethnicity of its owner, did not affect its performance.

Sales in older firms grew more slowly than those in younger ones. But the greatest boost to sales growth came from larger firms and exporters. About one-third of medium firms and over one-half of the large firms are exporters. Higher export performance was an important source of growth. For every 5 percent increase in the proportion of sales exported, overall sales grew by 1 percent. The strong link between the proportion of sales exported and growth indicates that exports are a critical source of growth for globally competitive firms as they relax the demand constraint that otherwise limits the size of the market for nonexporters. The percentage of the workforce that could use computers served as a proxy for the technical skills of a firm's employees. Sales grew by 0.67 percent for each 1 percent increase in the number of employees using a computer.

Empirical tests confirm a positive relationship between investment and sales growth. For each percentage point increase in investment, sales grew by 0.08 percent. Compared with the past when that link was missing, its emergence between 2000 and 2002 provides cause for optimism. Perhaps the investor response was delayed because even though the transition to a market economy began much earlier, it was only after a long lag that investors gained confidence in the government's commitment to reform and began investing in manufacturing.

Although policy makers can do little about a firm's location, sector, or characteristics of the owners, at least in the short term, policy levers are available and can influence the other determinants of firm growth: size, investment, export, and technical skills accumulation in the workforce to support the adoption of newer technologies such as those that enable the use of computers to raise labor productivity.

A better understanding of investment in Tanzanian firms can be gained from the study of Harding, Söderbom and Teal (2002). The authors find that from 1992 to 2001, investment rates were generally quite low. They explain that the low rates could be due to the lumpy nature of investment, which leads many firms to make large investments once every four years. Microeconomic evidence from the 2003 Regional Program on Enterprise Development firm survey data validates shorter trends: on average, investment in firms grew at 0.2 percent per year from 2001 to 2002, and the variance was large. About one-half of all manufacturing firms invested in 2001 and 2002. Growth in investment increased corresponding with a firm's age and size. Consistent with the theory of firm growth, firms age 10 years or less invested almost 10 times more than the average. Investment growth in smaller firms was nearly zero, compared to 2.1 percent in large firms. Exporters invested substantially more than nonexporters; exporters with positive export growth outperformed all other firms, with investment growth rates of 2.15 percent.

Investment decisions are influenced by a variety of intricately linked factors. Because the firm dataset contains more than 100 of those factors, the latter were listed under five broad categories, with each category containing about 15 to 40 different but strongly correlated variables. The leading constraints to investment are as follows:

1. Access to and price of financial capital

2. Access to superior technology

3. Infrastructure

4. Labor skills and productivity

5. Investment climate.

Econometric testing shows that firm characteristics defined by age, size, sector, location, and nationality of ownership explain some of the investment growth across all firms. Because policy makers can do little directly about those characteristics, we control for them in our analysis and turn to the other policy-responsive determinants of investment.

Constraint 1: Access to and Price of Financial Capital

Empirical analysis indicates that access to financial capital is largely determined by the nationality or ethnicity of the firm's owner and the share of foreign equity in the firm. Easier access to financial capital enabled exporters and larger firms to transcend constraints such as availability of bank financing and higher interest rates that otherwise constrain the majority of domestically owned firms. Typically, firms with access to bank loans for start-up capital could also use bank financing for investment and working capital.

Most of the start-up capital for nearly all firms is sourced from internal savings or retained earnings rather than from bank financing. Among nonexporters, about 77 percent of the equity was held by the domestic private sector, 16 percent by foreign owners, and less than 5 percent by the government. In contrast, exporters obtained almost twice as much equity from foreign firms, which also facilitated access to investment and working capital. They relied less on bank loans despite considerably lower interest rates. From 2001 to 2002, the interest rates available to them were 10 percent, compared to more than 16 percent for nonexporters. In general, use of bank loans was limited. Loan applications had a high transaction cost, and most domestic applicants were rejected. Only 20 percent of the domestic firms had access to bank loans, which they used to finance about 14 percent of their total investment and 10 percent of their working capital during those years. Exporters used bank loans more for working capital. Empirically, a positive nexus existed between bank loans and investment growth at that time, especially among younger firms. However, because most firms did not have access to bank capital, private finance remained the foremost constraint to start-up capital.

There are policy priorities. Enhancing access to credit requires the pursuit of macroeconomic policies and financial sector reforms that support a deepening of the financial sector and reduce the cost of credit by increasing the efficiency of the financial sector. Chapter 10 discusses financial sector issues in more detail.

Constraint 2: Access to Superior Technologies to Improve Productivity

Empirically, the three key technology-related determinants of investment in the manufacturing sector are (a) the proportion of a firm's machinery that is no more than

10 years old (the larger the share, the better the performance and effect on investment growth); (b) the ratio of a firm's capital assets to employment, which reflects the capital intensity of production (the higher the ratio, the more negative the effect on investment growth); and (c) the proportion of firms that invest to acquire newer technologies. The last determinant contributes the most to investment growth and is strongly related to the proportion of employees using a computer, as well as to the level of investment in research and development (R&D) to develop or acquire new technologies. Capacity utilization and the proportion of firm machinery that is no more than 10 years old are strongly correlated factors because older machines require more maintenance and lead to frequent operational disruptions compared with younger machines.

About 48 percent of all firms, including 65 percent of the exporters, invested in the purchase of newer technologies in the period from 2000 to 2002, especially in agroindustry, chemicals, and plastics. About 37 percent of the large firms licensed newer technologies from a foreign-owned company, and 22 percent of all firms invested in R&D to develop new technologies. About 30 percent of exporters, compared to 19 percent of the nonexporters, invested in acquiring new technologies, indicating that export orientation introduces incentives for firms to maintain their globally competitive edge. Average spending on R&D varied from T Sh 300,000 in small firms to T Sh 5.0 million in large firms. Relative to the average of T Sh 3.9 million for all sectors, firms in agroindustry and metals invested T Sh 10.0 million each. On average, only 5 percent of the workforce is computer literate; in larger firms, computer literacy is more frequent—about 8 to15 percent of the employees use computers. Relative to exporting firms, more employees in nonexporting firms use computers. On average, 12 percent of all firms were certified by the International Standards Organization (ISO), with the highest proportion among large firms (37 percent) and exporters (24 percent). Firms manufacturing plastics, textiles, construction materials, and agricultural products had higher levels of ISO certification than did other firms.

There is a policy priority. Given the critical need for access to newer technologies to raise productivity and export competitiveness, policy makers should explore what, if anything, the government can do to promote the adaptation and adoption of superior technologies at the firm level. In that context, the experience of other developing countries such as Chile and those in East and South Asia may be instructive. Lessons from Fundación Chile, a nonprofit institution, and from India's institutes that facilitate technology for exporting grapes may be useful (see Chandra 2006). Chapter 9 provides a more in-depth discussion of the drivers of innovation and technological change.

Constraint 3: Infrastructure

Firms located in industrial estates do not appear to benefit from superior infrastructure, although such benefits were the intent of development of such infrastructure. Measured in terms of a single eight-hour period, power outages amount to at least 18 working days per year. For some firms, the disruptions last 56 working days per year. Around 54 percent of the firms have installed private power generators at costs ranging from T Sh 172,700 to T Sh 812,500 per employee. Private provision of water entails additional costs of construction in channeling water to factories. About

40 percent of industrial water is obtained from private sources. About 34 percent of the firms own a well, 31 percent have invested in their own water infrastructure, and about 12 percent share a water source with the local community. For a country with a rich rural hinterland that supports agroindustry, the shortage of reliable freight transportation by road, rail, and air is also a direct constraint to growth. About 41 percent of the firms lose between 1 and 50 percent of their cargo in transit because of spoilage, breakage, and so forth. At least 10 percent of the firms invest in private roads; 18 percent have invested in freight transportation to cart goods back and forth. About 26 percent of the firms have invested in transportation for employees to compensate for lack of good public transportation to and from the workplace.

Another area with problematic infrastructure is telecommunications. Only 49 percent of the firms have Internet connectivity, but power outage–related spillovers diminish the ability of those firms to access information in a timely manner. Firms pay about T Sh 11,428 per employee per year in telecommunications bills. Although that amount may seem meager, the opportunity cost of regular and easy access to information technology is yet another factor that constrains Tanzanian firms from developing and maintaining better links with global markets in pursuit of faster growth.

Empirical analysis indicates that the main constraints in infrastructure are related to electricity, water, road transportation, and factors such as telecommunications, Internet connectivity, and waste disposal facilities. Overall, infrastructure-related factors explain a significant proportion of investment growth, especially for younger firms, mostly because of the exacerbated effect of water- and transportation-related constraints. Poor public infrastructure has driven many firms to invest in and substitute private infrastructure for public infrastructure, but at a high opportunity cost as measured by forgone investment for expansion. That situation is evident from the negative effect of electricity, water, freight, and cargo transport constraints on private investment. Private provision of these public goods imposes higher fixed costs per unit of installation necessary to operate electric generators, water wells, and transportation, among others. In contrast, the provision of private roads, Internet access, and telephone connections affects firms' decisions to invest positively. It is plausible that public goods such as roads and telephone connections, which require high up-front investment but have low maintenance costs, serve as assets and encourage future private investment; whereas public goods such as generators, water infrastructure, and freight transport, which require high up-front investment but also have high recurrent and replacement costs, crowd out private investments that expand firms.

There are policy recommendations. Improving the supply and regularity of electricity and water and the supply and quality of freight transport would develop and enhance the infrastructure needed for growth. Chapter 10 provides an analysis of the challenges Tanzania faces in expanding access to infrastructure.

Constraint 4: Labor Skills and Productivity

Empirical analysis indicates that the key human capital–related determinants of firms' decisions to invest are associated with a skilled labor force proxied by higher education and training. Compared with less-skilled individuals, skilled workers are better at adapting to the new technologies of production that can raise firm productivity even for simple goods such as T-shirts. The larger the share of the workforce with secondary and vocational education, graduate and postgraduate education, and formal training, the more likely that a firm will invest in a particular year.

Unfortunately, data problems prevent a meaningful analysis of the effect of HIV/AIDS on firms' investment rates. However, other sources of information suggest that the pandemic is inflicting severe costs on firms through decreased labor productivity.

Between 2000 and 2002, about 44 percent of the manufacturing workforce had completed primary education, 25 percent had secondary education, 12 percent had some vocational education, and 7 percent had tertiary education or a diploma. In fast-growing firms such as exporters, the proportion of graduates or postgraduates was twice as high (10 percent) as in firms that sell domestically. Exporters also offer more training: 71 percent of their workforce had received some type of formal training, compared to only 47 percent of that of nonexporters. The high cost of firm-level training discourages large-scale training, especially of workers who have only primary education. The larger the share of employees with graduate, technical, or tertiary education is, the more willing firms are to invest in their training, which probably explains why firms in Tanzania and other Sub-Saharan African countries invest less in training than firms in East Asia.

If the creation of human capital is not accelerated, Tanzania's manufacturing sector is at risk of either not attracting investors or attracting investors shopping only for low-skilled workers. Both possibilities are detrimental to investment growth in manufacturing, likely to generate low-wage employment, and a deterrent to economic diversification through an expansion in manufacturing that can move workers out of poverty. The last requires firms to graduate into higher value added production that needs skilled workers. More important, Tanzania's advantage of low labor costs is not permanent. With increasing integration into global markets, its low-skilled, low-cost workers will have to compete with high-skilled, low-cost workers from other competitors, especially those in Asia. Early signs of that competition are apparent from the stagnant investment rates in manufacturing, especially in the garments subsector, and highlight further the sector's unsustainable growth.

There are policy recommendations. Although expansion of primary and secondary education is necessary, it is not sufficient to attract investment in manufacturing. Public investment in tertiary and technical education is critical for Tanzania to create the large pool of skilled labor needed to encourage firms to invest, to diversify production, and to increase export competitiveness. Public investment is also necessary to facilitate the use of superior technologies, promote technological learning among workers and firms, and enhance productivity at the labor and firm levels. Although the effect of HIV/AIDS does not emerge in our empirical analysis, we would be unrealistic to ignore timely public interventions that can increase prevention and treatment of HIV/AIDS among workers and their families. The opportunity cost of not doing enough is high for both the government and the firms.

Constraint 5: Investment Climate

Although Tanzania's manufacturing sector faces a plethora of problems in areas such as access to financial capital and to superior technologies, infrastructure, and human capital, the investment climate–related constraints are less problematic.

Whereas delays for most processes for starting or renewing business permits seem reasonable, bribes and excessive delays for many exporters and larger firms are problem areas. For example, instead of a normal period of 20 days for customs clearances, the delays lasted 97 to 150 days for many exporters and larger firms. Exporters wait much longer than nonexporters for inspection certificates, utility connections, and construction permits. The bribes paid ranged from T Sh 35,000 for a water connection, to T Sh 50,000 for a telephone line, to T Sh 150,000 for an import license. Delays for registration or re-registration for business permits for larger firms last as long as 180 days. The bribes paid for such permits are correspondingly high, ranging from T Sh 50,000 to T Sh 180,000, with the outliers in the range of T Sh 500,000 to T Sh 2.4 million. Eighty-four percent of all firms hire a company or an agent to assist with registration.

Ongoing reforms are already redressing the following areas:

- Transaction costs of numerous licenses and permits are being reduced as government officials are trained to operate a one-stop shop for all investors.

- Legislative reforms to protect private property rights and an efficient judicial system are necessary for attracting larger investors.

- Longer-term leases (100 years) are an option for attracting fixed investment in land and buildings, as well as commercial courts that can speedily resolve disputes.

Enhancing the Export Performance of the Manufacturing Sector

Tanzania's exports of manufactured goods have recovered since 1999. The share of nongold exports in total exports is 52 percent. The share of manufactured exports in nongold exports increased to 17 percent in 2004 (US$120 million) from 6 percent in 1999. Although a favorable trend in the real exchange rate between 2001 and 2004 supported the growth in manufactured exports, an equally if not more critical factor was the wide-ranging reforms to generate efficiency. These reforms led to accelerated production and boosted the competitiveness of Tanzanian exports.

If exporters are defined as firms that export at least 10 percent of their production, only 19 percent of Tanzanian firms are exporters. They are the key drivers of the manufacturing sector, which grows at 0.2 percent for every 1.0 percent of additional production exported. Only 11 percent of small firms are exporters, compared to 55 percent of large firms. In 2001 and 2002, the growth of exporting firms was about 24 percent per year, compared to 8 to 11 percent per year for nonexporters. A large variation exists in the proportion of the output that firms export. Approximately

25 percent of the exporters channel almost 100 percent of their production to foreign markets, thus underscoring the point that market demand is not the binding constraint for firms that are competitive. In Tanzania's small open economy, with all else remaining the same, exporters can sell, in the short term, all that they can produce. If the domestic constraints to production are relaxed further, manufactured exports can yield some rapid short-term gains, as evidenced by the double-digit growth experienced in recent years. In the medium to longer term, the ability to export will be determined, as in any other country, by the global competitiveness of manufacturing firms. Their presence today is no guarantee of their future place in the global market.

Existing exporters rely more on foreign sources of financing, especially from parent companies or private capital. For most existing exporters, 61 percent of the equity is private and domestically owned, and 31 percent is foreign owned. For nonexporters, 75 percent of the equity is private and domestically owned, and only 16 percent is foreign owned. Clearly, local firms that are limited to private sources of start-up and investment capital are also potentially constrained from entry into the exporting business. Existing exporters enjoy increased access to bank financing for working capital, commercial loans through overdraft privileges, and lower interest rates.

In contrast to nonexporters, exporting firms employ a workforce with relatively higher education levels—graduate, technical, and vocational—a proxy for skills. The ratio of skilled to unskilled workers in exporting firms is 1.6 times that of nonexporters. Exporters pay a premium for higher skills, averaging 20 percent for managers, 37 percent for professionals, and 19 percent for those with technical skills. They pay about 6 percent less for unskilled workers. On average, they have five times more (10 percent) workers with computer skills than do nonexporters (2 percent). Given the higher share of skilled workers, more exporters (71 percent) invest in formal training than do nonexporters (47 percent). Exporters also have a larger proportion of foreign managers with more experience.

In the absence of publicly provided infrastructure and basic services, at least twice as many exporters as nonexporters, especially smaller firms, are able to privately finance their infrastructure. Exporters and large firms have equal ability to compensate for the poor public infrastructure through the private provision of roads and transport and water wells, although this ability must come at the cost of investment.

Seventy percent of Tanzania's manufactured exports are destined in equal proportions to two main regional markets: (a) Western Europe and (b) the regional African market, which is dominated by Kenya and Uganda. About 66 percent of the exporters each sell nearly 35 percent of their exports to those two regions, suggesting, at the very least, that a sizable share of existing Tanzanian exporters are as globally competitive in Western Europe as they are in the African market, where competition from low-income Asian exporters such as China is rising. Considering that only 19 percent of all firms exported more than 10 percent of their output, one is encouraged to find that exports to markets in industrial countries are not dominated by one or two large firms, as is often the case in many low-income countries.

What are the determinants of manufactured exports? By measuring the share of output exported, an empirical analysis reveals that the key determinants of export growth are as follows.

- Firm size matters. As exporters are mostly large firms, sales growth in large firms also translates into export growth. Compared with smaller firms, large firms in Tanzania's manufacturing sector have several advantages that enable higher rates of productivity, which, in turn, raise efficiency and growth. They have a higher rate of investment made possible by (a) a larger share of own-financing from retained earnings and private capital, (b) greater foreign equity, and (c) easier access to bank loans for start-up and working capital. Their size creates spillovers that more than compensate for the longer delays they face at ports and in obtaining licenses and permits to do business. By exploiting economies of scale, they can pay higher remuneration to attract more skilled workers. Higher rates of computer skills in the skilled workforce enable larger firms to license modern technologies that boost competitiveness and increase their capability to export.

- Relative to firms in the garments and textiles sector, firms in agroindustry contribute significantly to exports.

- Larger firms, especially Kenyan-owned firms, are the main drivers of exports relative to all other nationalities. Ethnicity also matters; relative to European firms, the export performance of African-owned firms is below average.

- Export experience is important. Firms that acquired exporting skills in the past five years are able to export a larger proportion of their output. Similarly, given the complexity of exporting, new entrants in the Tanzanian market with prior foreign experience as exporters perform better.

- High interest rates reduce use of bank loans for investment and start-up capital and negatively affect export expansion.

- The availability of workers with graduate and postgraduate education is important and indirectly supports the development of computer skills. This is natural as more manufacturing processes, especially in heavy industries such as chemicals, paper, metals, and machinery, are capital intensive and need more sophisticated skills, including computer capabilities.

- Exports destined for the Southern African Development Community or the local regional markets in Kenya do not grow as fast as those destined for markets outside Africa, such as Western Europe, Eastern Europe, the United States, and Asian countries. The size and purchasing power of the latter are much larger than low-income African markets, where competition from other regional African exporters selling similar products is high.

- The government offers about 12 export promotion programs. However, less than 25 percent of the exporters use any of them. Among the export promotion programs that are most popular and used by at least 10 percent of the firms are (a) retention of export proceeds in a foreign country, (b) the bonded warehouse scheme, (c) the customs duty drawback, (d) duty certificates, and (e) the profit tax exemption scheme.

Policy Recommendations

Reinforcing the ability to produce and export is key to overall growth in Tanzania's manufacturing sector. For every 5 percentage point increase in the proportion of output exported, manufacturing growth increases by 1 percent. An important aspect of export growth is the strong link between large firms and exporters. Empirically, though most exporters are large firms, it would in practice be incorrect to consider domestic sales growth as a substitute for export growth. Relative to Tanzania's small domestic market, its export markets offer unlimited opportunities for growth. In fact, for rapid and sustained growth of the manufacturing sector, there is no alternative to export growth. We recommend the following policies:

- Two types of discrete export promotion incentives are needed: (a) those that can retain existing firms and facilitate their ability to export more and (b) those that can attract new entrants into the export business, especially exporters equipped with globally competitive technologies needed to penetrate new markets and grow faster. Targeting incentives at large firms, both domestic and foreign, should be most effective in raising export growth. With appropriate design, such a policy should also encourage learning between existing firms and internationally competitive ones to promote export competitiveness.

- Scaling up exports requires more and larger exporters. However, with the exception of foreign firms that have access to cheaper capital from retained earnings or parent companies, domestic manufacturing firms' access to start-up and investment capital is constrained by private savings. For firms that have access, high interest rates limit use of bank capital. Financial policies that increase credit for fixed investments for large firms are required. The government could learn from policies adopted in East and South Asia: using the ability to export as the measuring rod, proactive governments were able to preempt government failure by using credit expansion and lower interest rates as effective policy levers for export expansion.

- Given the weak state of infrastructure countrywide, an option for the government is to target infrastructure provision to export processing zones and the main industrial areas to maximize agglomeration economies and reduce the cost of private infrastructure for exporters. As industrial areas house large firms, such a policy should support the entry of new exporters from larger firms, as well as the scaling up of existing exporters.

- The role of technical and tertiary education in enhancing export competitiveness is critical. Policies with a longer-term vision to substantially scale up technical and tertiary education are the most important levers for improving labor productivity and technological upgrading to achieve global competitiveness and sustained export growth. This recommendation also implies more investments in primary and secondary education to enhance the quality of the throughput to higher education.

- The prevailing policy attention on export competition with neighboring Kenya is myopic when the true competition in the home and neighboring markets is with low-income large Asian exporters such as China. A shift in policy focus is warranted to think outside of the Africa box—away from export markets within Africa and toward non-African markets. Three differentiated export promotion policies tailor-made for the various export sectors are required. First, for heavy industry that relies on local natural resources, public policies to support expansion and raise productivity should be of high priority. Second, agroprocessing of local nontraditional produce (such as fish and fruits) is also natural resource–based but requires meeting complex phytosanitary standards to gain entry into markets in industrial countries. Moving up the value chain requires policies that reduce the high costs of information, marketing, compliance with global standards, facilitation of newer technologies, and technological capacity building. Third, for labor-intensive exports such as garments and furniture, policies that enable firms to link with global supply chains such as those that attract foreign multinational corporations into local assembly and manufacturing are needed. Lesotho and Madagascar are good examples. A proactive policy stance to signal the government's new commitment to promote exports—especially exports to non-African markets—is needed.

- Selectivity is recommended: strengthen the few export promotion incentive programs that firms actually use (bonded warehouse scheme, retention of foreign exchange, duty drawbacks, profits tax exemption scheme, and duty certificates) and rationalize the remainder, but most important, design special programs to support export penetration in non-African markets. Additionally, a concerted monitoring of the one-stop shop to eliminate delays in issuing permits to exporters will help.

Conclusions and Recommendations for a Manufacturing Sector Growth Strategy

A growth strategy based on supporting the manufacturing sector—and within it larger firms, especially exporters—has nontrivial poverty implications for the large proportion of unemployed and relatively less-skilled Tanzanians. In the past, faster rates of growth in the sector contributed to higher growth in the overall economy and to the largest proportion of better-paying jobs relative to jobs in the agricultural and informal sectors, which fetch incomes that typically fall below the poverty line. For example, in 2001, manufacturing generated about one-third of nonagricultural private employment. How can policy makers maximize the sector's growth potential? Empirically, larger firms are the *drivers* of growth and employment within the manufacturing sector. In absolute terms, in a sample of 276 firms, larger firms with more than 30 employees generated 29,000 jobs relative to only 1,700 in smaller firms. Employment in larger firms grew at 8.5 percent a year relative to only 3.0 percent in smaller firms. Unsurprisingly, larger firms systematically paid significantly higher wages. The median wage for professionals in larger firms was T Sh 240,000 relative to T Sh 100,000 in smaller firms. For skilled workers, the median wage was T Sh 90,000 in larger firms, compared to T Sh 60,000 in smaller firms, and for unskilled workers, it was T Sh 60,000 in larger firms relative to T Sh 50,000 in smaller firms. Larger firms also paid significantly higher compensation rates.

Empirical analysis of the determinants of manufacturing firm growth shows that the two leading contributors to firm growth are a technically skilled labor force and growth of large firms, which also represent the majority of the exporters. A 1 percent increase in the technical skills of the workforce increases firm growth by 0.7 percent, and a 5 percent increase in the output exported delivers almost a 1 percent increase in firm growth, which, in turn, raises employment growth. The third important determinant of growth in manufacturing firms is investment growth (growth elasticity is 0.08). The jump in firm growth is intricately tied to growth in exports because of limited purchasing power in the domestic market; therefore, an aggressive and proactive policy stance for promoting manufactured exports is likely to have the biggest effect on manufacturing growth in Tanzania and is recommended. The rationale for that selective approach is motivated by today's global reality: if a firm cannot compete in the global market (that is, export), it is unlikely to survive for too long in Tanzania's domestic or Africa's regional markets, which are flooded with cheaper imports from low-cost, high-skills producers such as those from East and South Asia.

Firm size is a critical determinant of firm growth in Tanzania. And, as many larger firms are also exporters, and most exporters are larger firms, policies targeting larger firms should have large payoffs in helping to expand existing firms and promote new entrants in the export sector. Although policies that favor large firms also favor exporters, export promotion strategies are important in their own right, given the limited purchasing power in the Tanzanian market. This recommendation requires a strategic, two-pronged approach: one that targets large firms, and another that targets existing and potential exporters.

- Policies are needed that redress domestic supply constraints associated with disproportionately higher transaction costs of investment faced by large firms and exporters. Policies that increase investment and a program that reduces obstacles associated with finance, infrastructure, technology, and skills are required. All of that may seem tantamount to recommending everything—that is, redressing all barriers to production currently facing all manufacturing firms in Tanzania. It is not. To circumvent the high financial and time costs and the government's weak implementation capacity, we recommend focus and pragmatism in catering to larger firms. In delivering physical inputs such as infrastructure and financial inputs such as more accessible bank financing, the government could identify spatial locations where manufacturing and export activity is most prevalent. It could then reinforce the delivery of public inputs and services to those locations. Spatial identification helps in targeting exports. Similarly, to attract potential exporters, the government could identify special areas, such as industrial districts and export processing zones, where larger firms interested in exporting would be able to benefit from improved infrastructure and service delivery, as well as financial support. That approach would render public support in a financially feasible and timely manner for fast-growing exporters and potential new entrants into the export business. The manufacturing sector cannot afford to wait until the constraints to investment are resolved economywide.

- Although the entry of firms into the export sector can be facilitated, much more is needed to sustain them in the business. Creating and nurturing firms' ability to export implies grappling with the challenge of improving productivity and spurring competitiveness to export to non-African markets, where competitiveness is best tested. That challenge requires a different set of externally oriented policies that exploit Tanzania's latecomer advantage to leapfrog into the global marketplace. The starting point should be direct public support to facilitate the delivery of the two key public goods: (a) superior technologies of production through adaptation and (b) development of technical, tertiary, and managerial skills needed to apply them. Public-private partnerships have served as the best mechanism to deliver those two public goods. The ability of Fundación Chile to promote technology transfer and adaptation and that of the Indian Institutes of Technology and Management to deliver critical skills offer useful lessons. Additionally, financial incentives are needed to reduce the high fixed cost of entry into export markets and to attract firms and sustain them in the export business. Special incentives to promote exports out of Africa are likely to have the highest payoff and sustainability. Those challenges require creativity (that is, thinking outside of the Africa box) and political commitment. Lessons from East and South Asia are good starting points, especially in the area of agroprocessing and light manufacturing.

7

The Tourism Industry

Annabella Skof

Tanzania is an up-market tourism destination. The country is endowed with a variety of tourism assets, including six World Heritage sites and numerous wildlife parks, beach resorts, coral reefs, and spectacular mountain scenic views. Twenty-eight percent of Tanzania's landmass is protected area, consisting of 15 national parks, the Ngorongoro Conservation Area, 31 game reserves, and 38 game-controlled areas.

Currently, wildlife is the prime tourist attraction. The Northern Circuit, including the Ngorongoro Crater, the Serengeti National Park, and Mount Kilimanjaro, is still the principal destination for wildlife-viewing safaris. However, the government is encouraging the development of the Southern Circuit, including the Selous Reserve, which is among the world's largest natural reserves, to prevent overexploitation of the Northern Circuit. Other principal tourist destinations include the beach resorts, mainly on the island of Zanzibar. Wildlife safaris and beach resorts are offered as single-destination attractions and combination packages.

Starting in the early 1990s, leadership of commercial development in the tourism industry shifted from the government to the private sector. The government formulates policies, regulates and promotes investment and services, and facilitates the supporting infrastructure.

Economic Contribution of Tourism

The Tanzanian government regards tourism as a priority sector. The contribution of the tourism industry to the gross domestic product (GDP) rose from 7.5 percent in 1995 to 12 percent in 2001 and to around 16 percent in 2004. In 2004, the tourism industry generated nearly 25 percent of total export earnings. Throughout the 1990s, the tourism sector has performed very well and shown high growth rates (see figure 7.1). From 1990 to 1999, tourist arrivals and foreign exchange earnings from tourism increased by an average annual rate of 15.15 percent and 27.41 percent, respectively. However, in 2000, the tourist arrival rate fell by 2.2 percent, partly as a result of the terrorist attack in Dar es Salaam in August 1998. Since 2000, tourist arrivals and foreign exchange earnings have grown only modestly at average annual growth rates of

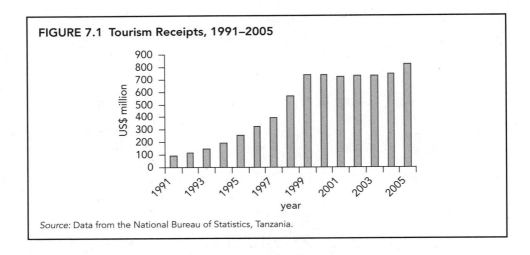

FIGURE 7.1 Tourism Receipts, 1991–2005

Source: Data from the National Bureau of Statistics, Tanzania.

4.1 percent and 2.1 percent, respectively. Tourism also plays an important role in attracting foreign direct investment (FDI). In 1999, it brought in 13 percent of the total FDI.

In 2005, Tanzania's average hotel occupancy rate was 48 percent, down from a peak of 64 percent in 1999 (table 7.1). However, there are regional differences. In general, the Northern Circuit rates (70 to 80 percent) are higher than the Southern Circuit rates (40 to 45 percent). In 2001, Europeans accounted for 31 percent of the visitors to the mainland and for 75 percent of the visitors to Zanzibar, whereas Africans made up 40 percent of the visitors to the mainland.

An estimated 40 to 50 percent of holiday visitors come overland from Kenya to Tanzania. That percentage constitutes a significant change from 1996, when it was estimated that some 60 percent of holiday visitors came through Nairobi. According to the European tour operator survey, three-fifths of respondents indicate that Tanzania is now sold as a standalone destination, rather than an add-on to a Kenya program (Ministry of Natural Resources and Tourism 2002).

Tourism contributes not only directly to growth but also indirectly through its links with other sectors of the economy. The effect of an increase in tourism expenditure on economic activity in a country (such as output, income, or employment) can be measured by using multipliers. For Tanzania, the output multiplier is estimated at 1.83, meaning that an increase of T Sh 1 million in tourism output causes the output in the economy to increase by T Sh 1.83 million, implying that other sectors expand to service the tourism industry. The backward multiplier for tourism in Tanzania is 1.16, which measures the stimuli given to supplying sectors because of increased tourism demand. A backward link of 1.16 requires the output of supplying industries to rise by T Sh 1.16 million, with a T Sh 1 million increase in tourism output (Kweka, Morrissey, and Blake 2003). Both multipliers are higher than the respective multipliers for agriculture, manufacturing, and other services. Tourism requires 44 percent of its inputs from other sectors, a rate that is above the average of all sectors. The most important input sectors for tourism in Tanzania are agriculture, livestock, poultry, fisheries, dairy,

TABLE 7.1 Key Tourism Statistics, 1991–2005

Statistic	1991	1995	2000	2001	2002	2003	2004	2005
Number of tourists	186,800	295,312	501,669	525,122	575,000	576,000	582,000	613,000
Total earnings (US$ million)	95	259	739	725	730	731	746	823
Average earnings per tourist (US$)	507	879	1,473	1,169	1,270	1,269	1,282	1,342
Average daily expenditure per tourist (US$)	72	122	184	173	172	127	128	140
Number of hotels	205	210	326	329	465	469	474	495
Number of hotel rooms	5,484	6,935	10,025	10,325	25,300	30,600	30,840	31,365
Number of hotel beds	9,878	12,145	17,303	18,284	45,500	55,500	55,932	56,562
Total tourist bed nights in hotels	1,031,136	1,662,542	1,888,000	1,955,000	8,430,000	9,600,000	9,625,000	10,630,000
Average hotel occupancy rate per year (%)	56	57	54	59	51	47	47	48
Number of employees in the tourist sector	45,000	96,000	156,050	156,500	160,200	160,500	198,500	199,000

Sources: Data from the Ministry of Natural Resources and Tourism and the National Bureau of Statistics, Tanzania.

manufacturing, nonperishable foods and dry goods, ground transportation, and hand-icrafts. Many of the products are sourced locally but are not necessarily produced in Tanzania. Furthermore, even though some products are locally produced, tourism op-erators often choose to import such products because of limited domestic availability of variety and quantity and because of relatively lower quality.

The tourism sector employed 160,750 people in 2004 compared with 96,000 in 1995. Overall, tourism has a relatively high employment multiplier, 5.39, which is the number of employees for each T Sh 1 million increase in final demand for tourism. About 75 percent of the effect on employment is to the benefit of other sectors, given the high links of tourism to those sectors. A study of Northern Circuit hotels and lodges conducted by the Multilateral Investment Guarantee Agency (MIGA 2002) found that each room is estimated to create two jobs directly. In addition, the study found that 27 percent of revenues go to imports, 36 percent to expenditures on goods and services produced in Tanzania, 15 percent to income, and 24 percent to gov-ernment taxes. The average daily expenditure per tourist was US$172.58 in 2001, which has risen steadily from US$122.00 in 1995.

Given the backward links of tourism, that sector has a large potential for increas-ing value added in the economy. Therefore, tourism is important for reducing poverty in Tanzania. Households that are involved in tourism are 10 percent less likely to be poor and therefore show lower poverty rates than food crop or fish producers and min-ing sector households. Households close to protected wildlife areas also have a poten-tial to earn tourism income. A study found that the number of households receiving income from tourism varies from 3 percent for households near the Loliondo Game-Controlled Area to 12 percent for those near the Ngorongoro Conservation Area (Homewood and others 2001). However, tourism is rarely the principal source of in-come, and the earnings are highly skewed toward the elite. Another study found that the combined (labor and nonlabor) income multiplier for tourism is 0.66, the lowest compared with other sectors in Tanzania (Kweka, Morrissey, and Blake 2003). How-ever, the tourism sector has the highest value of the labor income multiplier (0.45), which indicates the relative prevalence of paid labor in that industry. The generally low val-ues of income indicators reflect low levels of wages, employment, or both.

Tanzania has a tax multiplier of 0.08 for tourism—again higher than in agriculture, manufacturing, and other services. That multiplier is probably rather high because of the relative ease of taxing hotels and restaurants, which implies that the most efficient way to tax tourism is through taxing tourist expenditure in the country. Another study found that tourism has an unambiguously favorable effect on tax revenue (Kweka 2004). A 10 percent tax on all tourist expenditures increases government revenue by 2 percent, real GDP by 0.3 percent, and total welfare by 0.2 percent.

The Tanzanian Tourism Industry Compared with That of Other Countries

In terms of tourism assets, Tanzania can be compared with Kenya because both coun-tries feature a number of game parks, mountains, and lakes, as well as beaches on the Indian Ocean. However, in 2004, Kenya received about 780,000 visitors more than

Tanzania (figure 7.2), although Tanzania has more than four times the landmass conserved as national parks. In addition, Tanzania's wildlife is considered to be superior in terms of quality, quantity, diversity, and visibility to that in competing destinations.

One reason for the differential in visitor arrivals is that Tanzania targets higher-income tourists and tries to avoid the style of mass tourism fostered in Kenya. Mass tourism is not seen as an option for Tanzania because of the fragility of its natural assets. In addition, targeting low-volume, high-yield tourism allows Tanzania to keep the image of exclusivity, which is feasible because of its assets.

Tanzania's tourism industry shows better results if compared in terms of earnings from tourism. In 2004, Tanzania received US$746 million in tourism earnings, while Kenya earned US$495 million. Tanzania's performance in terms of growth of tourism receipts by far surpassed that of Kenya during the 1990s: from 1990 to 1995, Tanzania showed an average annual growth of receipts of 31.8 percent, while Kenya's receipts grew by 1.9 percent annually. From 1995 to 2000, Tanzania's average annual growth of receipts slowed to 23.3 percent, and Kenya marked an average annual decrease in receipts of 10.7 percent.[1] Kenya picked up growth in the period from 2000 to 2004, experiencing an average annual growth rate of receipts of 18.9 percent, far surpassing Tanzania's slow average annual growth rate of 0.24 percent.

In terms of the hotel occupancy rate, Tanzania shows similar figures to Kenya. On average, both Kenya and Tanzania have an occupancy rate of about 50 percent. However, Tanzania shows better results during the low season: 34.5 percent as compared with 27.6 percent in Kenya (table 7.2).

According to the World Travel and Tourism Council Competitiveness Monitor 2004,[2] an online database (http://www.wttc.org/NU_compmon/compmon04/Intro.htm), Tanzania is less competitive overall than Kenya, Mauritius, or Thailand (figure 7.3).

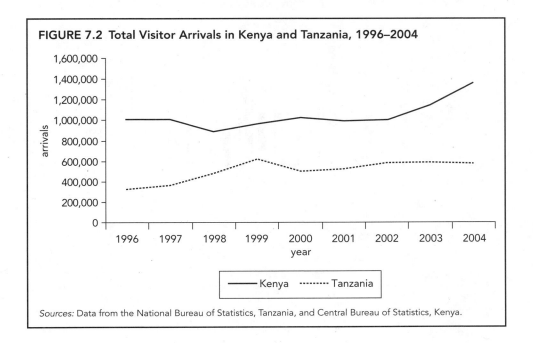

FIGURE 7.2 Total Visitor Arrivals in Kenya and Tanzania, 1996–2004

Sources: Data from the National Bureau of Statistics, Tanzania, and Central Bureau of Statistics, Kenya.

TABLE 7.2 Hotel Occupancy Rate

(percent)

Time of occupancy	Kenya	Tanzania	Uganda
Average 2002/03	50.10	50.85	47.50
High season	75.78	72.92	72.30
Low season	27.61	34.52	24.04

Source: World Bank 2005d.

Tanzania's price level is higher than that of Kenya and Thailand. Even though the tourism infrastructure in Tanzania is slightly better than in Kenya, it is still very weak. The levels of technology, education, openness toward trade and visitors, and social factors are very low in Tanzania, resulting in international rankings in the lowest third.

Competitiveness in tourism is determined by price, product, infrastructure, and enabling environment. A market survey of tour operators found that the quality of tourist services was perceived as a major weakness of the product (Murphy and Henegan 2002). Furthermore, respondents indicated that a lack of training could be detected and that service orientation should be more professional.

Infrastructure services are a major obstacle to the tourism sector in Tanzania. Almost 47 percent of the surveyed tour operators perceive electricity services as poor or very poor (table 7.3). In Kenya, roads, waste disposal, and security are regarded as bigger problems than electricity.

The recent Investment Climate Survey for Tourism in East Africa found that the inadequate provision of electricity is perceived as a major obstacle in the business envi-

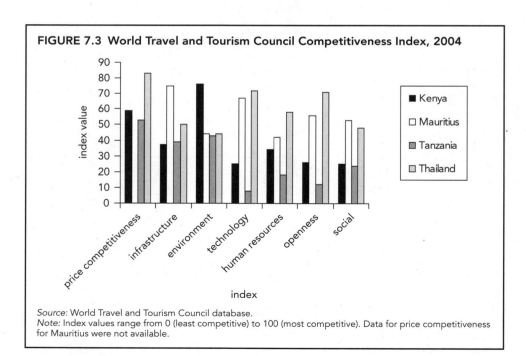

FIGURE 7.3 World Travel and Tourism Council Competitiveness Index, 2004

Source: World Travel and Tourism Council database.
Note: Index values range from 0 (least competitive) to 100 (most competitive). Data for price competitiveness for Mauritius were not available.

TABLE 7.3 Perception of Infrastructure Services

Service	Percentage of respondents ranking services poor or very poor		
	Kenya	Tanzania	Uganda
Roads	**64.70**	**37.88**	**28.60**
Waste disposal	**61.80**	**33.33**	17.90
Security	**38.20**	18.18	17.90
Water	35.30	28.79	10.70
Land telecommunications	32.40	6.06	14.30
Railways	29.40	1.52	7.10
Electricity	23.50	**46.97**	**21.40**
Mobile telecommunications	17.60	4.55	3.60
Postal service	14.70	1.52	11.10
Air freight	11.80	4.55	**33.30**
Trucking	2.90	1.52	18.50

Source: World Bank 2005d.
Note: **Bold** typeface indicates the three poorest services in each country.

ronment. With 62.1 percent of businesspeople surveyed ranking that problem as major and very severe, the provision of electricity is a significantly greater problem in Tanzania than in Kenya and Uganda (table 7.4). Tax administration is also ranked more often as a major or very severe obstacle in Tanzania than in Kenya or Uganda. Tax rates, however, constitute a major obstacle in Tanzania as well as in Kenya and Uganda.[3]

TABLE 7.4 Obstacles Encountered in the Business Environment

Obstacle	Percentage of respondents ranking obstacles major and very severe		
	Kenya	Tanzania	Uganda
Telecommunications	23.5	10.6	0.0
Electricity	32.4	**62.1**	**37.0**
Transportation	26.5	27.3	14.8
Access to land	9.1	33.3	**37.0**
Tax rates	**61.8**	**69.7**	**63.0**
Tax administration	29.4	**56.1**	37.0
Customs and trade regulations	11.8	28.8	14.8
Labor regulations	11.8	18.2	11.1
Skills and education of workers	11.8	28.8	37.0
Business licensing and operating permits	11.8	33.3	11.1
Access to financing	23.5	45.5	33.3
Cost of financing	**61.8**	47.0	**55.6**
Economic and regulatory policy uncertainty	32.4	40.9	22.2
Macroeconomic instability	**44.1**	**51.5**	22.2
Corruption	**50.0**	48.5	**44.4**
Crime, theft, and disorder	**47.1**	28.8	14.8
Anticompetitive or informal practices	23.5	18.2	25.9

Source: World Bank 2005d.
Note: **Bold** typeface indicates the worst five obstacles in each country.

Growth Potential

The government of Tanzania has set a target of 1 million tourists by 2010 bringing US$1.5 billion in receipts. In the medium term, the objective is to increase the average annual growth rate of the tourism sector to 8 percent by 2005/06.

Tanzania's tourism potential is largely underexploited; the sector can therefore make a greater contribution to growth and poverty reduction. As noted earlier, Kenya has received more visitors than Tanzania, but Tanzania has both more landmass conserved as national parks and superior wildlife compared with Kenya. Tanzania also targets higher-income tourists and avoids mass tourism, which allows it to protect its fragile natural assets. In addition, Tanzania's low-volume, high-yield tourism strategy maintains its image of exclusivity.

Nevertheless, much unexploited potential exists in new destinations and activities, in particular in niche markets. Moreover, the capacity of tourist services in the southern part of the country is not fully used. Likewise, the potential that marine assets on the coast area offer has not yet been fully transformed into tourism products. Any further exploitation of Tanzania's tourism potential must ensure long-term sustainability, requiring activity by public and private actors.

Several structural constraints hamper the realization of the tourism industry's growth potential. The tourism sector is highly concentrated. Few operators control demand and volume to products such as the Ngorongoro Conservation Area, the Serengeti National Park, and the island of Zanzibar. Because of saturation, growth in the package holiday segment is limited. To increase growth in the tourism industry, the restructured *Tourism Master Plan* identifies investments in infrastructure, enhanced products, improved efficiency and competitiveness of suppliers, and an improved enabling environment (Ministry of Natural Resources and Tourism 2002). The plan, however, lacks a specific focus while offering several growth strategy options.

The tourism industry has great potential to increase its indirect contributions to economic growth and poverty reduction because significant opportunities exist for strengthening and increasing tourism backward links in the agriculture, manufacturing, and services sectors. Backward links can be increased both in volume and through inclusion of additional industries. Many of the tourism sector's suppliers are small, often informal operators with limited capacity and limited access to capital and expertise. For example, in the existing and important fruit and vegetable link, suppliers are mostly informal with little opportunity to expand their business. Thus, the potential for increasing the value added of the products by processing fruits and vegetables remains largely unrealized. Similarly, improved techniques, increased capacity, and better-trained employees would strengthen sector-to-sector links. The *Tanzania Diagnostic Trade Integration Study* (World Bank 2005f) has identified a number of detailed and specific recommendations aimed at increasing the economic contribution of tourism by strengthening links.

Furthermore, the potential exists to increase the number of households receiving income from tourism. For example, in Talek, Kenya, near a gate to the Masaai Mara Nature Reserve, 86.4 percent of the households earn income from tourism, compared with 12 percent of those near the Ngorongoro Conservation Area.

Recommendations

Several recommendations can be made on the basis of these findings.

Development of Innovative Tourism Packages and Niche Products

Tanzania has not yet fully exploited its potential in value-added niche products such as adventure tourism, including climbing and trekking, deep-sea fishing, scuba diving, cultural tourism, bird watching, and hunting.

Currently, community awareness and participation are almost nonexistent. The Tanzania Ministry of Natural Resources and Tourism has recently enacted Wildlife Management Area regulations to enable participation of local communities in conserving wildlife. Community-based tourism offers great potential to reduce rural poverty. Wildlife-based tourism can be used as a revenue source for rural communities. This form of tourism could be combined with cultural tourism and sold as a package.

Investment in Supporting Infrastructure

The tourism sector would benefit from investments made in transportation, telecommunications, electricity, and health services.

Transportation Infrastructure

Tanzania's international access by air is inadequate and expensive. Many visitors to the Northern Circuit fly to Nairobi, Kenya. KLM Royal Dutch Airlines has had a direct flight from Amsterdam to Kilimanjaro for more than 30 years, and British Airways serves Dar es Salaam. In its current condition, the airport on Zanzibar is inappropriate for landing jumbo jets from Europe. The lengthening of the runway is under way; however, airport facilities and safety are inadequate. A public-private partnership is recommended to improve management and efficiency of airport facilities and safety. Domestic transportation also needs great improvement. Furthermore, to exploit the tourism potential of remote destinations, in particular in the Southern Circuit, Tanzania must improve road and air transportation to allow better access.

Telecommunications and Electricity

The costs for telecommunication services and electricity are high in Tanzania. In general, only about 7 percent of Tanzania's population has access to electricity, whereas the Dar es Salaam area consumes about half of the country's electricity. The Tanzania Electric Supply Company's predominantly hydroelectric system is prone to shortages caused by conditions such as poor rainfall. Moreover, the southern part of Tanzania has no access to the national electricity grid. Most lodges in Tanzania's national parks and game reserves rely on generators and alternative solutions such as photovoltaic cells. However, they are not likely to have access to the grid in the medium term. Even where there is access to electricity, the provision is not reliable. Tanzania experiences,

TABLE 7.5 Electricity Provision Indicators

Indicator	Kenya	Tanzania	Uganda
Outages (days)	82.90	91.85	—
Duration (hours)	31.00	4.55	—
Firms with generator (%)	88.89	74.24	60.71
Share of electricity from generator (%)	17.54	35.33	3.26
Firms with damaged equipment (%)	63.89	50.00	35.71
Value of damaged equipment (US$)	21,114.04	8,565.51	7,274.12

Source: World Bank 2005g.
Note: — = not available.

on average, nearly 92 days of outages, almost 10 days per year more than Kenya. However, the duration of outages is shorter in Tanzania (table 7.5).

Health Services

The availability of heath services is also very important to the tourism industry, in particular for up-market tourism. A better provision of health clinics and medical evacuation facilities is needed to meet the requirements of the tourism business (for example, decompression chambers for diving). Tourists must protect themselves from malaria by using nets treated with insecticide and other prophylactic measures.

Investment in Human Resources

In Tanzania, no written policy and objectives toward human resource development in tourism exist. Investment in human resources is indispensable if the quality of tourism services and the professionalism of the industry are to improve.

Notes

1. Average annual growth rates of receipts are calculated by the World Tourism Organization.
2. The tourism Price Competitiveness Index is computed using the Hotel Price Index and Purchasing Power Parity Index. The Infrastructure Index shows the level of infrastructure development, combining the Road Index, the Sanitation Index, and the Water Access Index. The Environment Index combines the Population Density Index, CO_2 Emission Index, and Environmental Treaties Index. The Technology Index unites the Internet Index, Telephone Index, Mobile Index, and HiTech Index. The Human Resources Index is proxied by using the Education Index obtained from the 2004 United Nations Development Programme report, consisting of the adult literacy rate and the combined primary, secondary, and tertiary gross enrollment ratios. The Openness Index is an aggregate index including the Visa Index, Tourism Openness Index, Trade Openness Index, and Taxes on International Trade Index. The Social Index is a combination of the Human Development Index, Newspaper Index, Personal Computer Index, and Television Index.
3. See chapter 8 on the informal economy for a more detailed discussion of the business environment for small and medium enterprises in Tanzania.

8

The Informal Economy

Annabella Skof

International estimates that include informal activities in agriculture suggest that Tanzania's informal economy accounts for about 60 percent of the Tanzanian gross national income (Schneider 2004). The informal sector is thus relatively large in both regional and international comparisons (figure 8.1). Data from the Tanzanian "Integrated Labour Force Survey, 2000/01" (National Bureau of Statistics 2001) that exclude informal sector activities in rural agriculture suggest that the informal sector employs about 16 percent of the total labor force. The Instituto Libertad y Democracia (ILD 2005) found that about 98 percent of economic activities in Tanzania were within extralegal boundaries in the informal economy and that 89 percent of all such activities are held extralegally. According to ILD, the Tanzanian informal economy has assets worth US$29 billion.

Many small enterprises in Tanzania operate under a semiformal legal status without the necessity of registration with state authorities (table 8.1). Semiformal operators appear on a list of operators at the local authorities, and they pay taxes that are collected by local authorities. How long informal operators may remain at any level of informal or formal status differs widely in Tanzania. An operator may progress through a semiformal stage or move directly from informal status to the official registration.

Informal economy operations can be found in most sectors in Tanzania. According to the National Bureau of Statistics (2001), people whose main economic activity is in the informal economy are most often employed in these sectors: retail trade of agricultural products, meat, and chicken (20.7 percent); stationery, photography, and general retail (18.8 percent); retail trade of processed food (10.5 percent); and restaurants and hotels (12.4 percent). The majority of people whose informal activity is a secondary activity are employed in crop growing (94.4 percent).[1]

Generally, for households engaged in informal economic activities in urban areas, such activity tends to be their main activity, whereas such activity is more likely to be secondary in rural areas. According to the National Bureau of Statistics (2001), one in three households was active in the informal economy in 2000/01, as opposed to one in four households in 1990/91. The survey shows that the number of households with informal economy activities grew during the 1990s from 42 percent of the total households in urban areas to 61 percent. In rural areas, 27 percent out of the

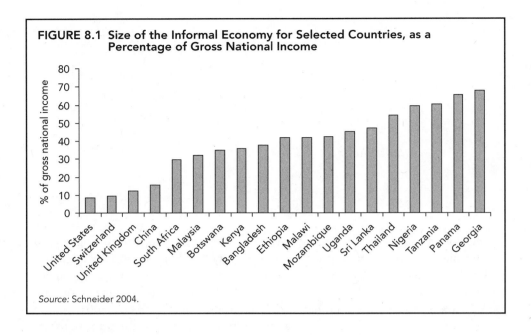

FIGURE 8.1 Size of the Informal Economy for Selected Countries, as a Percentage of Gross National Income

Source: Schneider 2004.

TABLE 8.1 Typology of Forms of Enterprise in Tanzania

Formal status	Legal form	Description and subcategories
Illicit	None	An enterprise for which there is no legally permitted, licensed, or registered counterpart.
Informal	None	An activity (for which there is a formal counterpart) that does not comply with requirements of the regulatory system regarding licenses, permits, certificates, notification, or registration of the activity.
Semiformal	Local authority–licensed enterprise	An activity carried on by an operator who appears on a local authority list of licensed operators of enterprises but who is not registered with the state registrar. Existing forms of licenses include those for (a) hawkers, (b) businesses, and (c) market stalls.
Formal	State-registered enterprise	Persons registered to conduct business activities under a registered business name. For example, an activity enumerated on a state register as a sole ownership enterprise, a private limited company, or a joint stock company open to public subscription shareholdings.

Source: Nelson and de Burijn 2005.

total households had informal economy activities in 2000/01, as compared to 21 percent in 1990/91. Also, in terms of employment, the informal economy holds a bigger share in urban areas than in rural areas. In Dar es Salaam, for instance, 36 percent of the total labor force is employed in the informal economy.

The vast majority of persons in the informal economy are self-employed without employees. Eighty-two percent[2] are self-employed in the main activities, while 88 percent are self-employed in the secondary activities.

The level of education of informal business operators is generally low. According to the National Bureau of Statistics (2001), 64.2 percent of operators in the main activities and 53 percent of those in the secondary activities have completed primary school. In the main and secondary activities, 16.7 percent and 43.5 percent, respectively, of the operators have no education or have dropped out of primary school.

The National Bureau of Statistics (2001, 58) suggests that the growth of the informal economy during the past decade "is possibly a result of economic hardships households have been facing that have forced them to join the sector as a survival strategy." Accordingly, 44.5 percent of people whose main activity is in the informal economy stated that the major reason for involvement in that sector is the inability to find work. For those for whom the informal economy is a source of secondary activity, the main reason is the need for additional income for families (43.9 percent). Such data indicate that survivalists constitute a considerable part of the Tanzanian informal economy. A study by the International Labour Organization (ILO), the United Nations Industrial Development Organization (UNIDO), and the United Nations Development Programme (UNDP) therefore differentiates between survival types of operators and growth-potential types of businesses in the Tanzanian informal economy (ILO, UNIDO, and UNDP 2002).

The National Bureau of Statistics (2001) further notes that informal economy activities as main employment are more concentrated in urban areas because of problems of unemployment, whereas in rural areas the informal economy predominantly provides opportunities for secondary activities. As stated before, crop growing is the sector employing the majority of the people whose informal activity is a secondary activity. The National Bureau of Statistics' (2002) "Household Budget Survey 2000/01" finds that 75.8 percent of the people in rural areas are mainly active in farming, raising of livestock, or fishing. In rural areas, agricultural income accounts for the primary source of income with a share of 60.4 percent, which means that almost 40 percent of the income is derived from sources outside farm production. Sixty-five percent of rural households report more than three income sources.

In general, income tends to be much lower in the informal sector than in the formal sector. Tanzania is no exception. According to the National Bureau of Statistics (2001), the average income for paid employment of households in Dar es Salaam that do not undertake informal activity is T Sh 191,662, while it is T Sh 85,960 for households with informal activity. Income in rural areas is much lower, averaging T Sh 76,800 for households not involved in activities in the informal economy and T Sh 47,874 for households with informal activity.

Nonetheless, the informal economy thrives in Tanzania because it provides opportunities for income generation to the poor and unemployed and because it offers a low-cost ground for experimentation with business ideas that might lead to growth and formal enterprises. Forced formalization risks incurring the cost of damaging fragile enterprises and livelihoods for very little benefits and suppressing business experimentation and development. The decision of a small-scale informal operator to formalize should be a voluntary one.

Our poverty analysis presented in chapter 2, as well as other research such as Owens and Teal (2005), suggests that the informal sector—especially urban self-employment—has been an important path out of poverty for many Tanzanians. Not only did the share of self-employed persons in the adult population increase from 4.8 percent to 8 percent,[3] but expenditures by households headed by self-employed individuals grew by 18 percent between 1991/92 and 2000/01, compared with a much more modest growth of expenditure of agricultural households, which grew by only 7 percent during that period. In Dar es Salaam, the growth of expenditures by households headed by a self-employed person was even more dramatic at 65 percent, which was even higher than the average growth in expenditures of 60 percent experienced by households headed by a person in paid employment (see table 2.16).

Constraints to Growth of Enterprises in the Informal Sector and Formalization

Micro and small enterprises in Tanzania, most of them in the informal sector, are not only an important means to generate income; they are also an important entry point for the development of a strong private sector in Tanzania. As such, it is important to consider how growth of such enterprises and their transition into the formal sector can be facilitated.

Informal operators state the existence of a number of constraints to growth of their businesses. Most important, they are often not in a position to afford permanent premises for their businesses. Second, they lack access to credit. A lack of business management skills and very limited access to new technology also are detrimental to the growth of informal businesses. Often, informal entrepreneurs face harassment by local authorities. That situation has improved considerably since 2003, but it is still a problem. Some businesses are demolished, property is taken away, and in the worst cases, entrepreneurs face charges.

Furthermore, advocacy is needed for the informal economy. Currently, three associations represent the interests of informal economy operators: the Small Industries and Petty Traders Association (Vikundi vya Biashara Ndogondogo, or VIBINDO), an umbrella organization; the Tanzania Small Industrialists Society (TASISO); and the Tanzania Food Processors Association (TAFOPA). However, sectoral associations are still weak. The ILO Syndicoop project facilitated the formation of a national steering committee that includes the Trade Union Congress of Tanzania, the Tanzania Federation of Cooperatives, the Savings and Credit Cooperative Union, the government, and individual informal economy groups.

VIBINDO states that the biggest constraint to formalizing a business is access to affordable permanent premises. There are a number of success stories of informal operators formalizing their businesses after the municipal authorities provided or assisted in the access to permanent premises.

The costs of starting and operating a formal business are high in Tanzania. According to the World Bank's *Doing Business 2007* (World Bank 2006), entrepreneurs in Tanzania can expect to go through 13 steps to launch a business, which on average take 30 days and cost 92 percent of the US$340 per capita income, compared to 11 percent, 46 percent, and 114 percent of per capita income in Botswana, Kenya, and Uganda, respectively, or 6.5 percent in Organisation for Economic Co-operation and

Development (OECD) countries. However, the minimum capital required to obtain a business registration number in Tanzania is 6 percent of per capita income, which is considerably lower than the regional average (297.2 percent) or the OECD average (28.9 percent).

The ILD (Instituto Libertad y Democracia) found that the costs and burdens of the procedure to legally incorporate a private Bureau of Change in Mbeya include 10 stages, 103 steps, 379 days, and US$5,506, whereas the respective figures for Dar es Salaam are 95 steps, 283 days, and US$3,816 (ILD 2005). ILO, UNIDO, and UNDP (2002) calculated that the cost of coping with regulatory and nonregulatory constraints would amount to as much as 75 percent of monthly sales of informal operators in the firewood and charcoal sector, which explains the decision to remain informal.[4]

To register a business, entrepreneurs must travel to Dar es Salaam, where the Business Registration and Licensing Agency is located. ILO, UNIDO, and UNDP (2002) show that business licensing is equally cumbersome, because it requires various procedures in different offices at regional and district levels. Both processes, licensing and registration, are required and often involve bribing officials, further increasing the cost of starting a formal business. Costs of formalization are often increased even more because some officers are reported to be unhelpful, obstructive, and uncaring (ILO, UNIDO, and UNDP 2002).

De Soto (2001) explains that a major problem faced by the informal economy is its inability to convert what he refers to as dead capital (untitled assets) into capital that can be used, for example, as collateral for loans. Registering property is an expensive and time-consuming undertaking in Tanzania: it takes 12 steps and 61 days, compared to 4 procedures and 33 days in OECD countries. The cost of registering property amounts to 12.2 percent of the property value, which is considerably higher than in OECD countries (4.7 percent). ILD (2005) found that the procedure to allocate land for urban purposes and to obtain a building permit takes 13 stages and includes 68 steps, which take eight years to complete and cost US$2,252.

Also, enforcing formal contracts costs on average 5.3 percent of the debt, compared with the OECD average of 10.9 percent. According to ILD (2005), claims for a debt at Tanzania's Commercial Court Division take 9 stages, 96 steps, and 390 days and cost US$11,964. Likewise, collection of a debt by executing a court decree takes 1,286 days and costs US$1,022. In addition, hiring or firing employees is comparatively difficult in Tanzania. However, because employment regulations are not enforced, ILO, UNIDO, and UNDP (2002) did not identify them as a severe constraint.

Tax rates, which are perceived as too high, often act as a disincentive to formalize. A recent study shows a number of anomalies with the tax regime for small businesses, in particular that the system is regressive for nonrecordkeepers (FIAS 2006). Moreover, the study states that the "tax environment encourages expansion of the informal economy," because "small businesses face a proportionately higher time and financial costs to comply with administrative requirements and therefore may not see any benefit of joining the tax net" (FIAS 2006, 18). Furthermore, newly registered businesses must pay taxes up front, which further increases the required starting capital.

The marginal effective tax rate is higher for small businesses than for large firms. Local governments still levy a large number of taxes, fees, and charges. Local taxation

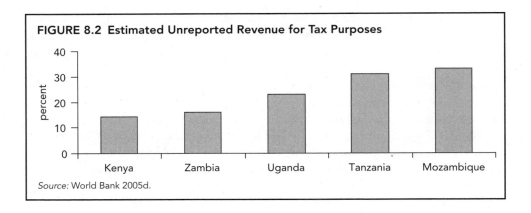

FIGURE 8.2 Estimated Unreported Revenue for Tax Purposes

Source: World Bank 2005d.

is seen as a major constraint to formalization. In addition, bribes are estimated to add up to more than 5 percent of total sales. Comparative investment climate survey datasets collected by the World Bank (2004e) suggest, however, that the share of revenue that Tanzanian businesses deliberately fail to report for tax purposes is more than 30 percent, compared with around or less than 20 percent in Kenya, Uganda, and Zambia (figure 8.2). However, one should note that informal entrepreneurs do pay taxes to local authorities. For example, in Dar es Salaam, a local tax of T Sh 100 per day is collected from every informal operator.

In sum, another reason for the large size of Tanzania's informal economy is that for microenterprises the benefits of formality are dwarfed by its costs. "Whether in monetary terms (direct cost or income foregone), or in terms of time and energy, the cost of compliance turns out to be too high for most starting businesses, who are therefore obliged to start informally" (ILO, UNIDO, and UNDP 2002, 3). In other words, the state fails to provide an institutional environment that is conducive to investment in the formalization of informal enterprises. Therefore, the "current regulatory set up (a) fails to meet [the] objective of ensuring quality control for the majority; and (b) traps the entrepreneurs in low quality settings, puts their upgrading and growth too far out of reach, and limits the contribution of the subsector to poverty reduction and national growth" (ILO, UNIDO, and UNDP 2002, 35).

Benefits of Increasing Formalization

The most obvious benefit to the government of increasing formalization is higher tax revenue. Furthermore, the government's ability to implement policies and the effectiveness of government programs aimed at the private sector will rise because informal enterprises operate outside of the government system of regulation.

From the perspective of business operators, formalization of their business increases the trustworthiness for customers, a benefit that has been mentioned by several entrepreneurs who formalized their business. Furthermore, formalization creates the basis for formal transactions with other entities, including financial intermediaries for access to credit, the public sector for the provision of public services, and clients and suppliers for contract-based transactions. Given the rigidities, costs, and attitudes of formal sector regulators and service providers, the access of informal entrepreneurs to important public goods, such as electric and water utilities, and to other inputs and services is limited.

Furthermore, operators in the informal economy cannot convert dead capital in the form of untitled assets into productive economic currency, such as collateral for loans to start or expand a business. According to ILD (2005), there is US$29 billion in dead capital in Tanzania. Moreover, operators' access to the capital market is very limited. Formal registration is generally a prerequisite for access to credit and small business loans (US$15,000 to US$30,000). Therefore, informal sector operators are destined to remain small without being able to exploit potential economies of scale. As a result, productivity tends to be low. In general, the labor productivity is lower in Tanzania than in many other African countries—the median value added per worker is US$2,061, as shown in panel (a) of figure 8.3. Panel (b) of figure 8.3 indicates that, in the case of microenterprises (most of which are informal), labor productivity is even lower.

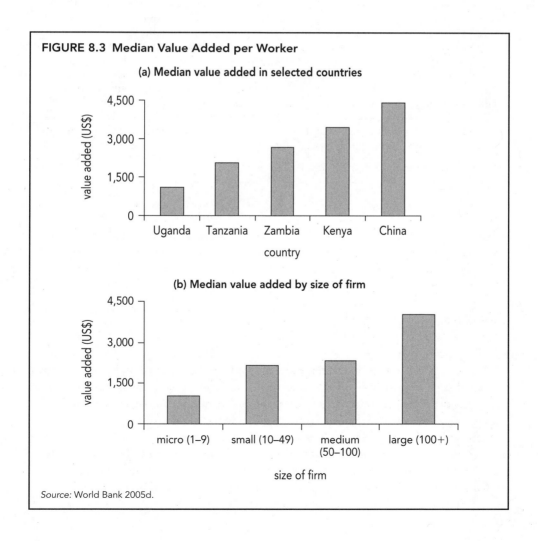

FIGURE 8.3 Median Value Added per Worker

(a) Median value added in selected countries

(b) Median value added by size of firm

Source: World Bank 2005d.

BOX 8.1 Examples of Voluntary Formalization

Alan Mungo experimented with operating an informal insurance agency and a clothes shop. He eventually progressed to producing wine and operating a safari tour company. Having developed a marketable product and identified market opportunities for expansion, he decided it would be in his interest to legitimize his enterprise. However, after preliminary inquiries, he found that the premises he used, an automobile garage on the grounds of his dwelling house, would not be approved by health inspectors, which meant he would not be able to apply for an operator's license.

Around this time, he attended a meeting of representatives of the Tanzanian Food Processors Association, the local trade licensing officer, and a representative of the Ministry for Agriculture, Food Security, and Cooperatives. That meeting produced an agreement that small-scale food processors who could not comply with regulations would not be forced to cease their operations. Instead they could continue to operate without licenses, but they would still be subject to supervision by health inspectors. That condition incidentally implied the advantage of being off the database of operators liable for formal taxes. The acknowledged reason for the ministry's decision was that Tanzania's food-processing industry was important; that it relied mainly on small-scale producers, most of whom were not licensed; and that it would be forced to close if regulations were enforced. Mungo was able to continue operating, and licensing costs were deferred until after his premises reached the standard about one year later. At that point, his formalization costs were very low.

Dan Himba formalized his business after an activity period of 29 years. He conducted informal enterprise activities as a supplement to his salaried employment. During that period, he enjoyed a long run of starting informal enterprises, maximizing profits while he could, and abandoning those enterprises when they showed signs of having run their most profitable life cycle. When the conditions of his employment deteriorated, a full-time entrepreneurial career became more attractive to him and increased the stimulus to formalize. He subsequently abandoned his job for a career in private enterprise.

Source: Nelson and de Burijn 2005.

The decision to formalize an informal business depends on expected benefits from formalization (box 8.1). Often, informal businesses are too small to be able to pay the costs of formalization.

Implications for Policy

To allow for a low-cost arena for business experimentation, as well as a means of income generation for poor and unemployed people in the absence of a state-provided safety net such as unemployment benefits, the Tanzanian government should tolerate and support informal economic activities. Governments can reduce informality by reducing the costs and increasing the benefits associated with becoming formal. By reducing corruption, for example, they can increase enterprises' willingness to deal with public institutions. In addition, governments can encourage firms to become formal by reducing the burden imposed on formal enterprises by such factors as barriers to entry, business regulations and inspections, and labor regulations.

In addition, providing for an adequate institutional framework that is conducive to and provides incentives for voluntary formalization of informal businesses is important. Possible incentives are the abolishment of up-front payment of taxes or free training on procedures of formalization. Alternatively, an agency to assist entrepreneurs in registration procedures could be set up. Moreover, local governments should provide more permanent premises at low rents (such as market stalls in Ilala, Dar es Salaam) for informal entrepreneurs. The Small and Medium Enterprise Development Policy of 2002 addresses the problem of infrastructure requirements and calls on local authorities to allocate and develop land for small and medium enterprises, to develop industrial clusters and trade centers, and to identify and allocate underused public buildings to such enterprises. A higher degree of realization of this policy would be very beneficial.

The focus of government has been primarily on encouraging formalization of businesses, while paying relatively less attention to supporting small-scale, informal sector activities. In addition to the review of laws and regulations that may unduly impinge on small-scale informal activities, that effort also requires a change in mindset of public officials to recognize the value and importance of informal sector activities for Tanzania's economic development. In particular, local authorities, who deal with the informal sector on a daily basis, would benefit from capacity building in that area.

Access to credit poses severe constraints to informal entrepreneurs. Often, informal businesses find even microfinance schemes hard to comply with. Alternative credit schemes include rotating savings and credit societies, such as savings and credit cooperatives (SACCOs). Developing and improving occupational SACCOs can be an effective alternative to formal banks. In the long run, SACCOs could function as a way to connect informal savings with the formal financial sector.

The government has already started to implement measures to reduce the cost of doing business and to facilitate the formalization of businesses and property. In October 2004, it launched the Property and Business Formalisation Programme. The objective of the program is to identify assets and guarantee property rights. In fall 2005, at the conclusion of the diagnostic phase of the program, ILD (2005) presented a comprehensive report that commented on legislation governing property ownership and compiled data on the patterns of movable- and fixed-asset ownership. Formalization reforms will be designed on the basis of those findings.

The government has also taken important measures to reduce the burden of business licensing and registration, and a business activities registration bill was submitted to the Tanzanian parliament in 2005. The goal is to create a business licensing system that is transparent and efficient, aiming at registration rather than revenue collection and control in place. Furthermore, the license fee for small businesses was abolished in 2004/05. By simplifying and harmonizing legislation and streamlining regulations of business and property registration, the government should cut all costs of formalization in order to create an enabling environment. For example, the Business Registration and Licensing Agency should open branches throughout the country so that travel expenses of entrepreneurs who wish to license a business are kept at a minimum.

Officers of local and national government agencies should be well informed and trained to assist potential licensed business owners. They should pass on correct and useful information in order to facilitate business licensing. In particular, officers should be aware of legislative changes such as the new taxation schedule and comply with them.

In addition to government officers, potential and current informal entrepreneurs should have a fair understanding of the formalization process, as well as the benefits and opportunities of running a formal business. Informal workers should be encouraged to form cooperatives. Training for informal business operators in managerial skills through seminars and workshops is of the utmost importance and is very beneficial to fostering private sector development.

Notes

1. Those figures are calculated on the basis of the national definition of employment.
2. The figure of 82 percent was reached according to the standard International Labour Organisation definition of labor force, or 73 percent using the national definition.
3. Data from the Integrated Labour Force Survey (National Bureau of Statistics 2001) and the Household Budget Survey (National Bureau of Statistics 2002) provide different measures of informal sector activities, but the magnitude and trends provided by these two surveys present broadly similar pictures.
4. Regulatory constraints include complicated, lengthy, and unpredictable procedures; inadequate institutional arrangements; rent-seeking civil servants; unreasonable specifications and standards; and a multiplicity of taxes and levies. Nonregulatory constraints include, for example, poor clients, lack of access to financing, poor infrastructure, and unfair competition. The 75 percent figure is the highest average cost for coping with constraints that occurred in the firewood and charcoal sector. However, in the cloth-making sector, for example, the highest average cost calculated was 5.8 percent of monthly sales.

PART III
Elements of a Strategy for Shared Growth

9

Fostering Innovation, Productivity, and Technological Change

Anuja Utz and Jean-Eric Aubert

The application of knowledge, as manifested in areas such as entrepreneurship and innovation, research and development (R&D), and people's education and skill levels, is now recognized as one of the key sources of growth and competitiveness in the global economy. Developing countries such as Tanzania have ample scope to use new and existing knowledge and innovation to develop new products and processes, thereby enhancing technological change and improving productivity across all sectors of the economy. Innovation in Tanzania concerns not just the domestic development of frontier-based knowledge; more important, it relates to the application and use of existing knowledge to the local context. It requires a climate favorable to entrepreneurs that is free from bureaucratic, regulatory, and other obstacles and that fosters interactions between the local and outside business worlds, with different sources of knowledge, including universities, public laboratories, users, think tanks, industries, and indigenous communities.

Four pillars are generally considered to be important for countries to make effective use of knowledge for their overall economic and social development:

- An economic and institutional regime that provides incentives for the efficient use of existing knowledge, the creation of new knowledge, and the flourishing of entrepreneurship

- An educated and skilled population that can create, share, and use knowledge well

- A dynamic information infrastructure that can facilitate the effective communication, dissemination, and processing of information

- An efficient innovation system of firms, science and research centers, universities, think tanks, consultants, and other organizations that can tap into the growing stock of global knowledge, assimilate and adapt it to local needs, and create new knowledge.

BOX 9.1 Benchmarking Tanzania in the Global Context

Some recent indexes that have been developed to benchmark countries' performance in terms of competitiveness or knowledge readiness on a global basis include the following:

- *World Economic Forum's Global Competitiveness Report 2006–2007.* This report (World Economic Forum 2007) highlights World Economic Forum's new Global Competitiveness Index (GCI), which provides an overview of factors critical for driving productivity and competitiveness. The factors are grouped into nine pillars: institutions, infrastructure, macroeconomy, health and primary education, higher education and training, market efficiency, technological readiness, business sophistication, and innovation. Tanzania is ranked 104th (of 125 countries) on this new 2006 GCI, behind Kenya (94) but ahead of Uganda (113). World Economic Forum's Business Competitiveness Index (BCI) is another index that focuses on microeconomic factors that determine economies' current productivity and competitiveness. Tanzania is ranked 73rd (of 121 countries) on the BCI in 2006, ahead of Uganda (88) but again behind Kenya (68).
- *World Economic Forum's Africa Competitiveness Report 2004.* This report (World Economic Forum 2004) highlights the prospects for growth and the obstacles to improving competitiveness in 25 African economies. Tanzania ranks 9th of 25 countries on the overall global competitive index, surpassing Uganda, which is ranked 14th, and Kenya, which placed 15th.
- *World Bank Institute's Knowledge Assessment Methodology (KAM).* The figure below compares Tanzania's performance on the Knowledge Economy Index (KEI) with the performance of the African region, Tanzania's neighbors, and Botswana and South Africa, as well as with that of well-performing East Asian economies such as Malaysia and Thailand. It shows that between 1995 and the most current period (2004–05) Tanzania has made a substantial improvement in its overall knowledge readiness, as evidenced by positive changes in the KEI, particularly for the economic and incentive regime and the innovation pillars. In addition, it has made some improvement in information and communication technologies (ICTs). Also, Uganda has made strides in improving its economic incentive regime and in the ICT pillars, and Kenya has strengthened its information infrastructure over the past decade or so. Kenya's performance surpasses that of the African region, whereas the performance of Tanzania and Uganda does not. Botswana and Malaysia have slightly improved their recent performance over that in 1995, but South Africa and Thailand have

Effective use of knowledge in any country requires appropriate policies, institutions, investments, and coordination across these four pillars. A country's economic and incentive regime is critical because it describes the framework within which a society and an economy work—in other words, the rules of the game, both formal and informal. And the basic enabler for any country to use knowledge effectively is education—encouraging learning and the exploration of new knowledge, with innovation being a driver of technological change and information and communication technologies (ICTs) providing the mechanisms to reduce transaction costs. These three functional pillars—education, innovation, and ICTs—are the focus of this section. Box 9.1 provides a snapshot of how Tanzania fares in terms of its competitiveness on a global scale.

BOX 9.1 *(continued)*

not. Thus, this relative comparison shows that even though a country can make progress, it can still fall relatively behind because the world as a whole may have made much more significant improvement in the variables that are used to track knowledge- and innovation-related performance.

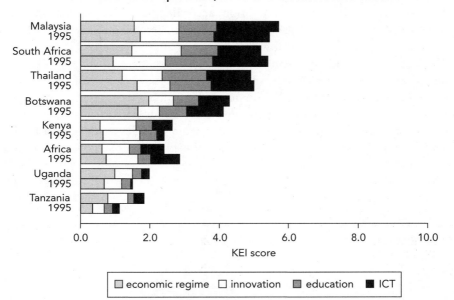

Tanzania and Comparators, 1995 and Most Recent Period

Source: World Bank's Knowledge Assessment Methodology, http://www.worldbank.org/kam.
Note: The two bars represent the aggregate KEI score for a selected country for the most recent year for which data are available and for 1995, split into four pillars: economic incentive regime (in light gray), innovation (in white), education (in dark gray), and ICT (in black). Each color band represents the contribution of a particular pillar to a country's overall knowledge readiness.

Education

Well-educated and skilled people are key for creating, sharing, disseminating, and using knowledge effectively to spur growth and innovation. Ideally, countries need to develop flexible education systems, starting with basic education, which provides the foundation for learning; moving next to secondary and tertiary education, which can develop core skills, including technical ones that encourage creative and critical thinking for problem solving and innovation; and moving finally to a system of lifelong learning. Developing countries such as Tanzania face many challenges in developing such systems. They include expanding coverage to achieve universal access to basic and secondary education; providing tertiary education, which is generally weak;

improving the links between formal and informal education systems and the labor market; and raising the overall quality of learning.

Tanzania's economy today is largely market oriented and has in place many elements required for private sector–led growth. However, it does not have the sound base of an adequately qualified and trained workforce, which is essential for rapid economic growth and effective diversification of its production and export bases. Figure 9.1 shows that in 2001 Tanzania's adult literacy rate (77 percent) was higher than that of Uganda (69 percent) but lower than that of Botswana (79 percent), Kenya (84 percent), and South Africa (86 percent). In addition, according to figure 9.2, Tanzania's average number of years of schooling in 2000 (3.4) was higher than in Uganda (3.22), lower than in Kenya (5.08), and far below the average in South Africa (7.22).

The recent focus on investment in primary and secondary education, if sustained, promises accelerated increases in literacy and average years of schooling in the medium to long term. In recent years, the Tanzanian government has recognized the need to raise educational levels in the population as a necessary condition for enhancing economic growth. The general education system in Tanzania includes seven years of primary education, four years of lower secondary education, and two years of upper secondary education. Appropriate programs for primary and secondary education have been put in place to enhance access to and increase the quality of education. Key measures so

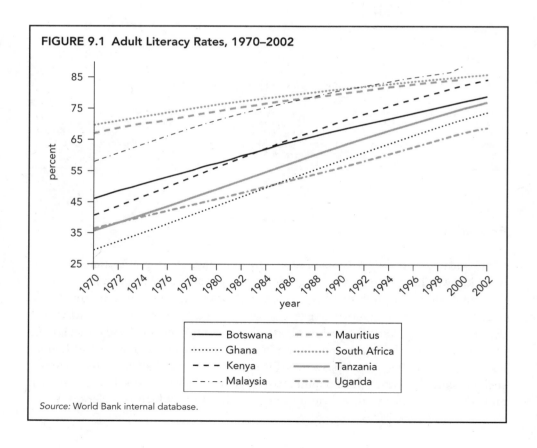

FIGURE 9.1 Adult Literacy Rates, 1970–2002

Source: World Bank internal database.

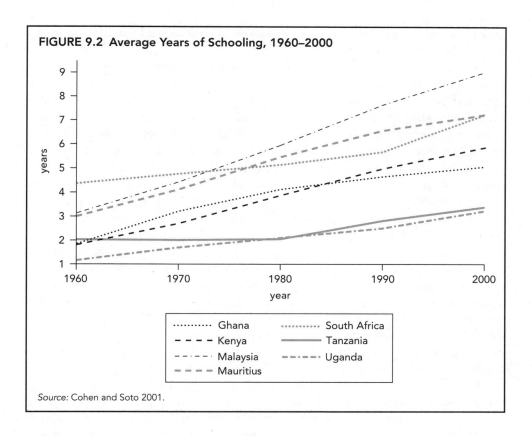

FIGURE 9.2 Average Years of Schooling, 1960–2000

Source: Cohen and Soto 2001.

far have included the abolition of primary school fees in 2001, significant increases in budgetary funding for primary education, and the implementation of the Primary Education Development Program (PEDP). Under this program, Tanzania's gross enrollment ratios for primary education increased from 78 percent in 2000 to 106 percent in 2004. The net enrollment ratio increased from 59 percent in 2000 to 91 percent in 2004. Girls represent 49 percent of the total.

A key challenge for government is to focus more on improving the quality of primary education. In terms of inputs, the availability of textbooks has also improved. On average, before the PEDP was launched, eight students shared one book on each subject. In 2003, the book-to-pupil ratio improved to 1:4. The government's target was to reach a ratio of 1:1 by 2006. Teachers' knowledge and mastery of the curriculum have also improved through preservice and in-service teacher training interventions. The proportion of grade A teachers (those with secondary-level education) increased from 46 percent in 1999 to 58 percent in 2004. However, more qualified teachers are still needed (World Bank 2005c). The PEDP has strengthened institutional capacity and management of education, as measured by the enhanced capacity in the Ministry of Education and Culture to provide policy and guidelines and monitor education delivery. It has led to decentralization and delivery of primary education through regional administration offices, district wards, and schools and has strengthened community participation and school-level management and accountability. Resource availability and use of resources have also improved, as measured by increased nonsalary expenditures in the primary school budget.

With respect to secondary education, Tanzania has one of the lowest net enrollment ratios in Sub-Saharan Africa. Only about 9 percent of the relevant age group attends secondary education, compared with an average of 27 percent for Sub-Saharan Africa in 2000, including about 11 percent in lower secondary school and less than 2 percent in upper secondary school. Only 22 percent of primary school leavers in Tanzania have a chance to continue their education at the secondary level, compared with 50 percent in Uganda in 2001. Secondary enrollment ratios are low for all population groups, but especially for low-income youth and students in rural areas. Few government schools have been established, and inadequate incentives exist to provide nongovernment schools in rural communities, because households are unable to pay the fees required (World Bank 2004d).

Three main challenges face Tanzania in secondary education: increasing access, raising quality, and reducing costs. To support reforms in secondary education, the government has launched the Secondary Education Development Program (SEDP), which has among its aims increasing the proportion of the relevant age group completing lower and upper secondary education, expanding enrollment with equity, improving the learning outcomes of students (especially among girls), and enabling the public administration to manage secondary education more effectively. To expand enrollment with equity, the SEDP includes measures to make more efficient use of resources, provide development grants to schools and communities (mainly those in underserved areas), expand teacher supply, lower household costs for secondary education, expand the scholarship program for students from poor families, and enhance the partnership with the nongovernmental sector. The program for quality improvement includes curricula and examination reforms, provision of textbooks and teaching materials through capitation grants to schools, and quality improvements in preservice teacher training together with establishment of a system for professional in-service teacher development. The program also includes institutional reforms and capacity building at the central, region, district, and school levels for more efficient operation of the secondary education system.

The results of the Southern and Eastern Africa Consortium for Monitoring Educational Quality (SACMEQ) II (2000–03)[1] for primary schools show high reading and math scores for Tanzania's mainland compared with other countries. In reading, Tanzania's mainland placed third, behind Seychelles and Kenya, while on math scores, it is fifth, behind Mauritius, Kenya, Seychelles, and Mozambique (figure 9.3).

In tertiary education, Tanzania's performance is very weak: tertiary gross enrollment ratios stood at 0.94 percent in 2002, compared with 3.24 percent for Uganda and 3.52 percent for Kenya in 2001 and 4.69 percent for Botswana and 15.05 percent for South Africa in 2002.[2] In the 2000/01 academic year, there were 6,117 students at the University of Dar es Salaam and 13,442 in total in the country's three universities (University of Dar es Salaam, Sokoine University of Agriculture, and the Tanzania Open University). In April 2001, an education fund was established to sponsor children from very poor families to complete higher education. But in the past 10 years, a number of private universities have also emerged, and today the country has nine

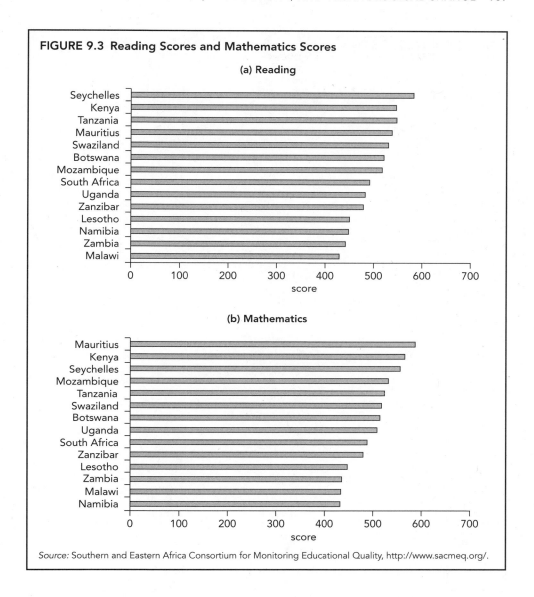

FIGURE 9.3 Reading Scores and Mathematics Scores

(a) Reading

(b) Mathematics

Source: Southern and Eastern Africa Consortium for Monitoring Educational Quality, http://www.sacmeq.org/.

private universities, mostly small and denominational, which award diplomas in financial and business management, wildlife management, community development, social welfare and cooperatives, and transport and media operations (ESRF 2002).

Söderbom and others (2004) examined the returns to education in the manufacturing sector in Tanzania. Their findings suggest that the marginal returns to education for primary and secondary education are rather limited. However, the data suggest a sharp increase in the returns for people who have a tertiary education (figure 9.4). One of the implications of these findings is that the effect on growth in the manufacturing sector of more primary and secondary education is likely to be small, but greater investment in tertiary education has higher payoffs (Söderbom and others 2004).

FIGURE 9.4 Predicted Earnings in Manufacturing Sector Based on Manufacturing Firm Surveys

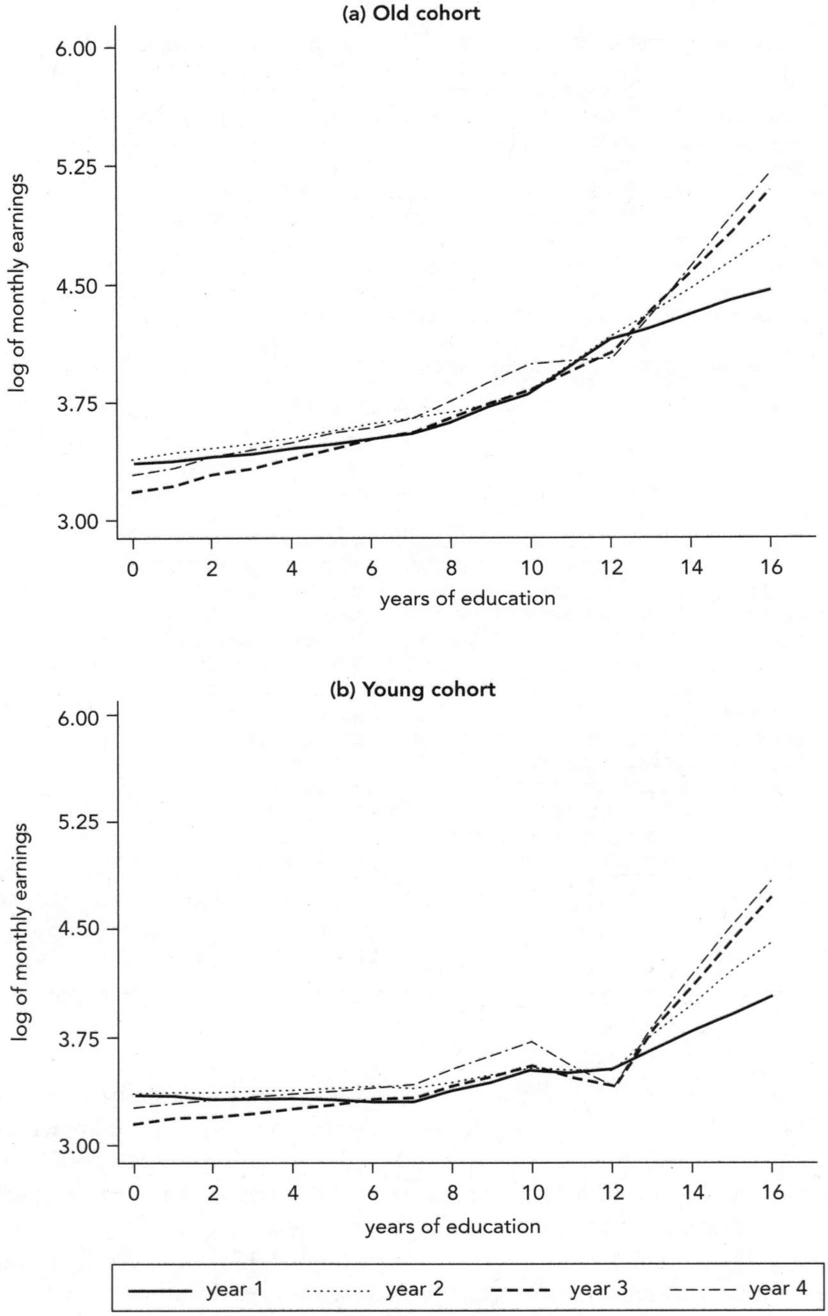

Source: Söderbom and others 2004.

The analysis of the 2000/01 Integrated Labor Force Survey in Tanzania shows the value of secondary education to the individual Tanzanian (figure 9.5). In a sample of more than 3,000 wage earners between the ages of 18 and 65, more than half had completed primary education, a quarter had completed lower secondary (form IV), and 5 percent had completed upper secondary (form VI). Of the sample, 33 percent were female and 23 percent resided in rural areas. The average hourly wage for these wage earners amounted to approximately T Sh 400, but it ranged from roughly T Sh 200 for those with primary education to more than T Sh 700 for those with secondary education. Disparities between rural and urban earners and between genders were sizable (World Bank 2004d).

The difference in the profile of marginal social returns to education for workers in the manufacturing sector and for workers in the overall labor force may suggest that at the tertiary level certain degree programs are well rewarded by the manufacturing sector but that many other degree programs result in lower-paying jobs. The implication would be to shift the supply of higher education to those programs that seem to be in demand by the manufacturing sector. The difference in the profiles of social returns to education also suggests that, for the manufacturing sector, a limited supply of workers with relevant tertiary education is a constraint, while for other sectors the limited supply of workers with secondary education may be more of a constraint.

The government has been the major financier of technical and vocational education and training (TVET), with assistance from donors. But the TVET system faces several problems in terms of inefficient use of resources, inequitable distribution of

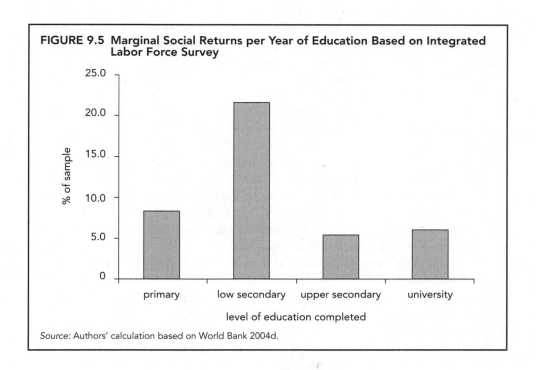

FIGURE 9.5 Marginal Social Returns per Year of Education Based on Integrated Labor Force Survey

Source: Authors' calculation based on World Bank 2004d.

educational opportunities, poor links to the labor market, and lack of coordination between donors and the government. The unsustainable costs of training appear to be caused not only by low use of capacity, but also by low student-to-faculty ratios, whereas the inequitable distribution of education opportunities is biased toward primary schools for students from wealthier backgrounds. Recognizing that the TVET system had failed to produce graduates who were suited for the labor market, the government introduced policy changes in 1996 that emphasize its continued responsibility for the provision and financing of more and better basic education, coupled with a reduction in untargeted subsidies through increased cost sharing, liberalization of private education and training at all levels, and decentralization of authority. The Vocational Training and Education Authority, set up in 1994, is working to ensure that the training that is provided is responsive to the labor market (Gill and Dar 1998).

Africa is a capital-scarce region, and the loss of this limited resource is widely considered detrimental to the prospects of sustained growth and development. There is a significant parallel to this problem on the side of human capital. Weakness in human capital—and particularly skill deficiency—is a drag on investment and growth in Africa. Progress in overcoming shortages of skilled and trained workers seems to be disappointingly slow, despite the substantial resources devoted by both governments and donors to this effort during the past three decades. This deficiency is sustained at a time when Africa is losing a very significant proportion of its skilled and professional workers to other markets and increasingly depending on expatriates for many vital functions. Although comparatively Africa is the smallest source of immigration to the industrial world, a high proportion of its migrants is made up of highly skilled professionals. For example, it has been estimated that more than 30 percent of highly skilled professionals in a number of African countries are lost to the countries of the Organisation for Economic Co-operation and Development (OECD). Nearly 88 percent of adults who emigrate from Africa to the United States have at least a high school education. More African scientists and engineers work in the United States than in Africa. The emigration of technically skilled people has left 20,000 scientists and engineers in Africa serving 600 million people.

Tanzania is no stranger to brain drain. The most vulnerable professions at the national level include medicine, accounting, law, engineering, and science. As a proxy for the national picture, data from two premier institutions of higher learning provide some interesting evidence. Out of a teaching staff of about 861, about 149 staff members (17.3 percent) left the University of Dar es Salaam between 1990 and March 2002. The majority of those who left were from the Faculty of Arts and Social Sciences (38), followed by the Faculties of Medicine (17), Engineering (13), Law (11), Science (10), and Commerce (9). Most of them exited at the senior lecturer and lecturer levels. The same was true at the Sokoine University of Agriculture. Out of a staff of 239 people, about 50 (21 percent) left in the same period. Again, the majority who left were either lecturers or senior lecturers (ESRF 2002).

In medicine, Tanzania is also facing a massive skills loss, especially of doctors and scientists. Low salaries for doctors are the principal reason driving the brain drain—and those who remain seek higher wages in private hospitals in large urban centers, leading to a lack of doctors in some of the country's district hospitals. In a bid to increase the number of health professionals in the country, the Tanzanian government

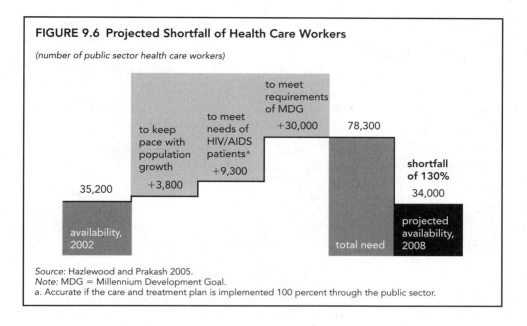

FIGURE 9.6 Projected Shortfall of Health Care Workers

(number of public sector health care workers)

to meet
requirements
of MDG

to meet
needs of
HIV/AIDS
patients[a]

to keep
pace with
population
growth

+30,000   78,300

+9,300

+3,800

35,200

availability,
2002

shortfall
of 130%

34,000

projected
availability,
2008

total need

Source: Hazlewood and Prakash 2005.
Note: MDG = Millennium Development Goal.
a. Accurate if the care and treatment plan is implemented 100 percent through the public sector.

has recently promised to cover all training costs for medical students in both public and private universities (Balile 2003).

The brain drain also has an effect on the development of human resources in Tanzania, especially given the AIDS crisis. A recent article (Hazlewood and Prakash 2005) reiterates the fact that Tanzania faces an acute shortage of health care workers. Low pay, poor working conditions, and limited training programs contribute to the problem, which is exacerbated by the rising burden of treating HIV/AIDS patients. Hazlewood and Prakash estimate that Tanzania will have to find nearly 10,000 more workers to address the rising needs of HIV/AIDS patients and three times that number to meet the Millennium Development Goals (MDGs) (figure 9.6). However, improving the productivity of individual health care workers and of the health care system as a whole could increase Tanzania's capacity by two-thirds, even without additional workers. Some improvements, such as providing telephones and motorbikes for better communication, would be relatively easy to make; others, such as managing the flow of patients more satisfactorily and implementing planning and accounting tools, would require more investment and training. Making these changes requires that health organizations and the government increase the capacity of their training programs by at least half to ensure a sustainable workforce and aggressively recruit trained workers to alleviate the immediate shortages.

Innovation

Innovation can be understood as the diffusion of a new or improved technology or practice in a given environment. Two levels of innovation are particularly relevant for developing countries: at the micro level, there is the diffusion of available technologies for use by firms, individuals, or households to help improve their productivity, welfare, living conditions, and so on; at the sectoral level, there is the development of new industries, generally based on foreign technologies, that can be a source of new jobs, income, and exports. Thus, innovation can contribute to poverty reduction by

- fueling economic growth, as it forms the basis of new activities, industries, or services that can generate wealth and jobs;

- inducing productivity gains, which are also a source of wealth as well as a means of maintaining jobs from foreign or other types of competition; and

- maintaining the self-sustainability of local communities, for example, through the adoption of appropriate technologies.

Role of the Government

A recent study by the World Bank (Chandra 2006) focuses on examples of innovation from low- and medium-income countries and identifies a host of government actions that are essential to the development of competitive industries.[3] In order of importance, first are actions that make available appropriate skills and provide support for technology acquisition and development. Next are actions of a regulatory nature, such as those relating to standards and quality control. Then come the various types of support that can be provided to enterprises and industry organizations for export promotion, investment, and so on (table 9.1).

Major Issues in Innovation in Tanzania

The innovation climate in Tanzania presents serious weaknesses. First and foremost is a generally poor business environment coupled with mediocre infrastructure, bureaucratic hurdles, and corruption. The technical culture of the population is also not very developed, as evidenced by high illiteracy rates. In the past, Tanzania had no deliber-

TABLE 9.1 Role of the Public Sector in Fostering Innovation

Industry/country	Spinoffs	Export and investment promotion	Technical acquisition and development	Regulation and compliance	Support to industry organizations	Technical skills development
Electronics, Malaysia	X	X	X			X
Electronics, Taiwan, China	X		X			X
IT, India		X	X	X	X	X
Maize, India			X	X		X
Grapes, India			X	X	X	X
Oil palm, Malaysia	X	X	X	X	X	X
Salmon, Chile	X		X	X		X
Wine, Chile	X	X	X		X	X
Nile perch, Uganda			X	X		X
Cut flowers, Kenya				X	X	X

Source: Based on Chandra 2006.

ate strategies or plans for appropriate selection, acquisition, and transfer of technology or for effective integration of imported technologies with local capacity for R&D. However, in 1985, it enacted the first National Science and Technology policy, which was revised in 1995. The major thrust of this policy was to establish relative priorities and programs to generate new knowledge and to determine strategies for science and technology (S&T) development. The government also established the Tanzania Commission for Science and Technology in 1986 and the Centre for the Development and Transfer of Technology (CDTT) in 1994, in an effort to institute workable mechanisms for coordinating capacity-building efforts, adopting new technologies, strengthening R&D, and facilitating information exchange and extension services.[4] Although these are laudable initiatives, the reality is that these institutions, especially the CDTT, lack adequate resources, infrastructure, equipment, and trained personnel to respond to the increased needs of the local entrepreneurial society and to develop a coherent science and technology policy.

The low level of R&D as a percentage of gross domestic product (GDP)—only 0.2 percent (comparable with other African countries)—reflects the modest nature of Tanzania's research and innovative effort. Other more sophisticated indexes such as the United Nations Development Programme's Technology Achievement Index, which includes measures of the diffusion of new technologies (such as computers) as well as of the technical qualifications of the population, confirm the low technological capabilities of the country (box 9.2).

Research and Development in Tanzania

There are about 62 R&D institutions in Tanzania, covering agriculture, including livestock and forestry (28); industry (11); health care (11); wildlife and fisheries (4); and universities and other higher learning institutions (9) (ESRF 2002).[5] Most of these entities are government institutions; objectives include conducting scientific research and designing and manufacturing machinery and equipment for agriculture, as well as appropriate technologies for rural businesses and small and medium-size industrial enterprises.

However, these institutions lack real incentive schemes for researchers to conduct this type of research; as a result, only a few researchers tend to be very instrumental in R&D activities. In the main, there is a crucial lack of resources for R&D institutes, as a result of a deliberate liberalization policy of the government. Such institutes are increasingly facing reduced support from the government and are therefore undertaking reforms to become independent executive agencies. They are looking for new lines of business that could make a profit and thus enable them to meet their personnel and operational expenses. This trend is worrying because it distracts these institutions from conducting research of a more public goods nature that could benefit society as a whole. Mechanisms for technology diffusion are also modestly developed, with a near absence of decentralized structures such as agriculture extension services.

Foreign direct investment (FDI) is an important source of technological upgrading in developing countries. There is no doubt that in Tanzania, FDI—which is relatively high compared with other African countries—has played a key role in the modernization of important sectors of the economy such as trade (retail), banking, tourism, and

---

BOX 9.2 The United Nations Development Programme's Technology Achievement Index

In its *Human Development Report 2001*, the United Nations Development Programme (UNDP) introduced the Technology Achievement Index (TAI), which tries to capture how well a country is creating and diffusing technology and building a human skill base—reflecting its capacity to participate in the technological innovations of the network age. This composite index is not a measure of which country is leading in global technology development but focuses on how well the country as a whole is participating in creating and using technology. The index recognizes that a nation's technological achievements are larger and more complex than any index can capture. It is impossible to reflect the full range of technologies—from agriculture to medicine to manufacturing. Many aspects of technology creation, technology diffusion, and human skills are hard to quantify. And even if they could be quantified, a lack of reliable data makes it impossible to fully reflect them. For example, important technological innovations occur in the informal sector and in indigenous knowledge systems, but they are not recorded and cannot be quantified.

Thus, the TAI focuses on three dimensions of innovation at the country level: creation of new products and processes through R&D, use of new technologies and old in production and consumption, and availability of skills for technological learning and innovation. Countries are ranked in four categories: leaders, potential leaders, dynamic adopters, and the marginalized. The results show three trends: a map of great disparities among countries, with TAI values ranging from 0.744 for Finland to 0.066 for Mozambique; diversity and dynamism in technological progress among developing countries; and a map of technology hubs superimposed on countries at different levels of development. Tanzania and Kenya are both listed as marginalized (below 0.20)—which means that technology diffusion and skill building have a long way to go in these countries and that large parts of the population have not benefited from the diffusion of technology.

Source: UNDP 2001.

---

the telecommunication networks. It has also been crucial in the take-off and growth of new industries such as fishing and gold mining. But, as shown by the international experience, it takes time to build an indigenous innovative capability through foreign investment. It requires explicit mechanisms such as the employment of large contingents of local cadres in managerial positions, as well as programs to closely link local suppliers of components and materials to upgrade the suppliers' equipment and the quality of their products. Such mechanisms do not exist in Tanzania; consequently, the transfer of knowledge and technology from foreign sources remains modest. Box 9.3 provides an example of constraints to technology access in the horticulture sector in Tanzania.

Policy Proposal for Developing a Nationwide Innovation Support Scheme

In addition to improving the overall business environment and upgrading the education system, Tanzania must develop specific actions for the promotion of innovation and technology diffusion in order to put its R&D infrastructure at the service of the country's development. There is a need for a systemic approach that provides complementary support on three basic aspects: financial, technical, and regulatory.

BOX 9.3 Constraints to Technology Access in the Horticulture Sector in Tanzania

The horticultural sector has become an important contributor to exports in Tanzania. Nonetheless, Tanzania's performance significantly lags behind that of Kenya, which has made important strides in increasing its market share for horticultural exports. It is useful to analyze the constraints to technology access in this sector and, in particular, the barriers to the introduction of improved varieties of seeds and pest control technologies, with the aim not only of identifying constraints, but also of deriving some lessons for other sectors.

The most important finding is that it is not formal import restrictions that pose constraints to the introduction of technologies used in other countries to Tanzania, but rather the underlying regulations and institutions that impede such access, as well as a lack of information. In the case of access to pesticides, for example, the most impeding factors are the unclear institutional framework governing registration processes and the cumbersome, long, and expensive registration process. The registration of agrochemical pesticides can cost up to US$7,550 and can take as long as two years. Furthermore, the horticultural sector in Tanzania, as compared with that in Kenya, suffers from a backlog of registered pesticides that are urgently needed. The introduction of biological control agents is even more cumbersome and time consuming. Different issues are at stake concerning the introduction of new seed varieties. The transfer of knowledge regarding new seed varieties often does not take place because smallholder farmers buy from stockists, who have little knowledge of how to handle these seeds. Another constraining factor is the lack of awareness regarding the recently adopted Plant Breeder's Rights (PBRs).

Some recommendations that can help to improve the introduction of improved varieties of seeds and pest control technologies include the following:

- *Streamline legislation.* After the review by the Natural Resources Institute, University of Greenwich, has been completed, legislation should be streamlined in line with recommendations in order to close loopholes and make the process of registration more transparent. Clear institutional arrangements regarding the Tropical Pesticides Research Institute and the registrar are needed.
- *Create harmonization within the East African Community.* Working groups on pesticides exist in the East African Community (EAC). Reciprocal recognition of registration within the EAC should be encouraged as an important outcome of this process.
- *Recognize Kenyan registration.* Given that the process of reciprocal recognition among EAC countries may take time, Tanzania should automatically register pesticides that are already registered in Kenya.
- *Implement quality control inspections of and provide training to stockists.* Stockists should be frequently inspected to ensure the quality of seeds and pesticides. These inspections would help to eliminate the circulation of counterfeit products. Stockists and smallholder farmers should receive training to increase awareness of the benefits of hybrid seeds and use of improved varieties. Public-private partnerships are an option, given the interest of seed importers in increasing sales of their products.
- Dissemination of information about the PBRs. Given the domestic as well as international lack of awareness that Tanzania now has the PBRs in place, efforts to inform stakeholders are essential. Efforts should also be increased at an international level to attract foreign direct investment and to stimulate innovation in this area.

Source: Skof 2006.

Financial Support

There is a crucial lack of resources on the demand side for accelerating the design, testing, use, and dissemination of technologies. We suggest that Tanzania establish two complementary schemes, which are based on simple matching fund principles. The schemes would provide—in grant form—50 percent of the funding required for the development (R&D phase) of small and medium-size projects (for example, up to US$20,000):

- *User scheme.* This scheme would allow particular groups and communities to buy needed technologies and provide, if appropriate, complementary in-kind funding (labor for community purposes).

- *Developer scheme.* This scheme would fund 50 percent of technical services or R&D projects undertaken by small and medium-size enterprises with R&D institutes (public, academic, and so forth). It would thereby help—indirectly, but more effectively—the R&D institutes use their competencies to serve communities. (This type of scheme is in place in a number of industrial countries.)

It is important that the management of such support schemes be carried out primarily at subnational levels. Regional and local commissions would screen and select projects with the support of appropriate experts (including foreign ones). This screening and selection process is a primary condition that is necessary to have efficient management and to reduce the bureaucracy that would ineluctably affect schemes administered at the central level. The central level, however, would have to have oversight and control the overall process.

Technical Support

On the basis of experience accumulated in industrial countries, we suggested that a network of locally based and owned structures be established to serve the needs of rural and urban communities for technical advice, information, and assistance (in design, marketing, and so forth). These structures should be adapted to different sectors (for example, extension services for agriculture and design and manufacturing workshops for industry). They should also be conceived and operated as antennas of central bodies to which they would be strongly connected through information technology (IT), databases, and the like. They should be established on a clearly expressed demand from local communities and funded on a 50/50 cost-sharing basis, with local organizations (municipalities, business or farmer associations, and so forth) matching the resources put in by the central government.

Regulatory Support

Regulatory-related actions must be implemented to deal with several issues:

- Proposed actions that aim to stimulate service-based contracts and formalize new links between the business sector and the R&D infrastructure require the establishment of clear legal and administrative procedures. We therefore recommend reviewing, adjusting, and standardizing appropriate models for such relationships. Many issues may be involved, including the use of public or university laboratory equipment and personnel by firms, the temporary employment of university researchers by business enterprises, and intellectual property rights.

- In many sectors, there is a need to develop quality awareness and quality control, as well as related accreditation and certification procedures. A program should be implemented to raise awareness of these issues, because doing so could yield important results in a short time span.

- Firms or individuals that are first producers face major financial problems and frequently do not get access to credit from the banking system. The government's recently established credit guarantee mechanism, which is supposed to mobilize the banking and financial sector, does not seem to be working well. An audit needs to be undertaken to examine in detail the mechanisms that can be put in place to complement this incentive, such as microcredit schemes; equity investment procedures (such as the Dutch Program for Cooperation with Emerging Markets, which supports 30 percent of the investment of individual firms in the flower industry); and the like.

An Innovation Multipurpose Facility

To efficiently implement and fund the multicomponent program proposed here, Tanzania could do well to establish a new ad hoc facility—an innovation multipurpose facility—that is endowed with a critical mass of funds and that operates with maximum flexibility in the use of the types of policy actions outlined above. The facility could be administered at the level of the president's office. Funding needs can be estimated at US$10 million to US$15 million per year. If matched by equivalent spending from the private sector (which currently spends almost nothing), this amount would double the current national S&T expenditure, reaching 0.5 percent of GDP. That expenditure could reach full scale three to four years after an initial pilot phase, which would possibly be focused on a few specific industries (discussed next). The effect on the economy would become evident within five years or so. It is suggested that this government support mechanism be modeled on the Tanzania Social Action Fund, which has been efficiently administered at the president's level.

Promotion of Specific Industries

The scheme for an innovation multipurpose facility could be focused on specific priority industries, including the tourism sector and the agro-foods industry. The first is already an important source of income; the second would take advantage of the large agriculture base. Systemic, well-focused action is needed in both industries.

- In tourism, such actions include a general campaign of quality control and accreditation of hotels and related facilities throughout the country, efficient enforcement mechanisms for ensuring the respect for and compliance with the defined standards, an international campaign of marketing and promotion of the tourism advantages of Tanzania in selected countries of the industrial world, and adequate financial support to Tanzanian firms and organizations intending to improve or create new services.

• For the agro-foods sector, it is important to consider the different types of production (vegetables, cereals, fruits, meat, and so forth) and the missing links that need to be constituted or consolidated, from the basic producer level to the market (both local and export). Adequate actions then must be undertaken, including food quality control and insurance, improvement of testing facilities, support of packaging enterprises and distribution channels, and systematic scouting of foreign knowledge and technologies of potential use in Tanzania. These measures should be closely coordinated with programs that aim to improve agricultural productivity and diversity, notably as funded by the World Bank (such as the Second Tanzania Agricultural Research Project).

The involvement of foreign enterprises in both sectors is crucial. These enterprises provide access to foreign markets, provide management competencies, and introduce up-to-date technologies. It is important to establish a liaison with Tanzanian enterprise associations, which are efficient organizations for negotiating and partnering with foreign businesses. Clear contracts regarding technology licensing, personnel training, and access to export markets should be developed. On the whole, a two-pronged action strategy combining both upgrading and developing domestic capabilities and involving foreign actors would be essential for a successful innovation intervention to help improve Tanzania's growth prospects.

Information and Communication Technologies

Rapid advances in ICTs are dramatically affecting economic and social activities, as well as the acquisition, creation, dissemination, and use of knowledge. These advances are affecting the way in which manufacturers, service providers, and governments are organized and how they perform their functions. As knowledge and innovation become increasingly important elements of competitiveness, the use of ICTs is reducing transaction costs and time and space barriers, thereby allowing the mass production of customized goods and services and substituting for limited factors of production. The pervasive and global ICT revolution is disrupting all kinds of relationships, helping build new types of organizations, widening the knowledge and productivity gap, and posing serious risks for the unprepared. It thus calls for countries such as Tanzania to develop capabilities to master the new technologies and harness the full potential of ICTs for all sectors of the economy for education, innovation, and learning; public sector management; private sector competitiveness; and capacity building.

Research also shows strong links between ICTs and growth. Compelling evidence exists that strengthening telecommunications infrastructure and service is pivotal in promoting trade and economic growth. It is estimated, for example, that a 10 percent decrease in the bilateral price of phone calls is associated with an 8 percent increase in bilateral trade (Fink, Mattoo, and Neagu 2002). In Africa, significant evidence suggests that if the telephone growth rate were 10 percent instead of 5 percent (and if growth in electricity generation were 6 percent instead of 2 percent), the increase in Africa's growth rate would be at least 0.9 percent higher (Estache 2005).

Information infrastructure consists of telecommunications networks, strategic information systems, and policy and legal frameworks affecting their deployment, as well as skilled human resources needed to develop and use it. In the ICT domain, Kenya, Tanzania, and Uganda are all at a very nascent stage of application and use. It is not surprising that all three countries lag Botswana, Malaysia, and South Africa by a huge margin, as can be seen in figure 9.7. Mauritius, by contrast, has been doing better than Botswana and South Africa on telephony and personal computer (PC) penetration and is close to the level of Malaysia. In the case of Internet hosts, South Africa and Malaysia are the undisputed leaders.

A recent report by the United Nations Conference on Trade and Development (UNCTAD) also provides some insights into the international digital divide. It evaluates ICT development using a range of indicators to benchmark connectivity, access, ICT policy, and overall ICT diffusion in 165 countries. In the benchmarking analysis, OECD countries continue to dominate the upper rankings, while South Asian and African countries occupy the lower half of the rankings. The more developed African countries enter the rankings relatively early, with Mauritius 52nd and South Africa 66th. Botswana comes in 80th, while Kenya is ranked 115th, Tanzania 135th, and Uganda 154th, indicating that many Sub-Saharan Africa countries have a considerable way to go in terms of ICT connectivity and diffusion (UNCTAD 2005).

Tanzania has been making some progress. In 2003, it published a cross-sectoral National ICT Policy (http://www.moct.go.tz/ict) that relates ICTs to relevant sectors of the economy, such as education, manufacturing, health, and tourism. The policy was developed in response to the poor harmonization of initiatives that has led to random adoption of different systems and standards, unnecessary duplication of effort, and waste of scarce resources, especially through the loss of potential synergies. The policy notes that the weak ICT infrastructure and the lack of adequately trained and skilled personnel are the main barriers to increased adoption of ICTs in Tanzania. This broad-based national strategy is designed to correct these weaknesses by addressing Tanzania's developmental agenda and calling for the creation of appropriate institutional arrangements to ensure that all stakeholders can rise to the challenge of implementing the ICT policy. It is worth mentioning that stakeholder discussions on ICT policy and related issues were held mainly through an e-mail list of e–think tanks— an ICT fraternity, comprising representatives from government, the private sector, and civil society.

Even though the government's ICT policy addresses issues related to rationalization and coordination, it fails to loop in the productive economic sectors. Expenditure on

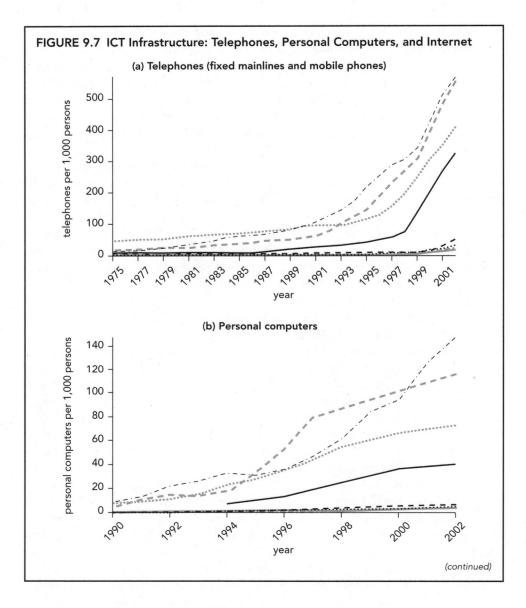

FIGURE 9.7 ICT Infrastructure: Telephones, Personal Computers, and Internet

(a) Telephones (fixed mainlines and mobile phones)

(b) Personal computers

(continued)

building infrastructure and training should be strategic investments after the needs and demands of the private sector are addressed—specifically, which firms can benefit the most from ICT, leading to appropriate allocation of scarce resources.

In the telecommunications sector, the policy, legal, and regulatory framework has been encouraging private sector participation.[6] This sector is regulated by the Tanzania Communications Regulatory Authority (TCRA). The performance of the Tanzanian Telecommunications Company Limited (TTCL) has improved considerably since February 2001, when a Dutch-German consortium, Celtel, took a 35 percent stake in it. The remaining shares were allocated to local financial institutions (14 percent),

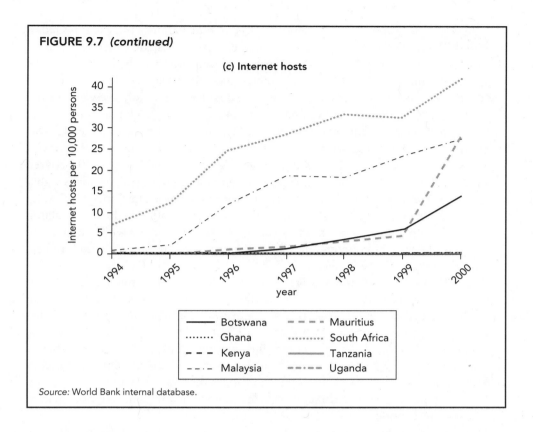

FIGURE 9.7 *(continued)*

(c) Internet hosts

Source: World Bank internal database.

international financial institutions (10 percent), and TTCL employees (5 percent); the government retained a 36 percent stake. At present, TTCL has about 250,000 operational lines (InfoDev 2005).

The sector liberalization and the privatization of TTCL have had a significant effect on the market dynamics, particularly in the supply of telecommunications services. Market revenues grew from US$143 million in 1998 to US$389 million in 2003. The compound annual growth rate is 19 percent. Overall teledensity grew from 0.3 in 1998 to 2.57 in 2003, and the mobile market has grown 21.19 percent since liberalization and the introduction of competition, new products, and new services.

Despite the competition, tariffs remain high and teledensity is one of the lowest in the South African Development Community (SADC), in part due to the poor interconnection framework and the lack of regulatory independence and also because of other issues, such as lack of infrastructure sharing. Thus, in general, Tanzania's postal and telecommunications services are weak, and the provision of fixed telephone lines has been meager. An inadequate regulatory framework persists, and competition has been hampered by various issues, such as inadequate interconnection agreements and directives, high fees and royalties levied by the TCRA, and the absence or nontransparency of regulatory oversight.

Progress made under the 1997 National Telecommunications Policy is expected to continue. The mobile telephone market is fully competitive. Significant liberalization has also taken place in various segments: private operators now provide basic, mobile, data, paging, Internet, payphone, and other value-added services. The mobile telephone market involves a number of operators and is growing rapidly. New mobile operators have committed significant financial resources to the development of a state-of-the-art telecommunications infrastructure. Four providers operate under 15-year licenses: MIC Tanzania, Zanzibar Telecoms, Vodacom, and Celtel. As a result, overall teledensity—mainlines plus mobile phones—increased to 24 per 1,000 between 1996 and 2003 (table 9.2). Tanzania's mainline and mobile phone penetration is higher than Uganda's. Anecdotal evidence also exists that mobile phones are increasingly being used in Tanzania to get business-related information and to reduce transaction costs. For example, traders in Dar es Salaam now can place orders with producers of bananas throughout the country—thus linking demand and supply in real time and enhancing the efficiency of markets.

Tanzania also has a comprehensive Internet service, including three licensed data-service providers and 21 Internet service providers. Most users access the Internet from urban Internet cafés—the Internet is not very accessible in the rural areas. Tanzania in 2003 had twice as many Internet users (250,000) as Uganda (125,000). The government has developed a fairly comprehensive national Web site (http://www.tanzania.go.tz/), which provides considerable background information on the economy and political structure of the country; it hopes the site will help raise the country's international profile and attract foreign investment. In addition, a number of ministries, state institutions, and embassies have their own sites.

In terms of developing human resources in IT, training centers that focus on the development of ICT knowledge workers are only now beginning to emerge. For example, the Soft Tech Training Center, established in 1993, is committed to developing local expertise through ICT skills enhancement. The government has also initiated plans to encourage Tanzanians to develop content that is relevant to local interests, and Tanzania has implemented several ICT applications relevant to its national objectives.

TABLE 9.2 ICT Indicators for Tanzania and Comparators

Country	1996–2003 (per 1,000)				2002 Personal computers (per 1,000)	2000 Internet hosts (per 10,000)	2003 Internet users (per 1,000)
	Mainlines	Mobile telephones	Radios	Televisions			
Botswana	87	241	150	44	40.7	13.99	50[a]
Kenya	10	42	221	26	6.4	0.32	200[a]
South Africa	107	304	336	177	72.6	41.94	2,890[a]
Tanzania	5	19	406	4	4.18	0.16	240
Uganda	2	16	122	18	3.32	0.07	125
Sub-Saharan Africa, average	15	37	198	69	11.90	3.10	6,233

Source: World Bank 2004a, 2005a.
a. Denotes data for 2001.

Examples of such initiatives include an information system to strengthen the capacity of wildlife institutions and a computerized case-flow management system that has facilitated an increase in transparency and professionalism in the judiciary system (Accenture, Markle Foundation, and UNDP 2001).

Summary of Issues and Recommendations

Some measures that can help strengthen Tanzania's performance in the three functional pillars are highlighted here.

Education

Key challenges facing Tanzania in this domain include the following:

- Sustaining and improving the quality of education as enrollments increase by recruiting teachers, constructing classrooms, increasing preservice teacher training, and providing subsidies for purchasing teaching and learning materials.

- Ramping up secondary education, including improving its quality and relevance to the needs of the economy.

- In higher education, strengthening the governance and administration of the country's three public universities in terms of financial sustainability, up-to-date content, and teacher training.

- Using the potential of distance education to expand access to education services while improving equity. The Open University of Tanzania offers degree programs by correspondence and also in regional centers. The costs are low because the state covers tuition, but enrollments are low, partly because of lack of content and partly because of a dearth of partnerships with international academic institutions that could provide degree programs online. Combining distance-education modalities with extended face-to-face interactions with Tanzania's other public universities may be one way to boost enrollments and increase access to higher education.

- Reforming teaching methods and the curriculum at all levels to include skills and competencies (communication skills, problem-solving skills, creativity, and teamwork) to meet the new needs of the economy.

- Increasing the interface between industry and education and offering differentiated curricula that better meet the new skill demands of industry, generated by changing markets and technologies.

- Harmonizing the technical education offered in secondary schools with that offered in technical colleges and then linking these schools with the proposed zonal and regional institutes and colleges. These institutes and colleges should offer differentiated products to meet the differing needs of industries, such as mining, fisheries, major cash and food crops, external trade, and metal.

- Devising strategies to proactively deal with problems of skills lost through brain drain.

Innovation

To encourage innovation, Tanzania needs to focus on the following efforts:

- Improving the overall business environment (regulatory, tax, bureaucracy, and other aspects) and the basic infrastructure (especially for transport and power), both of which currently create considerable hindrances to any form of innovative activity, even the most modest ones.

- Improving the overall technical culture of the population and notably the technical skills at all levels (from primary schools to university colleges), with particular attention to vocational and professional schools.

- Facilitating access to and use of foreign knowledge and technology by attracting foreign investors and stimulating appropriate transfer through personnel employment and training, links with local suppliers of components, and the like.

- Increasing the resources of the R&D institutes (public and university based), linking them to users' demands and needs.

- Strengthening structures, incentives, and regulations to facilitate the diffusion of up-to-date and appropriate technologies throughout the economy.

- Creating an ad hoc mechanism to promote technological innovation throughout the country and facilitate the dissemination of improved and new technologies. This mechanism would make concrete and focus the overall effort of innovation promotion. Such a scheme, based on decentralized structures and initiatives, should address altogether the financial, technical, and regulatory needs of enterprises as well as those of local communities. At the same time, it should help support the R&D infrastructure by orienting it toward the service of the country's needs. The scheme should give priority to a few important industries such as agro-foods and tourism.

- Conducting a comprehensive nationwide innovation and R&D survey to establish concrete factors that either facilitate or hinder innovative activities in the country. The outcome of the survey can serve to put in place concrete innovation policies and strategies.

Information and Communication Technologies

To strengthen its information infrastructure, Tanzania should continue to pursue the following goals:

- Finalizing and adopting the new electronic communications bill, which is key to defining the ground rules for sector development (including rural areas).

- Implementing the new converged licensing framework, which will ensure further liberalization of the market.

- Reviewing and modernizing telecommunications policies and regulations to generate fair competition and reduce high communication and operational costs.

- Building capacity to undertake such reforms, including through the establishment of systems and processes to review the performance of the regulatory institutions. For example, given the great demands and expectations placed on the regulator (TCRA) by telecommunications sector reforms, the Swedish government, through the Swedish International Development Cooperation Agency, is helping TCRA create capacity to meet its existing and future challenges and learn from its experiences in operating in a more competitive market.

- Supporting the development of rural telecommunications infrastructure, such as by developing universal access schemes. Rural areas lack telecommunications services or have only limited access in areas adjacent to main towns and on major trunk roads. This effort requires developing content in local languages (such as Swahili).

- Enhancing technical and business-related skills development among the population using ICTs through technical institutes and vocational centers. For example, the University of Dar es Salaam is offering IT training in its computer center to the public.

- Continuing to use global experiences to enhance the efficiency of the telecommunications sector. In many areas of telecommunications reform, Tanzania has benefited by adopting best practices from both industrial and developing countries. The functions and roles of the national regulator (TCRA) are the best example. Further benefits from global experience and best practices depend on the capacity of TCRA and other institutions to learn from the experiences of other countries.

Notes

1. In terms of monitoring education quality, the SACMEQ monitors and evaluates the quality of education in selected southern and East African countries. The SACMEQ II Project (2000–03) has been completed in 13 countries: Botswana, Kenya, Lesotho, Malawi, Mauritius, Mozambique, Namibia, the Seychelles, South Africa, Swaziland, Tanzania (separate assessments on both the mainland and Zanzibar), Uganda, and Zambia.

2. These statistics should be viewed in perspective: the countries differ in their systems of postsecondary education. Tanzania has many students enrolled in postsecondary nonuniversity courses; perhaps these schools are not counted in the official statistics.

3. The studies cover the extremes of the industrial spectrum: wheat and maize in India, salmon and wine in Chile, Nile perch in Uganda, oil palm in Malaysia, cut flowers in Kenya, medium-tech electronics in Malaysia, high-tech electronics in Taiwan (China), and software exports from India. The industries are chosen based on exceptional comparative performance in the past decade, large contributions to overall growth, and the role that technological change played in its success (Chandra 2006).

4. For more information, see the science and technology section of the Tanzania Country Profile on Tanzania's national Web site: http://www.tanzania.go.tz/science_technology.html.

5. Tanzania's S&T infrastructure includes education infrastructure and R&D institutions such as the University of Dar es Salaam; Sokoine University of Agriculture; the University College of Lands and Architectural Studies; Muhimbili University College of Health Science;

Rwegalulira Water Resources Institute; and the National College of Mbeya, Arusha, and Dar es Salaam Institute of Technology.

6. For example, Draka Comteq—which consists of 11 companies in Denmark, Finland, France, Germany, the Netherlands, Norway, Singapore, the United Kingdom, and the United States—has recently won a US$30.2 million turnkey project in Tanzania, involving the supply and installation of two long-distance links, covering some 2,300 kilometers of optical fiber cable and 500 kilometers of optical power ground wire (Economist Intelligence Unit 2004a).

10
Enhancing the Business Environment

Michael Wong, Ravi Ruparel, and Peter Mwanakatwe

The quality of the business environment affects the cost of doing business and thus a country's attractiveness to investors and its international competitiveness. The costs of an inefficient business environment are estimated to be very high in Tanzania in international comparisons. They amount to 25 percent of sales and include the cost of contract enforcement difficulties, regulation, bribes, crime, and unreliable infrastructure (figure 10.1).

Figure 10.2 compares the cost structure of firms in a sample of selected countries, dividing the cost of businesses into labor, capital, input, and indirect costs. The effect of a poor business environment on firms is often reflected in high indirect costs. Many African firms incur heavy costs for transport, logistics, telecommunications, water, electricity, land and buildings, marketing, accounting, security bribes, and so forth. Indirect costs as a percentage of total costs, on average, are more than 20 percent in Tanzania, equal to the average cost of labor. In a global economy, where Tanzanian products compete with those of countries such as China and India, high indirect costs are a severe impediment to economic activity. In China, indirect costs are only about 8 percent of total costs; in Tanzania, they are about 24 percent of total costs. In addition, factors that affect indirect costs also affect the costs of other inputs and thus lead to a loss of competitiveness in the economy that exceeds the loss at the firm level.

An investment climate assessment carried out in 2003 (World Bank 2004c) suggests that the tax system, high-cost credit and limited access to credit, limited availability and poor reliability of infrastructure services, and red tape in the public sector are the principal constraints to even higher growth rates (figure 10.3).

This chapter focuses on three aspects of the business environment that promise the highest gains in terms of economic growth if appropriate action is taken: the provision of complementary infrastructure, the cost of and access to finance, and the cost arising from bureaucracy and corruption in the interaction of the private with the public sector.

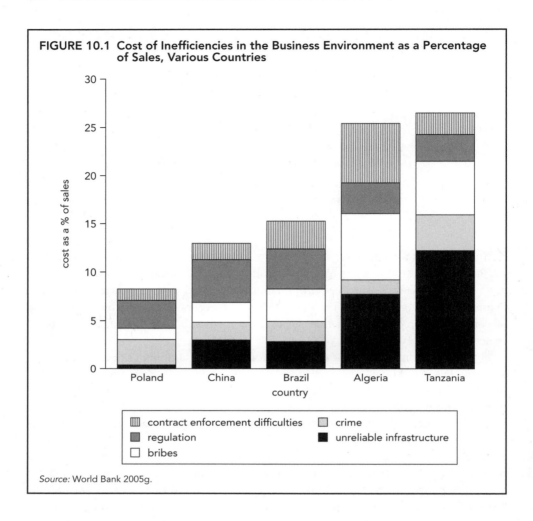

FIGURE 10.1 Cost of Inefficiencies in the Business Environment as a Percentage of Sales, Various Countries

Source: World Bank 2005g.

Scaling Up Access to Infrastructure

This section assesses the extent to which infrastructure is a binding constraint on growth in Tanzania, its role in promoting growth and poverty reduction, and the key issues in scaling up investment in infrastructure.

Investing in infrastructure is important for growth. The experience of fast-growing developing countries such as China shows that infrastructure can contribute significantly to growth. Infrastructure affects growth through its effect on enterprise productivity, the cost of doing business, market access, and profitability. Analysis of firm-level data identifies access to infrastructure services as a key determinant of enterprise growth and investments. For a low-income country such as Tanzania, where the majority of the rural poor are smallholder farmers, reliable and affordable infrastructure (particularly rural roads) is a critical factor in improving market access and enhancing the capacity of farmers to commercialize and diversify into higher-value economic activities to improve incomes.

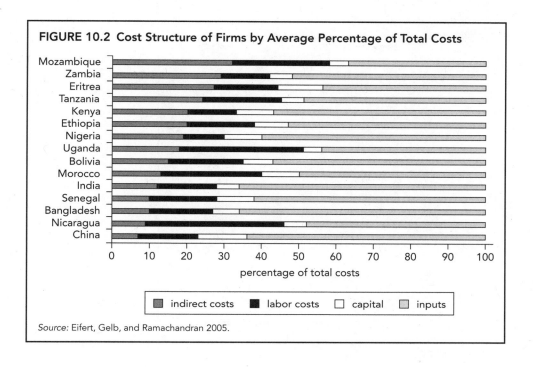

FIGURE 10.2 Cost Structure of Firms by Average Percentage of Total Costs

percentage of total costs

indirect costs   labor costs   capital   inputs

Source: Eifert, Gelb, and Ramachandran 2005.

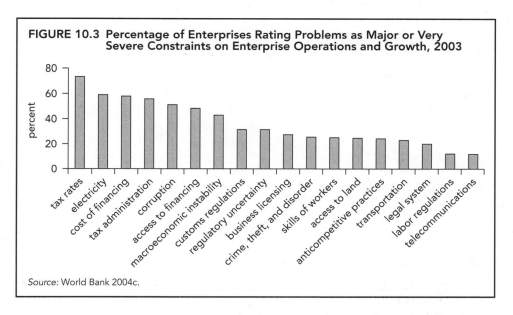

FIGURE 10.3 Percentage of Enterprises Rating Problems as Major or Very Severe Constraints on Enterprise Operations and Growth, 2003

percent

tax rates, electricity, cost of financing, tax administration, corruption, access to financing, macroeconomic instability, customs regulations, regulatory uncertainty, business licensing, crime, theft, and disorder, skills of workers, access to land, anticompetitive practices, transportation, legal system, labor regulations, telecommunications

Source: World Bank 2004c.

Tanzania's infrastructure is weak and inadequate. Although Tanzania has started re-forming its infrastructure sectors and public spending (especially on roads) has in-creased, the country's infrastructure indicators are still among the lowest in the world (figure 10.4).

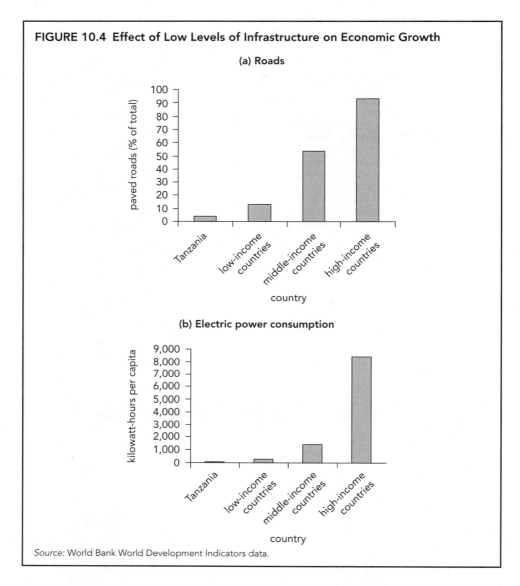

FIGURE 10.4 Effect of Low Levels of Infrastructure on Economic Growth

(a) Roads

(b) Electric power consumption

Source: World Bank World Development Indicators data.

Thus, infrastructure continues to pose a major policy challenge. According to the 2004 Investment Climate Assessment, infrastructure ranks among the three top constraints on business enterprise growth. Power supply, in particular, is perceived as the most serious infrastructural constraint. These constraints have driven business enterprises in Tanzania to invest in their own infrastructure. The Investment Climate Assessment has reported that about 55 percent of enterprises own generators to provide backup power supply. These generators represent a significant additional cost of doing business, given that they are expensive to buy and run. The indirect costs of poor infrastructure and private provision of infrastructure have been estimated at 25 percent of sales, compared to 7 to 10 percent in Asia and 18 percent in Uganda.[1] As pointed out in an independent operations evaluation report by the International Finance Corporation (IFC 2000), unreliable and expensive electricity, high transportation costs, and poor communications are major factors underlying Tanzania's lack of external competitiveness.

The extent to which infrastructure is a binding constraint on Tanzania's growth can be partly assessed from returns to infrastructure. Because infrastructure is widely believed to be such a binding constraint, one would expect high economic rates of return to this type of public investment. To get an idea of the magnitude of the returns to infrastructure in Tanzania, we looked at estimates of rates of return on 26 road rehabilitation and upgrading projects that the government has identified as part of its transport sector investment program. The rates of return ranged from 9 percent to 103 percent, and the average was 32 percent, which is high. The ex post economic rates of return on completed infrastructure projects financed by the World Bank, as presented in its Implementation Completion Reports and Operations Evaluation Department reports, however, show a somewhat mixed picture. A number of the selected projects had exceptionally high ex post rates of return: for example, the Sixth Highway Project yielded a rate of return of 37 percent; the Fourth Power Project, 23 percent; the Telecommunication Project, 50 percent; and the road and storm water component of the Urban Sector Rehabilitation project, 33 percent. A few had low or even negative rates of return. The Highway IV Project, for example, yielded an economic rate of return of 4 percent.

The infrastructure constraint in Tanzania is region and geography specific: The rates of return to infrastructure in Tanzania are, generally, high.[2] However, the large variation in the size of the returns in each sector—especially roads—suggests that the infrastructure constraint in Tanzania is geography specific. The magnitude of returns and the growth effect also depend on the type and quality of infrastructure. Generally, returns on rural roads linking production areas with markets are higher than on other categories of roads.

Relationship of Infrastructure to Growth and Poverty Reduction

Several studies have been carried out to estimate the contribution of public spending on infrastructure to growth and poverty reduction in developing countries on the basis of marginal returns and cost-benefit ratios. A recent study on public investment and poverty reduction in Tanzania attempted to compute marginal returns and cost-benefit ratios for the various types of public investments, using household data.[3] The marginal returns and the benefit-cost ratios were disaggregated by geographic zone and compared across the various categories of public spending. The preliminary conclusion was that investment in rural roads has a high payoff, with an average benefit-cost ratio of 9:1. The study also found that roads have diverse effects across regions. The policy implication is that targeted public infrastructure is required if the effect on growth is to be maximized. Further analytical work on rates of return to infrastructure in Tanzania using more robust data and methodologies would provide greater insight into the growth and poverty effects. To shed more light on the infrastructure challenges, the following section elaborates on the constraints in the infrastructure sectors and the related poverty and policy issues.

Transport is of strategic importance to growth and poverty reduction: Given Tanzania's geography and the dispersal of areas of economic activities, roads are particularly critical for the country's growth. The total road network is estimated at 85,000 kilometers.[4] Although road maintenance has improved since the creation of the Road Fund Board and the Tanzania National Roads Agency (TANROADS), the overall condition of the road network remains poor because of underfunding and capacity constraints. Table 10.1 depicts the condition of the road network. Of the 85,000 kilometers of road, only 27 percent is judged to be in good and fair condition. The situation of rural roads is even worse, with only 15 percent of the road network in good and fair condition.

Figure 10.5 is also revealing because it shows that only 38 percent of the rural population in Tanzania lives within 2 kilometers of an all-season road, which is lower than the average for low-income countries.

TABLE 10.1 Road Network, February 2004

(kilometers)

Portion of network	Good and fair condition	Poor condition	Total
Trunk roads	5,563	4,371	9,934
Regional roads	9,276	9,682	18,958
Subtotal managed by TANROADS	14,839	14,053	28,892
Urban roads	1,715	735	2,450
District roads	5,000	13,658	18,658
Feeder roads	1,000	34,000	35,000
Subtotal managed by local governments	7,715	48,393	56,108
Total network	22,554	62,446	85,000

Source: United Republic of Tanzania 2005b.

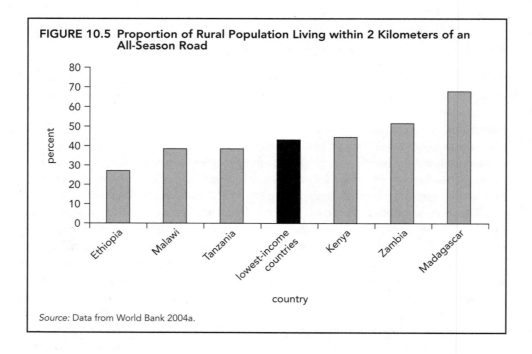

FIGURE 10.5 Proportion of Rural Population Living within 2 Kilometers of an All-Season Road

Source: Data from World Bank 2004a.

Poor rural road infrastructure impedes growth and poverty reduction. The poor road infrastructure in the rural areas of Tanzania is worrying, considering that the growth needed to reduce poverty is expected to come from agriculture and nonfarm rural activities, such as agroprocessing. The experience of other developing countries has shown that improving rural infrastructure does have positive effects on agricultural production, incomes, and poverty reduction (Vietnam is a case in point). When the quality of rural roads improves, the effect can be significant, for example, in increasing the use of fertilizers and the uptake of new agricultural technologies. This finding is relevant to Tanzania, where the quality of infrastructure is closely related to agricultural growth and the incidence of poverty. Those zones where poverty incidence is the highest—the south and the central zones—are the least connected, while poverty is considerably lower in well-connected Dar es Salaam and the southern highlands.

Road quality has a significant effect on producer prices, the length of the supply chain, competition, and access to basic social services. A recent study of the logistics costs of rural marketing (Nyange 2005) has shown that villages in areas with poor roads are less well served by freight and public transport, as evidenced by fewer traffic arrivals, the limited tonnage of trucks, and the more pronounced seasonality of traffic. Villages with poor roads do not have regular transport and are accessed by transporters only during the peak season for crop marketing, thus denying farmers the opportunity to benefit from higher prices in the early and late seasons. Moreover, there is far less competition in villages with poor roads, as evidenced by the smaller number of crop agents and export companies operating in those villages. Consequently, the producer prices received by farmers in villages with poor roads are less than the prices received by their counterparts in villages with fair roads. This situation has a disincentive effect on production in the less accessible villages. The survey also underlines the importance of roads in improving access to basic social services. As expected, well-connected villages are better served with basic social and economic services, such as schools, health facilities, and grain milling plants.

Thus, more investment in the rehabilitation and maintenance of the road network is needed for Tanzania to achieve its long-term growth objectives and poverty reduction goals. To get the core network required for poverty alleviation into maintainable condition, about US$3 billion is required over the next 10 years (World Bank 2004b). Currently, Tanzania spends about US$100 million to US$150 million per year in the road sector, which is far from adequate. The funding problems have been compounded by weak road administration capacity at the local government level and weak local private contracting capacity. For Tanzania to achieve its goal of having about 45,000 kilometers in maintainable condition, a large amount of additional financing is required. However, it is important that Tanzania accelerate road sector reforms to ensure effective use of the funds earmarked for road rehabilitation and maintenance. In particular, the government needs to (a) enact a new Roads Act to transform TANROADS into an independent authority and (b) redefine the responsibilities of institutions in the sector to prevent duplication.

Improved rail services would lower freight transport costs. Although the rail system share of freight traffic is far less than the road system share, the rail system provides an important link between inland regions and ports and is a cheaper alternative for transporting agricultural produce over long distances. For more than a decade now, the railway has faced major infrastructural and operational problems. Large sections of track are obsolete, and the available wagons and locomotives are not sufficient to sustain a reliable and efficient rail service. Exporters complain of delays and the uncertainty in allocation of locomotives, especially for crop haulage. The low rail transport capacity is a source of major logistical problems in the economy and has contributed to congestion at the port. It is, therefore, vital that the privatization or concessioning of the railways and rehabilitation of the infrastructure be undertaken as planned in order to improve efficiency and reduce freight transport costs. Furthermore, improving rail services will help reduce pressure on the road infrastructure, leading to lower costs for road rehabilitation and maintenance.

The power sector in Tanzania has problems. For many years, Tanzania has experienced the effects of droughts, high technical and commercial losses in the grid system, and (until recently) poor collection of receivables and low tariffs. Per capita power consumption in Tanzania is estimated at 62 kilowatts, much lower than in comparator countries such as Kenya (120 kilowatts per capita), India (380 kilowatts per capita), and China (987 kilowatts per capita). Hence, there is scope for a significant increase in power consumption. Currently, hydropower is the major source, accounting for 70 percent of the country's grid generation capacity of 773 megawatts. The remaining 30 percent comes from thermal plants. The thermal plants that use imported fuel (diesel and heavy fuel oil) for power generation, mainly the Tegeta plant, are very expensive to run compared with those now using indigenous natural gas.

An unreliable power supply is perceived by investors as a severe constraint on enterprise operations and growth. The poor performance in the power sector is reflected in frequent power outages. According to the recent Investment Climate Assessment, the median number of power outages experienced by enterprises in 2002 was estimated at 48, compared to only 21 in Kenya and 20 in Uganda. The high frequency of power outages and poor quality of supply caused by low voltage impose high financial costs on businesses through loss of production, wastage in the production process, and damage to equipment. Perhaps not surprising, electricity is the infrastructure constraint that enterprises are most concerned about.

There is an urgent need to expand the power supply, as well as its reliability, and the efficiency of the energy sector through sector reform and investment, to meet the growing demand by industry and the service sector. The government has been implementing a power sector reform program aimed at improving efficiency in power supply through commercialization and private sector participation. Since 2002, the management of the Tanzania Electric Supply Company (TANESCO) has been contracted to a private company, Net Group. This arrangement has resulted in strengthened financial management of TANESCO, which, however, remains vulnerable to external shocks such as the drought experienced in 2005/06. Unfortunately, the technical turnaround has not yet been achieved—hence the continued problems in power supply.

The recent establishment of the Energy and Water Utilities Regulatory Authority (EWURA) marks an important step in the ongoing implementation of power sector reforms. However, to improve the performance of the power sector, further reforms and substantial investment in transmission and distribution are needed. In this regard, it is important that the government develop a clear strategy and detailed implementation plan for executing the remaining aspects of the power sector reform. The key actions to be undertaken include (a) promulgation of the revised electricity legislation that would allow private participation in the extension of electricity services; (b) measures to ensure the financial viability of TANESCO; and (c) eventual concessioning of TANESCO, depending on the market situation. Tanzania is already encouraging private sector participation in generation expansion and needs to build on this effort. In addition, the country can benefit from regional power integration through transmission interconnectors, notably with Kenya and Uganda.

Currently, less than 5 percent of the rural population has access to electricity, and the overwhelming majority continues to rely on fuelwood for energy. The low electricity access rate for the rural population constrains the development of nonfarm activities and the improvement of the quality of life in rural areas. However, extending the main grid to rural areas is expensive, and the rural poor are unlikely to afford electricity without subsidies, at least to cover the capital portion. To improve access, Tanzania should consider investing in independent grids using small hydro systems (pico, micro, or mini), as well as natural gas, as in Somanga. But for more intensive uses than lighting for households, a better substitute for biogas could be liquefied petroleum gas. The other option is to promote the use of solar photovoltaic systems in small communities. Such systems would meet rural areas' lighting needs with respect to basic social services such as health and education and allow the running of small water pumps.

Inadequate water supply affects both growth and human development. Although Tanzania is endowed with abundant freshwater resources, the provision of water for domestic and industrial use is inadequate. More than 15 million of the 35 million Tanzanians lack a safe water supply. Despite recent improvement, only 50 percent of the rural population has access to clean sources of water, and only 70 percent of the urban population does. Inadequate water supply in Tanzania stems from underinvestment, past neglect of maintenance of facilities, and weak water resource management and institutional capacity. Currently, 30 percent of rural water supply facilities are unreliable or not functional. Some 20 to 40 percent of urban water is unaccounted for because of technical and commercial losses. The low domestic water supply coverage—especially in rural areas—affects quality of life, as evidenced by the high incidence of waterborne disease, especially among women and children. Apart from its direct effect on social outcomes, poor water supply also affects rural productivity, because the time spent by women fetching water could be spent on more productive activities. As in other infrastructure sectors, meeting the long-term targets for service provision will be challenging. The Millennium Development Goals needs assessment for Tanzania shows that, to reach the water and sanitation target, investment per capita must double, to US$12 in 2015 from the projected US$6 in 2006. Further institutional reforms in the water sector are also critical for achieving the long-term sector goals.

Policy Recommendations for Scaling Up Investment in Infrastructure

There is no doubt that scaling up investment in the rehabilitation and expansion of existing infrastructure is necessary to promote sustained growth. However, in scaling up infrastructure investment, the government must consider some policy issues to ensure that the investment yields positive effects on growth and on poverty reduction:

- While public financing, including donor financing, will be critical for improving basic infrastructure such as roads and rural water, sectors such as railways, ports, and energy offer greater potential for private sector participation through the public-private partnership model. However, to attract private investors, the regulatory framework must be strengthened and the regulatory bodies must be provided greater autonomy. Strengthening Tanzania's capacity to monitor the effect of infrastructure privatization on expanding access to infrastructure services will also be important.

- Reforms in the road and power sectors will be critical in ensuring that investment in infrastructure contributes effectively to efficiency-based growth and poverty reduction. It is particularly important that a new Road Act be passed, along with the Electricity Act. The benefit incidence of electricity consumption clearly shows that electricity is almost exclusively consumed by people in the higher-income quintiles. Thus, the rationale for subsidies to the power sector is weak, which underlines the potential for private sector investment in the power sector to meet the growing urban demand.

- Tanzania's infrastructure requirements are large and must be properly prioritized. Given budgetary constraints, it is not possible for Tanzania to improve the quantity and quality of infrastructure across the board. Therefore, it is important that the large infrastructure investment requirements be properly prioritized through the existing sector and the medium-term expenditure planning and budgeting process. In prioritizing infrastructure projects (particularly roads), the main considerations should include the need to (a) strengthen connectivity between potential high-growth areas and domestic and regional markets and (b) connect the poor to emerging growth opportunities and improve access to basic social services. Priorities in road sector investments should thus focus on upgrading rural roads (to open up areas of high economic potential) and rehabilitating and maintaining major transport corridors and regional roads to enhance integration and connectivity to domestic markets.

- Infrastructure needs and constraints in rural areas vary, reflecting the diversity in economic activities, population densities, remoteness, and other factors. The policy implication is that infrastructure interventions must be regional or area specific to better reflect local growth needs and priorities. Part of the regional infrastructure development strategies could entail clustering infrastructure investments in areas of growth potential, which would enable producers to exploit economies of scale and lead to faster growth.

- The infrastructure planning process must take into account synergies between the different types of infrastructure, as well as links with other growth and poverty reduction initiatives. The effect of infrastructure on growth is likely to be enhanced if an integrated approach in planning is adopted. For example, in the case of transport, a logistical corridor approach integrating ports, maritime and coastal shipping, railways, road freight, terminals, and warehouses and distribution centers is likely to promote greater efficiency by lowering logistical costs.

- The selection of infrastructure projects must be based on economic efficiency criteria and demonstrated poverty effects: The pressure to scale up investments in public infrastructure may compromise the quality of public investments. It is therefore important that the selection of public infrastructure projects be guided, first and foremost, by efficiency criteria. Priority should then be given to infrastructure projects that meet the economic efficiency criteria and benefit the poor.

- Appropriate balance needs to be maintained between new investment, rehabilitation, and recurrent maintenance. Although road sector spending has increased, it is still insufficient to maintain the existing road network. Therefore, as Tanzania scales up investment in infrastructure, an appropriate balance needs to be established between new investment and maintenance. Building new roads is expensive; appropriate maintenance of existing roads is necessary to ensure the cost-effectiveness and long-term sustainability of the infrastructure benefits.

- Scaling up investment in infrastructure may have adverse short-term macroeconomic consequences. The high domestic content of large-scale infrastructure construction such as roads may affect relative prices between tradables and nontradables. In the longer run, however, the effect is likely to be more than compensated for by the economywide productivity gains from the investment. Nonetheless, this potential downside needs to be managed carefully. To avert these short-term "Dutch disease" effects, those choosing infrastructure spending also need to consider the import content and the gestation period of the investment. A higher import content reduces the likelihood and magnitude of adverse Dutch disease effects. Investments with a short gestation period that result in a quick improvement of Tanzania's competitiveness can also contribute to staving off any negative short-term effects.

Scaling Up Access to Capital and Finance

Access to capital and finance is a critical determinant of investment and economic growth. Countries with well-developed financial systems (banks, stock markets, and bond markets) tend to grow faster than countries with less well-developed systems. Causation appears to run from financial sector development to growth, not from growth to financial sector development (Beck, Levine, and Loayza 2000). The analysis of both the agriculture sector and the data from the enterprise survey confirms that this finding holds true for Tanzania, with a significant positive relationship between access to finance and enterprise investment and growth. The International Monetary Fund's "Financial System Stability Assessment" (IMF 2003) concluded that the depth and efficiency of Tanzania's financial system fell well short of what is needed to help support economic growth.

The Tanzania investment climate assessment (World Bank 2004c) identified the cost of financing and access to finance as two of the main obstacles to enterprise operation and growth. Only 20 percent of the firms in the investment climate survey reported having loans from a financial institution. Investment is financed primarily through retained earnings (68 percent of new investments). Close to two-thirds of enterprises that invested did not use the financial sector. Financing enterprise growth through retained investment results in lower levels of investment and, therefore, reduced business growth and competitiveness.

First-Generation Financial Sector Reform

Tanzania has undertaken substantial financial sector reforms since 1991. These reforms included liberalization of the banking system to allow the entry of private and foreign banks, enhanced financial sector legislation, and strengthened supervision of banking by the Bank of Tanzania. State ownership of financial institutions has been significantly reduced with the sale of the National Bank of Commerce and the conclusion of the first phase of the privatization of the National Micro-Finance Bank, involving the sale of 49 percent of its shares to a consortium led by Rabobank of the Netherlands. The legal and regulatory environment for microfinance has been reformed, including the approval of new microfinance regulations in 2004. In addition, the payment and clearance system has been strengthened in recent years with the establishment of an electronic clearinghouse, an electronic funds transfer system, and real-time gross settlement facilities offered by the Tanzania interbank settlement system. A credit reporting system is under development, and a credit bureau has been launched. Recent reforms of the land legislation, which now provides for land to be used as collateral, represent important steps in supporting access to credit.

These reforms have resulted in a diverse financial system and significant changes in financial and monetary indicators. The financial system comprises 21 banks; 9 nonbank financial institutions; several pension funds, 2 of which invest in financial assets; 14 insurance companies; 63 foreign exchange bureaus; about 650 savings and credit cooperatives (SACCOs); several other microfinance institutions; and a stock exchange. Foreign equity participation accounts for about two-thirds of banking system capitalization, and 57 percent of total banking assets are in banks that are majority owned by foreign banks.

Access to financial services for households has declined over the past decade. In the early 1990s, 19 percent of all households had a member with a savings or current account. The restructuring of the banking system, during which a number of bank branches were closed, contributed to a decline in access in 2001 to only 6.4 percent of all households and 3.8 percent of households in rural areas.

Table 10.2 presents monetary statistics for 1997 to 2005, using gross domestic product (GDP) as a scaling device. Net foreign assets more than doubled between 1997 and 2005. This growth is primarily attributable to the rapid increase in international reserves held by the Bank of Tanzania. By contrast, net domestic assets of the financial sector declined from 12 percent of GDP in 1997 to 3 percent in 2003, mainly because of the sharp reduction in lending to the government by the Bank of Tanzania. Subsequently, the rapid increase in credit to the private sector led to a recovery of domestic assets of the banking sector to 10 percent of GDP.

Financial intermediation by commercial banks has increased from 14 percent of GDP in 1997 to about 21 percent in 2005. The most dramatic developments occurred with

TABLE 10.2 Financial Variables as a Percentage of GDP, 1997–2005

Variable	Percentage of GDP[a]						
	1997	2000	2001	2002	2003	2004	2005
Monetary survey							
Net foreign assets	8	9	12	13	17	18	19
Net domestic assets	12	8	6	6	3	4	10
Domestic credit	9	9	8	7	8	9	12
Net claims on government	5	5	3	2	2	1	2
Credit to private sector	3	4	5	5	6	8	10
Other items (net)	3	−1	−2	−2	−4	−5	−2
Liquidity paper (issued by the Bank of Tanzania)	0	−4	−2	−1	−1		
Broad money (M3)	20	17	18	19	21	22	29
Currency in circulation	6	5	5	5	4	5	6
Deposits	10	8	9	10	10	11	14
Foreign currency deposits	4	4	5	5	6	6	8
Commercial banks							
Foreign assets	5	6	7	6	6	6	6
Foreign liabilities	0	0	0	0	0	0	0
Reserves	1	2	2	2	2	3	2
Domestic credit	9	10	8	10	10	11	15
Claims on government (net)	5	5	3	4	2	2	5
Claims on private sector	3	5	5	6	8	9	10
Demand deposits	4	4	4	5	5	5	6
Time and savings deposits	6	5	6	6	6	6	7
Foreign currency deposits	4	4	5	6	6	6	8

Source: Bank of Tanzania, various years.
a. End-of-year value as percentage of GDP for the preceding year.

respect to the structure of credit. Overall credit by commercial banks increased from 9 percent of GDP in 1997 to 15 percent in 2005. This expansion of credit was accompanied by a dramatic change in the composition of credit. In 1997, the bulk of credit (5 percent of GDP) still went to the public sector, while credit to the private sector amounted to only 3 percent of GDP. By 2005, credit to government was still about 5 percent of GDP, but credit to the private sector had increased to 10 percent.

Table 10.3 shows trends in the sectoral composition of lending by commercial banks between 1997 and 2005. In 2005, mining and manufacturing and trade accounted for almost 50 percent of bank lending. Agricultural production and the transportation sector together accounted for another 20 percent. Credit between 1997 and 2005 grew at an average annual rate of 29 percent. Credit to agricultural production, building and construction, tourism, and specified financial institutions saw the fastest increases. Credit for marketing and exporting agricultural produce completely disappeared during that period. It is also worthwhile to note that the increase in credit to the private sector is not reflected in an increase in private sector investment, because most of the credit finances working capital. The sectoral pattern of increases in credit is also consistent with the sectoral GDP growth patterns, where the fastest-growing sectors also experienced the largest increase in credit.

TABLE 10.3 Commercial Bank Lending to Some Sectors, 1997–2005

(percent)

| Sector | Share in total domestic lending | | | | Average growth rate |
	1997	2000	2003	2005	1997–2005
Public sector	3	2	2	1	14
Agricultural production	8	6	12	12	37
Mining and manufacturing	24	31	26	23	28
Building and construction	2	3	5	6	45
Transportation	8	13	9	8	28
Tourism	1	1	2	2	38
Marketing of agricultural produce	1	0	0	0	
Export of agricultural produce	2	0	0	0	
Trade in capital goods	0	0	0	0	
All other trade	24	26	23	24	29
Specified financial institutions	0	2	4	6	84
Other	27	13	17	19	23
Total	100	100	100	100	29

Source: Bank of Tanzania, various years.

Figure 10.6 shows real interest rate developments between 1993 and 2005. Real interest rates on savings were around –5 percent until 1998. Subsequently, between 1998 and 2005, real interest rates on savings were higher, although still negative in most years. The development in the real savings rate seems to be closely related to domestic sav-

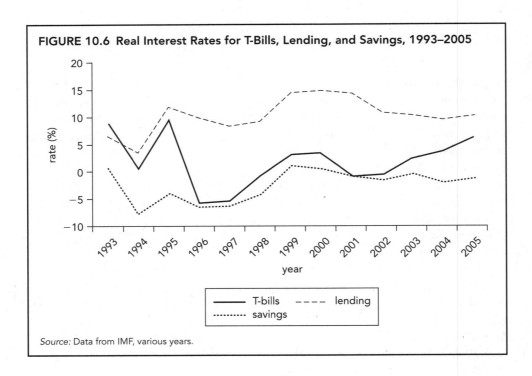

FIGURE 10.6 Real Interest Rates for T-Bills, Lending, and Savings, 1993–2005

Source: Data from IMF, various years.

ing, which also has risen as real interest rates have increased. Interest rate spreads have declined in recent years, from 18.4 percent in 1997 to 11.5 percent in 2005.

Despite these signs of progress, including growth in lending and increased competition in microfinance, credit to the private sector remains very small and mostly short term, interest spreads are high, and banks accumulate extensive holdings of government paper and sizable offshore dollar placements. Unfinished privatization and, most of all, a number of structural impediments to lending (including a poor credit culture, difficult and slow enforcement of creditor rights, and lack of suitable collateral) are the main factors limiting financial intermediation.

Second-Generation Financial Sector Reform

The financial system is ineffective in supplying long-term funds to the private sector. A large proportion of the long-term liabilities of the pension funds are invested in bank deposits, treasury bills, or short-term bonds. As such, one important supply of long-term funds to finance private sector development fails to be passed through.

A key issue is the distribution of liquidity. Although there is a perception of excess liquidity, this is not the case for all the banks. Ninety percent of the excess liquidity is concentrated in three banks, and a large part of this liquidity comes from government deposits. Moreover, a large portion of this liquidity is invested in government securities.[5] This situation implies that the commercial banks are not being provided the opportunity to compete for government deposits and that intermediation using these funds is not taking place.

Overall, the picture reflects the low level of development of the financial sector in Tanzania. In particular, access to credit is limited to a small number of enterprises with solid collateral in key urban areas, while small and medium enterprises (SMEs) and firms located outside the main urban areas are virtually excluded.

To address the challenges, the government has developed a roadmap for the Second-Generation Financial Sector Reform Program. This program includes an implementation plan that is based on the recommendations of the Financial Sector Assessment Program and was prepared by an interinstitutional committee. Implementation of the reform program involves a three-pronged approach: (a) strengthening the lending environment and the financial infrastructure, primarily through policy changes and institution strengthening; (b) facilitating the increase in lending to SMEs and long-term lending by commercial banks through selective interventions by the government; and (c) giving direct support to providers of financial services for micro and small enterprises.

Strengthening the Lending Environment and Financial Infrastructure

This aspect includes completing the task of divesting state-controlled entities in banking and insurance; strengthening the legal and judicial framework that supports lending; clarifying and deepening the regulatory and information and technology infrastructure for households and microenterprises; and encouraging long-term pension and insurance funds to finance longer-term private investments.

Facilitating the Increase in SME and Long-Term Lending

The government is undertaking efforts to further improve the availability of medium- and long-term credit to key sectors of the economy. With the assistance of the World Bank, it is taking initiatives in five areas:

- It has launched an SME Credit Guarantee Scheme to encourage commercial bank lending for SMEs.

- It is expected to launch a development finance guarantee facility, which will be managed initially by the Bank of Tanzania and will provide partial government guarantees to commercial banks for their loans to development- and export-oriented projects.

- It hopes to facilitate the creation of a privately owned and managed long-term financing facility that would channel funds from nonbanks or banks and potential development partners (without government guarantee) to be lent to commercial banks on a long-term basis.

- It will introduce a development finance institution, most likely incorporating the Tanzania Investment Bank. The institution would channel multilateral and bilateral donor funds and perhaps use government seed money from the budget, but it would not take any new deposits from the public.

- It will advance reforms in the pension fund sector in order to unify the legal and regulatory framework for all pension funds, along with investment guidelines. It is expected that this effort, particularly the development of investment guidelines, will facilitate the channeling of pension funds' resources into longer-term lending through commercial banks.

Giving Direct Support to Providers of Financial Services for Micro- and Small Enterprises

The Second-Generation Financial Sector Reform Program also includes initiatives related to micro and rural finance. These initiatives are designed to respond to the government's vision for the development of pro-poor finance in Tanzania, as articulated in the national microfinance policy. Some of these initiatives, such as strengthening the regulatory framework, will be addressed as part of strengthening the lending environment and financial infrastructure. Others will require direct support to the providers of financial services. It is expected that a large part of this support will be provided by the Financial Sector Deepening Trust, funded by four bilateral development partners.[6] The trust will provide assistance for the transformation of nongovernmental organizations focused on microfinance, the strengthening of networks of SACCOs, and the development of links between banks and microfinance institutions.

Achieving the Plan

To achieve the objectives of the Second-Generation Reform Program, the government must fully commit to timely implementation of the action plan. Considerable efforts have gone into developing the strategies and building consensus. The challenge is now to implement the plan.

With continued reform, it is reasonable to expect the expansion of credit to continue. The solid expansion of credit, both in aggregate terms and to a wider range of small-scale borrowers, can be expected to continue given the growing confidence by lenders that the credit environment has improved. Increasingly vigorous competition and the availability of deposit resources point to the likelihood that banks will reach down further into serving small-scale clients. These efforts will be supported by continuing the thrust of the overall financial sector policy environment.

Enhancing the Public-Private Interface

The public-private interface covers two important aspects of the business environment. The first relates to the quality of regulation of private sector activities. The second, whose importance for economic growth has only recently been stressed in the literature (for example, Rodrik 2004), relates to the quality of collaboration and coordination between the public and private sectors in an effort to foster economic growth.

Regulatory agencies, tax revenue authorities (including customs), business and land registries, and the judicial system all form part of the public interface with the private sector, which has an important bearing on the costs, risks, and barriers to business in Tanzania. The costs influence the range of opportunities that are profitable. Because investments are forward looking, risks and uncertainty determine the types and nature of investments. Entry restrictions limit innovation and the efficient provision of goods and services.

The quality of the public-private interface also is critical for ensuring that the government can play a supportive role in growth efforts led by the private sector. This role relates to the flow of information between the private and public sectors, allowing the government to play a supportive role by removing obstacles, collaborating in the identification of growth opportunities, and ensuring that the provision of public goods and services (especially infrastructure) is well aligned with private sector needs. An efficient public-private interface is part of the second-generation reforms that will determine the private sector's response to productivity-based opportunities.

Factors that affect the public-private interface overlap with the broader concept of governance. Box 10.1 describes the different aspects of governance: voice and accountability, political stability, government effectiveness, regulatory quality, rule of law, and control of corruption. Figure 10.7 shows that in each of these aspects, Tanzania performs better than other low-income countries. For all indicators except political stability/no violence, Tanzania registered improvements between 1996 and 2005. With respect to control of corruption, Tanzania moved from being perceived as among the most corrupt countries to a position in which about 29 percent of the 200 countries assessed are perceived as doing worse than Tanzania in controlling corruption. The slight deterioration in Tanzania's rating of political stability/no violence is likely related to continued political tensions between the ruling and the main opposition parties.

The World Bank's annual *Doing Business* report provides an objective assessment of the regulatory environment in 175 countries by measuring the number of procedures,

---

BOX 10.1 Aspects of Governance

Many researchers and practitioners have tried to produce aggregate statistics that make it possible to compare the quality of governance across countries and over time. Few of these studies cover the entire world or all topics. Furthermore, the questions used to elicit responses are usually not comparable across surveys. To increase country coverage, Kaufmann, Kraay, and Mastruzzi (2006) combined information from as many as 60 mostly subjective indexes from other sources to produce six measures that capture different aspects of regulation, corruption, and governance:

- *Voice and accountability.* The extent to which citizens of the country are able to participate in the selection of the government.
- *Political stability.* The likelihood that the government will be destabilized or overthrown by possibly unconstitutional or violent means, including terrorism.
- *Government effectiveness.* The quality of public service provision and the government bureaucracy, the competence and independence of the civil service, and the credibility of the government's commitment to announced policies.
- *Regulatory quality.* The quality of government policies. This measure focuses on the prevalence of market-unfriendly policies, such as price controls or inadequate bank supervision, and on perceptions of the regulatory burden facing businesses.
- *Rule of law.* The extent to which individuals have confidence in and abide by the rules of society. This measure includes perceptions about the incidence of crime (both violent and nonviolent), the effectiveness and predictability of the judiciary, and the enforceability of contracts.
- *Control of corruption.* The extent of corruption (that is, the illegal use of public power for private gain).

---

time required, and cost imposed on businesses through government regulation. In 2006, Tanzania ranked 142 among the 175 countries, which suggests that doing business in Tanzania is handicapped by severe weaknesses in the regulatory environment. The business licensing regime, employment regulations, and registration of property are particularly problematic areas. The situation is somewhat better with respect to the administrative cost and procedures related to trading across borders and the enforcement of contracts, although even in these areas there is significant scope for improvement in order to enhance the attractiveness of Tanzania for investment. However, *Doing Business 2007* (World Bank 2006) also recognizes the efforts Tanzania is undertaking to improve its business environment. Indeed, Tanzania is assessed as being among the top 10 reformers in 2005/06. Recent reforms include simplification of the business licensing regime; reduction in the cost of registering property; revision of the Companies Act to give investors greater protection; and reform of customs administration through the introduction of risk management techniques, electronic data interchange systems, and border cooperation agreements.

The indicators reported in *Doing Business 2007* provide an objective assessment of the regulatory environment. Information from the investment climate assessment carried out in 2003 (World Bank 2004c) provides complementary information on the extent to which weaknesses in the regulatory environment constrain enterprise growth.

FIGURE 10.7 Governance Indicators for Tanzania, 1996–2005

(a) Comparison between 1996 and 2005

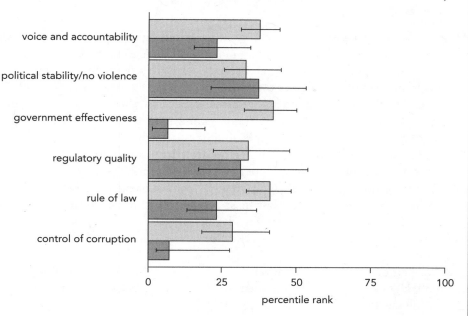

(b) Comparison with low-income country average, 2004

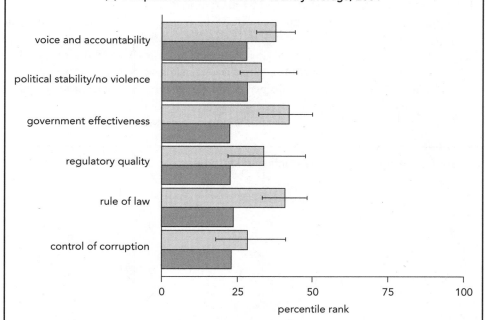

Source: Kaufmann, Kraay, and Mastruzzi 2006.

Note: The figure depicts the percentile rank on each governance indicator. Percentile rank indicates the percentage of countries worldwide that rate below the selected country (subject to margin of error). The selected comparator (if any) is depicted by the lower bar for each governance indicator. In the bar chart, the statistically likely range of the governance indicator is shown as a thin black line. For instance, a bar of length 75 percent with the thin black lines extending from 60 percent to 85 percent has the following interpretation: an estimated 75 percent of the countries rate worse and an estimated 25 percent of the countries rate better than the country of choice. However, at the 90 percent confidence level, only 60 percent of the countries rate worse, whereas only 15 percent of the countries rate better. Higher values imply better governance ratings.

Barriers to Entry

Although some entry restrictions are necessary—requiring enterprises to register with tax authorities, for example—others do more harm than good. Several recent studies have shown that entry restrictions encourage firms to remain informal by making it difficult and expensive to enter the formal sector (see figure 10.8).[7] Entry restrictions can also lead to corruption and reduce competition, thereby hurting economic performance in other ways.[8] Within the Organisation for Economic Co-operation and Development (OECD), for example, multifactor productivity and investment are significantly lower in sectors that have greater restrictions on entry.[9]

Most enterprises in Tanzania did not rate business licensing as a serious obstacle to enterprise operations and growth. Only about 27 percent of enterprises said that it was a major or very severe problem. But these results probably understate the effect of such regulations. Businesses that are already operating are much less likely to view entry restrictions as an obstacle. Indeed, they may even welcome regulations that limit competition.

According to World Bank data on the cost of doing business,[10] in 2006, it took about 30 days to fulfill all legal requirements for starting a business in Tanzania (table 10.4). Although the same process takes five days or fewer in some OECD countries, such as Australia, Canada, or Denmark, or the United States, this period is not exceptionally burdensome when compared with the time required in other developing countries. For example, business licensing takes about 35 days in China and India, 54 days in Kenya, and 30 days in Uganda. But the monetary cost of this process as a percentage of per capita gross national income (GNI) is higher in Tanzania (92 percent) than in some of the comparator countries. In contrast, business licensing costs 9 percent of per capita GNI in China, 74 percent in India, 46 percent in Kenya, and 114 percent in Uganda.

Legal restrictions are not the only barrier to entry that new firms face. Access to infrastructure—especially electricity—is another important obstacle. The median wait for

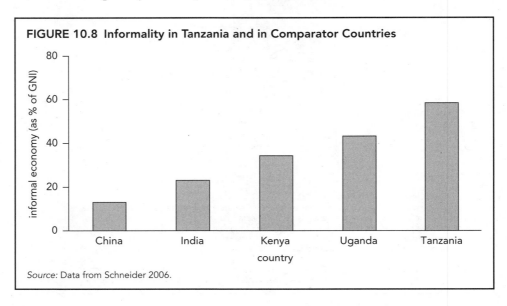

FIGURE 10.8 Informality in Tanzania and in Comparator Countries

Source: Data from Schneider 2006.

TABLE 10.4 *Doing Business Indicators*

Indicator	Tanzania	Botswana	Kenya	Malaysia	Thailand	South Africa	Uganda
Ease of doing business (rank)	142	48	83	25	18	29	107
Starting a business							
Procedures (number)	13	11	13	9	8	9	17
Time (days)	30	108	54	30	33	35	30
Cost (% of per capita income)	91.6	10.6	46.3	19.7	5.8	6.9	114.0
Minimum capital (% of per capita income)	5.5	0	0	0	0	0	0
Dealing with licenses							
Procedures (number)	26	24	11	25	9	17	19
Time (days)	313	169	170	281	127	174	156
Cost (% of income per capita)	3,796.6	457.7	37.6	78.2	11.1	33.5	832.8
Hiring and firing workers							
Difficulty of hiring index (0–100)	100	0	33	0	33	44	0
Rigidity of hours index (0–100)	40	20	20	20	20	40	20
Difficulty of firing index (0–100)	60	40	30	10	0	40	0
Rigidity of employment index (0–100)	67	20	28	10	18	41	7
Nonwage labor cost (% of salary)	16	0	4	13	5	2	10
Firing cost (% of salary)	32	90	47	88	54	24	13
Registering property							
Procedures (number)	10	4	8	5	2	6	13
Time (days)	123	30	73	144	2	23	227
Cost (% of property value)	5.5.2	4.9	4.1	2.4	6.3	8.9	6.9
Getting credit							
Strength of legal rights index (0–100)	5	7	8	8	5	5	3
Depth of credit information index (0–6)	0	5	2	6	5	5	0
Public registry coverage (% of adults)	0	0	0	42.2	0	0	0
Private bureau coverage (% of adults)	0	43.2	0.1	—	21.7	53.0	0

(continued)

TABLE 10.4 *(continued)*

Indicator	Tanzania	Botswana	Kenya	Malaysia	Thailand	South Africa	Uganda
Protecting investors							
Extent of disclosure index (0–10)	3	8	4	10	10	8	7
Extent of director liability index (0–10)	4	2	2	9	2	8	5
Ease of shareholder suits index (0–10)	7	3	10	7	6	8	4
Strength of investor protection index (0–10)	4.7	4.3	5.3	8.7	6.0	8.0	5.3
Paying taxes							
Payments (number)	48	24	17	35	46	23	31
Time (hours per year)	248	140	432	190	104	350	237
Total tax payable (% of gross profit)	45.0	53.3	74.2	35.2	40.2	38.3	32.2
Trading across borders							
Documents for export (number)	3	6	11	6	9	5	12
Time for export (days)	24	37	25	20	24	31	42
Cost to export (US$ per container)	822	524	1,980	481	848	850	1,050
Documents for import (number)	10	9	9	12	12	9	19
Time for import (days)	39	42	45	22	22	34	67
Cost to import (US$ per container)	817	1,159	2,325	428	1,042	850	2,945
Enforcing contracts							
Procedures (number)	21	26	25	31	26	26	19
Time (days)	393	501	360	450	425	600	484
Cost (% of claim)	51.53	24.8	41.3	21.3	17.5	11.5	35.2
Closing a business							
Time (years)	3.0	1.3	4.5	2.3	2.7	2.0	2.2
Cost (% of estate)	22	15	22	15	36	18	30
Recovery rate (cents on the U.S. dollar)	21.9	64.7	14.6	38.7	42.6	34.4	40.4

Source: World Bank 2006.
Note: — = not available.

an electricity connection was 30 days in Tanzania, compared with 3 days in China, 14 days in Uganda, and 15 days in Kenya. Micro, small, and medium-size enterprises faced much longer median delays (30 days) than large enterprises (21 days) and very large enterprises (3 days). Obtaining a water connection also took longer in Tanzania than in any of the comparator countries, but the median delay—7 days—was far shorter than the wait for electricity. Getting a telephone connection was somewhat more time consuming, but the median wait of 14 days was considerably shorter than in Kenya (60 days).

Business Regulations and Inspections

Business regulations and inspections may impose significant cost on businesses and encourage enterprises to operate informally. Tanzania's licensing regime is among the most burdensome, according to the *Doing Business 2007* data (World Bank 2006). For example, obtaining all the permits to build a warehouse involved 26 procedures that required together 313 days with a cost of 3,797 percent of GNI. In most other countries, fewer procedures that consume less time are required, and the cost of obtaining the required permits is significantly lower. In Kenya, the cost is only 38 percent of GNI, and in Thailand it is only 11 percent.

According to the information from an enterprise survey (World Bank 2004c), on average, enterprises in Tanzania reported that senior managers spent about 15 percent of their time dealing with government inspections, regulations, and paperwork. This figure was slightly higher than in Kenya (13 percent) and China (12 percent) and significantly higher than in Uganda (4 percent). Similarly, the median enterprise in Tanzania reported 15 inspections or meetings with government agencies (including tax officials) per year, significantly more than in Uganda and India (5 and 6 inspections, respectively). However, enterprises in China and Kenya each reported a slightly greater number of inspections (16). Finally, the bureaucratic burden associated with regulation is much higher for exporters. The numbers of inspections and days spent dealing with regulatory issues are higher for exporters (47 and 20, respectively) than for non-exporters (28 and 14). Figure 10.9 shows the types of inspections that may take place.

Overall, inspections do not appear to vary greatly by sector. The vast majority of establishments are inspected by government agencies. For example, 92 percent of manufacturing firms, 85 percent of tourism establishments, and 71 percent of construction firms reported tax inspections (table 10.5). But firms in the construction sector were less likely to be inspected than enterprises in other sectors, while firms in the manufacturing sector were most likely to be inspected. For firms that were inspected, the average number of inspections was similar across sectors. For example, the median firm in all sectors was inspected seven times by the tax inspectorate in 2002.

Customs and Trade Regulations

Exporting and importing in Tanzania are both hampered by poor customs administration. Among enterprises that engaged in foreign trade, the median firm reported that it took 14 days on average for imports to clear customs and 7 days for exports, once

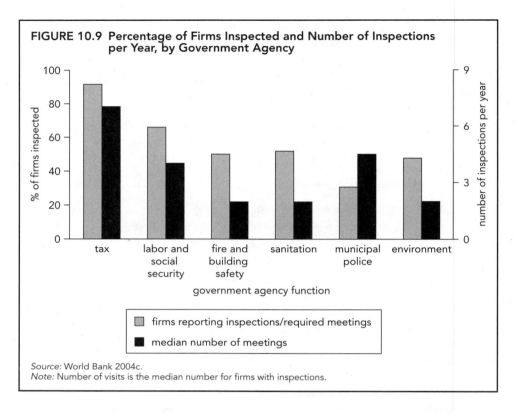

FIGURE 10.9 Percentage of Firms Inspected and Number of Inspections per Year, by Government Agency

Legend:
- firms reporting inspections/required meetings
- median number of meetings

Source: World Bank 2004c.
Note: Number of visits is the median number for firms with inspections.

TABLE 10.5 Percentage of Firms Inspected and Median Number of Inspections, by Sector

Indicator	Tax	Labor and social security	Fire and building safety	Sanitation	Municipal police	Environment
			Type of inspection			
Percentage of firms with inspections						
Construction	71	30	19	19	21	19
Tourism	85	58	23	48	18	32
Manufacturing	92	66	50	52	31	48
Median number of inspections for firms with inspections						
Construction	7	2	2	3	5	2
Tourism	7	3	1	3	5	2
Manufacturing	7	4	2	2	5	2

Source: World Bank 2004c.

they had reached the point of entry or exit.[11] The median wait was considerably shorter than the average typical wait because several enterprises reported exceptionally long delays.[12] Managers also reported that clearance times were unpredictable, forcing them to hold additional inventory in anticipation of worst-case scenarios. For imports, the median enterprise reported that the longest delay was 21 days—considerably longer than the typical 14-day wait. For exports, the median enterprise reported that the longest delay was 12 days.

Port and customs delays are considerably longer in Tanzania than in any of the comparator countries. The median delays for imports and exports in China were less than half as long—five and three days, respectively. Similarly, reported delays for imports and exports were seven and four days, respectively, in Kenya and seven and three days, respectively, in India.

Poor customs administration and overly restrictive trade and customs regulations discourage enterprises from exporting. Indeed, as noted previously, trade and customs regulation partially explain why enterprises in Tanzania export less than similar enterprises in Kenya. Because exporting has been linked to improved productivity—as well as an improved balance of trade—these delays and restrictions can have a real effect on enterprise performance.

Land Registration

Land constitutes one of the most important asset bases for investments. The provision of information on land in the form of a title and a certificate of occupancy or ownership can transform potential assets into tradable assets of capital. However, the value of these assets and their economic potential are often jeopardized by the insecurity of property rights. The transaction costs of using land as collateral are high. The title registration system is inefficiently administered and maintained, and poor security of the physical files has provided opportunities for fraudulent and corrupt activity, compromising the integrity of the title registry. A poorly functioning land registry makes it costly to verify the status of a land title, which in turn affects the ability to sell land or associated real estate. Existing title holders and banks have reported that it takes an average of three months to register a title for a mortgage in the land registry.

Legal System

Since embarking on economic reforms in the mid-1980s, Tanzania has witnessed significant social and economic changes, including the emergence and growth of a vibrant private sector that has been able to stimulate economic growth and increase the country's competitiveness, as well as to provide a variety of goods and services to citizens— previously the domain of the state or state-run institutions. However, reform of the country's legal sector to sufficiently support and enhance economic growth and efficiency led by the private sector has not taken place at the same pace as economic reform. The present legal system is mainly based on English laws introduced when Tanganyika was a British mandate; in many aspects, it is outdated. In addition, a substantial part of the legislation and the institutions, even where subsequently amended, were fashioned for the centrally planned economy and therefore cannot be efficacious in a competitive market system. With globalization, regionalization, and technological advances, the problem is more compounded as—inevitably—new demands are placed on the economy and the conduct of its agents, creating the need for a more conducive environment for competitiveness.

Reform of the country's legal sector began in 1997 when the government accepted the recommendations submitted by the Legal Sector Task Force in 1996. Since then, the government has designed strategies for implementation to ensure that priority needs in the legal sector are addressed accordingly. Problems identified by the Legal Sector Task Force, which are widely acknowledged, include inordinate delays in resolving disputes and dispensing justice in the justice system, inaccessibility of the justice system for the majority of poor and disadvantaged Tanzanians, low levels of public trust in the justice system, and excessive prevalence of unethical behavior (United Republic of Tanzania 2004b). The key challenges identified for the sector include the rapid social, political, economic, and technological changes taking place in the country and internationally and, in particular, the need to rapidly develop a legal system to facilitate the efficient development of a private sector, market-led economy and provide due protection of consumer rights.

Taxation

Tax administration was the area of regulation that enterprises were most likely to identify as a serious problem, more than half of them rating it as a major or very severe obstacle. Some 92 percent reported that they had required meetings with tax inspectors; the median firm within this subset reported seven meetings per year. Fewer enterprises reported having required meetings or inspections from other agencies, and the number of required meetings was lower for those that did.

Almost 73 percent of enterprises in Tanzania rated tax rates as a major or very severe constraint on enterprise performance and growth—considerably more than rated any other obstacle as a major constraint and more than in any of the comparator countries (figure 10.10).[13] Among the countries where investment climate assessments were completed by the end of 2003, in only two (Brazil and Ethiopia) were enterprises more likely to rate tax rates as a serious obstacle. Fewer enterprises in Tanza-

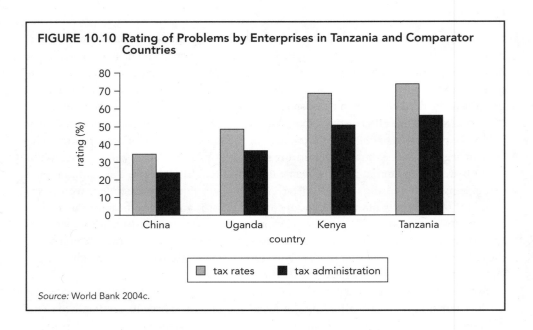

FIGURE 10.10 **Rating of Problems by Enterprises in Tanzania and Comparator Countries**

Source: World Bank 2004c.

nia (58 percent) rated tax administration as a serious problem. However, tax administration ranked high among enterprises' serious concerns, falling just below tax rates, electricity, and costs of financing.

Problems with tax rates and tax administration were not unique to any one group of enterprises. Medium, large, and very large enterprises all rated tax rates as the greatest obstacle to enterprise operations and growth (that is, tax rates were the obstacle rated as major or very severe by the largest number of enterprises in each group). Enterprises in tourism and construction also rated tax rates as a serious problem, as did foreign-owned and domestically owned firms and both exporters and nonexporters. In addition, each group ranked tax administration among the top obstacles it faced.

The data from *Doing Business 2007* (World Bank 2006) put the information from the enterprise survey into perspective. In Tanzania, entrepreneurs there must make 48 payments, spend 248 hours, and pay 45 percent of gross profit in taxes. Although the number of payments is higher in Tanzania than the average for the region and for OECD countries (41 and 15, respectively), the amount of time spent and the effective tax rate are not too different from the regional and OECD averages (336 days and 203 days and 71 percent and 48 percent, respectively). This information suggests that while entrepreneurs (not unexpectedly) feel that taxation is a major burden on their businesses, the system is not significantly more burdensome than that of many other countries.

Informality and Evasion

It is difficult to draw strong conclusions about tax evasion from investment climate surveys—enterprise managers being unlikely to be forthcoming in this respect. However, the evidence from the survey is consistent with the macroeconomic evidence. Evasion appears to be a greater problem in Tanzania than in the comparator countries. Managers in Tanzania estimated that the typical firm in their area of activity reported 69 percent of its sales for tax purposes.[14] By contrast, the average estimates in Uganda and Kenya were 77 percent and 86 percent, respectively. The high level of evasion is especially striking given that enterprises in Tanzania face a greater number of tax inspections and required meetings than enterprises in most of the comparator countries.

Estimates of amounts reported for small, medium, large, and very large enterprises ranged between 68 and 83 percent of sales. Reporting rates were highest among very large enterprises and lowest among microenterprises (about 25 percent). Consistent with the observation that informal microenterprises were far less concerned about tax rates and administration than other enterprises, they reported the smallest share of sales to tax authorities—19 percent, compared with 28 percent for formal microenterprises. The relatively small gap between informal and formal microenterprises may reflect the fact that informality is a continuum, with many enterprises being informal to some degree.[15]

One approach that the government could take to combat evasion would be to reduce the tax burden on formal enterprises. However, since the government's fiscal discipline has underpinned Tanzania's impressive macroeconomic performance, rate cuts would need to be combined with steps to improve revenue mobilization. One way for the government to do this would be to reduce costly tax exemptions and incentives (IMF 2003). Another would be to encourage informal firms to enter the formal sector—and in so doing broaden the tax base—by reducing the regulatory burden on formal enterprises.

As a first step in improving revenue mobilization, the government must improve tax administration, which remains problematic (IMF 2003). For example, the value added tax (VAT) efficiency ratio (the ratio of VAT revenues to GDP divided by the VAT rate) in Tanzania (0.20) lags the average for Sub-Saharan Africa (0.27). The government has already taken some steps to strengthen administration, including the establishment of the Large Taxpayer Unit in 2001, the introduction of taxpayer identification numbers in 2000, and the five-year corporate plan for the Tanzania Revenue Authority.

Tax Administration

Improving collection should not be the only goal of tax administration reform. The government should also reduce the burden that tax administration imposes on enterprises. Enterprise managers in Tanzania reported that in 2002/03, they spent about seven days dealing with inspections or required meetings with tax officials. In comparison, enterprise managers in China, Kenya, and Uganda reported spending two to three days on such tasks. Despite recent reforms, managers generally did not report any reduction in this administrative burden. Although 36 managers reported fewer meetings with tax officials in 2002 than in 2001, 59 managers reported more meetings, and 149 reported the same number.

The burden of tax administration is particularly high on more productive firms, which tend to be larger and are more likely to be both foreign owned and exporters. This acts as a tax on efficiency. In addition to discouraging firms from becoming more efficient, it also discourages them from taking actions that might signal their efficiency, such as entering export markets.

In addition, the government should combat corruption in tax administration. Despite recent reform efforts, 21 percent of enterprises that had required meetings with tax inspectors reported that gifts or informal payments to inspectors were expected or requested.[16] The corresponding figures for the comparator countries were 7 percent in Uganda, 21 percent in China, and 38 percent in Kenya. The median value of the gift or informal payment was T Sh 400,000 (about US$400 in mid-2003).

Corruption

The government appears to have made some progress in reducing corruption since 1996, when a presidential commission led by Judge Joseph Warioba produced the Warioba Report.[17] It is implementing a national anticorruption strategy and has strengthened the institutional framework—notably through the Finance Act of 2001 and the Public Procurement Act of 2002—and adopted a clear zero-tolerance position on corruption (ESRF and FACEIT 2002). Nonetheless, corruption continues to have an important effect on businesses.

Grand Corruption

Enterprise managers in Tanzania see grand corruption—payments made to policy makers or senior bureaucrats to win government contracts and influence lawmaking—as a serious problem (figure 10.11). Approximately 45 percent of managers said that payments to government officials that affected the content of government decrees had at least a moderate effect on their businesses, while 47 percent said the same of payments to members of parliament that affected their votes. These figures were higher than in Kenya (which reported 40 percent and 26 percent, respectively) and Uganda (which reported 30 percent and 20 percent, respectively).

Informal payments to secure government contracts also appear common in Tanzania. Of enterprises that did business with the government, about 33 percent reported that unofficial payments were needed to secure government contracts. Within the subset of firms reporting that payments were needed, the median firm reported that about 10 percent of the contract value was needed to secure government work. This result was similar to the median percentages reported in Uganda and Kenya (both 10 percent), but significantly higher than the median percentage reported in China (2 percent). The amount paid in bribes is strongly correlated with firm performance: firms with faster sales growth and higher productivity pay larger bribes. Because corrupt officials often target the most productive and profitable enterprises, corruption can act as a tax on efficient firms.

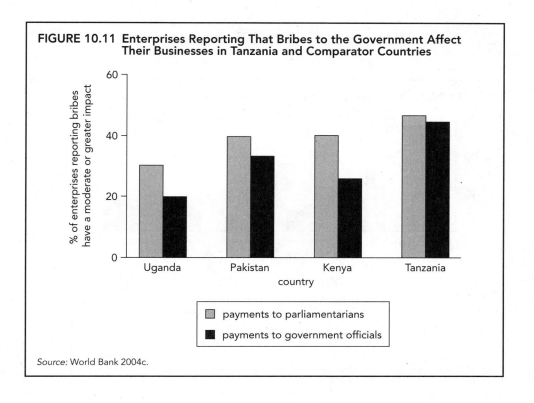

FIGURE 10.11 Enterprises Reporting That Bribes to the Government Affect Their Businesses in Tanzania and Comparator Countries

Source: World Bank 2004c.

Petty Corruption

Enterprises are also affected by petty corruption—payments made to lower-level government officials to "get things done" in connection with customs, taxes, licenses, and other services. About 35 percent of enterprise managers said that informal payments were typically needed for firms like theirs. Of the enterprises that reported that informal payments were needed, the median payment was about 0.3 percent of sales. Bribes were fairly common for many transactions, such as getting utility connections and applying for import licenses (table 10.6).

Informal payments and gifts were also common during inspections and mandatory meetings with government officials. About 21 percent of enterprises that had inspections or meetings with officials from the Tanzania Revenue Authority reported that

TABLE 10.6 Likelihood of Reporting That Bribes Were Needed to Get Things Done, by Size of Enterprise

(percent)

Report		Size of enterprise			
	Micro	Small	Medium	Large	Very large
Bribes needed to "get things done"	23	30	44	41	36	
Gifts or payments required					
Mainline telephone connection	—	26	27	14	0
Electrical connection	27	32	35	27	14
Water connection	33	22	24	13	0
Import license	—	0	19	12	9
Operating license	34	15	30	14	6

Source: World Bank 2004c.
Note: — = not available.

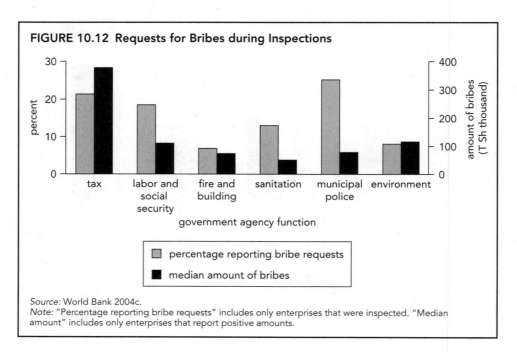

FIGURE 10.12 Requests for Bribes during Inspections

Source: World Bank 2004c.
Note: "Percentage reporting bribe requests" includes only enterprises that were inspected. "Median amount" includes only enterprises that report positive amounts.

bribes were requested, with the median amount being T Sh 375,000 (figure 10.12). Similarly, 25 percent of enterprises dealing with the municipal police reported requests for bribes. The median payment in that case was T Sh 80,000. About 18 percent of enterprises reported requests from labor or social security officials, 13 percent from health and sanitation inspectors, 8 percent from environmental inspectors, and 7 percent from fire and building safety inspectors. Payments to these other inspectors were generally lower than payments to tax officials.

Microenterprises are less likely than larger enterprises to find corruption a major or very severe constraint. Only 18 percent of informal microenterprises and 30 percent of formal microenterprises found corruption to be a serious problem, compared to 48 to 58 percent of small, medium, and large enterprises. Microenterprises were particularly unlikely to face requests for bribes. Only 15 percent of informal microenterprises reported that bribes were needed to get things done, compared with 38 percent of formal microenterprises.

Although microenterprises were less likely to report that bribes were needed to get things done, they were no less likely to report that bribes were needed for typical transactions. For example, 34 percent of microenterprises reported that bribes were needed to get an operating license, compared with 15 percent of small, 30 percent of medium, 14 percent of large, and 6 percent of very large enterprises. The most plausible explanation is that microenterprises are far less likely to interact with bribe-taking institutions but at least as likely to encounter corruption when they do. For example, only 5 percent of microenterprises reported getting an electricity connection in the two years before the survey, compared with 30 percent of larger enterprises (figure 10.13). Microenterprises were also less likely to get operating licenses, water connections, and fixed-line telephone connections.

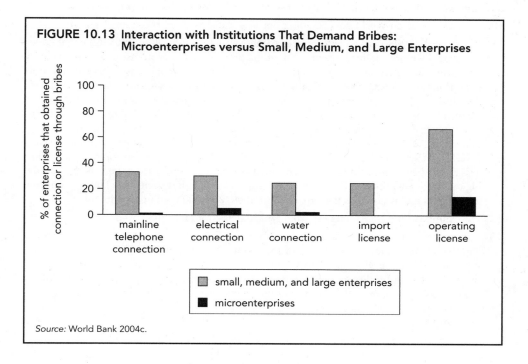

FIGURE 10.13 Interaction with Institutions That Demand Bribes: Microenterprises versus Small, Medium, and Large Enterprises

y-axis: % of enterprises that obtained connection or license through bribes

x-axis categories: mainline telephone connection; electrical connection; water connection; import license; operating license

Legend:
- small, medium, and large enterprises
- microenterprises

Source: World Bank 2004c.

Notes

1. These estimates are drawn from Chandra, Kacker, and Li (2005).

2. The ex post rates of return of the selected infrastructure projects should be interpreted in the context of the policy and institutional environment during the particular time period. It is also important to note that economic rates of return may not fully capture all the benefits of infrastructure investment, especially if those benefits occur in the form of externalities (see Canning and Bennathan 2003).

3. The preliminary results of this study are contained in Fan, Nyange, and Rao (2005).

4. The core road network required for poverty alleviation (that is, the network that provides reliable access for roughly 90 percent of the population) is 45,000 kilometers long. This figure represents more than half of the existing network—emphasizing the importance of roads for poverty reduction.

5. It is estimated that in April 2005, almost 50 percent of the T-bills were held by two banks.

6. Canada, the Netherlands, Sweden, and the United Kingdom.

7. Using data from the World Bank's Doing Business database for 85 developing and developed economies, Djankov and others (2002) find that informality is greater in countries with greater barriers to entry.

8. Broadman and Recanatini (2001) find that corruption is higher in transition economies, where entry barriers, which they measure using subjective data from the World Business Environment Survey, are higher. Djankov and others (2002) find similar results using different data.

9. Using data from 17 high-income OECD economies for several manufacturing and business service industries between 1984 and 1998, Scarpetta and Nicoletti (2003) show that multifactor productivity is lower in sectors where regulation is stricter. Alesina and others (2003) present results for investment. Because the measures of regulation are sector specific and are measured over time, both this study and Scarpetta and Nicoletti (2003) control for country- and sector-specific effects that might affect investment and productivity.

10. Data are from the World Bank's Doing Business database.

11. World Bank (2005d) asked enterprise managers how long it takes from the time that goods arrive at the point of entry or exit to the time that they clear customs. It did not ask how much time was attributable to customs processing and how much was attributable to port operations because managers typically do not have access to this information. However, for the most part, the problems in Tanzania appear to be related to customs, rather than port performance. For example, the Economist Intelligence Unit (2004b, 26) notes, "One of the more successful privatizations carried out by the government is that of Dar es Salaam container port. This is now being run by Tanzania International Container Terminal Services (TICTS), a company that is financially controlled by a Hong Kong-based company. . . . While TICTS has benefited from the long-term project embarked on by the government in dredging the port's entry channel, its own investment in facilities has been a key factor in improving services and it now has the capacity to handle 250,000 containers annually."

12. For example, nine enterprises reported typical delays of more than 50 days.

13. For example, enterprises in Tanzania were more likely to rate high tax rates as a major problem than firms in almost two-thirds of the countries in the 1999 World Business Environment Survey. The survey asked firms in all surveyed regions about infrastructure, access to finance, policy instability and uncertainty, inflation, exchange rates, the functioning of the judiciary, street crime, and organized crime. The survey also asked about regulatory constraints, including high tax rates and tax administration.

14. Enterprise managers were asked about the "typical firm" in their industry rather than their own firm so that they could avoid implicating themselves (World Bank 2004c).

15. It may also reflect the way that the question was asked. If registered enterprises felt that unregistered enterprises in the same sector and of similar size were an "enterprise like yours," they may have included those enterprises in their responses.

16. Reforms included the establishment of the independent Tanzania Revenue Authority in 1996, and measures designed to limit political interference in tax administration and to allow the authority to pay salaries that were higher than would have been possible had the agency remained part of the civil service (Fjeldstad 2002).

17. See ESRF and FACEIT (2002) for a general summary of the Warioba Report and progress against corruption over the preceding decade.

11

Harnessing Natural Resources for Sustainable Growth

Kerstin Pfliegner

Natural resources in Tanzania constitute a wealth asset. Since 1996, mining, fisheries, and tourism have been the most dynamic sectors in the economy. Although tourism development is a success story in macroeconomic terms, local development spin-off effects could be explored more fully. Most known mineral deposits are already being tapped, but new mineral stocks are being discovered. The fisheries sector is still growing, but there are signs of decline in the catch per boat in Lake Victoria and the catch of fish and prawn in the coastal zones, which point toward a deceleration of growth in the medium and long terms.

Forestry, wildlife, and marine fisheries resources, though declining, are still relatively abundant and have largely untapped growth potential. Although these natural resources, like labor and capital, contribute to the economy and the subsistence base of the rural population, their value and potential are underestimated. This underestimation is partly based on missing markets for public goods, imperfect competition, distortions caused by government interventions, and pricing of natural resources below market value. The result of all these market failures leads to suboptimal economic decision making and loss of income to the country.

The National Strategy for Growth and Poverty Reduction of 2005 subscribes to the principles of sustainable and equitable development. The operational starting points of these principles include the following:

- Renewable resources should be exploited on the bases of maximizing profits and sustaining yields. Resources should not be driven to extinction, regardless of the dictates of present value maximization. Hence, harvesting rates should not exceed regeneration rates and waste emissions should not exceed absorptive capacities.

- Nonrenewable resources should be exploited at a rate equal to the creation of renewable substitutes. Revenue from the exploitation of nonrenewable resources should contain an income component and a capital component. The capital component should be used to invest in building up a new renewable asset to replace the nonrenewable one at the point of its exhaustion.

• Revenue generated from natural resources should be shared equitably, in particular with the rural communities on whose land these resources are located.

The macroeconomics of sustainability require integrating qualitative development and growth in gross domestic product (GDP) more fully, giving equal weight to the need for pro-poor growth and the maintenance of a sustainable natural resource base. Because of policy failures, Tanzania's natural resource endowments are not harnessed in an optimal way to achieve both economic growth and poverty reduction.

On the contrary, owing to weak governance regimes in revenue-generating sectors, resources are offered below market price to the benefit of a few powerful winners and the loss of the majority of the rural population. Yet these natural resources provide substantive potential for income to communities in rural areas. The weaknesses in governance regimes in forestry, wildlife, and fisheries include primarily (a) the lack of transparency and accountability in issuing rights to extract resources and accrue revenues from them, (b) inequitable sharing of benefits with communities, and (c) weak monitoring and surveillance of stocks. In all four principal sectors providing natural capital in the growth equation—forestry, wildlife, fisheries, and mining—royalties are set arbitrarily and do not reflect scarcity. Royalties are hence not used as a policy instrument of intertemporal resource pricing and sustained yield management.

As long as these weaknesses are not addressed, a substantial base of economic growth will slowly erode and poverty reduction objectives are unlikely to be achieved.

Contribution of Natural Resources to Growth and Government Revenue

Commonly for forestry, wildlife, and fisheries, a great share of the economic contribution does not enter GDP and export statistics and is hence not taken into account in analyses of growth. A general problem is the unavailability and poor quality of data.

An overview of annual revenue earned by the Ministry of Natural Resources and Tourism (MNRT) from its key departments in 2003 and 2004 is presented in table 11.1. Although revenue is an important measure for growth, it does not capture all contributions to economic and rural development by the respective sectors.

Forestry provided more than T Sh 5 billion in government revenue in 2003 and 2004, as table 11.1 shows. It officially contributes 2 to 3 percent to GDP and 10 to 15 percent to export earnings. Estimates that include unaccounted-for services and nonindustrial forestry reach 10 to 15 percent of GDP.

Forests provide about 75 percent of building materials and 100 percent of indigenous medicinal plants and supplementary food products. In addition, forests provide an important component of value added to national income through their ecosystem service functions—providing for industrial and domestic water and energy supply.

TABLE 11.1 Ministry of Natural Resources and Tourism Annual Revenue, 2002/03 and 2003/04

Revenue source	Amount of revenue (T Sh billion)	
	2002/03	2003/04
Forestry	5.29	5.82
Wildlife	9.17	9.55
Fisheries	6.99	9.70
Tourism	0.83	0.96

Source: Ministry of Natural Resources and Tourism 2004.
Note: Amounts include revenue collected and retained at source.

Some 95 percent of Tanzania's energy consumption is in the form of fuelwood; that consumption includes major input factors in rural industries such as tobacco curing and fish smoking. Forests provide watershed functions for major rivers feeding into the national hydropower dams. The lack of reliable power and water supplies can hamper growth in the long term and is already being cited as a serious constraint in attracting private investment.

Further to their "source" functions, forests also have "sink" functions, absorbing and neutralizing the negative externalities of economic growth—most importantly pollution. The value of carbon sequestration services provided by Tanzanian forests is estimated to be between US$700 and US$1,500 per hectare. Additional environmental service functions include inputs from land and forests into agricultural production.

Revenue generated from wildlife resources accrues to the MNRT mainly from hunting licenses; it was more than T Sh 9 million during 2003 and 2004 (table 11.1). An independent study (Baldus and Cauldwell 2004) of the sector cites annual earnings in 2001 of about US$30 million from tourists' hunting and an additional US$9 million generated by the private companies that lease hunting concessions from the government. In 2002, earnings from live animal exports amounted to roughly US$170,000.

The largest income earner is the nonconsumptive use of wildlife resources: game viewing by international tourists. In 2001, Tanzanian national parks drew more than 100,000 international visitors. This tourism generated receipts of almost 5 percent of GDP, equivalent to about US$400 million.

In addition, wildlife provides unaccounted-for subsistence values. Well over two-thirds of the people eat wild game, with up to 95 percent of the rural population claiming it as their most important meat protein source.

Tanzania's production in the fisheries sector has grown at 4 percent annually between 2000 and 2005. In 2005, the value of caught fish amounted to T Sh 339 billion, compared to T Sh 78 billion in 2000. About 75 percent of revenue comes from freshwater fisheries, and only 25 percent from marine fisheries. However, the number of foreign vessels licensed to operate in the Exclusive Economic Zone (EEZ) on the mainland and Zanzibar has increased from fewer than 10 in 1998 to more than 170 in 2004, corresponding to revenue of US$3.3 million. In terms of export earnings, fisheries contributed 8 percent of total exports in 2005 (US$142 million), the export value of Nile perch alone being US$129 million.

A great share of the marine catch does not enter GDP and export statistics but plays an important role in livelihood support. The official number of artisanal fishermen has doubled since 1995, reaching close to 115,000 in 2005.

Although the contribution of mining to GDP was still not more than 2.8 percent in 2005, it is the single most important earner of foreign exchange. About 50 percent of export earnings accrue from minerals, predominantly from gold mining by large-scale, foreign-owned operators. In addition, mineral resources are important to the artisanal mining sector.

Public Investment in Natural Resource–Based Growth

It is obvious from these data that these natural resource–based sectors make an important contribution to both the formal and the subsistence economies. However, of the three natural resource sectors, only fisheries represent a net contributor to the Treasury. Forestry and wildlife are subsidized through government allocations to cover their recurrent expenditures and through foreign grant allocations to finance their development budgets. Table 11.2 shows the government recurrent budget allocations to the sectors: forestry and wildlife each received 29 percent of the MNRT budget in 2003/04, followed by fisheries (18 percent) and tourism (11 percent).

There is a mismatch between foreign resource allocation for sectoral development activities and national funding allocation for recurrent expenditures. The large degree of underspending of the development budgets in both sectors is a possible indication of constraints on capacity to absorb foreign funding and institutional inefficiencies, aggravated by the uncoordinated policies of the development partners. In the forestry sector, a planned sectorwide approach is supposed to address the last problem.

There is a tendency to draw government allocation away from these sectors, because they should finance themselves and move toward privatization. However, there are trade-offs to this trend. There is a need for government to control and regulate, setting and enforcing fiscal and market instruments to ensure sustained growth and incorporation of externalities. Although the recurrent government budget allocations to

TABLE 11.2 Budget of Ministry of Natural Resources and Tourism, as Distributed by Subsector, 2002/03–2003/04

Subsector	2002/03		2003/04	
	T Sh thousand	Percent	T Sh thousand	Percent
Forestry and beekeeping	4,897,656	24	7,633,912	29
Wildlife	6,593,025	33	7,586,736	29
Fisheries	3,688,280	18	4,648,202	18
Tourism	2,208,073	11	2,880,761	11
Other	2,856,131	14	3,507,741	13
Total	20,243,165	100	26,257,352	100

Source: Ministry of Natural Resources and Tourism 2004.
Note: Total includes other subsectors not listed here. The amounts are only recurrent expenditures.

these sectors are getting smaller and there is a trend toward privatizing some government functions, the need for sectorwide environmental management functions is increasing. Environmental impact assessments; market-based instruments for environmental protection (such as taxes, subsidies, standards, and permits); monitoring of stocks; and legal enforcement are becoming more important as the economy grows. Because of institutional failures, these overarching environmental management functions have basically been lacking in Tanzania for the past decade.

Although the new Environmental Management Act provides the necessary environmental framework law, the country is still a long way from seeing the effects of its implementation. Increased public investments are needed to support these broad-based environmental management activities.

Untapped Growth Potential

With regard to nonconsumptive use of wildlife for game-viewing tourism, the potential in the southern parks remains untapped. Although the Northern Circuit has supposedly reached maximum carrying capacity in terms of numbers of visitors, places such as Ruaha and Katavi National Parks are still fairly unknown. Shifting marketing and infrastructure development to those areas would provide new growth potential for the tourism sector. In addition, there is scope to increase the concession fees of international tour operators and lodges, which currently account for only 2 percent of the revenue of Tanzania National Parks (TANAPA).

Marine fisheries have recorded a sharp rise in revenue from licensing of foreign vessels in the EEZ (figure 11.1). Some sources estimate that the present revenue does not reflect the amount that the government could earn and that the real catch is much higher than what has been assumed as the basis for setting license fees (between 200 and more than 400 tons per day per boat). Notably, there is no catch-based license or fee, and vessels are allowed unlimited catch if they have a valid license. Although the annual revenue, as shown in figure 11.1, is considerable, it is low compared with the estimated value of fish caught by foreign vessels in Tanzanian waters and sold in foreign markets. One must thus assume that there is scope for revenue increases.

With regard to freshwater fisheries, past growth rates are based mainly on Nile perch exports from Lake Victoria. Other lakes, such as Tanganyika and Nyasa, are commercially underdeveloped, as is the harvesting of other species.

Diversification could also be sought in terms of exploring additional export markets. Risks and vulnerability increase when export earnings in a sector depend entirely on a single market. For example, fisheries exports from Lake Victoria are destined mainly for the European Union. Following an unfavorable assessment of sanitary standards by the European Union, Tanzanian fish-processing plants had to halt all production for several months in 1999 because of a temporary ban.

Despite high growth in the fisheries sector and despite local production of fishnets, 95 percent of fishnets are imported. Hence, an important backward link to the industry and an employment opportunity remain unexploited.

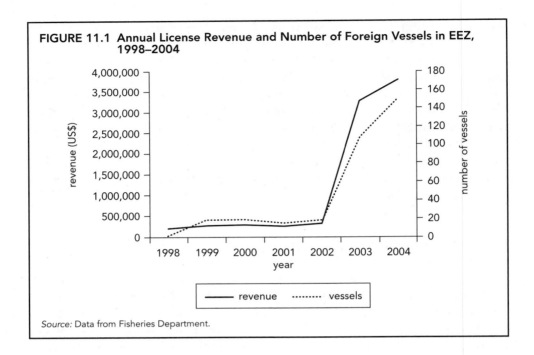

FIGURE 11.1 Annual License Revenue and Number of Foreign Vessels in EEZ, 1998–2004

Source: Data from Fisheries Department.

Commercial fisheries present an important, emerging revenue source for the country and the sector. If the sector is well managed, commercial fisheries can have positive effects on economic growth and poverty reduction at the same time. Principles of management need to include retention and reinvestment of revenue into the sector and safeguarding of the artisanal fisheries to protect their rights and access to the resource.

Potential for Local Spinoff Effects

Local spinoff effects are missing for marine fisheries in the EEZ. While new fisheries agreements are being negotiated with foreign countries, no fish are expected to be landed ashore, and few supplies will be sourced from within Tanzania. If no such spinoff effects are created, the net effect of commercial fisheries on poverty reduction may be negative, increasing competition with artisanal fisheries over the same resource.

The fact that Tanzania is a net importer of forest products is a sign of lost opportunities for income generation for the local economy. Similarly, the mining sector seems to have had limited influence on reducing poverty in the local economy. Employment in the large-scale mining sector is limited, although younger employees especially may receive significant salaries. The majority of those employed in the mining sector are self-employed in the small-scale sector, typically as artisanal miners. Returns are very low, especially when one considers the hardship associated with this kind of employment. It seems, furthermore, that an increasing income disparity is emerging between those employed in the small-scale mining sector and those employed in the large-scale one. To the extent that those recruited by the large-scale mining sector are recruited outside the local community, the local community is thus restricted to opting for poorly paid employment opportunities in the small-scale sector.

Large-scale mining may have positive effects for local communities through the improvement of basic infrastructure. There is, however, no indication that expansion in the mining sector triggers significant growth in the local economy, because mining operations generally are detached from local supply chains and therefore primarily create employment in the services sector.

Potential for Poverty Reduction

In addition to their potential for generating government revenue, wildlife, fisheries, and forestry resources provide the nonagricultural subsistence base for rural communities in remote locations. Increased emphasis on natural resources–related enterprises has the potential to create additional income opportunities for the rural population.

For example, in Loliondo Division in Ngorongoro District, seven villages earn more than US$110,000 per year from joint ventures with wildlife tour operators. In Ololosokwan village, tourism revenue totals about US$55,000 per year. The income from payments by one of four tour operators in Ololosokwan is shown in figure 11.2. If the

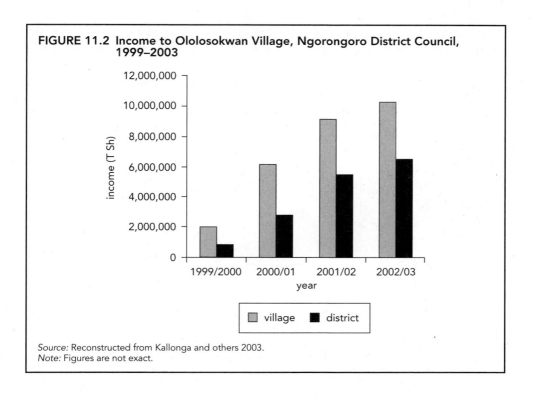

FIGURE 11.2 Income to Ololosokwan Village, Ngorongoro District Council, 1999–2003

Source: Reconstructed from Kallonga and others 2003.
Note: Figures are not exact.

effects of elite capture are avoided and income is equitably distributed within the communities, this income has large poverty reduction potential in a dryland area that does not offer many other opportunities for diversification.

Although Ololosokwan is an exceptional example, the potential for local development from wildlife-related tourism has not been fully tapped in other areas. In the Mara-Serengeti ecosystem, the number of households earning any income from tourism varies from 86 percent in Talek, Kenya, to 12 percent and 3 percent at the Ngorongoro Conservation Area and Loliondo Game Reserve on the Tanzanian side.

In the Southern Circuit, tourism is growing, offering potential scope for positive effects on local economic development. Participatory wildlife management in communities close to Ruaha National Park in Iringa District generated T Sh 15 million in local income in 1999, accrued through earnings from the residents' hunting quota. An additional T Sh 4.1 million was earned from the 25 percent share of license fees from tourists' hunting (figure 11.3).

The income from hunting quotas was sufficient to triple village-level communal income, enabling villages to pay district-level taxes that would otherwise be levied on households, as well as to carry out social infrastructure investments. One of the success factors identified was that the project has emphasized institutional capacity building at village and intervillage levels.

Similarly, community-based forest management has provided revenue to villages across Tanzania. The 2002 Forest Act authorizes villages to sell timber from their own forest reserves, potentially providing a new source of forest revenue that would accrue directly to the communities.

Despite the conducive policy framework in both the wildlife and forestry sectors, weak governance systems at both the central and local levels have so far limited the realization of the potential for poverty reduction through community-based natural

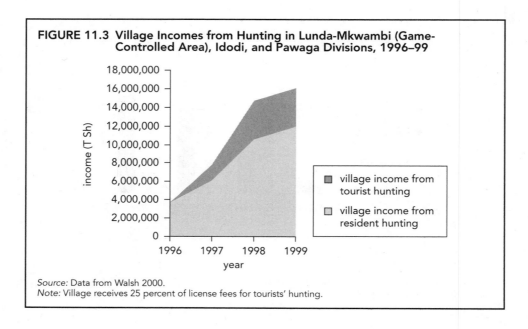

FIGURE 11.3 Village Incomes from Hunting in Lunda-Mkwambi (Game-Controlled Area), Idodi, and Pawaga Divisions, 1996–99

Source: Data from Walsh 2000.
Note: Village receives 25 percent of license fees for tourists' hunting.

resources management. The main focus in community wildlife management has been on institutions and the distribution of benefits rather than on enterprise opportunities at the household level. Fear of inequity has led to the relative neglect of entrepreneurship in Tanzania, reflecting a persistent and much broader philosophical bias against private enterprise.

Sustainability of Growth

In the context of sustainability of natural resources–based growth, several constraints are emerging that lead to revenue loss and possible deceleration of growth in the long term:

- Underpricing of resources, thereby not allowing the capture of resource rents

- Weak environmental governance systems

- Limited knowledge of stocks, their values, and changes over time.

Underpricing of Resources

Sustainable growth based on renewable resources requires that the cost of extracting a resource and the notional cost of replacing a unit of the resource, commonly known as *resource rent*, be evaluated so that the wealth base is not eroded. Although royalties are the most important source of government revenue in forestry (83 percent), wildlife (96 percent from hunting licenses), and fisheries (84 percent from royalties and 15 percent from export licenses), they are set arbitrarily and capture neither market values nor resource rents.

Similarly, in the mining sector, licenses to foreign investors do not take the capital component into account. Tax incentives for foreign investors have been generous, to attract capital investment and to open the market, at the expense of sustainability principles. In this scenario, the acceleration of growth comes at the expense of pricing resources below market value, which leads to loss of income, erosion of critical stocks, and an associated deceleration of growth in the long term.

Estimates of resource rents from marine fisheries, computed from license fees as a percentage of the value of revenue through licenses for foreign vessels fishing in the EEZ, show that gross resource rent is approximately 2.2 percent. That percentage is less than half of what might be expected in a Western industrial fishery. The current license fee arrangements of private fisheries agreements in the EEZ generate not insignificant amounts of revenue, and the level is too low to result in a reasonable return of revenue (more than 5 to 7 percent of gross revenue) to capture a resource rent.

Similarly, in forestry, royalties have been fixed arbitrarily. The 2002 Forest Act demands the determination of royalties based on market value, profitability, and principles of sustainable harvesting. Improvement of the Forest Produce Pricing System should include market-based pricing of forest produce and public auctions or tendering for timber lots. Royalties could also be used as an instrument to divert harvests from pressured species toward lesser-known species.

In the wildlife sector, the concession component of TANAPA's earnings is only 2 percent, which most likely underrepresents the value of these concessions compared with the income they generate for the foreign investor. Loss of revenue and unsustainable use are also fostered through hunting quotas that do not reflect true market values and are not based on ecological monitoring to maintain critical stocks. Presently, concessions are leased at rates far below true market value irrespective of size, quality, or income potential. This situation represents a massive loss of income to the Wildlife Division (estimated at more than US$7 million). The system promotes subleasing to foreigners, with the result that much of the income generated by the industry never enters the country and substantial tax revenue is lost.

Weak Environmental Governance

In forestry, an undercollection of 5 to 10 percent of revenue is reported to be due to inefficiencies in revenue collection and to corruption in the sector. The 2004 logging scandal in Rufiji revealed that illegally harvested logs were valued at T Sh 382.65 million.

In marine fisheries, it is alleged that Zanzibar licenses for foreign vessels are registered in Muscat, Oman, the fees thus escaping the Zanzibar authorities. In EEZ fisheries, the lack of transparency is attributed to a large degree to the lack of catch reporting by foreign vessels. The governance regime in EEZ fisheries is unique in that it imposes responsibilities for transparency and accountability on other nations whose fisheries cover distant water.

In the wildlife sector, a nontransparent system of quota setting for the hunting industry by the government leads to imperfect competition in the market. There is no competitive bidding for hunting concessions, but distribution through autonomous government decision making. Effective market forces are hence not applied to optimize revenues. This policy intervention leads to a monopoly of knowledge by the Wildlife Division and an oligopsony in access to the resource, a situation in which a small number of large buyers controls the market. Consequently, quotas are sold below market value, leading to a loss in revenue. Although imperfect competition usually benefits a few powerful players, it usually disadvantages the majority of the population. It leads to loss of income and livelihoods for rural communities.

Limited Knowledge of Resources Stock Values and Stock Changes

The optimal scale of natural resource–based economic growth must be at a sustainable level. Hence, a general macrolevel constraint of growth is that the optimal scale is the one at which the long-run marginal cost of expansion equals the long-term marginal benefits of expansion. This constraint cannot be operationalized if the true costs of resource extraction are unknown.

Commonly in fisheries, forestry, wildlife, and mining, there are neither inventories of the full availability of stocks nor complete information about their value. In addition, stock changes are not monitored comprehensively. In the absence of stock and flow data, limits of extraction and quotas associated with licenses can be set only arbitrarily. Hence, they are not based on sound ecological calculations and realistic projections. For example, in marine fisheries, there are no catch limits attached to licenses, allowing vessels to take as many fish as are available, and foreign fishing vessels return only scant information on actual catch. Similarly in forestry, land coverage, deforestation, and values represented in the country's forest estate are a matter of speculation.

There is already a government effort in the fisheries and forestry sectors to address some of these problems. For example, the Fisheries Department has lately increased its monitoring, control, and surveillance with support from a South African Development Community regional project. The Forestry Department is in the process of developing a national forest monitoring facility and database.

Externalities

Consideration and efficient control of externalities is important to reflect the true cost of the use of resources and to prevent their overexploitation. In addition, externalities can cause trade-offs between economic growth and poverty reduction because they can negatively affect local people's access to natural resources. Finally, control of externalities can realize cost savings in monies otherwise spent on pollution control. Examples are abundant:

- Economic growth is associated with an increased need for energy and water supply for domestic and industrial purposes. Currently, 95 percent of energy supply comes from biomass energy. Because of incorrect pricing, the price of charcoal does not represent the full value of the wood being harvested. In terms of providing value added to growth through energy and water supply, Tanzania's forests provide critical capital. Catchment forests are an example, and their conservation is clearly a binding constraint to be addressed.

- Increased agricultural production and intensification can create externalities. Large commercial rice farming in the Usangu Plains has reduced the dry season flow of the Great Ruaha River through intensified year-round irrigation, which is negatively affecting water use by small-scale farmers downstream.

- Commercial fish production for export markets at Lake Victoria erodes a base of livelihood and food supply for local fishing communities. Similarly, the penetration of foreign vessels into territorial seas affects the catch of artisanal fisheries.

- Mining poses a number of threats to and possibilities for local communities, as well as for the miners themselves. The nature and extent of the threats and opportunities cannot be assessed in detail because of the lack of reliable data. There are concerns that large commercial mining crowds out the artisanal sector. Also, there are indications of a number of negative social effects, notably child labor, HIV/AIDS, and gender imbalances.

• The evidence about the environmental effects of large-scale mining suggests that mining communities may suffer a number of severe effects, from direct and observable noise and erosion to longer-term pollution of air, water, and soil, which in turn may have serious health consequences. Still, the evidence does not allow for extrapolation; more comprehensive analysis is required to get a better idea of the environmental implications of large-scale mining in Tanzania.

The current policy framework does not provide for sound management of natural resources and mitigation of externalities. Instruments applied at present for revenue generation do not address externalities, nor are they used as instruments to capture rents from natural resources. Rather than employing fiscal instruments to steer the exploitation of resources, there is, allegedly, tax evasion within the revenue-generating sectors themselves.

Hence, in the present regime of environmental governance, increased growth will come at the cost of running down the resource stocks, impeding long-term growth opportunities. To ensure a positive net effect of accelerated growth on poverty reduction, a careful balance needs to be preserved between increasing export earnings and maintaining the resource base for the artisanal sector. In particular, in fisheries, certain safeguards need to be put in place for the artisanal fisheries to protect their rights, access to the resource, and livelihoods.

Recommendations

Making sustainable development operational is an international political challenge. In particular, in the context of globally shared resources such as fisheries, responsibilities apply to both harvesting and host countries. True factor pricing and resource rent capture are policy instruments that even some Western countries grapple with. Yet some basic principles of governance are missing in Tanzania, which, if applied, could regain some of the lost opportunities described in this chapter.

The single most important recommendation for capturing and maintaining natural resource–based growth in Tanzania is to reform environmental governance so as to achieve good governance, rule of law, and equity. Such reform includes ensuring greater coherence between different national policies and instruments, particularly community-based wildlife management, tourism development, rural growth strategies, investment regulations and incentives, and poverty reduction strategies.

In addition, Tanzania needs to make investments in the improvement of its human capacity and capital stock so that value-added processing of natural resources can take place more often within the country. This investment is required to comply with the principle stated in the National Strategy for Growth and Poverty Reduction that policies should be designed so that benefits from high-growth sectors are transmitted to the poor in the form of better livelihood opportunities—for example, supporting supply links with local producers.

The recommendations below are divided into general recommendations, which apply equally to all natural resources sectors, and sector-specific recommendations.

General recommendations:

- Strengthen capacity for data collection, recordkeeping, monitoring, control, and surveillance and enforce punitive measures to control illegal practices.

- Control externalities through fiscal instruments, royalties, and resource pricing and increase revenue from rent capture rather than uncontrolled exploitation.

- Increase efficiency in revenue collection and administration, as well as full transparency and accountability over revenue generation and distribution.

- Promote market-based principles when appropriate, ensuring local spinoffs and allowing competition and entrepreneurial development.

Fisheries:

- Put in place a regulatory framework and sound governance regime for marine fisheries, comprising the EEZ and near-shore fisheries.

- Safeguard rights and livelihoods for coastal communities, for example, through demarcation of a community territorial sea.

- Conduct a fisheries sector review to assess the economic and social, ecological, and fiscal perspectives and policy options. The review could inform policy makers and influence the strengthening of the regulatory framework.

- Establish some form of EEZ inspectorate patrol to build a more accurate picture of available resources.

- Investigate the potential for exports of marine products and for value adding of these products to promote growth in the coastal zone.

Forestries:

- Introduce taxes for wood lot and plantation owners—in particular an income tax based on timber sales and a property tax based on the average productive capacity of different land categories.

- Enforce the collection of royalties and fees and eliminate the exemption for industries such as tobacco and fishing.

- Improve the forest produce pricing system through market-based pricing, public auctions or tendering for timber lots, and cheaper royalties for lesser-known species.

- Increase domestic and foreign private sector investment through reduction of bureaucracy in the licensing system, clear investment guidelines, clearly defined ownership of all forestland, tax incentives, credit facilities, and technology transfer.

- Increase the capacity utilization of the sector to reverse the trade balance to net exports of forest products.

- Introduce new revenue sources, such as watershed management fees from hydropower stations, sale of genetic resources, and carbon credits.

Wildlife:

- Encourage attitudinal change toward wildlife at the policy level so that policy makers see it as an asset for rural development and poverty reduction rather than as something looked after by conservationists. Such an attitude change will include a shift in the emphasis of community wildlife approaches to focus on creating enterprise opportunities.

- Ensure that local communities are the principal decision makers for allocation of concessions and quota setting for hunting on their land and that they receive and manage the funds generated on their land.

- Reform the tourist hunting industry to realize its true revenue potential. Such reform includes the introduction of market-based competition in the commercial hunting industry through competitive bidding for concessions. It may have the positive side effect of naturally controlling subleasing and related revenue losses.

- Introduce performance-based independent monitoring of the hunting industry, possibly through certification, to ensure that certain standards are adhered to. Criteria should be set to consider the maximum income from the least number of animals hunted and contributions toward protection and community involvement.

- Revise the quota-setting system on the basis of more objective criteria, computerization of hunting data, and monitoring of trophy quality and age.

- Conduct a review (by the Ministry of Finance) of the financial management and taxation procedures of the Wildlife Division to assess strengths and weaknesses. This review would include an inventory of the true value of hunting licenses.

Tourism:

- Integrate opportunities for pro-poor tourism into tourism strategies; set objectives in terms of local development effects, not just numbers of tourists or foreign exchange earnings.

- Establish a pro-poor tourism growth program to place attention on company practices, destination management, infrastructure development, procurement patterns, national training, and regulation.

Mining:

- Improve data collection on externalities in the mining sector (for example, through more rigorous and systematic enforcement of environmental impact assessments).

- Revise the pricing system to capture the capital component of nonrenewable mining resources.

12

Enhancing the Capacity of the Poor to Participate in Growth

Johannes Hoogeveen

This chapter examines what strategies would enable poor people to participate in growth. The most important assets of poor Tanzanians are labor and, in rural areas, land. A strategy that aims to enhance the capacity of the poor to participate in growth should therefore focus on an intensification of the use of labor and land while permitting poor Tanzanians to build up human and physical capital.

We first focus on those aspects that build human capital: education, nutrition, health, and fertility. Next, we discuss aspects that allow poor people to build physical capital and, in particular, the exposure to risk and the role of financial markets. Finally, and starting from the realization that certain people may not be able to benefit from growth, we discuss social protection and inequity.

Improving Human Capital of the Poor

Levels of human capital are low in Tanzania, and building human capital is an important element of the poverty-reducing strategy for at least two reasons. First, by building human capital, the foundation is laid for higher growth in the future (Barro 1991; Mankiw, Romer, and Weil 1992). Second, by building the human capital of the poor, the pattern of growth will be pro-poor.

In this section, we discuss three elements of human capital: education, nutrition, and population (health care and fertility).

Education

Twenty-nine percent of Tanzanians age 15 and above are illiterate (National Bureau of Statistics 2002), and according to the 2002 census, the average number of years of education of the working population (ages 20 to 64) is 5.1. Not only is the lack of education one of the factors contributing to Tanzania being one of the poorest economies in the world, but within Tanzania, differences in education are strongly associated with income levels. In rural areas, where poverty is highest, the average level of education of heads of household is 4.3 years, compared to 7.8 years in Dar es Salaam, where poverty incidence is lowest (National Bureau of Statistics 2002). Consumption regressions show that individuals living in Dar es Salaam in households headed by someone who completed secondary education have a per capita income that is 49 percent higher than those in households headed by someone with no education. In rural areas, the difference is even larger: 70 percent (table 12.1).

Education is associated not only with income but also with nonincome dimensions of poverty. Low levels of education lead to higher total fertility, lower levels of child nutrition (Lindeboom and Kilama 2005), higher child mortality (Rafalimanana and Westoff 2001), and an intergenerational transfer of poverty because children from poor households are less likely to attend school themselves. The total fertility rate of women ages 40 to 49 is 6.5 if they do not have any education but drops to 4.9 if they completed at least primary education (National Bureau of Statistics and Macro International 2000). Evidence from Kagera shows that children with educated parents have better nutritional outcomes (Alderman, Hoogeveen, and Rossi 2006). And according to the Household Budget Survey (HBS), 52 percent of Tanzanian children ages 7 to 10 attended school, but only 44 percent from the first two quintiles did so (National Bureau of Statistics 2002).

With the prevailing low levels of education, one can see that educational attainment needs to be raised in order to reduce poverty and to raise income in general. In recent years, important initiatives to that end have been undertaken, of which the Primary Education Development Program (PEDP), introduced in July 2001, and the Secondary Education Development Program (SEDP), started in September 2004, are the most important. PEDP's aim is to increase overall gross and net enrollment of girls and boys. In recognition that some parents fail to send their children to school because of cost or distance, the program has abolished all school fees and other mandatory parental contributions and started an investment program in school buildings and classrooms. SEDP's main objective is to ensure that more of the increased numbers of primary school graduates can be absorbed into secondary schools.

Under PEDP, enrollment in standard I in primary schools increased tremendously (figure 12.1). With a net enrollment rate of 90 percent (and a gross enrollment rate that exceeds 100 percent), Tanzania has now put in place one of the essential preconditions

TABLE 12.1 Increase in Per Capita Consumption Relative to Households Headed by Individuals with No Education

(percent)

Level of education of head of household	Dar es Salaam	Other urban areas	Rural areas
Some primary education	25	19	17
Completed primary education	57	30	42
Some secondary education	36	42	48
Completed secondary education	49	52	70
Postsecondary education	90	73	90
Adult education only	43	−1	−2

Source: Author's calculations based on National Bureau of Statistics 2002.

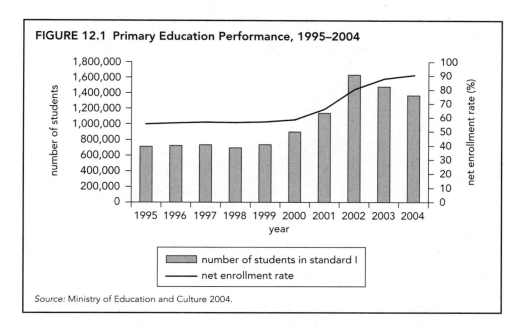

FIGURE 12.1 Primary Education Performance, 1995–2004

Source: Ministry of Education and Culture 2004.

to attain the Millennium Development Goal of ensuring that, by 2015, children will be able to complete a full course of primary schooling.

Not only did net enrollment increase dramatically with PEDP from 59 percent in 2000 to 91 percent in 2004, evidence from Kilimanjaro and Ruvuma suggests that inequalities in access to primary education have disappeared. Figure 12.2 presents, for rural Kilimanjaro, concentration curves for 2001 and 2003. In panel (a), the concentration curve for 2001 shows how pre-PEDP access to primary education was unequally distributed: children from wealthier households attended school relatively more often than children from poorer households. The distribution of access was as unequal as the distribution of consumption, represented by the Lorenz curve. With PEDP, inequalities in access to education disappeared, and the concentration curve coincides with the 45-degree line. Though not shown in the figure, results for Ruvuma are comparable.

Despite major progress in enrolling children and in addressing aspects of the gender gap (box 12.1), implementation of PEDP lags behind in certain regions, particularly the poorer and more isolated ones, as is evident from net enrollment figures. In 2004, enrollment was 90 percent for the country as a whole, but in Tabora it was only 68 percent and in Kigoma, 77.2 percent, whereas in Dar es Salaam it was 93.1 percent. Interestingly, some poor regions do particularly well. For example, Ruvuma has a net enrollment of 99.3 percent; thus, poverty is not the only explanatory factor for the divergence in performance.

After an intense focus on expanding access to primary education, there is now increased focus on addressing concerns about the quality of education. Teacher-pupil ratios of 1:52 (up from 1:46 in 2001) are hardly an enabling environment for learning. The availability of textbooks leaves much to be desired as well, although it improved from 8 students per textbook in 2001 to 4 students per textbook in 2004. That lack

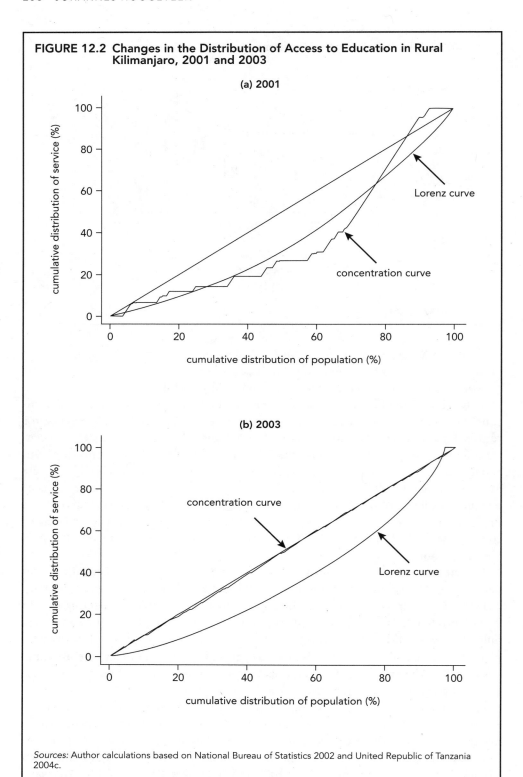

FIGURE 12.2 Changes in the Distribution of Access to Education in Rural Kilimanjaro, 2001 and 2003

Sources: Author calculations based on National Bureau of Statistics 2002 and United Republic of Tanzania 2004c.

BOX 12.1 Gender Differences in Education

With PEDP, some gender biases in education disappeared. Gender parity in enrollment has almost been attained: 49 percent of those attending primary schools are girls (Ministry of Education and Culture 2004). Information from the 2002 census also suggests that the gap in education attainment has been closed. As the figure below indicates, although women age 60 and above received only 30 percent of the education of men of the same age, girls below age 15—the youngest age cohorts—are actually better educated than boys of the same age.

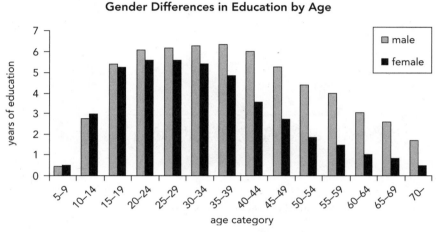

Gender Differences in Education by Age

Source: Data from 2002 census.

However, not all gender differences disappeared. Pass rates for girls at the Primary School Leavers Exam are lower than those for boys. In 2004, 48 percent of all boys passed, compared to 33 percent of all girls. That 15 percentage point gap in pass rates has persisted over the past 10 years and leads to a gender imbalance at the end of the primary curriculum, which is corrected at enrollment in secondary school in form I. Form I enrollment data for 2004 show, again, a near gender balance at entry level. Yet gender imbalances reappear later. Between form I and form IV, the girl-to-boy ratio drops gradually until it reaches a ratio of one girl to two boys in form VI (United Republic of Tanzania, Vice President's Office 2005).

---

of quality is reflected in the pass rate at the Primary School Leavers Exam. At 62 percent in 2006 (up from 22 percent in 2000), the pass rate remains low, which implies that more than one-third of the students do not learn the material expected for primary school. However, pass rates are only a proxy of quality and do not really reflect what children learn.

In secondary education, there have been improvements in recent years. The number of primary school leavers entering secondary school increased from a low of 3.4 percent in the mid-1980s to 22 percent at the start of the millennium. By 2004, that number had increased further, and approximately 30 percent of those who finished primary school got a place in a secondary school (figure 12.3). As a result of the expansion of public secondary schools, the share of private secondary schools in total secondary education has gradually dropped from 60 percent in the early 1990s to about

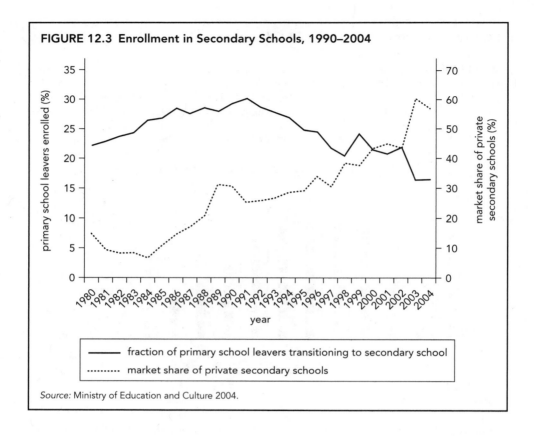

FIGURE 12.3 Enrollment in Secondary Schools, 1990–2004

— fraction of primary school leavers transitioning to secondary school

·········· market share of private secondary schools

Source: Ministry of Education and Culture 2004.

33 percent in 2004. Nonetheless, secondary education remains a relatively exclusive affair that is skewed toward the nonpoor, which the HBS data illustrate. The probability that a child age 14 to 18 attends secondary school is 2 percent if the child is from a household in the first consumption quintile and 13 percent if the child comes from a household in the top quintile.

Investing in human capital has a long lead time, and it will take many years before the current investments in education translate into higher income and reduced poverty. Even if, over the coming 10 years, those ages 10 to 19 manage to raise education levels to 7 years and those ages 5 to 9 raise education levels to 10 years, the average level of education in the working population (ages 15 to 65) will have risen from 5.1 years to only 6.8 years. Levels of education among the youth (ages 15 to 29) will have risen considerably, however, from 5.6 years now to 8.1 years, which should enhance their ability to escape poverty.

The long lead time before current investments in education will pay off in higher income and reduced poverty is reason to consider whether levels of education of those in their productive years can be raised through adult or youth education. According to the HBS, in 2000/01 26 percent of households were headed by someone with no education, which demonstrates a need for education (National Bureau of Statistics 2002). And youth and adult education potentially has a large effect on a household's earning capacity. That effect can be illustrated by the consumption level of those who benefited from some primary education: it is 17 to 25 percent higher than the consumption level of those who did not receive any education (table 12.1). In Dar es Salaam, consumption levels in households in which the head received adult education only are 43 percent higher than in households in which the head has no education. A word of caution seems justified however, as the data show no significant beneficial effect of adult education in rural and other urban areas.

Nutrition

Improving the nutritional situation of Tanzania's population is another element in a strategy aimed at building human capacity for growth and poverty reduction. The prevalence of undernutrition in Tanzania is high. As of 2004, nearly 40 percent of the children ages 0 to 59 months are chronically undernourished or stunted (low height for age) (figure 12.4). About 3 percent are wasted (low weight for height), and 22 percent of children are underweight (low weight for age), which is a composite measure of long- and short-term undernutrition and one of the Millennium Development Goal indicators.

Nutrition rates are worst among the poor. According to the 1999 Tanzania Reproductive and Child Health Survey (TRCHS), 50 percent of children in the bottom two quintiles are stunted and 34 percent are underweight. In comparison, 23 percent of children from the top quintile are stunted and 22 percent are underweight. Tanzanians are

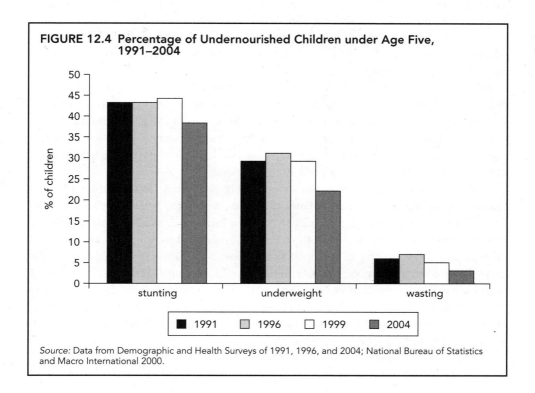

FIGURE 12.4 Percentage of Undernourished Children under Age Five, 1991–2004

Source: Data from Demographic and Health Surveys of 1991, 1996, and 2004; National Bureau of Statistics and Macro International 2000.

not only affected by protein-energy malnutrition, but many suffer from deficiencies of micronutrients such as iodine, iron, and vitamin A (National Bureau of Statistics and Macro International 2000). According to the 2004 Tanzania Demographic and Health Survey (DHS), only 43 percent of households used adequately iodized salt, and 46 percent of children ages 6 months to 59 months benefited from vitamin A supplementation in the six months preceding the survey (National Bureau of Statistics and ORC Macro 2005). Approximately two-thirds of children and 43 percent of women are anemic.

Both types of nutrient deficiencies have negative consequences for the ability to be economically active. Undernutrition retards physical growth directly as well as indirectly by increasing the susceptibility to disease. It affects cognitive and mental development and educational attainment and leads to reduced productivity and reduced income. Iron-deficiency anemia, for instance, has been shown to reduce productivity by 5 to17 percent, with the higher percentage holding for the heavier manual work such as farming, typically carried out by the poorer segments of the population (Horton 1999; Horton and Ross 2003).

Undernutrition is closely associated with the inability of HIV/AIDS-infected people to undergo antiretroviral treatment. It is also associated with under-five mortality. A high correlation exists at the regional level (a correlation coefficient of 0.27) between the fraction of children ages zero to five that are underweight and the under-five mortality rate. The correlation with stunted children is even higher at 0.57 (figure 12.5).

Undernutrition is a factor that stretches across generations. Evidence from Kagera suggests, for instance, that parents of small stature are more likely to have children of small stature as well (Alderman, Hoogeveen, and Rossi 2006). And children who are stunted at a young age are shorter later in life (figure 12.6).

In the face of high rates of undernutrition, large-scale interventions to address nutrition deficiencies are limited even though most nutrition interventions have attractive benefit-cost ratios (table 12.2).

Interventions that focus on micronutrients, improve infant and child nutrition, or reduce low birth weight have the highest benefit-cost ratios. However, the more challenging interventions, such as mother-child care programs or integrated child care programs, also have attractive benefit-cost ratios. In fact, if one were to consider large-scale interventions, such challenging interventions would have to be part of the package because of the nature of Tanzania's nutrition problems.

Undernutrition in Tanzania takes shape during pregnancy (many babies are born underweight) and during the first months following birth. According to the 1999 TRCHS (National Bureau of Statistics and Macro International 2000), the proportion of stunted children increases more than fivefold between 0 to 6 months and 13 to 24 months (from 9 percent to 53 percent). The proportion of severely stunted children increases more than sevenfold (from 3 percent to 21 percent) (figure 12.7). A strong negative association exists between nutritional status and being born during the rainy season, when demands on labor are highest and illness is most prevalent (Alderman, Hoogeveen, and Rossi 2006; Lindeboom and Kilama 2005). There is a strong positive association of nutritional status with breastfeeding, but a negative one exists for low birth weight, the birth interval, and long duration of breastfeeding because children need additional nutrients after six months of age (Lindeboom and Kilama 2005).

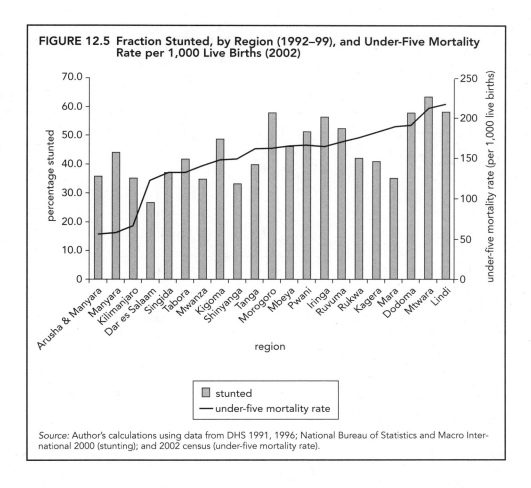

FIGURE 12.5 Fraction Stunted, by Region (1992–99), and Under-Five Mortality Rate per 1,000 Live Births (2002)

Source: Author's calculations using data from DHS 1991, 1996; National Bureau of Statistics and Macro International 2000 (stunting); and 2002 census (under-five mortality rate).

Evidence also suggests that children living in households consuming more milk are better nourished (Beegle, De Weerdt, and Dercon 2006; Lindeboom and Kilama 2005). No correlation (even a negative one) exists between food insecurity as measured in the HBS and the incidence of malnutrition at a regional level. Because undernutrition rates are high even in the wealthiest households, undernutrition seems to be less the result of a lack of food availability than one of dietary knowledge, hygiene, and care for pregnant women and young children (UNICEF 1990).[1] That pattern is consistent with global experience.

Not only are community interventions attractive for their rate of return and from a human development perspective, but they are also likely to be pro-poor. Because nutrition problems affect poor households more severely, the poor stand to benefit more from interventions. Evidence to that effect comes from Kagera, where it has been shown not only that community-based interventions had a considerable beneficial effect on nutritional status (Alderman, Hoogeveen, and Rossi 2006), but also that poor households benefit disproportionately (figure 12.8).

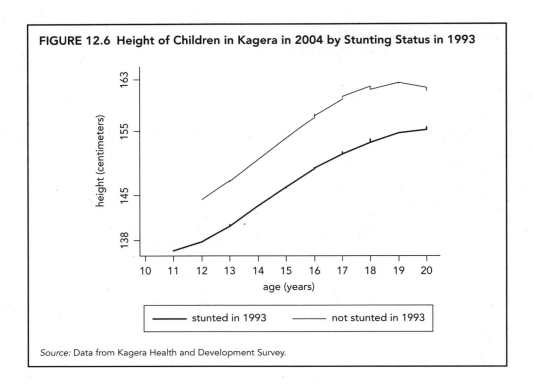

FIGURE 12.6 Height of Children in Kagera in 2004 by Stunting Status in 1993

Source: Data from Kagera Health and Development Survey.

TABLE 12.2 Benefit-Cost Ratios of Nutrition Interventions

Type of intervention	Benefit-cost ratio	
	Low	High
Improving infant and child nutrition		
Breastfeeding promotion in hospitals in places where infant formula is normally used	5.6	67.1
Integrated child care programs	9.4	16.2
Intensive preschool program with considerable nutrition for poor families	1.4	2.9
Reducing micronutrient deficiencies		
Iodine (per woman of childbearing age)	15.0	520.0
Vitamin A (child under age six years)	4.3	43.0
Iron (per capita)	176.0	200.0
Iron (pregnant women)	6.1	14.0

Source: Behrman, Alderman, and Hoddinott 2004.

The challenge for community interventions, however, is less whether they can be successful than whether they can be introduced in such a way that they are sustained over time. Evidence to date suggests that vertical, project-type interventions are difficult to maintain and hard to scale up (TFNC 2004a). Interventions that are integrated within the sectors (health, agriculture, and education) and that facilitate increased human and financial resource allocation to nutrition at subregional and community levels should be considered.

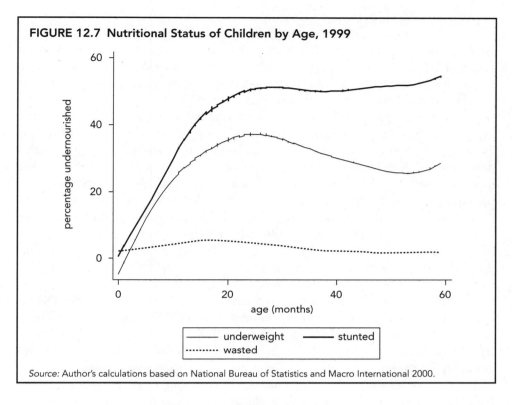

FIGURE 12.7 Nutritional Status of Children by Age, 1999

Source: Author's calculations based on National Bureau of Statistics and Macro International 2000.

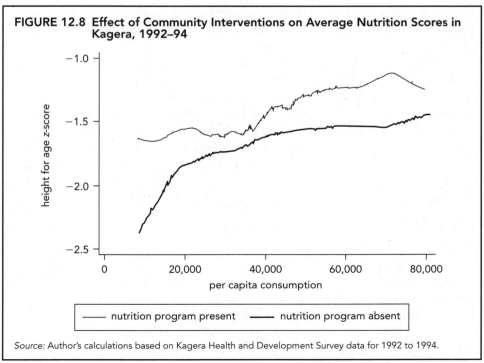

FIGURE 12.8 Effect of Community Interventions on Average Nutrition Scores in Kagera, 1992–94

Source: Author's calculations based on Kagera Health and Development Survey data for 1992 to 1994.

Health

Health is another important determinant of human capacity. Many factors affect the health of individuals, including where one lives, the state of the environment, genetics, nutritional status, income, and education. Access to and use of health care services are another determinant of health outcomes.

In recent years, progress was made in improving the health of Tanzanians. According to the 2002 census, life expectancy increased from 44 years in 1978 to 49 years in 1988 and to 54 years for males and 56 years for females in 2002. Infant mortality dropped in all regions (figure 12.9), and nationally it fell from 115 per 1,000 in 1988 to 95 per 1,000 in 2002.[2] In addition, child malnutrition, which remained unchanged over the course of the 1990s, declined rapidly between 1999 and 2004 (figure 12.4). Other health indicators saw less progress or even deterioration. Maternal mortality, which was 529 per 100,000 births in 1996, did not decline and may even have increased, though the increase to 578 in 2004 is not statistically significant. The fraction of blood donors infected by HIV/AIDS increased from 7 percent in 1994 to 12 percent in 2003 for women and from 5 percent to 8 percent for men.[3]

The prevalence of illness in Tanzania remains high. According to the 1999 TRCHS (National Bureau of Statistics and Macro International 2000), 35 percent of children under age five were affected by fever in the preceding two weeks, 12 percent were affected by diarrhea, and 14 percent experienced acute respiratory infections. The HBS 2000/01, which reports on adults and children, stated that 27 percent of its respondents indicated having experienced illness in the preceding four weeks (National Bureau of Statistics 2002). Malarial fever and diarrhea are the most common types of illness. Such high levels of illness have economic consequences. Almost one in four people missed at least one week of school or work as a consequence of illness, and that finding is evenly distributed across consumption quintiles (table 12.3).

One-third of those who reported being ill in the preceding four weeks indicated not having consulted a health provider. And of those who had been unable to work for at least two weeks, 17 percent did not consult a health provider. Among those who did not consult a health care provider, 7 percent indicated that care is too expensive and 2 percent stated that it is too far away.[4] Households from the poorest quintile were more likely to mention cost as an obstacle to seeking health care than were households from the top quintile, but the difference is not very pronounced (8 percent versus 6 percent). And the percentage of households from the poorest quintile that mentioned distance as an obstacle to seeking health care was as high as that among the wealthiest quintile (2 percent).

The percentage of households indicating that distance or cost is an obstacle to seeking health care seems low but may be underestimated. One could conceive that among the 91 percent of respondents who indicated no need for health care despite being sick, some may have done so because of the distance to health care providers, the opportunity costs of time, the confidence in the providers, and the quality of care provided. Because 9 percent of the population lives more than 10 kilometers from a dispensary or health care center, the importance of distance in seeking health care is likely underestimated (table 12.4).

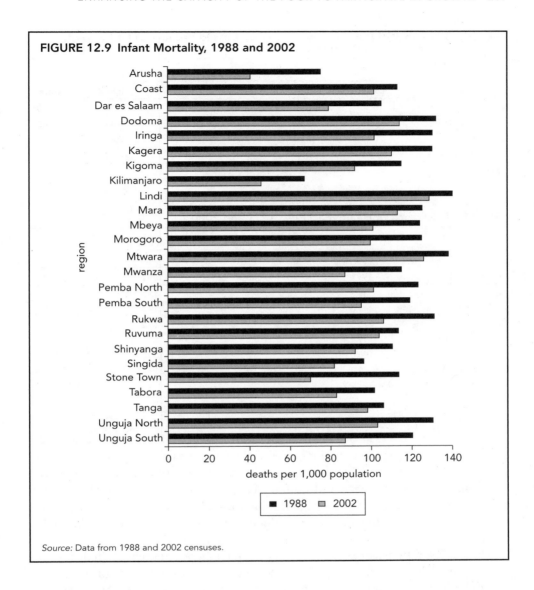

FIGURE 12.9 Infant Mortality, 1988 and 2002

Source: Data from 1988 and 2002 censuses.

Likewise, costs probably play a more important role than the responses from the HBS suggest. The legislation of private practice and the introduction of user fees likely contributed to a doubling in the share of health expenditures in nonfood consumption during the 1990s to about 8 percent. That percentage is almost identical across quintiles, suggesting that, in absolute Tanzanian shillings, poor households spend considerably less on health than do wealthier households. Such spending is unusual and deserves consideration, because poor households typically spend a greater share on health.

More than one-half of the individuals who consulted a health care provider visited a government provider. Use of private services is highest in Dar es Salaam, but in rural

TABLE 12.3 Number of Days of School or Work Missed Because of Illness, by Consumption Quintile

Days missed	Lowest	Second	Middle	Fourth	Highest	Average
			Consumption quintile			
None	0.30	0.31	0.29	0.30	0.32	0.30
One week or less	0.45	0.46	0.46	0.46	0.43	0.45
One to two weeks	0.13	0.11	0.11	0.12	0.13	0.12
More than two weeks	0.13	0.11	0.11	0.12	0.13	0.12

Source: Author's calculations based on National Bureau of Statistics 2002.

TABLE 12.4 Distance to Health Facilities, 1991 and 2000

Distance (km)	Percentage of population living at a distance			
	Dispensary or health care center		Hospital	
	1991	2000	1991	2000
Less than 2	34.3	37.9	13.6	13.3
2–5.9	41.0	37.5	18.4	19.1
6–9.9	15.3	15.9	10.2	13.5
10+	9.4	8.6	57.7	54.1
Total	100.0	100.0	100.0	100.0
Mean distance	4.4	3.9	19.7	21.3

Source: National Bureau of Statistics 2002.

areas, private providers also play an important role with traditional healers and missionary facilities. Poor and nonpoor households have a remarkably even use of private and public health care providers: poor households tend to visit traditional healers relatively more frequently, whereas the differences between visits to public facilities and private or mission facilities are negligible, as illustrated by the fact that the concentration curves for visits to those institutions almost coincide with the 45-degree line in figure 12.10.

Though few differences exist between poor and nonpoor households in their exposure to major diseases like malaria, diarrhea, or respiratory infections or in the fraction of budgetary expenses for health services, health outcomes differ considerably by wealth status. Infant and child mortality is 15 to 20 percent higher among the poor than among those in the top quintile (table 12.5). The difference for nutritional indicators is even larger: 30 to 50 percent. The one indicator in which poor households do substantially better than nonpoor households is HIV prevalence, which is 3.4 percent among those in the poorest quintile and 10.5 percent among individuals in the wealthiest quintile.

The health outcome differential may be explained in part by differences in coverage of preventive health services. Poor children, for instance, are less likely to be reached by vaccination services, and women from poor families are almost three times less likely to have their birth attended by trained medical personnel than are nonpoor women (table 12.6).

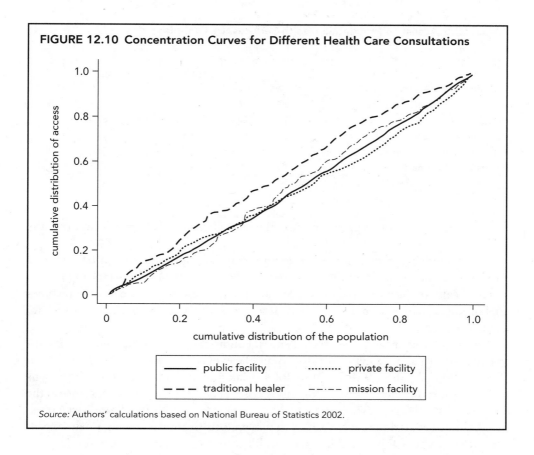

FIGURE 12.10 Concentration Curves for Different Health Care Consultations

Source: Authors' calculations based on National Bureau of Statistics 2002.

TABLE 12.5 Differences in Health Outcomes, by Quintile

	Quintile					
Indicator	Lowest	Second	Middle	Fourth	Highest	Average
Infant mortality rate (deaths per 1,000)	114.8	107.5	115.4	106.8	91.9	107.8
Under-five mortality rate (deaths per 1,000)	160.0	159.3	192.7	155.0	135.2	161.1
Stunted children under age five (%)	49.5	52.5	45.0	36.6	23.4	42.7
Underweight children under age five (%)	32.2	35.1	28.8	23.9	21.7	28.8
HIV prevalence (%)	3.4	4.5	5.6	9.4	10.5	7.0

Sources: Gwatkin and others 2003 from 1999 DHS data; HIV prevalence, from Tanzania HIV/AIDS Indicator Survey 2004 data.

Differences in behavior or economic circumstances also explain differences in health outcomes between poor and nonpoor households. For instance, poor individuals have less access to clean water and are less well educated. Children from the poorest quintile are five times less likely to sleep under a bednet than children from the top quintile. Individuals living in poor households are less likely to consume iodized salt, and women in the poorest quintile are almost three times more likely to

TABLE 12.6 Access to Preventive Health Services, by Quintile

(percent)

Preventive health service	Quintile					
	Lowest	Second	Middle	Fourth	Highest	Average
Bacille Calmette-Guerin coverage	88.8	96.9	87.3	93.7	99.9	92.7
Measles coverage	63.4	84.2	72.2	88.4	89.0	78.1
Diphtheria-pertussis-tetanus coverage	66.2	86.1	78.5	91.1	88.7	81.0
Fully immunized (diphtheria-pertussis-tetanus)	53.1	74.3	61.7	80.8	78.4	68.3
Birth attended by a medically trained person	28.9	35.0	33.3	48.4	82.8	43.8

Source: Gwatkin and others 2003 from 1999 DHS data.

have experienced female genital cutting than are those from the wealthiest quintile (table 12.7).

In acknowledging that nonhealth factors play an important role in determining health outcomes, one can put into perspective the role of the health sector in improving the health of the poor (and the population at large). Improving the health outcomes of Tanzanians requires a broadly shared effort across different sectors, including health, education,[5] and water.

The health sector faces several challenges. Funding is one. Though funding has improved—the total per capita allocation of public expenditure to health increased from T Sh 5,100 in 2001 to T Sh 7,374 in 2004 (Makundi and others 2004)[6]—it remains extremely low. Furthermore, with the rising costs of drugs, the observed increase in the budget (45 percent) overstates the possibility of providing additional care. Drug resistance to antimalarials and increasingly to tuberculosis treatment demands new, expensive drugs, thereby inflating the cost of health care without offering new services.

Another challenge is the high cost of treatment for HIV/AIDS, which creates pressure on the overall budget. Moreover, because of the pattern of HIV/AIDS, which affects nonpoor households much more than poor households, increasing the share of financing that supports treatment will make the health budget less pro-poor.[7]

Some developments also work in the opposite direction. The current allocation formula for the distribution of the health budget across districts, for instance, takes the degree of poverty into account. Other efforts to provide greater financial protection of poor households that seek medical care are ongoing.

TABLE 12.7 Socioeconomic Aspects of Health, by Quintile

(percent)

Socioeconomic aspect	Quintile					
	Lowest	Second	Middle	Fourth	Highest	Average
Access to piped water	30.9	31.3	34.2	43.6	56.1	39.2
Children under five who use a bednet	9.4	12.1	12.2	27.8	52.2	22.3
Availability of iodized salt in the household	52.1	60.0	61.7	71.3	86.0	66.9
Female genital cutting	29.2	16.4	16.7	18.2	11.0	17.7

Source: Access to piped water, National Bureau of Statistics 2002; female genital cutting, Tanzania HIV/AIDS Indicator Survey 2004 data; other indicators, Gwatkin and others 2003 from 1999 DHS data.

In addition, a serious human resource crisis affects the health sector. Only one-third of the positions for medical officers (going by the staffing norms) are filled and only 23 percent of the positions for assistant medical officer and public health nurse are filled (Makundi and others 2004). That human resource crisis goes back to the mid-1990s, when the total health workforce was about 67,000. By 2002, however, it had decreased to 49,000, with the population increasing during the same period from 25 million to 33 million inhabitants. That decrease affects people living in poor areas especially, because in the absence of additional incentives, motivating medical personnel to take up positions in areas with a lack of houses, with poor schools, and with low-quality medical facilities is difficult.

Household Size and Fertility

A strong association exists between nutritional outcomes and household size (Lindeboom and Kilama 2005), between educational attainment and household size, and between consumption poverty and household size (Mkenda 2005). With respect to the last, children living in a household with three people have a 16 percent probability of living in poverty, whereas children living in a household with six people have a 35 percent probability of living in poverty.[8]

Living in a large household not only increases the risk of poverty, but it affects other dimensions of welfare as well. Even if one controls for the consequences of household size on income, living in a large household has negative consequences for a child's educational outcomes.[9] Those consequences are illustrated in table 12.8, which presents a regression of the education gap[10] for children ages 8 to 11 as a function of household size. It shows that the education gap increases for children with more siblings ages 0 to 6. The regression also illustrates the direct effect of income on educational attainment: relative to those in the poorest quintile, children from households in the wealthier quintiles have a smaller education gap.

TABLE 12.8 Ordinary Least Squares Regression of the Education Gap of Children Ages 8–11

Indicator	Coefficient	T-statistic
Number of household members ages 0–6	0.0502	6.0
Number of household members ages 7–15	0.0036	0.5
Number of household members age 16 and above	−0.0168	−2.9
Age of child	0.4961	50.3
D-second wealth quintile	−0.1998	−7.0
D-third wealth quintile	−0.4484	−14.6
D-fourth wealth quintile	−0.6218	−18.5
D-fifth wealth quintile	−0.9130	−22.5
Constant	−3.0194	−30.9

Source: Author's calculations based on National Bureau of Statistics 2002.
Note: The education gap measures the number of years missed by the child and is defined as the years of education minus the age of the child minus 7.

The strong correlation between human resource outcomes and family size is reason to consider one of the key determinants of family size: fertility. One is not surprised to see that the strong association between income poverty and household size is found between household wealth and fertility as well (figure 12.11). The total number of births is more than twice as high in the poorest quintile as in the wealthiest quintile. The difference in the number of births is also distinct between the poorer rural and the wealthier urban areas.

There are additional reasons to consider the consequences of high fertility. Having a large family (or high dependency ratio) lowers—all other factors being the same—the savings rate, which means that the capital stock cannot expand as fast as it could have. High fertility thus leads to a decline in per worker output, which, as empirical analysis has shown, results in the decline in the growth of per capita income (Mkenda 2005).

High fertility is also associated with short birth intervals, which, in turn, cause higher child mortality. However, if preferred rather than actual birth spacing prevailed, then the fraction of children with a birth interval of less than two years would drop by 27 percent (from 13.2 percent to 9.6 percent), which would lead to an estimated decline in neonatal mortality of 7 percent and in under-five mortality of 3 percent (Rafalimanana and Westoff 2001).

High fertility also contributes to inequalities. It causes gender inequalities because, in a society where female life expectancy at birth is 56 years and where women from the poorest quintile have a total fertility rate of close to eight (not counting unsuccessful pregnancies), about one-half of a woman's adult life is spent either carrying a child in her womb or breastfeeding it (Dasgupta 1995). And because poor families spend less on their children's human resource endowments than do wealthy families, and because well-endowed children stand a better chance of earning higher income, high fertility contributes to the perpetuation and possibly even worsening of existing inequalities.

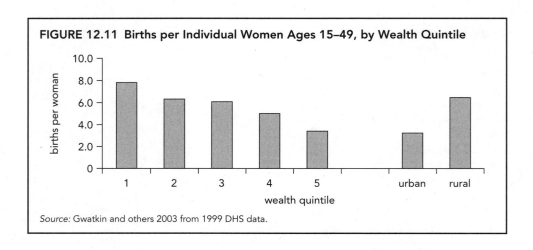

FIGURE 12.11 **Births per Individual Women Ages 15–49, by Wealth Quintile**

Source: Gwatkin and others 2003 from 1999 DHS data.

The fact that high fertility can engender negative consequences for human resource building, inequality, and economic growth is already recognized in policy. The National Population Policy states, "Rapid population growth tends to increase outlays on private and public consumption, drawing resources away from saving for productive investment and, therefore, tends to retard growth in national output through slow capital formation" (United Republic of Tanzania 1992). The policy also recognizes the pressure on national resources that population growth engenders: "the strains caused by rapid population growth are felt most acutely and visibly in the public budgets for health, education, and related fields of human resource development. The need to feed a rapidly growing population also means that part of the gains from increased agricultural production [is] eroded" (United Republic of Tanzania 1992).

The contraceptive prevalence rate has increased. The length of actual birth intervals increased from 30 months in the 1970s to 33 months in the 1980s and 35 months in the 1990s. Yet after an initial drop in the fertility rate in the early 1990s, the decline stopped. Total fertility per woman declined from 6.3 in 1991 to 5.8 in 1996 and remained statistically unchanged thereafter. Total fertility was 5.6 in 1999 and 5.7 in 2004. In combination with a drop in infant mortality, the situation causes concern as it suggests an acceleration in population growth, which underlines the case for an active population policy. There is certainly scope for improvement. Total fertility could fall considerably, even if only the difference between the total wanted fertility rate and actual fertility were closed. The poor would benefit most from the gap's closing because the difference for them is largest: 5.6 versus 6.5.[11]

Building Physical Capital of the Poor

For the poor to participate in growth, building human capital alone is insufficient. Complementary assets need to be created.

In the longer run, one expects the economy to transform from an agricultural one to a service- and manufacturing-based one. A strategy that enhances human capital prepares for that transition, and building assets outside agriculture seems a logical first step. However, the majority of people work as own-account workers in agriculture (figure 12.12), and only a small fraction are employed in the secondary and tertiary informal and formal sectors. So to address poverty in the meantime (and how long does the meantime last?), a focus is needed on strategies that allow poor households to accumulate physical capital so as to expand and improve their on- and off-farm enterprises.

Such a rural development strategy has proved to be very successful elsewhere (Klasen 2003). Evidence from rapidly growing East Asian countries shows that poverty reduction is largest when growth makes use of the assets that the poor possess (Drèze and Sen 1989; Ravallion and Datt 1996). And when poor households build their physical capital and increase their incomes, a virtuous cycle is started of enhanced resources that are used for additional investments in physical and human capital, which, in turn, lead to higher incomes.

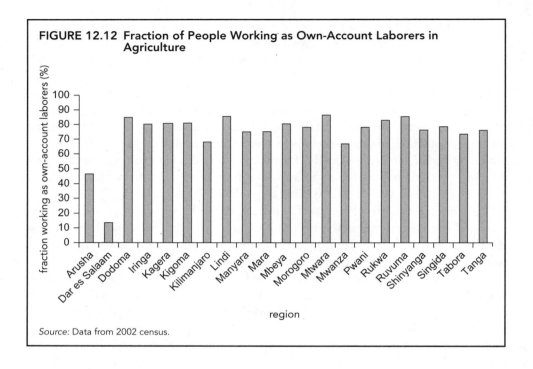

FIGURE 12.12 Fraction of People Working as Own-Account Laborers in Agriculture

Source: Data from 2002 census.

In previous chapters, we discussed various ways to strengthen the incentives to invest, such as higher agricultural prices, improved infrastructure, and greater access to markets. In short, those improvements in the business climate increase returns to income-generating activities and make investing in assets or new income-generating activities more attractive. As box 12.2 illustrates, investments in assets are less likely to be made without such improvements. This chapter focuses on one aspect of building physical capital that has received little attention so far: exposure to risk. We also discuss another aspect of building physical capital: access to financial markets.

Risk, Growth, and Asset Accumulation

Risks are pervasive in Tanzania. Disease, fluctuating prices, erratic availability of marketing opportunities, climate variability, uncertainty around governance, and the loss of major assets through theft, fire, death of livestock, or otherwise have major effects on the lives of poor and nonpoor Tanzanians. In Kilimanjaro, for instance, serious adult illness was found to lead to a reduction in per capita consumption of up to 17 percent (Christiaensen, Hofmann, and Sarris 2004). For Kagera, evidence shows that chronic illness leads to a 6 percent decline in consumption growth (Rossi 2004).

Exposure to risk contributes to large variability in well-being over time. Consider, for instance, table 12.9, which shows the transition between consumption quintiles for a sample of individuals from Kagera who were interviewed in 1994 and tracked and interviewed again in 2004.[12] It shows some persistence in that individuals remain in

---

BOX 12.2 Marketing Opportunities and Crop Adoption

Without proper incentives, investments in assets and improved production technologies will not be made. The adoption of improved banana varieties in Kagera was less successful in areas with limited marketing opportunities. Farmers living in areas where they had to travel far to sell their bananas preferred to hack their unsold bananas to pieces rather than carry the bananas on the exhausting journey home. That practice hindered the successful adoption of new banana varieties (personal communication, Joachim De Weerdt, March 2004, in Bukoba).

A qualitative study on income mobility (Kessy 2004) illustrates the consequences of lack of marketing opportunities well:

> During a village transect walk, the research team observed bananas left to rot in the farms. This was especially the case with matooke, the staple type of banana that is not used in local brewing. Not only was the banana market a problem: respondents mentioned that sometimes maize is used to feed chicken because there is no market. The market for cotton is also a problem but the situation is improving through private traders visiting the village. A market for tobacco is readily available.

TABLE 12.9 Consumption Transition Matrix in Kagera, 1994 and 2004

(percent)

Quintile, 1994	Quintile, 2004					Total
	Lowest	Second	Middle	Fourth	Highest	
Lowest	7	3	4	4	2	20
Second	6	4	4	3	3	20
Middle	5	3	4	3	5	20
Fourth	5	3	3	3	6	20
Highest	1	2	3	5	9	20
Total	24	15	18	18	25	100

Source: Author's calculations based on Kagera Health and Development Survey data for 1994 and 2004.

their initial quintile. Yet the percentages on the diagonal, which reflect no change in wealth status, are relatively low. Of those in the bottom quintile in 2004, one out of four (6 percent) originated from the top two quintiles in 1994. With such movements across wealth classes, it follows that considerable uncertainty exists about one's future well-being. Arguably, exposure to risk is such that considerations of risk inform many economic decisions, including the choice of the income portfolio, the amount to save, or the assets to invest in.

There are at least three ways in which exposure to risk affects income generation and the accumulation of assets. First and best known are the consequences (or ex post effects) that follow from the materialization of risk as a shock. A shock can lead to direct losses of assets (for example, livestock die) or indirect losses because the household is forced to lay off assets to deal with the crisis (for example, cattle are sold to buy grain after a harvest has failed).[13]

In addition to those ex post effects, exposure to risk has an effect on accumulation decisions even before it materializes. Those ex ante effects are potentially even more costly, though less visibly so, than the ex post effects. In the presence of risk, households may try to minimize their exposure and, in doing so, allow the composition of their income portfolio to be informed less by profitability and more by the security provided by the resulting income stream. Farmers, for instance, prefer to grow safe but low-return crops over high-return but risky crops. Households may opt to invest their savings in assets that can be easily sold during a crisis (cash and livestock) rather than in the most productive ones (bicycle, plow, or sewing machine).

Exposure to risk not only has static consequences in that the loss of assets pushes people back on their accumulation path or in that people opt for less profitable means of income generation, but it also has dynamic consequences. It may lead to lower growth because, in anticipation of risk, households may save and invest less than they would do otherwise.[14]

Little empirical work is available that estimates the effect of risk on asset accumulation, and no such evidence exists for Tanzania. Elbers, Gunning, and Kinsey (2003) estimate the effect of risk on smallholder farm households in Zimbabwe that rely on rain-fed farming. They find that the mean of the asset distribution is 46 percent lower than it would be in the absence of risk and that the annual growth rate would be 20 to 50 percent higher in the absence of risk. The ex ante effect is the most important and explains 33 percent of the growth shortfall: the remaining 13 percent is attributable to the ex post effect. Other empirical work (Rosenzweig and Wolpin 1993) similarly suggests large costs of exposure to risk.

Risk affects poor households disproportionately. One reason is that once shocks occur, poor households have less ability to cope. In Kilimanjaro, following the low coffee prices, for instance, poor households with few assets for coping were forced to uproot their coffee trees to make room for other crops. However, wealthier households were able to maintain their trees and wait for better prices (Christiaensen, Hofmann, and Sarris 2004).

In addition, because the poor have less ability to cope with shocks, ex post, they bear the high costs of an ex ante risk-avoidance strategy. In Shinyanga, for instance, households with limited options for consumption smoothing have been found to grow lower-return, safer crops such as sweet potatoes, sorghum, and millet. Wealthier households with a greater number of options for ex post coping are likelier to cultivate more profitable but risky crops such as cotton and paddy. The cost to the poor of such a diversification strategy is high. Depending on the area planted, some farmers forgo up to 20 percent of their income (Dercon 1996). It should be noted, however, that shocks can have positive consequences, as box 12.3 illustrates.

Reducing Risk

The negative consequences of exposure to risk for asset accumulation and growth and the disproportionate effect risk has on the poor are reasons to consider what can be done to reduce risk and exposure to it. To that end, one should consider the risks that

---

BOX 12.3 Positive Consequences of a Shock

Among the top two events that led to increased economic prosperity in Mkalanga village in Ruvuma was the outbreak of a crop disease known as gray leaf spot (GLS). The GLS outbreak occurred in 1998 and lasted four years. Together with the failure by the Mbinga Cooperative Union (MBICU) to pay farmers in 1997/98 and the breakup of MBICU in 1998, GLS was a major contributor to the hunger in Mkalanga village in 1998 and 1999.

The GLS outbreak, however, also led to innovations in the farming system. Before the outbreak, cassava was grown only in the bordering western lowland belt (Lake Shore) of Lake Nyasa. Because cassava appeared to be less susceptible to the disease, it became more widely adopted. Before then, many believed that cassava could not grow in the cold Livingstone Mountains, where Mkalanga is located. Since then, cassava has been growing very well, and it is now cultivated in large volumes.

Source: Kessy and Mashindano 2005.

---

affect households most. Information from Kagera is informative in that respect because households were asked to identify those shocks that had a major effect on their well-being during the past 10 years (table 12.10).

Death and illness make up about 50 percent of the major shocks affecting households; poor harvest and low crop prices explain another 25 percent of all shocks. Less important, but nonnegligible are shocks related to the labor market (7 percent). Some are risks that feature prominently in qualitative analyses but less so in the Kagera Health and Development Survey (Beegle, De Weerdt, and Dercon 2006). Those include

TABLE 12.10 Shocks with Major Consequences for Well-Being in Kagera, by Quintile, 1994–2004

(percentage of households experiencing incident)

Consequence	Quintile					Average
	Lowest	Second	Middle	Fourth	Highest	
Death of family member	31.4	29.6	31.1	30.7	34.3	31.3
Poor harvest because of weather	20.6	25.5	13.3	12.0	16.1	17.7
Serious illness	16.9	19.1	16.0	19.9	13.2	17.2
Loss of assets	6.1	4.9	5.8	6.4	7.1	6.0
Few opportunities for wage employment	5.0	4.6	3.8	7.7	8.6	5.7
Poor harvest (for other reasons)	2.8	5.4	5.0	3.7	1.1	3.8
Low crop prices	1.4	2.8	7.3	2.8	2.9	3.5
Eviction or resettlement	3.1	2.1	2.3	2.5	3.2	2.6
Off-farm employment	1.7	1.0	2.0	0.9	1.8	1.5
Remittances	1.4	0.0	3.8	0.6	1.4	1.5
Other	9.7	4.9	9.8	12.9	10.4	9.4

Source: Author's calculations based on Kagera Health and Development Survey data for 2004.

governance risks (Kessy 2004; United Republic of Tanzania 2004c), which vary from sins of omission, such as substandard service delivery (clinics that run out of medication, absence of veterinary services, extension workers who do not show up, and roads that are not maintained), to sins of commission, such as harassment by government officials or inhibiting rules and regulations. Theft—particularly of movable assets, livestock, bicycles, and cash—also features relatively prominently.

An important point is that many risks are preventable or their effect can be reduced. Governance-related risks can be avoided altogether because they are human made. The most important diseases and causes of death (table 12.11) can also be treated effectively (malaria, diarrhea, acute respiratory infections, and even HIV/AIDS) or are preventable (malaria, diarrhea, and HIV/AIDS) by stressing the importance of promoting insecticide-treated bednets and safe sex, by providing access to clean water, and by ensuring that the health sector can effectively deliver treatments for the most prominent diseases and causes of death.

Weather and price risks cannot be prevented, but their effects can be mitigated. One way is through irrigation. Another is through improved infrastructure, access to markets, and storage facilities. Especially in isolated markets, climatic shocks lead to large changes in prices. Especially after a weather shock, the livestock and food terms of trade tend to deteriorate because failed harvests result in an excess demand for food and an excess supply of livestock. The 2004 Participatory Poverty Assessment (United Republic of Tanzania 2004c) notes, for instance, how the price of cows expressed in maize declines to one-third the normal value during drought years and to one-twelfth the value during extreme droughts.

Agricultural research can also contribute to a reduced effect of weather shocks if high-yielding, drought-resistant crop varieties are developed. Experience from Dodoma suggests that even if high-yielding crop varieties are less marketable, farmers very much value the security provided, which, in turn, frees resources to invest more in higher-value activities.

That experience shows that much can be done to reduce risk through existing sector policies. It also shows that a key element of a strategy that reduces downward economic mobility and enhances growth opportunities for poor and nonpoor Tanzanians alike is an effort to reduce exposure to risk or its consequences in various sectors, including health, water, nutrition, agriculture, infrastructure, extension, and education.

TABLE 12.11 Five Main Causes of Mortality, by Age Group

Under 5	Ages 5–14	Ages 15–59	Age 60+
Malaria	Malaria	HIV/AIDS or tuberculosis	Malaria
Stillbirth	Diarrhea	Malaria	Diarrhea
Perinatal causes	HIV/AIDS or tuberculosis	Diarrhea	Heart problems
Diarrhea	Acute respiratory	Heart problems	Acute respiratory
Acute respiratory	infections	Unintentional injuries	infections
infections	Unintentional injuries		Neoplasms

Source: Lorenz and Mpemba 2005.

Asset Accumulation and Financial Markets

Another element in a strategy to promote investments is the improvement of financial markets. Financial markets play a crucial role in facilitating growth in at least three ways: (a) access to savings accounts permits people to store their cash in a safe place and to slowly build sufficient capital to buy expensive assets, (b) credit allows people to buy assets even before they have accumulated sufficient savings, and (c) access to insurance reduces the effect of risk on economic decision making.

Unfortunately, access to financial markets is very limited and virtually nonexistent in rural areas. Insurance and credit markets are ill developed, and even savings accounts are used very little. At a mean distance to a bank of more than 30 kilometers, households' limited use of savings accounts and other financial services is unsurprising. And with the restructuring of the banking sector during the 1990s, limited access to formal savings declined even further and was not compensated by an associated increase in informal savings groups (table 12.12).

Whereas the loss in access to formal savings increased the obstacles to asset accumulation, low inflation meant that cash could become a more attractive store of wealth. Kessy (2004) reports how cash savings are an important means for consumption smoothing. Christiaensen, Hofmann, and Sarris (2004) note that in Kilimanjaro monetary savings are the most important means of coping with the coffee price shock.[15]

Despite the great advantages that functional rural financial markets would bring, there are structural reasons for the highly imperfect financial markets in rural areas. Geographic isolation, moral hazard, and the high cost of information preclude forms of insurance that cover actual losses. Large fixed costs and volumes make futures markets unavailable for small farmers. The absence of collateral also prevents credit markets from developing. The credit and insurance that are provided are mostly informal and are based on high observability and repeated interaction.

That situation does not mean that formal forms of financial services cannot be developed. Greater access to formal savings mechanisms is possible, for instance, by relying on local institutions, such as funeral groups, that already manage financial resources (see Dercon and others 2004). Mobile banks and cell phone technology also present possibilities to increase access to savings. Numerous other initiatives exist that try to overcome the constraints to financial markets by focusing on group responsibility to overcome collateral constraints (microcredit initiatives), by offering insurance contracts against indexes (as is the case of weather-based insurance contracts), by using lease constructions, or by organizing rotating savings and credit associations (ROSCAs) and savings and credit cooperatives (SACCOs).

TABLE 12.12 Access to Savings Services in Rural Areas, 1991 and 2000

(percent)

Type of service	1991	2000
Savings or current account	12.9	3.9
Informal savings group	3.6	2.8

Source: National Bureau of Statistics 2002.

The literature on those various arrangements is adequately surveyed elsewhere (for example, Larson, Anderson, and Varangis 2004). Suffice it to say that financial markets do matter; that great gains can be reaped if they can be improved, even marginally; and that various very promising initiatives exist in that area that warrant attention.

Dealing with Vulnerability

One vision of economic growth considers poverty a transitory phenomenon. In the long run, everyone will converge toward an equilibrium steady state, and if investment opportunities with sufficiently high returns exist, then this steady state will lie above the poverty line. However, certain groups lack the ability to benefit from growth opportunities. In this section, we consider those vulnerable groups, which could comprise orphans, people with disabilities, and households headed by the elderly or a child, but which also could simply consist of a high concentration of poor people (Klasen 2003).

Social Protection and Vulnerable Groups

A common reflex in thinking about vulnerable groups is to call for a safety net. However, vulnerability is probably best addressed through a mix of economic growth, attention to risk reduction, and a selective use of safety nets. In an economy in which income is low and inequality limited, income growth is a prerequisite to moving people away from the poverty line.

However, as the poverty transitions of table 12.9 have shown, a large group of households experience downward mobility in wealth status. If such downward movement could be reduced, much poverty could be prevented. Hence, reducing risk is another important element in a strategy to reduce vulnerability. Such interventions not only are part of an economic growth strategy but also are essential to social protection.

Safety Nets

Returning to table 12.9, one sees that of those households in the bottom quintile in 1994, about one-half managed to improve their well-being and enter the middle quintile or higher. Surely a social protection strategy has to focus on those households that are not able to move upward. But how do we identify those households or individuals? A useful concept in this context is that of a poverty trap, which may be defined as a condition in which an individual is pushed below the poverty line and is unable to climb out of poverty without external assistance. Yet once assistance is provided, the individual should be able to sustain a living above the poverty line unless pushed back again.

The concept of a poverty trap is intuitive, until one asks why individuals are not able to climb out of poverty themselves. After all, in an environment where investments provide sufficiently high returns, people have a strong incentive to benefit from such opportunities. If that benefit requires investments, they will have a strong incentive to save to self-finance the investment. Because marginal returns to capital are also high, especially when few assets are available, one expects poor households to have a large incentive to save and invest.

By trying to understand how poverty traps come about, one can gain insight into the types of interventions that would allow people to move out of poverty. Typically, the presence of a poverty trap requires the existence of one or more critical wealth thresholds that people have difficulty crossing from below. The presence of a threshold by itself is not sufficient to explain the presence of a poverty trap, because even if investments are lumpy, households could slowly accumulate wealth and purchase the investment good later. Hence, the presence of a wealth threshold has to be compounded by something else—for instance, the lack of safe savings instruments, the inability to save from low income (because of minimum consumption requirements), or the malfunctioning of credit markets.

A typical threshold is minimum requirements in nutrition, education, and nonfood consumption items such as clothing that are needed before a person can participate in the labor market. Because borrowing is difficult in Tanzania in general—especially for poor people—once they are destitute, poor people may be permanently excluded from entering a home-based growth path or participating in the labor market.

Addressing poverty traps is attractive because the interventions are temporary and the benefits permanent. Social protection that manages to address poverty traps strengthens the economic self-reliance of the poor and their ability to invest.

It requires, however, the identification of a poverty trap, which is not always evident, especially because poverty traps are almost always the result of a combination of factors, typically including a threshold, imperfect credit markets, and the absence of safe assets. If the causes for a poverty trap have been identified, one needs to decide whether to assist those trapped (for example, through asset transfers) or to attack the causes of the trap itself. A few illustrations follow.

Lumpiness in combination with inadequate credit markets may prevent poor households from entering high-return activities (box 12.4). One response could then be transfers, in this case in the form of livestock. Another would be to address the lumpiness constraint by improving the means of capital accumulation by stimulation of ROSCAs and SACCOs; through the provision of credit or options for leasing; or, as is suggested in United Republic of Tanzania, Vice President's Office (2005), through vertically integrated agricultural production such as outgrower schemes, whereby a processor provides associated farmers with inputs and access to technology.

Lack of a clear regulatory framework, underpricing, and weak enforcement lead to an irreversible decline of common property resources, such as the fish stock in the Exclusive Economic Zone, a decline that threatens to permanently disenfranchise the local fishing communities from their main source of livelihood. Prevention through the promotion of good governance, a clear regulatory framework that is enforced, and proper pricing are policy interventions that may be preferred over the provision of transfers (COWI 2005).

BOX 12.4 A Poverty Trap in Shinyanga

In Shinyanga, cattle are a high-return investment (25 to 30 percent annually). Cattle are also a liquid asset that can be used for consumption smoothing, which makes cattle owner-ship attractive. But they are also a lumpy investment. Wealthier rural households have been found to specialize in cattle rearing, while poorer households derive a larger share of their income from off-farm activities. Differences in comparative advantage do not offer a convincing explanation for this phenomenon. Households specializing in off-farm activities have much lower incomes but are unlikely not to have the skills required because cattle rearing is a traditional activity in the area.

The lack of credit markets and the indivisibility of cattle imply that households must be able to put up relatively large amounts of money to invest in cattle rearing. However, poor households with low initial endowments from which only low incomes are earned find it hard to save enough to invest in cattle. That problem is exacerbated by the fact that, because of low endowments, the poor have limited ability to cope with shocks. Consequently, such households enter into safe, lower-return activities, making saving even harder. That combination of factors explains why poorer households specialize in off-farm activities (such as weeding or casual labor) that require few skills or investments but are safe. That pattern effectively traps poor households in poverty, despite the attractive investment opportunities that exist in the area.

Source: Dercon 1998.

Adults require a threshold of physical and human capital to be productive. That capital is typically obtained during childhood, when one is not yet able to decide for oneself or to borrow against future income. Hence, there is an economic argument to provide transfers in the form of education, nutrition interventions, or assistance to orphans and homeless children.[16]

Once one has identified the causes of a poverty trap and discovered why households are not able to deal with the poverty trap themselves (after all, doing so would be very attractive because it would allow people to attain their productive potential and escape poverty), one should obtain guidance on potential interventions. For instance, if difficulties in undertaking collective action explain the limited presence of ROSCAs and SACCOs, public interventions to convene people may help. But if the issue is one of lack of skills or the absence of safe places to store cash, an entirely different course of action should be taken.

Likewise, the high opportunity costs and discount rates of poor parents and the inability of young children to borrow for their own capacity building affect the human capital accumulation of children. One way to intervene is to eliminate any financial barriers to education, as was done with PEDP for primary education.

If one is clear as to why and how to intervene, then priorities may have to be set for whom to target. The HIV/AIDS crisis has placed much attention on the plight of orphans. According to the 2002 census, 493,000 children (or 1.5 percent of the total population) between ages 7 and 14 are double orphans, and their educational attendance lags behind that of nonorphans (figure 12.13). However, an almost equally large group of 438,000 children with disabilities receives a lot less attention despite their

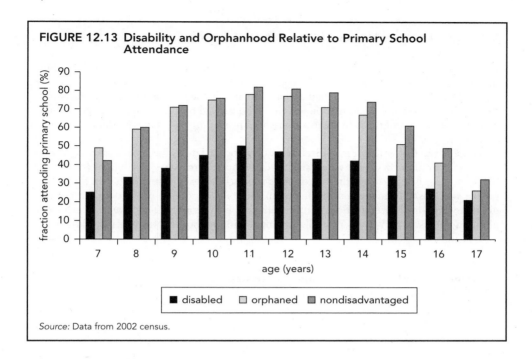

FIGURE 12.13 Disability and Orphanhood Relative to Primary School Attendance

Source: Data from 2002 census.

worse plight.[17] If the conclusion is that more attention should be paid to children with disabilities (see also box 12.5), then specific measures in the context of PEDP may be called for. But again, understanding the cause for nonaccess is most important. Depending on the type of disability, other measures, including medication (for diseases such as leprosy) or provision of prostheses, may be more effective.

Conclusions

Enhancing the capacity of the poor to participate in growth requires building human capital as well as accumulating physical assets. With regard to building human capital, considerable progress has been made in education—primary education especially. It will take time, however, for the current investments in primary education to contribute to poverty reduction, which is a reason to pay attention to adult education also.

Some progress has been made in health, but major challenges remain. Tanzanians are very often sick. Illness and untimely death have large social and considerable economic consequences. It has been argued that improving the health of Tanzanians is a responsibility that goes beyond the health sector and also involves sectors such as education, extension, or water.

Nutrition and population growth are areas receiving little policy attention, despite their importance for human capacity building. Whereas the trends with respect to fertility are encouraging, no improvements in nutritional status have been observed since the early 1990s. Because only limited benefits can be expected from the current episode

BOX 12.5 Analysis Helps Clarify Whom to Target

Few people would argue against the case for providing safety nets to people with disabilities. Yet a study by Lindeboom (2005) suggests that the incidence of poverty among people with disabilities is only somewhat higher than that among the population at large. Forty percent of those living in a household in which the household head is disabled are poor, compared to 34 percent of those living in a household headed by a person who does not have a disability.

As the figure below illustrates, disabilities often occur late in life. For most people, disabilities occur after the age at which they attend school; oftentimes, disabilities (for example, blindness) occur toward the end of one's productive life. The implication is that many people with disabilities are disadvantaged in their ability to earn an income but are not disadvantaged in their educational attainment or job experience. That situation helps explain, in part, why poverty is only slightly higher among households in which the household head is disabled.

Number of People in Different Age Groups Reporting Disability at the Time of the Census

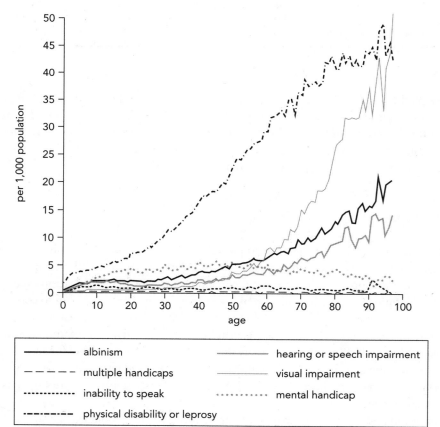

Source: Data from 2002 census.

BOX 12.5 *(continued)*

Further analysis, presented in the main text, shows that children with disabilities are se-verely disadvantaged in their schooling attainment. And in chapter 3, we have shown how educational attainment is one of the key determining factors for one's ability to earn an in-come. That evidence is cause for concern because the combination of having a disability and having low educational attainment probably presents a poverty trap that is hard to escape.

of high economic growth, large-scale interventions in nutrition seem justified. International evidence suggests that such interventions can be economically attractive because they are associated with very high benefit-cost ratios.

A prerequisite to building the physical asset base of poor households is a business climate that promotes competition, provides access to markets, and is embedded in an environment with predictable governance. Risk and financial markets are argued to be additional, important elements to a rural investment strategy.

Risk matters because it is a structural determinant of poverty and because its presence reduces the long-run value of the capital stock and, consequently, growth. We have shown that much can be done to reduce exposure to risk through sector interventions. Dealing with risk should therefore be considered an important crosscutting issue of relevance to many sectors, including health, infrastructure, agriculture, and water.

The financial sector plays an important role in promoting investments, especially when insurance instruments to deal with risk and access to credit can be provided. Because those products are difficult to develop, especially in a rural context, other financial products such as savings promotions or microcredit and leasing may be considered. And because many people resort to keeping savings in the form of cash, maintaining low inflation will allow poor households to accumulate through cash savings.

Finally, the discussion of social safety nets suggests that reducing risk is not only key for a growth strategy but also for social protection: reduced exposure to risk will prevent households from being pushed back on their accumulation path. Social protection therefore needs to look beyond safety nets and to engage sectors so as to promote risk-reducing policies (World Bank 2001). It has been argued that reducing the plight of vulnerable groups requires an understanding of poverty traps. Such an understanding will allow one to identify whether transfers are needed or whether bottlenecks should be addressed to allow vulnerable groups to participate in growth.

Notes

1. The finding that caring practices, diet, and hygiene are important determinants of under-nutrition explains why income growth alone will not be sufficient to address Tanzania's under-nutrition problems (chapter 4).

2. The decline in infant mortality is contested. Surveys carried out during the 1990s (the DHS and TRCHS) show a stagnation of mortality rates up to 1996 and a slight increase thereafter. Data from surveillance sites, on the other hand, support the decline in infant and child mortality. The 2004 DHS, which will be released soon, will shed more light on the actual trend.

3. There is some evidence of a decline in the infection rate among blood donors. Whether this finding is a statistical artifact or a reflection of an actual decline in the infection rate is not clear.

4. Those percentages are likely to be underestimates. Ninety-one percent indicated not needing health care, yet that percentage probably also comprises those who did not find it worthwhile to seek care because of concerns about distance, cost, or quality.

5. Apart from an intervention to teach students proper care practices, one low-cost nutrition intervention to reduce anemia would be deworming of all children on their first day of school.

6. Those amounts are in constant 2001 Tanzanian shillings. The nominal amount for 2004 is T Sh 8,815. The price index for 2001 to 2004 is calculated from table 11 of the United Republic of Tanzania (various years).

7. We are not saying that the use of antiretrovirals should not be promoted or that no pro-poor elements to antiretroviral treatment exist. Apart from the cost of the life-saving benefits, HIV/AIDS and the prolonged illness that precedes death from HIV/AIDS create a large economic burden. And because many infected urban people decide to go home, poor, rural households carry a disproportionate share of this burden.

8. Anand and Morduch (1996) and Lanjouw and Ravallion (1995) have urged caution in interpreting the apparent positive relationship between household size and poverty at the household level. They note that a scope for economies of scale exists at the household level afforded by the presence of public goods such that an increase in the household size leads to a less-than-proportionate need for consumption. However, the association between poverty and household size disappears only at a scale parameter of 0.6. And as Deaton and Zaidi (2002) argue, in a developing country where as much as three-fourths of the total household budget is spent on food, little scope exists for economies of scale, and an economies of scale parameter of close to 1 is to be expected. (In contrast, for industrial countries, a parameter of 0.75 appears reasonable.) Consequently, one can safely assume that the relation between poverty and household size is robust.

9. Such an association was not found for undernutrition.

10. The education gap is the difference between the number of years of education a child should have received and those actually received.

11. Being poor is approximated here by those with no education.

12. Some of the people interviewed in 1994 could not be reinterviewed in 2004. Some had passed away, could not be traced, or refused to be interviewed again. Ranking is done by the quintile in 1994 using consumption expressed in 1994 prices for those who were present in both rounds and thus does not refer to the overall population.

13. In an environment where negative and positive shocks occur and where the production function is concave, exposure to shocks has negative consequences for growth because of the asymmetric impact it has on production: a negative shock in assets leads to a greater loss in production than a positive shock of equal size would add to production.

14. Whether households save more or less following an increase in risk depends on the curvature of their utility function and is essentially an empirical matter. The evidence presented for Zimbabwe suggests that households save less.

15. Christiaensen, Hofmann, and Sarris (2004) and Kessy (2004) report that cash and savings are used in the more affluent villages; however, in poorer communities, households lack the monetary reserves to do so. Presumably, the opportunity costs in terms of forgone consumption are too high for poorer households to keep unproductive monetary savings.

16. Remarkably, no one disputes that investing in the education of children is wise, but investing in the nutrition or care for orphans or homeless children is less accepted.

17. Whereas orphans appear less disadvantaged in school attendance, Alderman, Hoogeveen, and Rossi (2006) show that orphaned children are significantly more prone to being stunted or underweight.

PART IV
Managing Policies and Expenditures for Shared Growth

13

Scaling Up Public Expenditure for Growth and Poverty Reduction

Robert J. Utz

Sustaining economic growth and reducing poverty will require increased levels of investment in public infrastructure and human capital. The United Nations (UN) Millennium Project (2005) estimates the annual cost of achieving the Millennium Development Goals (MDG) targets in Tanzania as increasing from US$82 per capita in 2006 to US$161 by 2015 (in constant 2003 dollars), as shown in table 13.1. Even though other methodologies (World Bank 2005e) produce significantly lower estimates of the resource requirements, there is nonetheless a growing consensus that achieving the targets for the MDGs and the National Strategy for Growth and Reduction in Poverty (NSGRP) will require a significant increase in public expenditure. Per capita government expenditure in 2004/05 is about US$90, of which about US$39 is directly related to the achievement of the MDG targets (both domestically and donor financed), according to the Millennium Project estimates.

Although there is uncertainty about the actual financing need and the capacity of Tanzania to scale up MDG-related activities, given human resource constraints, there is little doubt that significantly increased resource availability would be a necessary, although by no means sufficient, condition for accelerating progress toward the MDG targets. The challenge is to progress toward the targets while managing the macroeconomic implications for an overall favorable development outcome, with options strongly grounded in the microeconomic and sectoral underpinnings of the economy. In the following sections, we look at the prospects and implications of scaling up spending and resource mobilization.

Potential sources of financing for government expenditure are taxation, seignorage, domestic and foreign borrowing, and foreign aid. Each source has a different macroeconomic cost. Conceptually, as long as the marginal benefits of government spending are higher than the marginal cost of the resources, it is advisable to increase spending. The marginal benefit of additional government spending is likely to be

TABLE 13.1 Per Capita MDG Investment Needs and Financing Sources, 2006–15

Category	Amount (2003 US$)		
	2006	2010	2015
MDG investment needs			
Hunger	4	7	14
Education	11	13	17
Gender equality	2	3	3
Health	24	33	48
Water supply and sanitation	4	5	12
Improvement of lives of slum dwellers	3	3	4
Energy	14	15	18
Roads	13	21	31
Other	8	9	13
Total	82	111	161
Sources of financing			
Household contributions	9	11	17
Government expenditures	24	32	46
MDG financing gap	50	67	98
Current ODA for direct MDG support	15	15	15
Shortfall of ODA for direct MDG support over 2002 level	35	52	83

Source: U.N. Millennium Project 2005.
Note: ODA = official development assistance.

declining while the marginal cost of finance is increasing. Policy making in Tanzania is typically based on the assumption that the marginal costs of resources are relatively low for foreign aid inflows (but constrained by the amount donors are willing to provide) and for domestic revenue. Since 1995, when the government's primary objective was to achieve fiscal stabilization and sustainability, the costs of domestic borrowing (in the form of crowding out private credit and generating inflationary pressures) and of foreign, nonconcessional borrowing were considered exceedingly high. Thus, they were excluded from the financing package. However, as Tanzania has achieved macroeconomic stabilization and is putting more emphasis on achieving high growth, there is also scope to reconsider the appropriateness of fiscal deficit targets, especially in light of high needs for spending on economic infrastructure.

In the following sections, we look at the potential for expanding domestic resources and aid inflows. Cost sharing and private participation in service delivery, especially infrastructure, are important complements to public financing. However, these issues are not discussed in this section.

Domestic Resources

The NSGRP emphasizes the importance of domestic resource mobilization as the main source of financing its implementation. Domestic resource mobilization is also seen as important in the context of efforts to reduce Tanzania's aid dependency in the medium to long run. The amount of domestic resources available for reaching the MDG targets depends on three parameters: the rate of growth of gross domestic product (GDP), the share of GDP collected as revenue, and the share of revenue spent on MDG-related activities. Table 13.2 shows various scenarios of the evolution of domestic revenue and spending on MDG-related activities. Economic growth by itself is an important source of increased revenue. GDP per capita growth rates of 2, 4, and 6 percent would lead to increases in per capita government revenue to US$67, US$98, and US$144, respectively, by 2025. This projection assumes that the revenue-to-GDP ratio remains constant at 14 percent throughout the period. If revenue were to increase gradually to 20 percent of GDP by 2015 and remain at that level, available resources would be almost 50 percent higher by 2025 than if the revenue-to-GDP ratio holds constant.

These simulations underline the importance of economic growth as a means for generating resources for investment and poverty reduction. Although these simulations have focused on the effect of growth on available government revenue, the effect of growth on incomes for households and firms is equally important. More resources for households provide the means to spend on health and education and to save for investment. In an environment in which most investment is financed from own savings and retained earnings, such resources are particularly important. Efforts to raise the ratio of revenue to GDP should therefore carefully consider the effects of doing so on the competitiveness of Tanzanian businesses and on the ability of the private sector to save and invest. It is worth emphasizing that economic growth generates additional resources for growth and poverty reduction, whereas an increase in the revenue-to-GDP ratio only transfers resources from the private sector to the public sector. The marginal effect of private sector spending on growth and poverty reduction compared with that of public sector spending is thus critical in forming views on the appropriate level of revenue generation in the Tanzanian economy.

Domestic borrowing could be another source of finance. Until recently, during the period of macroeconomic stabilization, concerns about crowding out credit to the private sector and generating inflationary pressures have led the government to refrain from domestic borrowing. Those concerns remain relevant. In the context of the NSGRP, however, with increased emphasis on poverty reduction through high economic growth,

TABLE 13.2 Potential Contribution of Domestic Revenue to Finance MDGs, 2006–25

Per capita GDP growth (%)	Revenue per capita (2003 US$)			MDG spending per capita (2003 US$)		
	2006	2015	2025	2006	2015	2025
Scenario I: Constant revenue to GDP ratio						
2	45	55	67	24	29	36
4	45	66	98	24	35	53
6	45	80	144	24	43	77
Scenario II: Increase in revenue-to-GDP ratio to 20% by 2015						
2	45	78	95	24	42	51
4	45	95	140	24	51	75
6	45	115	205	24	62	110

Source: Author's calculations.

there is now scope to revisit the appropriate level of domestic borrowing—especially since domestic debt levels are relatively low in Tanzania. Because higher growth will require significant investments in infrastructure, an assessment of the appropriateness of the fiscal position should be undertaken. It should take into account the medium- to long-term effects of debt-financed infrastructure investment on future growth and government revenue, as well as the recurrent cost implications and the efficiency of government expenditure. Domestic resource mobilization has a critical role to play, but even under relatively optimistic scenarios it will be insufficient to meet all investment needs.

Scaling Up Foreign Aid

Domestic revenue is clearly insufficient to finance the implementation of the NSGRP and to reach the MDG targets. Official development assistance (ODA) plays an important role in the economy and is likely to remain important as long as Tanzania remains a low-income economy. The discussion of the financing needs of the MDG implementation clearly presumes a positive effect of ODA on economic growth and poverty reduction. In the short to medium term, aid-financed expenditures can provide an important demand-side stimulus to the economy. In the medium to long term, aid-financed investments in human and physical capital are intended to strengthen the supply side of the economy as the basis for sustained growth.

However, higher aid flows do not necessarily lead to higher economic growth and the achievement of targeted development objectives. Examples abound of countries that saw economic stagnation or decline despite high inflows of foreign aid.[1] International experience suggests that it is critical to manage two separate but related sets of problems that could undermine the positive effect of aid:

- Weakening of institutions
- Weakening of competitiveness through Dutch disease effects.

A weakening of institutions may occur if aid undermines accountability to domestic stakeholders, distorts incentives for public sector performance, or removes the pressure for an efficient revenue collection system. It is thus important that scaled-up aid goes hand in hand with reforms that improve governance and domestic accountability. In addition, the design of aid delivery mechanisms should support domestic accountability rather than replace it with accountability to donor agencies. In this respect, processes such as the Tanzania Assistance Strategy and the Joint Assistance Strategy have an important role to play in the development of appropriate accountability mechanisms. Efforts to fully integrate foreign aid into Tanzania's budget system and thus make aid subject to the same accountability process as domestic resources are also important.

The effect on competitiveness occurs through a spending effect and a resource movement effect, which are commonly labeled *Dutch disease* effects. A spending effect arises from the fact that unless all inflows are spent on imports or exportable goods, the real exchange rate will increase. This outcome implies a deterioration of a country's competitiveness. In addition, there is a resource movement effect, as resources move into the booming sector (that is, the government and development bureaucracy) and the nontraded sector.

The spending effect has typically received most of the attention in the literature. Aid inflows to Tanzania have fluctuated significantly since the 1990s, with no apparent statistical relationship between aid inflows and the real effective exchange rate (REER). As figure 13.1 illustrates, between 1990 and 1995, the REER was relatively stable, while aid inflows increased from US$1.166 billion to US$1.259 billion and then declined to US$745 million. Since then, aid inflows have been gradually increasing, to US$1.450 billion in 2003. The REER appreciated by about 50 percent between 1995 and 1998 and remained at that level until 2001. Since then, the REER has depreciated significantly and is now back to its 1995 level, which is estimated to represent equilibrium. Exports of manufactured goods increased from US$30 million in 1999 to US$80 million in 2004.

The absence of a clear relationship between foreign aid inflows and the REER is partly attributable to efforts by the government to sterilize these inflows through the sale of liquidity paper and the accumulation of reserves. Recently, however, the sale of bonds has exerted pressure on the interest rate and has the potential to crowd out private sector investment. It is noteworthy that sterilization through the sale of liquidity paper has been only partial and that aid flows have resulted in relatively high rates of monetary expansion. This rapid expansion of the money supply has been consistent with a low and declining rate of inflation, since it was accompanied by financial deepening of the economy. Continued financial deepening of the economy is thus a crucial element in increasing the capacity of the economy to absorb large inflows of aid without direct effects on the real exchange rate.

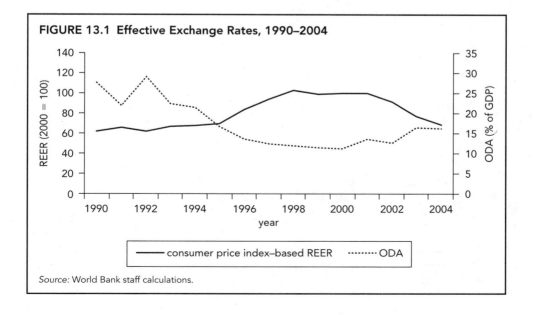

FIGURE 13.1 Effective Exchange Rates, 1990–2004

Source: World Bank staff calculations.

Although most of the discussion of Dutch disease focuses on real exchange movements, the ODA may primarily affect the relative growth of the tradable and nontradable sectors, without actually causing movements in the real exchange rate.[2] In Tanzania, sectoral and balance of payments developments since 1995 display symptoms that are frequently associated with Dutch disease. On the sectoral side, aside from the booming mining sector, growth appears to be heavily concentrated in the nontraded sector. The balance of payments shows a relative sharp decline in merchandise exports over the past decade, which could indicate a loss of competitiveness of the traded sectors versus the nontraded and so-called booming sectors. However, since 2000, exports of manufactures have been recovering, and more recently, agricultural exports have also started to grow (figure 13.2).

The resource movement effect works through two principal channels. The first concerns the direct involvement of Tanzanians in managing donor-related activities. Estimates suggest that there are more than 1,000 donor-funded projects on the ground, ranging from relatively simple technical assistance projects to complex, multimillion dollar projects. Management of donor assistance requires a staff in the offices of the donor agencies in Tanzania and a project staff, as well as a staff in the government that is devoted to managing and monitoring donor-funded activities and ensuring that a variety of donor requirements for financial management and reporting are met.

Salaries for local donor agency staff members and project staff members are typically highly competitive and thus draw the best-qualified staff to those activities. Gov-

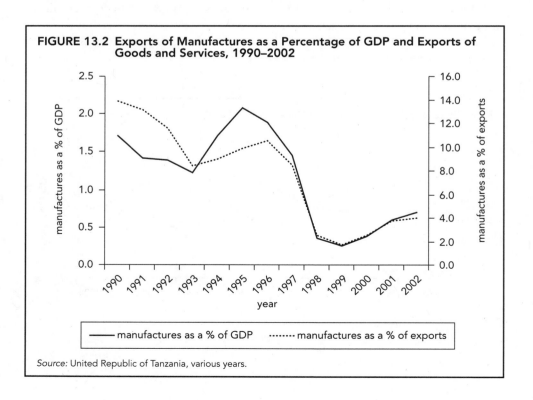

FIGURE 13.2 Exports of Manufactures as a Percentage of GDP and Exports of Goods and Services, 1990–2002

Source: United Republic of Tanzania, various years.

ernment staff members are frequently enticed with salary top-ups or specific benefits that derive from involvement in donor-funded activities. Not only do such enticements draw human resources away from regular private and public sector positions and tasks, but they likely also exert upward pressure on wages in the public and private sectors, with implications for Tanzania's competitiveness as well as for the cost of public service delivery.

Simulations of the effect of aid-financed increases in spending on HIV/AIDS of US$300 million (or 2.9 percent of GDP) and increases in spending on education of US$500 million (or 4.9 percent of GDP) show only a small appreciation of the real exchange rate as a result of these foreign exchange inflows.

Although it may be difficult to establish whether the low level of manufacturing exports and the poor growth of the tradables sectors in Tanzania are indeed directly related to the inflows of foreign aid and gold exports, both clearly highlight an international competitiveness problem. The recent recovery of manufactures exports gives some cause for optimism, but enhancing the competitiveness of the economy must be a central element of Tanzania's strategy to enhance and accelerate economic growth. In particular, the following set of measures should accompany scaling up of aid (Foster and others 2005):

- Ensure that increased aid-financed spending is accompanied by increased absorption of the foreign exchange, which (assuming that government spending continues to have a high local content) will probably require acceptance of exchange rate appreciation. Spending the aid without absorbing the foreign exchange does nothing to increase the real resources available to the economy, but it increases the likelihood that government will crowd out the private sector.

- Further liberalize imports to help increase absorption and reduce the need for real exchange appreciation or reserve accumulation.

- Focus on expenditures that will quickly release supply constraints and have a higher import content, including transport investments.

- Continue to improve the efficiency of the banking sector to ameliorate the need for high real interest rates.

- Consider adopting a more relaxed monetary policy.

- Coordinate exchange rate, monetary, and fiscal policy with the implications of aid inflows in mind.

Debt Sustainability

To the extent that scaled-up aid is in the form of concessional credits, the issue of debt sustainability needs to be considered. After Tanzania received HIPC (Heavily Indebted Poor Countries) Initiative debt relief in 2001 and further debt relief through the Multilateral Debt Relief Initiative, the ratio of the net present value (NPV) of debt to exports declined to about 64 percent. Panel (a) of figure 13.3 shows the

FIGURE 13.3 **Multilateral Credit Disbursements and Debt Sustainability: Net Present Value of Debt-to-Export Ratio, 2006–26**

(a) **Growth of multilateral credit disbursements by 2 percent**

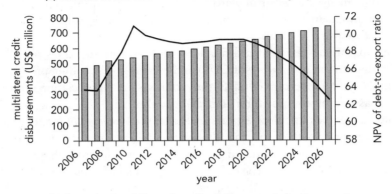

(b) **Growth of multilateral credit disbursements by 5 percent**

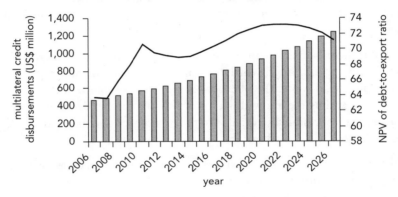

(c) **Doubling of multilateral credit disbursements in 2011**

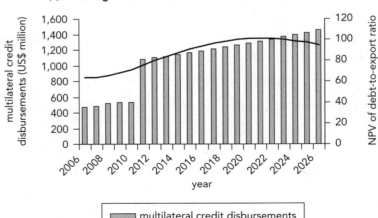

multilateral credit disbursements
—— NPV of debt-to-export ratio

Source: International Monetary Fund and World Bank staff estimates.
Note: NPV = net present value.

baseline projections of the net present value of exports-to-GDP ratio. The ratio is projected to increase initially to 71 percent by 2010, but to decline subsequently to 63 percent by 2026, assuming average export growth of 8.5 percent and annual growth of concessional credit disbursements (primarily from World Bank and African Development Bank credits) by 2 percent. Although debt ratios are relatively low, the debt sustainability analysis also suggests that Tanzania remains vulnerable to negative shocks on exports and GDP growth, which could lead to a significant deterioration in the debt indicators.

Panels (b) and (c) of figure13.3 show the effect of a significant scaling up of multilateral credit disbursements, which would allow a matching increase in imports. As shown in panel (b) of figure 13.3, if disbursements were to grow annually by 5 percent instead of 2 percent, the NPV of debt-to-exports ratio would increase from 64 percent in 2006 to 73 percent by 2021 and decline thereafter.

A doubling of multilateral credit disbursements in 2011 and subsequent annual growth by 2 percent would result in a gradually increasing NPV of the debt-to-export ratio, which would reach 101 percent by 2021 and decline thereafter.

In summary, from a debt sustainability perspective, there seems to be significant scope to expand Tanzania's fiscal space. However, doing so requires that expenditures financed through increased borrowing are indeed used to ensure the sustained growth of exports and GDP. The primary constraint is the availability of concessional funds rather than their effect on Tanzania's debt sustainability.

Reducing Aid Dependency

Dependency on foreign aid for financing public expenditures poses various risks for Tanzania:

- Distortion of Tanzania's development priorities

- Distortions in incentives in the public sector

- Exposure to fluctuations in aid flows

- Exposure to shortfalls in disbursements as compared with commitments.

The conventional approach to reducing aid dependency is to argue for an increased revenue effort. However, given the magnitude of Tanzania's aid dependency, increasing the revenue-to-GDP ratio is not going to address the issue. Indeed, the only way to reduce aid dependency is to increase economic growth and to reach a level of income at which an adequate level of infrastructure and service delivery can be financed from domestic resources. Raising the revenue-to-GDP ratio may have a negative effect on economic growth and thus prolong rather than reduce aid dependency. The key challenges for Tanzania and its development partners are thus the following:

- To adopt aid modalities that reduce the potential negative effect of aid dependency

- To develop mechanisms that allow Tanzania to deal with fluctuations in aid.

Tanzania has been a pioneer in developing modalities that reduce the potential negative effects of aid dependency. In particular, the NSGRP provides the overall framework that sets the priorities for both domestic and foreign resource use. The Tanzania Assistance Strategy sets out principles that would enhance ownership and aid effectiveness, and an increasing share of aid resources is fully integrated into the budget.

With respect to managing fluctuations in aid, most of the attention has been focused on reducing them up front. All development partners have made efforts to enhance the predictability of aid flows by providing more accurate information to the authorities and, in the case of general budget support, to provide the resources at the beginning of the fiscal year—July.

Relatively less attention has been paid to dealing with fluctuations after they happen. Indeed, with Tanzania's cash budget system, shortfalls in aid disbursements (or domestic revenue) result immediately in expenditure cuts. As argued in various Public Expenditure Reviews, though this mechanism has been instrumental in achieving macroeconomic stability, it has a severe negative impact on the implementation of expenditure programs. Domestic borrowing may be an appropriate way to deal with unexpected fluctuations in foreign aid.

Permanent changes in aid flows will require permanent adjustments in expenditure and revenue. Hence, on the expenditure side, the government needs to be cautious about the composition of expenditure and avoid a situation in which spending that is difficult to scale back, such as wages and salaries, dominates. Similarly, there is also a need to evaluate carefully the recurrent cost implications of donor-financed projects. Outsourcing and public-private partnerships may also be useful instruments to facilitate expenditure-side adjustments in case there is a shortfall in aid. They would also be a means for developing the private sector, by using aid inflows to provide business opportunities. On the revenue side, an appropriate strategy may be to not fully exploit the revenue potential but to focus on strengthening tax administration so as to be able to scale up revenue collection to compensate for a permanent decline in aid, if it were to occur.

Conclusions

Estimated resource requirements for achieving the MDG and NSGRP targets exceed available resources from both domestic and foreign sources. Increases in domestic resource mobilization should rely primarily on expanding the revenue base through sustained economic growth and further improvements in tax administration, with the objective of further progress toward an equitable and efficient tax system. Increasing revenue through tax policy measures needs to be approached carefully, considering the efficiency of investment and spending by the public sector compared with that of the private sector and households. Concerning external resources in the form of grants and concessional lending, under the assumption of sustained growth of exports and GDP, the binding constraint is likely to be the availability of these resources rather than debt sustainability. Although the effect of aid inflows on the REER seems to be moderate, raising the competitiveness of the Tanzanian economy remains nonetheless critical in order to offset any aid-induced loss in competitiveness and shifts to the nontradables sector.

Notes

1. Rajan and Subramanian (2005) provide a concise summary of the debate.
2. See discussion in Rajan and Subramanian (2005). In the standard Swan-Salter trade model with two traded goods and one nontraded good, aid reduces the size of the traded good sector without any changes in relative prices between tradables and nontradables. This result underscores the need to focus on quantities rather than prices.

14

Coordination of Economic Policy Formulation and Implementation

Robert J. Utz and Allister Moon

During the past decade, Tanzania has made significant progress in implementing economic reforms aimed primarily at macroeconomic stabilization, the liberalization of the economy, and the withdrawal of the public sector from commercial activities. The reforms have resulted in an acceleration of economic growth. To sustain economic growth, policy makers face two challenges.

The first is to continue these orthodox reforms, especially in areas in which progress has been limited and the marginal returns to reform promise to be high. They include a further reduction in rent-seeking opportunities for public officials who interfere with private sector activities and the improvement of the policy and institutional framework for infrastructure providers.

The second challenge arises from the changing role of economic management in Tanzania. To date, areas for economic reforms have been fairly easy to identify and implementation has required primarily political will to overcome vested interests and a minimum of technical competence in government, often supplemented by technical assistance. However, future economic management is likely to require (a) close collaboration between the private sector and the government, to make economic management more responsive to the proactive identification and pursuit of new opportunities by the private sector, and (b) stronger harmonization and coordination among government agencies to ensure consistent policies and the efficient use of scarce human and financial resources in pursuit of higher economic growth. This chapter assesses the state of affairs in these two areas and provides recommendations on how to strengthen the institutional framework for policy coordination and the dialogue between the private and public sectors.

Review of Institutions for Economic Policy

To understand Tanzania's situation with respect to policy coordination and planning, one may find it instructive to review approaches to policy coordination and planning since independence.

The first comprehensive statement of the country's economic policy after independence is found in the First Five-Year Plan for Economic and Social Development, published in 1965.[1] Central planning was introduced in Tanzania in the 1970s following the promulgation of the Arusha Declaration in 1967. As in other socialist countries, the Planning Commission, with the president as its chair, was at the center of planning, policy formulation, and coordination. Until the mid-1980s, the Planning Commission enjoyed significant power, particularly because it played a pivotal role in resource allocation and price setting.

The initial response to the economic crisis that emerged in the early 1980s was the formulation of a National Economic Survival Program (1981) followed by a home-grown Structural Adjustment Program (1982), and a campaign against economic saboteurs (1983). These programs tried to address Tanzania's economic crisis by intensifying the control regime and the degree of government intervention. Alongside these government-led efforts was an intensifying public debate on measures to overcome the economic crisis, which resulted in recognition of the failure of the centrally planned economy. The government started a process of reforms that would change Tanzania from a command to a market-driven economy. The failure of the efforts to address the crisis through more state intervention also led to a loss of confidence in planning and the role of the Planning Commission.

The introduction of far-reaching economic recovery programs in 1986 replaced medium-term planning with short-term economic management focused on fiscal and monetary stabilization as well as liberalization of the economy. This reform implied a shift in institutional responsibility and power from the Planning Commission to the Ministry of Finance and the Bank of Tanzania, which held the key responsibility for the implementation of the economic recovery programs. The initial efforts and relative successes in economic stabilization during the second half of the 1980s were not sustained during the second term of President Ali Hassan Mwinyi. The government's inability to control credit expansion to public enterprises, massive tax exemptions, poor revenue collection, and tax evasion resulted in severe macroeconomic disequilibria, such as large fiscal and balance of payments deficits, high inflation, and a decline in growth.

In 1996, the new, third-phase government under President Benjamin Mkapa made it a top priority to restore macroeconomic stability and to control corruption. In addressing these issues, the government made bold reassignments for economic management in an attempt to ensure that the capacity and credibility of institutions matched the task at hand. Specifically, an extraordinary amount of power and influence in the economic management of the country was transferred to the Bank of Tanzania. Not only was the bank responsible for monetary management, but with the introduction of a cash budget in 1996, it was also given the responsibility for determining monthly aggregate expenditure ceilings for the government in line with resources available from domestic revenue and foreign aid. The bank also took the lead in managing Tanzania's public debt. The reforms further weakened the Planning Commission, as the responsibility for preparing the development budget shifted from the Planning Commission to the Ministry of Finance in an effort to unify the budget and strengthen budgetary control. The Rolling Plan and Forward Budget, which until 1996 had been prepared by the Planning Commission but had since become virtually irrelevant for economic management, was replaced by the Medium-Term Expenditure Framework (MTEF), which is being prepared by the Ministry of Finance.

With the shift to a market-based economy, the government rightly embarked on efforts to replace government planning of the economy with a process based on greater dialogue between the government and the private sector. These efforts required strengthening private sector institutions that could effectively engage in this dialogue. The Tanzania Private Sector Foundation was established to represent the private sector.

The dialogue between the government and the private sector takes place in various forms. First, in most policy areas the government has adopted participatory processes that allow the private sector to feed its views into government policy making. Recent examples are consultations on the formulation of a new income tax act and the preparation of the rural development and agriculture sector strategies. In addition, the government has established the Tanzania National Business Council (TNBC), chaired by Tanzania's president, as the main forum for consultation between the government and the private sector. Since its establishment, the TNBC has very successfully organized annual international investor round tables, during which the government receives private sector input but also commits to and reports on progress in implementing specific policy reforms.

Another significant development with regard to economic management was the adoption in 2000 of the Poverty Reduction Strategy Paper (PRSP) process, which aims to align government policy and public resource allocation with Tanzania's objective of reducing poverty. The key responsibility within government for the preparation and monitoring of the PRSP was initially with the Vice President's Office, while the Ministry of Finance took the lead role in coordinating the PRSP implementation. This assignment of responsibilities implied a further weakening of the role of the Planning Commission (which was then the President's Office—Planning and Privatization) and a further fragmentation of economic management in Tanzania. However, with the creation of the Ministry of Planning, Economy, and Empowerment in early 2006, the responsibility for the PRSP was shifted to the newly created ministry, which also took over the responsibilities of the President's Office—Planning and Privatization.

Finally, ongoing decentralization efforts also have a significant effect on economic management in Tanzania as responsibilities for the formulation, coordination, and implementation of government programs are shifted from the national level to the district level. An example is the redefinition of the role of government in the agriculture sector. Under the Agriculture Sector Development Program, responsibility for the design of agriculture sector programs has shifted from the national level to the district level, which is now responsible for preparing district agriculture development plans. Similarly, responsibility and related resources for the development and maintenance of district roads have been shifted from the Ministry of Works to local government authorities.

Challenges

As we have mentioned, the focus of economic policy during the late 1990s and early 2000s has been primarily on macroeconomic stabilization and more recently on poverty reduction, with relatively little emphasis on the quality of economic growth and structural transformation. In addition, economic management has been fragmented among a variety of institutions, causing a certain lack of coordination of policy formulation and implementation. The new PRSP (the National Strategy for Growth and Poverty Reduction, or NSGRP) rightly puts greater emphasis on economic growth as a key mechanism for reducing poverty and suggests a more proactive role for government in the pursuit of economic growth. This increased focus on economic growth raises a number of important institutional issues that need to be addressed. We see six key challenges that need urgent attention to ensure that economic policy making can support and sustain high economic growth and react appropriately to the evolution of Tanzania's domestic and international economy.

Challenge 1: Strengthen Coordination of Economic Policy Formulation and Implementation

While the Ministry of Finance and Bank of Tanzania are doing a commendable job managing the economy for stability, coordinating and formulating the broader growth agenda exceeds their institutional mandates and capacities and also threatens to dilute their focus on their core responsibilities. Discussions with a variety of stakeholders reveal a clearly perceived lack of an institutional setup that could perform this coordination function.

Challenge 2: Create a Platform for a National Dialogue on Growth-Related Issues

In line with the transformation from a centrally planned to a market-oriented economy, the process and content of policy formulation and coordination clearly need to encourage dialogue and participation by stakeholders. Hence, the process must be an open one, rather than the preparation of strategies and plans behind closed doors. In various areas, Tanzania has been very successful in establishing processes that allow for continuous dialogue between the government and stakeholders and that draw on resources outside government for the formulation of plans and strategies. Such processes include the Public Expenditure Review and MTEF processes, in which the Ministry of Finance has opened up the budget process while establishing a framework in which analytic work by various parties is coordinated and brought to bear on government processes. Similarly, the Vice President's Office has complemented the broad consultative processes that take place during the preparation of the PRSP or progress report with the establishment of the Research and Analysis Working Group. The group serves as a platform for an ongoing dialogue between government and stakeholders on poverty-related issues and also as an instrument to coordinate analytic work in this area.

In the areas of economic and structural growth, such a platform is currently not available. This lack produces a situation in which a variety of initiatives proceed in parallel with minimal interaction or coordination. A setup similar to that of the Public Expenditure Review process could be envisaged in the areas of economic growth and policy formulation. An existing or a newly established institution would primarily serve as a convener of stakeholders for the coordination and formulation of economic policy, rather than as a mechanism for establishing a capacity to carry out all aspects of policy coordination and formulation.

Challenge 3: Ensure Adequate Governance Arrangements for Growth-Enhancing Government Interventions

Where market failures such as technological externalities, coordination externalities, or informational externalities exist, government interventions can play an important role in fostering private sector activities and economic growth. The government of Tanzania has recently launched several such initiatives, including targeted credit guarantee schemes, export processing zones, and targeted agricultural subsidies. However, experience with such interventions also has brought to the fore a range of potential government failures, which can reduce the effectiveness of such interventions. Government failures can be caused by (a) a lack of complete information about the nature, source, and magnitude of the relevant market failures; (b) the possible capture of policy interventions by firms whose behavior the interventions are aimed at regulating; and (c) the ability of the private sector to game policy makers when policies suffer from dynamic inconsistency (that is, when the promise to withdraw support from poorly performing activities lacks credibility).

Thus, to enhance the likelihood of success of government interventions, policy makers must put appropriate governance rules and monitoring mechanisms in place that would allow the weeding out of ineffective interventions. Box 14.1 provides a summary of such design rules, as proposed by Hausmann and Rodrik (2005).

Challenge 4: Redefine the Government–Private Sector Relationship

Recent research on economic growth (Rodrik and Hausmann 2003) highlights the importance of public-private sector interactions in finding appropriate approaches that result in higher growth at the micro- and macroeconomic levels. In particular, such an approach would require revisiting the private-public sector interface that takes place through central government institutions such as the Tanzania Investment Center, the Tanzania Revenue Authority, the Ministry of Industry and Trade, and the agriculture sector ministries, with a view toward redefining the interaction from a purely regulatory or administrative one to a problem-solving one.

Challenge 5: Strengthen Private Sector Institutions

As mentioned above, an important aspect of economic policy formulation is input by the private sector. Having such input requires the private sector to develop appropriate institutions to make its views heard. A variety of such institutions exists, including the Tanzania Private Sector Foundation; the Confederation of Tanzania Industries; the Tanzania Bankers Association; the Tanzania Chamber of Mines; the Tourism Council of Tanzania; the Tanzania Oil Marketing Companies; the Tanzania Chambers of Commerce, Industry, and Agriculture; the Tanzania Association of Consultants; and the Tanzania Chamber of Agriculture and Livestock. An important issue is to survey these institutions about their roles in the government–private sector dialogue, their satisfaction with the dialogue, and their capacity to effectively represent their constituents.

BOX 14.1 Governance Arrangements to Strengthen the Effectiveness of Growth-Enhancing Interventions

Hausmann and Rodrik (2005) suggest principles that provide an initial basis for formulating an effective program:

- *Clear criteria for success and failure.* Not all entrepreneurial investments in new activities will pay off. In fact, only a small fraction of business ideas are likely to be successful. From the perspective of the program objectives, however, one success can pay for scores of failures. The program must therefore clearly define what constitutes success and identify observable criteria for monitoring it. Otherwise, recipients of incentives can game public agencies and can continue to receive support despite poor outcomes. The criteria should ideally depend on productivity—both its progress and its absolute level—and not on employment or output. Although productivity can be notoriously difficult to measure, project audits by business and technical consultants at set intervals can provide useful indications.

- *Sunset clause.* The program must contemplate a built-in sunset clause. Financial and human resources should not remain tied up for a long time in activities that are not paying off. Every publicly supported project must have not only a clear statement ex ante of what constitutes success and failure, but also an automatic sunset clause for withdrawing support after an appropriate period has elapsed.

- *Targeting of activities rather than sectors.* Public interventions should support activities that suffer from externalities, not the sectors that confront them. This approach facilitates structuring the support as a corrective to specific market failures instead of as generic industrial policies. Rather than providing incentives, say, for electronics, tourism, or call centers, government programs should subsidize bilingual training, feasibility reports for nontraditional agriculture, infrastructure investment, adaptation of foreign technology to Tanzanian conditions, risk and venture capital, and so on. The government should not promote specific sectors but should support growth-enhancing activities that often span several sectors. Similarly, the deciding factor should not be the size of the recipient enterprises. A sectoral approach may be required, however, to get the right people around the table when coordination is an issue or when the relevant public goods and regulations have a sectoral nature. In principle, interventions should be as horizontal as possible and as sectoral as necessary.

- *Spillover and demonstration effects.* Subsidized activities need to have a clear potential for providing spillover and demonstration effects. Public support must be contingent on an analysis of the activity's ability to attract complementary investment or to generate information or technological spillovers. Moreover, supported activities should be structured in such a way as to maximize the spillovers.

- *Autonomous agencies.* The agencies carrying out promotion must be autonomous and, therefore, must have demonstrated their competence. Subject to certain constraints discussed below, the authorities responsible for carrying out promotion need to have enough autonomy and independence that they can insulate themselves from lobbying, design their work agenda appropriately, and have the flexibility to respond to changing circumstances. This requirement, in turn, means that the agencies selected for the purpose must have a prior track record of professionalism, technical competence, and administrative effectiveness. When administrative and human resources are scarce, it may be better to lodge promotion activities in agencies with demonstrated competence than to create new institutions from scratch, even if doing so restricts the range of available policy tools.

- *Monitoring.* The relevant agencies must be monitored closely by a principal who has a clear stake in the outcomes and has political authority at the highest level. Autonomy does

---

BOX 14.1 *(continued)*

not mean lack of accountability. Close monitoring and coordination of the promotion activities by a cabinet-level politician—a principal who has internalized the agenda of economic restructuring and shoulders the main responsibility for it—is essential. Such monitoring not only guards against self-interested behavior on the part of the agencies but also helps protect the agencies from capture by private interests. This principal might be the minister of the economy, for example, or the president. If he or she is not the president, the principal must have the ear of the president and must be viewed as the latter's associate rather than rival.

- *Communication with the private sector.* The agencies carrying out promotion must maintain channels of communication with the private sector. Autonomy and insulation do not mean that bureaucrats should isolate themselves from entrepreneurs and investors. Ongoing contact and communication allow public officials to establish a good basis of information on business realities, without which sound decision making would be impossible. This combination of bureaucratic autonomy and connectedness is what Evans (1995) terms *embedded autonomy* in his discussion of successful economic strategies in East Asia and Latin America.
- *Mistakes in the discovery process.* Public strategies of the sort advocated here are often derided because they may lead to picking the losers rather than the winners. However, an optimal strategy of discovering the productive potential of a country will necessarily entail some mistakes of that type. Some promoted activities will fail. The objective should not be to minimize the chances that mistakes will occur, which would result in no self-discovery at all, but to minimize the costs of the mistakes when they occur. If governments make no mistakes, it means only that they are not trying hard enough.
- *Flexibility in agency design.* Promotion activities need to have the capacity to renew themselves so that the cycle of discovery becomes an ongoing process. Just as there is no single blueprint for undertaking promotion, the needs and circumstances of productive discovery are likely to change over time. The agencies carrying out these policies must therefore have the capacity to reinvent and refashion themselves to fit the changing circumstances.

Source: Hausmann and Rodrik 2005.

Challenge 6: Strengthen the Capacity of Institutions at the Regional and District Levels

Tanzania is characterized by a high level of regional diversity with respect to potential sources of growth, access to infrastructure, and natural resource endowment. The lack of diversification of regional economies also makes them vulnerable to external shocks such as changes in commodity prices. A shared-growth strategy thus requires strong institutions not only at the national level but also at the local level to ensure that growth-enhancing measures are tailored to local circumstances.

Tanzania's ongoing decentralization process touches on important elements of the growth agenda. In particular, responsibility for service delivery in agriculture and infrastructure (district roads, water) is being shifted to local authorities, while the role of the central government in these areas is limited to policy formulation and monitoring. Funding for these activities is primarily provided through earmarked transfers from the central government. A formula-based system for budgetary transfers to the districts has been adopted that takes into account demographic and social indicators. It is important to ensure that local authorities play a supportive role for regional growth; therefore, the use of these resources must be guided by a regional growth strategy developed by a partnership of local authorities, the private sector, and other stakeholders. Strengthening of accountability arrangements at the local level needs to accompany increased resource flows to local authorities. Regional- or district-level growth strategies combined with strong accountability arrangements also form the basis for a successful switch from conditional to unconditional transfers, which is envisaged in the medium term. Unconditional transfers will provide local authorities with greater scope to implement a growth strategy that is tailored to the specifics of the district or region.

In this context, the division of revenue sources between the central government and local governments is also important. At present, the revenue sources for local authorities are limited to a closed list and typically provide only 10 to 20 percent of a district's revenue. The current system provides scope for redistribution of resources across districts. However, a system in which resource availability at the local level is more closely linked to revenue generation at the local level might provide more incentives for a greater focus on economic growth at the local level.

Implementation of the Growth Agenda of the NSGRP

The NSGRP, Tanzania's PRSP, has evolved as a broader instrument of national policy, with an explicit emphasis on the broader agenda of policies for shared economic growth. Links between the NSGRP and other instruments have also evolved:

- The government has continued to encourage an open process of consultation on these instruments of policy coordination.

- The decentralization process that is under way gives greater responsibility to local authorities, including for the management of infrastructure and water.

The task facing the government now is to translate the renewed emphasis on growth into specific strategies, detailed implementation plans, and proposed resource allocations. Several challenges arise in this task:

- The link between the NSGRP and the MTEF appears to have immediate potential for translating individual sector strategies into programs and expenditure plans. A higher degree of coordination may be needed to make this work for the relatively diffuse, cross-sectoral agenda that is the key for growth.

- Growth requires increasing public investment. It also requires enhanced capacity for scrutiny of public investment proposals, both at the sector level and in the overall coordination of public investment, ensuring maximum efficiency, complementarity with the private sector, and so on.

- The open process of consultation on policy coordination has attracted support of and interest, largely along sectoral lines, in sector programs. It is less clear that there is a strong and vocal constituency pressing the claims of an effective cross-sectoral strategy to promote growth.

- Numerous channels exist for interfacing with the private sector on issues that are highly relevant for growth but do not yet provide the forum for a coalition for growth across central agencies, sectors, civil society, and the private sector.

- This book underlines the specificity of growth opportunities at regional and district levels. A key challenge is to support regionally specific growth strategies that recognize these different opportunities while ensuring that institutions at regional and lower levels of government are consistent with this objective.

The broadened scope of the NSGRP offers an opportunity to review the institutions for coordinating policy on economic growth. The following may be some immediate entry points for strengthening the institutional environment for steering the growth agenda:

- Institutions related to the earlier narrower scope of the PRSP, such as the structure of the poverty monitoring system, require reorientation to a broader role so that they can capture the renewed emphasis on growth. This effort may also require evolution in the roles of the Vice President's Office, the Ministry of Planning, Economy, and Empowerment, and other central agencies involved in organizing NSGRP coordination and implementation.

- Implementing the NSGRP will require action plans based on its broad objectives. In most cases, at the sector level, action plans can be derived from individual sector strategies and programs, but there appears to be a case for stronger coordination of sector plans within a cross-sectoral growth strategy that adequately reflects the objectives of the NSGRP.

- The current budget guidelines do not appear to reflect the strong emphasis on growth-enhancing investment implied by the NSGRP. More work is needed to translate the NSGRP objectives in this area into detailed proposals, particularly for infrastructure investment, preferably in the course of developing the current year's MTEF.

- Reorientation of public expenditure toward a greater focus on growth will also have implications for the use of external financing. The dialogue in the context of the Public Expenditure Review process is an important opportunity to ensure that this strategic challenge is addressed.

Note

1. This section draws on Mjema (2000) and Muganda (2004).

Bibliography

Background Studies

Alderman, Harold, J. G. M. Hoogeveen, and Mariacristina Rossi. 2005. "Reducing Child Malnutrition in Tanzania: Combined Effects of Income Growth and Program Interventions." World Bank, Washington, DC.

Aubert, Jean-Eric, and Godwill Wanga. 2005. "Innovation in Tanzania: Insights, Issues, and Policies." World Bank, Washington, DC.

Chandra, Vandana, Pooja Kacker, and Ying Li. 2005. "Tanzania: Growth, Exports, and Employment in the Manufacturing Sector." World Bank, Washington, DC.

Christiaensen, Luc, Vivian Hofmann, and Alexander Sarris. 2004. "Coffee Price Risk in Perspective: Vulnerability among Small Holder Coffee Growers in Tanzania." World Bank, Washington, DC.

COWI. 2005. "Natural Resource Based Growth: Summary Paper." World Bank, Washington, DC.

Demombynes, Gabriel, and J. G. M. Hoogeveen. 2004. "Growth, Inequality, and Simulated Poverty Paths for Tanzania, 1992–2002." Policy Research Working Paper 3432, World Bank, Washington, DC.

Hoogeveen, J. G. M. 2004. "The Distributional Impact of the PEDP in Rural Kilimanjaro." World Bank, Washington, DC.

———. 2005. "Risk, Growth, and Transfers: Prioritizing Policies in a Low-Income Environment with Risk—The Case of Tanzania." World Bank, Washington, DC.

Kessy, Flora. 2004. "Rural Income Dynamics in Kagera Region, Tanzania." Economic and Social Research Foundation, Dar es Salaam.

Kessy, Flora, and Oswald Mashindano. 2005. "Moving Out of Poverty: Understanding Growth and Democracy from the Bottom Up—The Case of Ruvuma Region, Tanzania." Economic and Social Research Foundation, Dar es Salaam.

Kilama, Blandina, and Wietze Lindenboom. 2004. "Trends in Malnutrition in Tanzania." Research on Poverty Alleviation, Dar es Salaam.

Kopicki, Ronald. "Supply Chain Development in Tanzania." World Bank, Washington, DC.

Mahamba, Robert, and Jorgen Levin. 2005. "Economic Growth, Sectoral Linkages, and Poverty Reduction in Tanzania." World Bank, Washington, DC.

Mkenda, Adolf. 2004. "The Benefits of Malnutrition Interventions: Empirical Evidence and Lessons to Tanzania." University of Dar es Salaam, Dar es Salaam.

———. 2005. "Population Growth, Economic Growth and Welfare Distribution: An Overview of Theory, Empirical Evidence and Implications to Tanzania." University of Dar es Salaam, Dar es Salaam.

Mpango, Philip. 2005. "Subnational Dimensions of Growth and Poverty." World Bank, Washington, DC.

Simonsen, Marianne, and Louise Fox. 2005. "A Profile of Poverty in Tanzania." World Bank, Washington, DC.

Skof, Annabella. 2006. "Constraints to Technology Access in Tanzanian Horticulture: A Case Study of Barriers to the Introduction of Improved Seed and Pest Control Technologies." World Bank, Washington, DC.

Tanzania Food and Nutrition Centre. 2004. "Causes of Malnutrition and Tanzania's Nutrition Programs: Past and Present." World Bank, Washington, DC.

Utz, Anuja. 2004. "Fostering Innovation, Productivity, and Technological Change: Tanzania in the Knowledge Economy." Knowledge for Development Program, World Bank Institute, Washington, DC.

Utz, Robert. 2005. "Review of Growth Performance and Prospects." World Bank, Washington, DC.

van Dijk, Meine Pieter. 2006. "Urban Rural Dynamics in Tanzania through Informal Redistribution Mechanisms." World Bank, Washington, DC.

References

Abdulai, Awudu, and Dominique Aubert. 2004a. "A Cross-Section Analysis of Household Demand for Food and Nutrients in Tanzania." *Agricultural Economics* 31 (1): 67–79.

———. 2004b. "Nonparametric and Parametric Analysis of Calorie Consumption in Tanzania." *Food Policy* 29 (2): 113–29.

Accenture, Markle Foundation, and UNDP (United Nations Development Programme). 2001. "Case 7—Tanzania." In *Creating a Development Dynamic: Final Report of the Digital Opportunity Initiative*. http://www.opt-init.org/framework/ pages/contents.html.

Alderman, Harold, J. G. M. Hoogeveen, and Mariacristina Rossi. 2006. "Reducing Child Malnutrition in Tanzania: Combined Effects of Income Growth and Program Interventions." *Economics and Human Biology* 4: 1–23.

Alesina, Alberto, Silvia Ardagna, Giuseppe Nicoletti, and Fabio Schiantarelli. 2003. "Regulation and Investment." NBER Working Paper 9560. National Bureau of Economic Research, Cambridge, MA.

Anand, Sudhir, and Jonathan Morduch. 1996. "Poverty and the 'Population Problem.'" Center for Population and Development Studies and Department of Economics, Harvard University, Cambridge, MA.

ASDP (Agricultural Sector Development Programme) Working Group 2. 2004. "Report on Irrigation Development in Tanzania." ASDP Working Group 2, Dar es Salaam.

Baldus, Rolf D., and Andrew E. Cauldwell. 2004. "Tourist Hunting and Its Role in Development of Wildlife Management Areas in Tanzania." Paper presented at the Sixth International Game Ranching Symposium, Paris, July 6–9.

Balile, Deodatus. 2003. "Tanzania Pledges Support for Science Training." SciDev Net, June 19. http://www.scidev.net/dossiers/index.cfm?fuseaction=dossierReadItem&type=1&itemid=871&language=1&dossier=10.

Bank of Tanzania. 2004a. *Annual Report 2003/04*. Dar es Salaam: Bank of Tanzania.

———. 2004b. *Tanzania Investment Report of 2004*. Dar es Salaam: Bank of Tanzania.

———. Various years. *Quarterly Economic Review*. Various issues

Barro, Robert. 1991. "Economic Growth in a Cross Section of Countries." *Quarterly Journal of Economics* 106 (2): 407–41.

Barro, Robert, and Jong-Wha Lee. 2000. "International Data on Educational Attainment: Updates and Implications." CID Working Paper 42, Center for International Development, Harvard University.

Beck, Thorsten, Ross Levine, and Norman Loayza. 2000. "Financial Intermediation and Growth: Causality and Causes." *Journal of Monetary Economics* 46 (1): 31–77.

Beegle, Kathleen, Joachim De Weerdt, and Stefan Dercon. 2006. *Kagera Health and Development Survey 2004*. Washington, DC: World Bank.

Behrman, Jere R., Harold Alderman, and John Hoddinott. 2004. "Malnutrition and Hunger." In *Global Crises, Global Solutions*, ed. Bjørn Lomborg, 363–420. Cambridge, U.K.: Cambridge University Press.

Bosworth, Barry, and Susan Collins. 2003. *The Empirics of Growth: An Update*. Washington, DC: Brookings Institution. http://www.brookings.edu/views/papers/bosworth/20030307.pdf.

Broadman, Harry G., and Francesca Recanatini. 2001. "Seeds of Corruption: Do Market Institutions Matter? *MOCT-MOST: Economic of Policy in Transitional Economies* 11 (4): 359–92.

Canning, David, and Esra Bennathan. 2003. "The Social Rate of Return on Infrastructure Investments." Policy Research Working Paper 2390, World Bank, Washington, DC.

Carter, Richard C. 1999. "Private Sector Participation in Low Cost Water Well Drilling." *DFID-WATER*, November 1999. http://www.silsoe.cranfield.ac.uk/iwe/projects/lcdrilling/.

Chandra, Vandana. 2006. *Technology, Adaptation, and Exports: How Some Developing Countries Got It Right*. Washington, DC: World Bank.

Chandra, Vandana, Pooja Kacker, and Ying Li. 2005. "Tanzania: Growth, Exports, and Employment in the Manufacturing Sector." Background paper, World Bank, Washington, DC.

Christiaensen Luc, Vivian Hofmann, and Alexander Sarris. 2004. "Coffee Price Risk in Perspective: Vulnerability among Small Holder Coffee Growers in Tanzania." Background paper, World Bank, Washington, DC.

Cohen, Daniel, and Marcelo Soto. 2001. "Growth and Human Capital: Good Data, Good Results." CEPR Discussion Paper 3025. Centre for Economic Policy Research, London.

Collins, Susan, and Barry Bosworth. 1996. "Economic Growth in East Asia: Accumulation versus Assimilation." Brookings Paper on Economic Activity 2, Brookings Institution, Washington, DC.

COWI. 2005. "Natural Resource Based Growth: Summary Paper." Background paper, World Bank, Washington, DC.

Dasgupta, Partha. 1995. "The Population Problem: Theory and Evidence." *Journal of Economic Literature* 33 (4): 1879–902.

Datt, Gaurav, and Dean Joliffe. 1999. "Determinants of Poverty in Egypt: 1997." Discussion Paper 19, International Food Policy Research Institute, Washington, DC.

Datt, Gaurav, and Martin Ravallion. 1992. "Growth and Redistribution Components of Changes in Poverty: A Decomposition with Applications to Brazil and China in the 1980s." *Journal of Development Economics* 38 (2): 275–95.

Datt, Gaurav, and Thomas Walker. 2002. "Povstat 2.12: A Poverty Projection Toolkit—User's Manual." World Bank, Washington, DC.

Datt, Gaurav, Krishnan Ramadas, Dominique van der Mensbrugghe, Thomas Walker, and Quentin Wodon. 2003. "Predicting the Effect of Aggregate Growth on Poverty." In *The Impact of Economic Policies on Poverty and Income Distribution: Evaluation Techniques and Tools*, ed. François Bourguignon and Luiz A. Pereira da Silva, 215–34. New York: World Bank and Oxford University Press.

Deaton, Angus, and Salman Zaidi. 2002. "Guidelines for Constructing Consumption Aggregates for Welfare Analysis." LSMS Working Paper 135, World Bank, Washington, DC.

Demombynes, Gabriel, and J. G. M. Hoogeveen. 2004. "Growth, Inequality, and Simulated Poverty Paths for Tanzania, 1992–2002." Policy Research Working Paper 3432, World Bank, Washington, DC.

Dercon, Stefan. 1996. "Risk, Crop Choice, and Savings: Evidence from Tanzania." *Economic Development and Cultural Change* 44 (3): 485–513.

———. 1998. "Wealth, Risk, and Activity Choice: Cattle in Western Tanzania." *Journal of Development Economics* 55 (1): 1–42.

Dercon, Stefan, Tessa Bold, Joachim De Weerdt, and Alula Pankhurst. 2004. "Extending Insurance? Funeral Associations in Ethiopia and Tanzania." Working Paper 240, OECD Development Centre, Paris.

De Soto, Hernando. 2001. *The Mystery of Capital: Why Capitalism Triumphs in the West and Fails Everywhere Else.* New York: Basic Books.

Djankov, Simeon, Rafael La Porta, Florencio Lopez-De-Silanes, and Andrei Shleifer. 2002. "The Regulation of Entry." *Quarterly Journal of Economics* 117 (1): 1–37.

Drèze, Jean, and Amartya Sen. 1989. *Hunger and Public Action.* Oxford, UK: Clarendon Press.

Economist Intelligence Unit. 2004a. "Business Africa," September 1. Available online at http://db.eiu.com.

———. 2004b. "Country Report: Tanzania," May. Available online at http://db.eiu.com.

Eifert, Benn, Alan Gelb, and Vijaya Ramachandran. 2005. "Business Environment and Comparative Advantage in Africa: Evidence from the Investment Climate Data." World Bank, Washington, DC.

Elbers, Chris, Jan Willem Gunning, and Bill Kinsey. 2003. "Growth and Risk: Methodology and Micro Evidence." Discussion Paper TI 2003-068/2, Tinbergen Institute, Amsterdam.

ESRF (Economic and Social Research Foundation). 2002. "Background Note on Tanzania for the World Bank Institute." Paper prepared for the Policy Workshop on Knowledge for Development, Dar es Salaam, May 13–29.

ESRF (Economic and Social Research Foundation) and FACEIT (Front against Corrupt Elements in Tanzania). 2002. *Annual Report of the State of Corruption in Tanzania, 2002.* Dar es Salaam: ESRF and FACEIT.

Estache, Antonio. 2005. "What Do We Know about Sub-Saharan Africa's Infrastructure and the Impact of Its 1990s Reforms?" World Bank, Washington, DC.

Evans, Peter. 1995. *Embedded Autonomy: States and Industrial Transformation.* Princeton, NJ: Princeton University Press.

Fan, Shenggen, David Nyange, and Neetha Rao. 2005. "Public Investment and Poverty Reduction in Tanzania: Evidence from Household Survey Data." Development Strategy Governance Division Discussion Paper 18, International Food Policy Research Institute, Washington, DC.

FAO (Food and Agriculture Organization). 1997. *Irrigation Technology in Support of Food Security: Proceedings of a Regional Workshop.* Rome: FAO.

———. 2004. AQUASTAT database. FAO, Rome. http://www.fao.org/AG/agl/aglw/ aquastat/ water_res/index.stm.

FAO (Food and Agriculture Organization) and World Bank. 2001. *Tanzania Agriculture: Reaping the Benefits of Reform.* Rome and Washington, DC: FAO and World Bank.

FIAS (Foreign Investment Advisory Service). 2006. *Sector Study of the Effective Tax Burden—Tanzania.* Washington, DC: FIAS.

Fink, Carsten, Aaditya Mattoo, and Ileana Cristina Neagu. 2002. "Assessing the Role of Communications Costs in International Trade." Working Paper 2929, World Bank, Washington, DC.

Fjeldstad, Odd-Helge. 2002. "Fighting Fiscal Corruption: The Case of the Tanzania Revenue Authority." CMI Working Paper 2002:3, Chr. Michelsen Institute, Bergen, Norway.

Foster, Mick, Josaphat Kweka, Daniel Ngowi, Justine Musa, and Longinus Rutasitara. 2005. "The Macroeconomic Impact of Scaling Up Aid Flows: The Case Study of Tanzania." Overseas Development Institute, London.

Gill, Indermit, and Amit Dar. 1998. "Vocational Education and Training in Tanzania: Finance and Relevance Issues in Transition." Country Study Summary 19781, World Bank, Washington, DC.

Gresser, Charis, and Sophia Tickell. 2002. *Mugged: Poverty in Your Coffee Cup.* Oxford, U.K.: Oxfam International.

Gwatkin, Davidson R., Shea Rutstein, Kiersten Johnson, Eldaw Abdulla Suliman, and Adam Wagstaff. 2003. *Initial Country-Level Information about Socio-Economic Differences in Health, Nutrition and Population,* 2nd ed. Washington, DC: World Bank.

Haddad, Lawrence, Harold Alderman, Simon Appleton, Lina Long, and Yisehac Yohannes. 2003. "Reducing Malnutrition: How Far Does Income Growth Take Us?" *World Bank Economic Review* 17 (1): 107–31.

Harding, Alan, Måns Söderbom, and Francis Teal. 2002. "The Tanzanian Manufacturing Enterprise Survey 2002." Report REP/2002-04, Centre for the Study of African Economies, University of Oxford, Oxford, U.K.

Hausmann, Ricardo, and Dani Rodrik. 2005. "Self-Discovery in a Development Strategy for El Salvador." *Economía* 6 (1): 43–101.

Hazlewood, Judith G., and Srividya Prakash. 2005. "Tanzania's Health Care Crisis." *McKinsey Quarterly* 3: 9.

Hemming, Richard, Michael Kell, and Selma Mahfouz. 2002. "The Effectiveness of Fiscal Policy in Stimulating Economic Activity—A Review of the Literature." IMF Working Paper 02/208, International Monetary Fund, Washington, DC.

Homewood, K., E. F. Lambin, E. Coast, A. Kariuki, I. Kikula, J. Kivelia, M. Said, S. Serneels, and M. Thompson. 2001. "Long-Term Changes in Serengeti-Mara Wildebeest and Land Cover: Pastoralism, Population, or Policies?" *Proceedings of the National Academy of Science* 98 (22): 12544–49.

Horton, Susan. 1999. "Opportunities for Investment in Low Income Asia." *Asian Development Review* 17 (1–2): 246–73.

Horton, Susan, and J. Ross. 2003. "The Economics of Iron Deficiency." *Food Policy* 28 (1): 51–75.

Huppi, Monica, and Martin Ravallion. 1991. "The Sectoral Structure of Poverty in Indonesia during an Adjustment Period: Evidence for Indonesia in the Mid-1980s." *World Development* 19 (12): 1653–78.

IFC (International Finance Corporation). 2000. "Tanzania: Country Impact Review." IFC Independent Evaluation Group Report, February, Washington, DC.

ILD (Instituto Libertad y Democracia). 2005. *Program to Formalize the Assets of the Poor of Tanzania and Strengthen the Rule of Law: The Diagnosis.* Vol. 1. Lima: ILD.

ILO, UNIDO, and UNDP (International Labour Organization, United Nations Industrial Development Organization, and United Nations Development Programme). 2002. "Roadmap Study of the Informal Sector in Mainland Tanzania." ILO, UNIDO, and UNDP, Dar es Salaam.

IMF (International Monetary Fund). 2003. "Financial System Stability Assessment." IMF Country Report 03/241. IMF, Washington, DC.

———. 2004. "Tanzania: Selected Issues and Statistical Appendix." IMF Country Report 04/284. IMF, Washington, DC.

————. Various years. *International Financial Statistics.* Washington, DC: IMF.

InfoDev. 2005. "Improving Competitiveness in Tanzania: The Role of Information and Communication Technology." World Bank, Washington, DC.

Jaffee, Steven, Ron Kopicki, Patrick Labaste, and Ian Christie. 2003. *Modernizing Africa's Agro-Food Systems: Analytical Framework and Implications for Operations.* Africa Region Working Paper 44, World Bank, Washington, DC.

JICA (Japan International Cooperation Agency). 2002. *The Study on the National Irrigation Master Plan in the United Republic of Tanzania.* Tokyo: JICA.

Kallonga, Emmanual, Alan Rodgers, Fred Nelson, Yannick Ndoinyo, and Nshala Rugemeleza. 2003. "Reforming Environmental Governance in Tanzania: Natural Resource Management and the Rural Economy." Paper presented at the Inaugural Tanzania Biennial Development Forum, Dar es Salaam, April 24–25.

Kaufmann, Daniel, Aart Kraay, and Massimo Mastruzzi. 2006. "Governance Matters V: Governance Indicators for 1996–2005." World Bank, Washington, DC. http://www .worldbank.org/wbi/governance/pubs/govmatters4.html.

Kessy, Flora. 2004. "Rural Income Dynamics in Kagera Region, Tanzania." Background paper, Economic and Social Research Foundation, Dar es Salaam.

Kessy, Flora, and Oswald Mashindano. 2005. "Moving Out of Poverty: Understanding Growth and Democracy from the Bottom Up—The Case of Ruvuma Region, Tanzania." Background paper, Economic and Social Research Foundation, Dar es Salaam.

Klasen, Stephan. 2003. "In Search of the Holy Grail: How to Achieve Pro-Poor Growth?" *In Annual World Bank Conference on Development Economics—Europe: Toward Pro-Poor Policies: Aid Institutions and Globalization,* ed. Bertil Tungodden, Nicholas Stern, and Ivar Kolstad, 63–94. New York: World Bank and Oxford University Press.

Kweka, Josaphat. 2004. "Tourism and the Economy of Tanzania: A CGE Analysis." Paper presented at the Centre for the Study of African Economies Conference on Growth, Poverty Reduction, and Human Development in Africa, Oxford, U.K., March 21–22.

Kweka, Josaphat, Oliver Morrissey, and Adam Blake. 2003. "The Economic Potential of Tourism in Tanzania." *Journal of International Development* 15: 335–51.

Krugman, Paul. 1991. *Geography and Trade.* Leuven, Belgium: Leuven University Press, Leuven.

Lanjouw, Peter, and Martin Ravallion. 1995. "Poverty and Household Size." *Economic Journal* 105 (November): 1415–34.

Larson Donald, Jock Anderson, and Panos Varangis. 2004. "Policies on Managing Risk in Agricultural Markets." *World Bank Research Observer* 19 (2): 199–230.

Lindeboom, Wietze. 2005. *Disability and Poverty in Tanzania.* Dar es Salaam: Research on Poverty Alleviation.

Lindeboom, Wietze, and Blandina Kilama. 2005. "Trends and Determinants of Malnutrition in Tanzania." Paper presented at Research on Poverty Alleviation's 10th Annual Research Workshop, Dar es Salaam, April 7.

Lorenz, Nicolaus, and Cyprian Mpemba. 2005. *Review of the State of Health in Tanzania 2004.* Basel, Switzerland: Swiss Centre for International Health.

MAFS (Ministry of Agriculture and Food Security). 2001. *Agricultural Extension Reform in Tanzania.* Dar es Salaam.

Mahamba, Robert, and Jorgen Levin. 2005. "SAM/CGE Analysis of Tanzania's Economy." Background paper, World Bank, Washington, DC.

Makundi, E., P. Hiza, W. Kisinza, A. Mwisongo, J. Mcharo, K. Senkoro, G. Mubyazi, H. Malebo, S. Magesa, M. Munga, M. Kamugisha, J. Rubona, E. Kwesi, R. Mdoe, R. Kalinga,

D. Simba, M. Malecela, and A. Kitua. 2004. "Assessing Trends in the Overall Performance of the Health Sector in Tanzania." National Institute for Medical Research, Dar es Salaam.

Mankiw, N. Gregory, David Romer, and David Weil. 1992. "A Contribution to the Empirics of Economic Growth." *Quarterly Journal of Economics* 107 (2): 407–37.

MIGA (Multilateral Investment Guarantee Agency). 2002. "Tourism in Tanzania: Investment for Growth and Diversification." MIGA, Washington, DC.

Ministry of Education and Culture. 2004. *Basic Statistics in Education 1999–2003*. Dar es Salaam: Ministry of Education and Culture.

Ministry of Natural Resources and Tourism. 2002. *Tourism Master Plan: Strategies and Actions: Final Summary Update*. Dar es Salaam: Ministry of Natural Resources and Tourism.

———. 2004. *MTEF Budget of the Ministry of Natural Resources and Tourism, Vote 69*. Dar es Salaam: Ministry of Natural Resources and Tourism.

Mjema, Godwin D. 2000. "Strategic Long-Term Planning and Policy Management: Some Reflections from Tanzania." *DPMF Bulletin* 7 (2).

Mkenda, Adolf. 2004. "The Benefits of Malnutrition Interventions: Empirical Evidence and Lessons to Tanzania." University of Dar es Salaam, Dar es Salaam.

———. 2005. "Population Growth, Economic Growth and Welfare Distribution." University of Dar es Salaam, Dar es Salaam.

Muganda, Anna. 2004. "Tanzania's Economic Reforms (and Lessons Learned)." World Bank, Washington, DC.

Murphy, M., and A. Henegan. 2002. "European and United States Market Demand Survey for Tanzania." Paper prepared by CHL Consulting for the Ministry for Natural Resources and Tourism, Dar es Salaam.

National Bureau of Statistics. 1993. "Household Budget Survey 1991/92." National Bureau of Statistics, Dar es Salaam.

———. 2001. "Integrated Labour Force Survey, 2000/01—Analytical Report." National Bureau of Statistics, Dar es Salaam.

———. 2002. "Household Budget Survey 2000/01." National Bureau of Statistics, Dar es Salaam.

National Bureau of Statistics and Macro International. 2000. *Tanzania Reproductive and Child Health Survey 1999*. Dar es Salaam and Calverton, MD: National Bureau of Statistics and Macro International.

National Bureau of Statistics and ORC Macro. 2005. *Tanzania Demographic and Health Survey 2004/05*. Dar es Salaam: National Bureau of Statistics and ORC Macro.

Nehru, Vikram, and Ashok Dhareshwar. 1993. "A New Database on Physical Capital Stock: Sources, Methodology, and Results." *Revista de Análisis Económico* 8 (1): 37–59.

Nelson, Edwin G., and Erik J. de Burijn. 2005. "The Voluntary Formalization of Enterprises in a Developing Economy: The Case of Tanzania." *Journal of International Development* 17: 575–93.

Nyange, David. 2005. "Survey of Agricultural Marketing Logistics Costs in Rural Tanzania." Background paper for the *Tanzania Diagnostic Trade Integration Study*, World Bank, Washington, DC.

Owens, Trudy, and Francis Teal. 2005. "Paths Out of Poverty in Ghana and Tanzania in the 1990s." School of Economics, University of Nottingham, Nottingham, U.K.

Pritchett, Lant. 2000. "The Tyranny of Concepts: CUDIE (Cumulated, Depreciated, Investment Effort) Is Not Capital." *Journal of Economic Growth* 5 (4): 361–84.

Rafalimanana, Hanta, and Charles Westoff. 2001. "Gap between Preferred and Actual Birth Intervals in Sub-Saharan Africa: Implications for Fertility and Child Health." DHS Analytical Studies 2, ORC Macro, Calverton, MD.

Rajan, Raghuram G., and Arvind Subramanian. 2005. "What Undermines Aid's Impact on Growth?" IMF Working Paper 05/126, International Monetary Fund, Washington, DC.

Ravallion, Martin, and Gaurav Datt. 1996. "How Important to India's Poor Is the Sectoral Composition of Economic Growth?" *World Bank Economic Review* 10 (1): 1–25.

Rodrik, Dani. 2000. "Saving Transitions." *World Bank Economic Review* 14 (3): 481–507.

———. 2004. "Industrial Policy for the Twenty-First Century." Kennedy School of Government, Harvard University, Cambridge, MA.

Rodrik, Dani, and Ricardo Hausmann. 2003. "Discovering El Salvador's Production Potential." Kennedy School of Government, Harvard University, Cambridge, MA. http://ksghome.harvard.edu/~drodrik/ elsalvador.pdf.

Rosenzweig, Mark R., and Kenneth Wolpin. 1993. "Credit Market Constraints, Consumption Smoothing, and the Accumulation of Durable Production Assets in Low Income Countries: Investments in Bullocks in India." *Journal of Political Economy* 101 (2): 223–24.

Rossi, Mariacristina. 2004. "Consequences of Illness on Per Capita Consumption in Kagera." University of Rome Tor Vergata, Rome.

Scarpetta, Stefano, and Giuseppe Nicoletti. 2003. "Regulation, Productivity and Growth: OECD Evidence." Policy Research Working Paper 2944, World Bank, Washington, DC.

Schclarek, Alfredo. 2003. "Fiscal Policy and Private Consumption in Industrial and Developing Countries." Working Paper 2003:20, Department of Economics, Lund University, Lund, Sweden.

Schneider, Friedrich. 2004. "The Size of the Shadow Economies of 145 Countries All over the World: First Results over the Period 1999 to 2003." IZA Discussion Paper 1431, Institute for the Study of Labor, Bonn.

———. 2006. "Shadow Economies and Corruption All over the World: What Do We Really Know?" Working Paper 0617, Johannes Kepler University, Linz, Austria.

Sergeant, Andrew. 2004. "Horticultural and Floricultural Exports: Constraints, Potential, and an Agenda for Support." Report by Accord Associates for the *Tanzania Diagnostic Trade Integration Study*, World Bank, Washington, DC.

Shorrocks, Anthony F. 1984. "Inequality Decomposition by Population Subgroups." *Econometrica* 52 (6): 1369–88.

Skof, Annabella. 2006. "Constraints to Technology Access in Tanzanian Horticulture: A Case Study of Barriers to the Introduction of Improved Seed and Pest Control Technologies." Background paper, World Bank, Washington, DC.

Söderbom, Måns, Francis Teal, Anthony Wambugu, and Godius Kahyarar. 2004. *The Dynamics of Returns to Education in Kenyan and Tanzanian Manufacturing*. CSAE Working Paper WPS/2003-17, Centre for the Study of African Economies, University of Oxford, Oxford, U.K.

TFNC (Tanzania Food and Nutrition Center). 2004a. "Causes of Malnutrition and Tanzania's Nutrition Programs: Past and Present." TFNC, Dar es Salaam.

———. 2004b. *Vitamin A Report Based on Health Facility Data*. Dar es Salaam: TFNC.

UNCTAD (United Nations Conference on Trade and Development). 2005. *The Digital Divide: ICT Development Indices 2004*. New York and Geneva: UNCTAD. http://www.unctad.org/en/docs/iteipc20054_en.pdf.

UNDP (United Nations Development Programme). 2001. *Human Development Report 2001: Making New Technologies Work for Human Development*. New York: UNDP.

UNICEF (United Nations Children's Fund). 1990. "Women and Children in Tanzania: An Overview." UNICEF, Dar es Salaam.

UN (United Nations) Millennium Project. 2005. *Investing in Development: A Practical Plan to Achieve the Millennium Development Goals*. London: Earthscan.

United Republic of Tanzania. 1992. "National Population Policy." Dar es Salaam: Government of Tanzania.

——. 2002a. *Population and Housing Census: General Report*. Dar es Salaam: National Bureau of Statistics.

——. 2002b. "Agriculture Sector Development Programme Framework and Process Document." Government of Tanzania, Dar es Salaam.

——. 2003a. *Annual Survey of Industrial Production, Vol. III*. Dar es Salaam: Government of Tanzania.

——. 2003b. *Poverty and Human Development Report*. Dar es Salaam: Government of Tanzania.

——. 2004a. *Economic Survey*. Dar es Salaam: Government of Tanzania.

——. 2004b. *Legal Sector Reform Programme Medium-Term Strategy FY2005/6–FY2007/8*. Dar es Salaam: Government of Tanzania.

——. 2004c. *Vulnerability and Resilience to Poverty in Tanzania: Causes, Consequences and Policy Implications—Participatory Poverty Assessment*. Dar es Salaam: United Republic of Tanzania.

——. 2005a. *Budget Guidelines for 2005/06*. Dar es Salaam: Government of Tanzania.

——. 2005b. *Transport Sector Investment Programme*. Dar es Salaam: Government of Tanzania.

——. 2006. "Agriculture Sector Development Programme Document." Government of Tanzania, Dar es Salaam.

——. Various years. *Economic Survey*. Dar es Salaam: Government of Tanzania.

United Republic of Tanzania, Vice President's Office. 2005. *Poverty and Human Development Report, 2005*. Dar es Salaam: Government of Tanzania.

Walsh, Martin T. 2000. "The Development of Community Wildlife Management in Tanzania: Lessons from the Ruaha Ecosystem." Paper presented at the College of African Wildlife Management's conference "African Wildlife Management in the New Millennium," Mweka, Tanzania, December 13–15.

World Bank. 2000. *Entering the 21st Century: World Development Report 1999/2000*. Washington, DC: World Bank.

——. 2001. *Social Protection Sector Strategy: From Safety Net to Springboard*. Washington, DC: World Bank.

——. 2004a. *African Development Indicators, 2004*. Washington, DC: World Bank.

——. 2004b. "Staff Appraisal Report for the Central Corridor Transport Project." World Bank, Washington, DC.

——. 2004c. *Investment Climate Assessment: Improving Enterprise Performance and Growth in Tanzania*. Washington, DC: World Bank.

——. 2004d. "Tanzania: Secondary Education Development Program (SEDP)." Report 27631, World Bank, Washington, DC.

——. 2004e. "Tanzania: Second Agricultural Research Project." Implementation completion Report 30930, World Bank, Washington, DC.

——. 2005a. *African Development Indicators, 2005*. Washington, DC: World Bank.

——. 2005b. *Global Monitoring Report 2005*. Washington, DC: World Bank.

————. 2005c. "ICR on Primary Education Development Program in Tanzania." World Bank, Washington, DC.

————. 2005d. *Investment Climate Survey for Tourism in East Africa*. Washington, DC: World Bank.

————. 2005e. "Tanzania Aid Requirements to Accelerate Progress towards the MDGs." World Bank, Washington, DC.

————. 2005f. *Tanzania Diagnostic Trade Integration Study, June 2005*. Washington, DC: World Bank.

————. 2005g. *World Development Report 2005: A Better Investment Climate for Everyone*. Washington, DC: World Bank.

————. 2006. *Doing Business 2007: How to Reform*. Washington, DC: World Bank.

World Economic Forum. 2004. *Africa Competitiveness Report 2004*. Geneva: World Economic Forum. http://www.weforum.org/.

————. 2007. *Global Competitiveness Report 2006–2007*. Geneva: World Economic Forum. http://www.weforum.org/.

Wuyts, Marc. 2005. "Growth, Poverty Reduction and the Terms of Trade: A Comment on Tanzania." Paper presented at a Research on Poverty Alleviation discussion seminar, Dar es Salaam, September 2.

Index

Boxes, figures, notes, and tables are indicated by b, f, n, and t, respectively.

ate Due

ECO-AUDIT
Environmental Benefits Statement

The World Bank is committed to preserving endangered forests and natural resources. The Office of the Publisher has chosen to print *Sustaining and Sharing Economic Growth in Tanzania* on recycled paper with 30 percent postconsumer fiber in accordance with the recommended standards for paper usage set by the Green Press Initiative, a nonprofit program supporting publishers in using fiber that is not sourced from endangered forests. For more information, visit www.greenpressinitiative.org.

Saved:
- 9 trees
- 6 million Btu of total energy
- 799 lb. of CO_2 equivalent greenhouse gases
- 3,318 gal. of waste water
- 426 lb. of solid waste

green
press
INITIATIVE